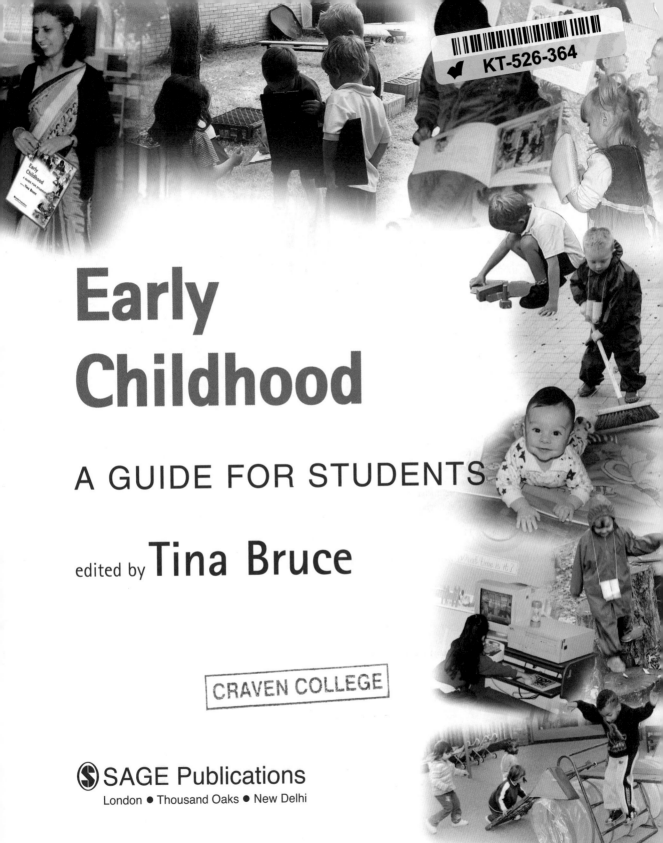

Early Childhood

A GUIDE FOR STUDENTS

edited by **Tina Bruce**

SAGE Publications

London • Thousand Oaks • New Delhi

First published 2006
Reprinted 2006

SAGE Publications Ltd
l Oliver's Yard
55 City Road
London EClY 1SP

SAGE Publications Inc.
2455 Teller Road
Thousand Oaks, California 91320

SAGE Publications India Pvt Ltd
B-42, Panchsheel Enclave
Post Box 4109
New Delhi 110 017

British Library Cataloguing in Publication data

A catalogue record for this book is available from the British Library

ISBN-10 1-4129-2075-2   ISBN-13 978-1-4129-2075-9
ISBN-10 1-4129-2076-0 (pbk)   ISBN-13 978-1-4129-2076-6

Library of Congress Control Number: 2006922116

Typeset by C&M Digitals (P) Ltd., Chennai, India
Printed in Great Britain by The Alden Press, Oxford
Printed on paper from sustainable resources

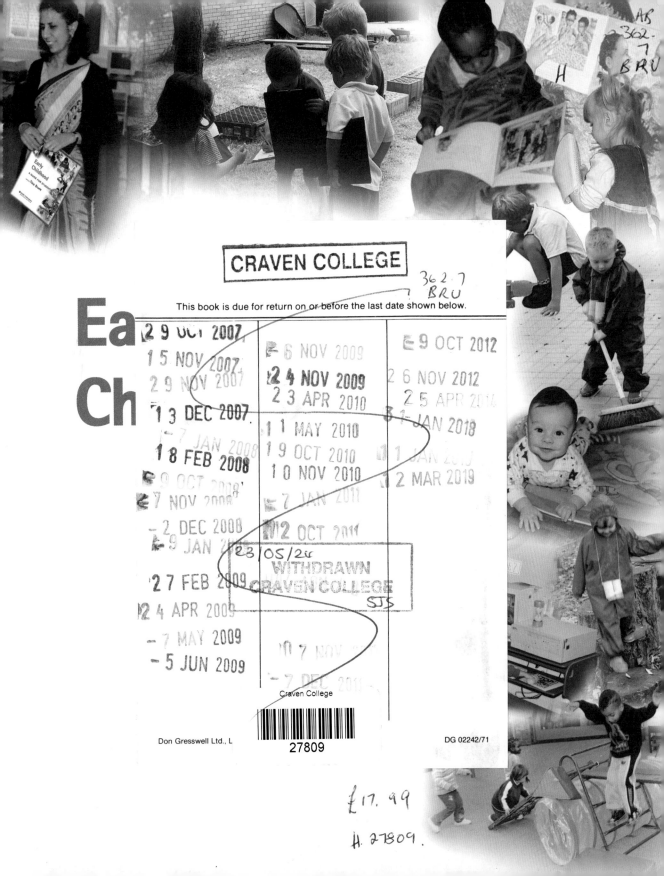

CONTENTS

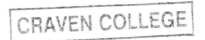

INTRODUCTION

This book is for those entering the field of early childhood practice, who are eager to up-skill their knowledge, and set it in a framework of practice that is embedded in time-honoured good practice, together with and supported by theory and current research and government documents.

Because it is an introductory book, it is written in very accessible and user-friendly ways, with contributions from some of the leading experts in the field. They have given of their time generously in writing chapters for this book, despite heavy and, by most standards, overwhelming workloads. The editor and authors of this book place a high priority on quality training. Young children, their families and carers require early childhood practitioners working with them who are well educated, mature, and highly qualified with appropriate training. Working with other people's children is not the same as spending time with your own children, and this needs to be addressed if children are to experience quality of the kind which supports, enhances and extends their development and learning in all its many aspects.

Quality training never separates theory from practice. It brings the two together, so that each feeds off and into the other. Because the modelling of the early years workforce is breaking new and pioneering ground, it is important to have textbooks which support its evolution in relevant and helpful ways. Many of the practitioners are already experienced in practice, and are entering new kinds of training and professional qualifications through non-traditional routes. It is therefore important that the book helps practioners to build on what they know, and to reflect on the practice they have encountered or have been involved in. There is a need to reaffirm what is already known, but also to reflect on established habits and ways of practice such that practitioners feel sufficiently supported and confident to challenge themselves. This requires maturity of approach.

In my experience, there are many practitioners of exactly this kind, hungry for more knowledge and understanding of how to help young children develop and learn, and to support and enhance the role of their families/carers in this. This book helps practitioners to study with a feeling of confidence that their knowledge to date is something they can build upon. The book helps them to see themselves, not just as practitioners, but as readers and writers, who are involved in academic study of the kind which takes forward quality practice. The book encourages readers to use what they know from their practitioner experience and their life experiences, and to make links with theory and research, and to see the importance of doing this if they are to enhance and develop their professional learning and gain further accreditation. The emphasis is on the Froebelian tradition of interweaving theory and practice, so that each illuminates the other, making connections with what is already known and understood, and transforming that knowledge in the process.

The book will be useful for those studying on Early Years Practitioner Courses, Foundation degrees or Early childhood degrees, as teacher assistants as well as those undertaking teacher training to work in the early years. It is a comprehensive textbook giving sufficient detail, but not so much so that it overwhelms. It encourages further exploration. It also helps students to become autonomous learners, undertaking work-based assignments, private study and distance learning.

The book is divided into eight sections.

In Section 1 (You and Your Learning), the first chapter, 'Managing yourself and your learning' by Sally Jaeckle, a Regional adviser for the Early Years Foundation Stage for the National Strategies, helps readers to locate themselves as learners, and to reflect on how they can build on where they are at this stage in their life-long learning journey. This chapter is important because most readers will be undertaking their study while working, rather than as full-time students. It gives helpful strategies of a practical kind, including well-being in the workplace. Maureen Brookson, lecturer in Early Childhood Studies in Norfolk, gives further help in Chapter 2, when she introduces some of the key aspects of study skills and information and communication technology (ICT) for adults. Ruth Pimentel, National Director for the Early Years Foundation Stage, writes about how practitioners can support children in developing their use and understanding of ICT in their development and learning.

Section 2 (Working with Children) contains a chapter by Vicki Hutchin, Regional Director for the Early Years Foundation Stage. She looks at meeting individual needs and the importance of observation that informs assessment. In the next chapter, Tina Bruce considers pioneers of early years practice, and Marion Dowling, President of Early Education, gives guidance on creating learning environments indoors and outdoors, both of which are crucial. Jenny Spratt, Head of Early Years in a local authority, describes work-based projects and their impact.

In Section 3 (Understanding Child Development) Professors Chris Pascal and Tony Bertram introduce the subject, which is complex, in easy to understand ways. This is followed by a chapter on symbolic development by Tina Bruce, which helps practitioners to understand its processes and how to work with young children to encourage it. Tina Bruce gives examples of practical situations and their issues in relation to transition in the final chapter of this section.

Section 4 (Birth to Five) begins with a chapter of central importance, written by Ann Langston, a key member of the team who developed the English *Birth to Three Matters* framework with Lesley Abbott. The remaining chapters in this and the next section look at the principles and practice of the *Curriculum Guidance for the Foundation Stage*, from 2008 the *Birth three Matters* and the *CGFs* documents will be embedded in the Early Years Foundation Stage. Helen Moylett, Senior Regional Adviser for the Early Years Foundation Stage, introduces readers to the first part of the core reference document. The chapter 'Diversity and Inclusion' is placed centrally. Tina Bruce sets out issues which address both different aspects of this fundamentally important concept.

In Section 5 (The Foundation Stage), Marian Whitehead considers communication, language and literacy. Maulfry Worthington and Elizabeth Carruthers, experts in this field, who are based in Devon, look at mathematical development, and include important examples of reasoning, problem-solving and numeracy. Katrina Foley, Headteacher of an Extended Maintained Nursery School, explores the importance of knowledge and understanding of the world. Penny Greenland, Director of the National Centre for Movement, Learning and Health writes about the importance of physical development, and Tina Bruce looks at creative development.

In Section 6 (Key Stage 1) Dr Kathy Goouch, University of Kent, introduces readers to the importance of supporting children in their development and learning. As in Section 5, there is a chapter on 'Inclusion and Diversity' (the concept examined in Section 5, and here reflected upon from a different angle). Tina Hyder, from Save the Children, emphasises the importance of inclusion and diversity from the perspective of gender, age, ethnicity and culture, while Julie Jennings, Early Year Development Officer, Royal National Institute for the Blind, focuses on children with special educational needs and disabilities. A chapter on curriculum and content guides readers in exploring mathematics, by Maulfry Worthington and Elizabeth Carruthers. Science is introduced by Chris Macro a freelance trainer for science and technology with a focus on the early years, and communication, language and literacy are introduced by Marian Whitehead.

Section 7 is concerned with 'Professional Development'. Maureen Brookson examines the role of the Teaching Assistant. In the next chapter, Wendy Russell, Senior Lecturer at the University of Gloucestershire, writes about Playwork. Dr Guy Roberts-Holmes, University of Kent, in a chapter which is very accessibly written and practical to carry into action, gives guidance on how to undertake practitioner research. Then follows an important chapter by Sue Owen, Director of the Early Year Unit at the National Children's Bureau, in which she brings together key aspects of the *Every Child Matters* agenda which will be embedded in the EYFS in 2008.

Section 8 is titled 'Leading and Managing'. Lesley Benson, a tutor on the 'Leading from the Middle' courses (National College of School Leadership), and a practising Headteacher, introduces important points for reflective practice in this area. This is followed by a chapter by Jenny Spratt, Head of Early Years in a local authority, who looks at 'Managing in context' which includes, among other things, the importance of preparing for inspections, self-assessment, and quality assurance. The final chapter, by Emeritus Professor Janet Moyles and Dr Siân Adams helps readers to develop and manage their professional role, locating it within the national framework, together with an examination of time-honoured approaches to quality in early childhood practice.

The book, with its eight sections, is organised so that readers may revisit ideas, thoughts and feelings as their understanding develops, and in doing so gradually deepen and consolidate their understanding of early childhood practice for children and their families/carers in the first seven years of living.

Editor's Note

When you read chapters relating to communication, language and literacy, or physical learning, or about the symbolic and creative aspects of development, you will need to be aware of the Rose Review, which, at the request of Ruth Kelly, the then Secretary of State for Education, looked at the teaching of reading, and reported on this in March 2006. The findings are being linked to the literacy and numeracy review of the strategies and will be integrated as the *Birth to Three* and *CGFs* documents become embedded in the Every Years Foundation Stage from 2008.

The Rose Review emphasises the importance for young children of:

- A rich learning environment.
- Multi-sensory learning (which means the co-ordinated and integrated development of learning through the senses and movement, rather than separate training of each sense or isolated physical exercise programmes.
- A systematic approach to the teaching of phonics which is well thought through and has consistency and inner logic, and which highlights discrete aspects in helping children to understand.

There is nothing here which undermines the approach taken in this book. The chapters which look at the importance of physical development, symbolic and creative development are inextricably linked with the chapters on communication, language and literacy and mathematical development, to form the basis of a rich learning environment. These chapters are underpinned with theoretical chapters such as those on *Birth to Three Matters*, or the general development of learning and reflections on teaching in the first five years, to be embedded in the EYFS from 2008, and also in Key Stage 1.

In this way, the emphasis on rich learning with a multi-sensory emphasis is central throughout the book. A rich learning environment requires a well thought through philosophy which is actively translated into practice wisdom. It needs to be consistent in approach, and to have inner cohesion. This applies to the teaching of phonics or any other aspect of pedagogy. Pedagogy is about the interface and interaction between adults and children, and children and children in relation to development, learning and teaching. The teaching of phonics must therefore be co-ordinated with every aspect of a child's developing learning; otherwise it is not a well thought through system. Phonics taught in isolation from a rich, multi-sensory learning environment will be unlikely to promote and result in the kind of learning that lasts for life that is valued by the authors of this book, and articulated, using an evidence based approach in its thirty chapters.

Acknowledgements

This book has been a team effort, from authors and publishers, especially Marianne Lagrange, Jeanette Graham and Beth Crockett and so huge thanks to all the participants. The authors have given shared expertise and experience, and have done so with clarity and evidence to support the views articulated. This has taken energy at a time when each and every one has been participating fully in a period of rapid change. Through their efforts they contribute to developing and improving the lives of children and families, and this book is part of that.

Thanks to Tom Bruce for his photography, Langford Extended Primary School, and Kate Greenaway Children's Centre maintained Nursery School, the families who welcomed us into their homes, and the families, children, childminders and staff in the settings in Peterborough Local Authority, Southway Nursery School and JABADAO.

CHAPTER

1

MANAGING YOURSELF AND YOUR LEARNING

Sally Jaeckle

Sally Jaeckle, currently a Regional Adviser for the Foundation Stage in the South West for the National Strategies, has worked as an early years teacher and Children's Centre manager both in this country and in the United States, and has been a lecturer in Early Childhood Studies and an Early Years Adviser.

Aims

To develop understanding of:

- ☐ the importance of being a reflective practitioner, and through this process identify your own strengths, interests and learning preferences
- ☐ and examine and develop your role as 'co-researcher' with colleagues and children in the workplace
- ☐ and explore the risks and challenges that this new learning will bring and identify strategies to manage this change.

Introduction: reflection on your learning journey so far

Effective practice in the early years requires committed, enthusiastic and reflective practitioners with a breadth and depth of knowledge, skills and understanding.

Effective practitioners use their own learning to improve their work with young children and their families in ways which are sensitive, positive and non-judgemental.

Therefore, through initial and ongoing training and development, practitioners need to develop, demonstrate and continuously improve their:

- relationships with both children and adults;
- understanding of the individual and diverse ways that children develop and learn;
- knowledge and understanding in order to actively support and extend children's learning in and across all areas and aspects of learning;
- practice in meeting all children's needs, learning styles and interests;
- work with parents, carers and the wider community;
- work with other professionals within and beyond the setting. (Key Elements of Effective Practice (KEEP) website)

In deciding to take up this opportunity you have already demonstrated your commitment to developing your own professional practice. In this chapter we will explore the importance of being a reflective practitioner and how this deepening self-awareness is at the heart of your continuing learning journey.

The importance of developing high-quality provision in the early years is indisputable, but first we need to stop and spend a few moments thinking about what this actually means. What does quality look like in practice and how will we recognise it when we see it? Do we all share the same vision? What is our role in making it happen? How will we go about it and where do we start?

All real learning is a dangerous business! It involves taking risks and overcoming challenges as the safety of old and familiar ways of thinking are left behind in the search for new layers of understanding. As you embark on your learning journey, you will be experiencing a range of emotions – from excitement to anxiety – but above all you are probably wondering about the impact this major commitment will have on your life and your practice. What changes will this quest for quality bring and how will it benefit the children and families in your school or setting? This chapter will attempt to answer both these questions, and will include exercises to explore your own thinking and case studies from practitioners who have already set out on their learning journeys and can see the difference that it has made.

EXERCISE 1.1

What is your personal goal in undertaking this course?
How will it help your colleagues?
How will it help the children you work with?
How will it help your friends and family?

Try to write down three points for each question. This could be the start of a reflective journal, so leave a space to add more thoughts as you proceed through the course.

Setting the context

The current direction of government policy recognises the importance of promoting high-quality early years provision. *Every Child Matters* (DfES, 2005b) establishes the government's commitment to improve the quality, accessibility and coherence of services so that 'every child and young person is able to fulfil their full potential'. The ten-year strategy for childcare 'Choice for parents, the best start for children' (HM Treasury website) sets out the government's vision for 'every child to get the best start in life' and establishes an aspiration to develop 'high-quality provision with a highly skilled childcare and early years workforce, among the best in the world'. This ambition is explored further in the 'Children's Workforce Strategy' consultation paper (DfES website).

The policy focus on quality has drawn significantly on recent research, and in particular the findings of the DfES-funded longitudinal study of Effective Provision of Pre-school Education (EPPE; Sylva et al., 2004) which has now shown the impact of early education on children's outcomes at the end of Key Stage 1. This research has shown that high-quality pre-school experiences do make a difference to children, particularly children from the most disadvantaged backgrounds, and that this difference can be sustained. The research has identified some particular indicators of quality provision including:

- highly qualified practitioners including trained teachers
- an equal balance of child-initiated and adult-led learning experiences
- adult–child interactions that encourage children to think deeply and express their ideas (sustained shared thinking)

- practitioners with knowledge of how young children learn and an understanding of the early years curriculum
- strong links between home and early years setting/school.

Your decision to develop your own professional practice and qualifications is an important step in making this vision of high-quality provision a reality.

E X E R C I S E   1 . 2

Reflecting on the Key Elements of Effective Practice (KEEP) and the characteristics of quality outlined above, list your strengths, interests and priorities for professional development. You may find it helpful to discuss this with a friend or colleague.

How will this new awareness improve your work with young children and their families? Note three aspects that you plan to develop in your practice.

What is a reflective practitioner?

If you do what you've always done, you'll get what you've always got. (Anon.)

Although the EPPE research begins to help us to understand some of the characteristics of effective pre-school provision, we still need to explore more deeply what this means for us in practice. Quality, like beauty can be said to be in the eye of the beholder. There can be no clear-cut, universally accepted definition because it is culturally determined and will mean different things to different people, depending on their own experiences, interests, beliefs and values. It cannot therefore be captured as a specific outcome that can be measured, or a goal that can be achieved. If 'quality' is viewed as a destination that can be reached once and for all, arrival would signal the end of the journey, and imply that there is no need for further thought, reflection or progress – a dangerous position in a rapidly changing world.

Instead, the pursuit of quality is really about the nature of the journey itself. It is an active process, a continuous seeking for improvement, dynamic and changing in response to our deepening awareness and growing understanding of how children think and learn. The reflective practitioner will set out on this journey with a strong commitment to making it the best that it can be for all concerned – children, families and fellow colleagues. This does not necessarily mean that they will take the most direct or easiest route but it will be the most meaningful and fulfilling. The journey will be planned flexibly in response to the interests, needs and learning preferences of fellow travellers, with plenty of time set aside to take in the views, check for progress and agree new paths where they are indicated.

Reflective practice is therefore the key to developing high-quality provision, but it is often easier said than done. The cycle of informed reflection, self-evaluation and development that lies at the heart of this process takes time, openness, and the capacity to step back and look at your practice with absolute honesty – warts and all! This is not a question of superficially ticking the boxes, but an altogether more demanding way of analysing what it is that you do. You will need to think in depth about those aspects of your practice that are effective, and why, checking that there is evidence to support the judgements you have made. You will also need to explore the elements that are less successful, and challenge yourself to make improvements.

This journey cannot happen in a knowledge vacuum. Practitioners also need regular opportunities to develop their professional expertise and extend their understanding of early learning and development. Access to recent and relevant thinking and research, through books and journal articles, learning networks, conferences and ongoing training, will establish a sound context for reflection and ensure that any analysis of practice is well informed.

Informed reflection, within the context of a developmentally appropriate curriculum and an understanding of how children think and learn, will help you to recognise and value your strengths, identify the areas in need of further development and establish priorities for action to move your practice forward. This process is at its most powerful when you are working collaboratively with others. 'Engaging in listening and dialogue is lively, enlivening – vivacious. In dialogue we meet many strong patterns of energy, tension, possibilities. We shape things and are shaped by them' (Edward Lorenz, in James Gleick, *Chaos – Making a New Science* and quoted in Bruce, 1991).

Perhaps the closest we can get to a definition of quality is the concept of a genuine learning community, where all participants – practitioners, children and their families – work together to develop their skills, knowledge and understanding through reflection, dialogue and a shared commitment to 'continually improving on their previous best'. When everyone in a school or setting is valued as a fellow traveller on this journey, respecting each other's contributions and different starting points, there is a buzz in the air and an excitement that is palpable.

In *Making Learning Visible* (Project Zero, 2001: 16) a learning group is described as: 'A collection of persons emotionally, intellectually and aesthetically engaged in solving problems, creating products and making meaning – an assemblage in which each person learns autonomously and through the ways of learning of others' or as a Year 8 pupil from Bradford so eloquently puts it: 'Schools should work together because its hard working on your own, but if you work as a team then you get a lot more done, and more ideas put in' (GTC and NCSL, 2005: cover).

The benefits of this approach are many. It has often been said that even the most effective early years practitioners sometimes find it difficult to explain exactly what it is that they do. In a nutshell, reflection, dialogue and self-evaluation will help you to deepen your understanding, clarify your thinking and sharpen your beliefs. Discussions with colleagues will help you to become better at finding the words to describe your practice and share your philosophy. Increased awareness will bring ownership and the confidence to encourage others in your team to make changes that improve the quality of practice in the setting. It will encourage action research and give you permission to take risks and try new approaches, safe in the knowledge that while not every new initiative will be successful, you can justify your principles and will analyse the impact – nothing ventured, nothing gained. You will know where you are in your practice, where you want to be and how you intend to get there.

Case Study 1.1

Sophie Robertson, full-time practitioner at a maintained nursery school with a high number of children from minority ethnic groups, new arrival families and asylum seekers:

By developing reflective practice I have learnt to continually challenge and question my own views, attitudes, values and pre-conceptions which in one way or another affect my practice with children and families. Without constant reflection, there is a danger that you are unable to give the children and people you work with the opportunities they deserve.

Walking the talk – planning your next steps

If we believe that children possess their own theories, interpretations and questions, and that they are co-protagonists in the knowledge building processes, then the most important verb in educational practice is no longer to talk, to explain or to transmit, but to listen. (Rinaldi, 1988)

As learners we all have much in common, whether we are children or adults. We share many of the same needs and the same entitlements, the same sense of eager anticipation and the same sense of anxiety. Your decision to return to study will help you to strengthen your understanding of the learning process and to develop your own sense of empathy. We have already discussed the many challenges that new learning brings and if we are to begin this journey with confidence, it will help to have an understanding of the close relationship between the emotional and cognitive aspects of learning – the relationship between self-esteem and achievement.

The images we have of ourselves as learners have far more to do with the perceptions we have of our competence than with any objective measure of ability itself. Carol Dweck's (1988) research on 'helpless' and 'mastery' learning styles helps us to understand the impact this can have on our attitudes to learning. These images and attitudes are shaped both by our personalities and by our previous academic experiences.

'Helpless' learners are goal orientated. They are focused on achievement and view this as a direct reflection of their competence. Their self-esteem is entwined with this idea of success and to protect themselves, they tend to keep their learning safe, only attempting what they know they can do. They avoid challenges, fearing failure and the negative judgements, humiliation and embarrassment that this might bring. Though 'helpless' learners can also be high achievers, these self-imposed limitations mean that they will never know the bounds of what could have been possible – they have had to keep their learning potential under wraps.

'Mastery' learners are fascinated by the journey itself. They are more interested in the process of learning than in any external goal or reward, embracing new challenges and delighting in finding innovative solutions for overcoming them. Failures and mistakes are viewed as opportunities for critical thinking, problem-solving and creativity, to be valued rather than feared – time to take stock, analyse and find new possibilities.

As a student, it is worth considering how you currently feel about yourself as a learner. Are you anticipating the excitement of the journey, open to new experiences and willing to take these on board? Or have you been more preoccupied with the outcomes – is the destination more important than the journey? Of course, both are important, everyone wants to achieve a successful outcome, but it is a question of balance and perhaps useful to explore how the attitudes you hold impact on the approaches you take – helping you to make the most of this new learning opportunity.

In an information-rich and ever-changing world, 'mastery' learning styles will become increasingly important. In the future, knowledge will be available at the touch of a button, but knowing how to discriminate, make connections and effectively apply that knowledge in new situations will be critical. An understanding of the skills and processes involved in learning to learn (meta-cognition) will become more important than simply acquiring a body of factual knowledge.

In *Building Learning Power* Guy Claxton (1999) talks about the 'Magnificent seven ways of being a good learner':

- resilience
- self-belief
- critical curiosity
- imagination and creativity (playability)
- making connections
- self-awareness
- managing dependence and independence.

These are some of the main attributes of 'mastery learning styles' and provide a good checklist for learners of all ages whether they are 3 or 93.

But confident, strategic thinkers do not develop in a vacuum; they flourish only when the emotional conditions for learning have been understood and prioritised. This will depend on shared ethos, values and principles but, most importantly, on the quality of relationships in any learning situation. Carl Rogers (1983) has identified the core characteristics of effective relationships as genuineness, trust, acceptance and empathy. A 'listening pedagogy' is therefore at the heart of a 'mastery' learning relationship. The knowledge that you are a valued member of the learning community with an important contribution to make, becomes a reality when your thoughts and views are both sought after and respected. When practitioners see themselves and children as co-researchers on the learning journey together, genuine relationships are established. Practitioners can 'walk the talk' both emotionally and intellectually, using their greater experience of the world to model relationships based on mutual respect, and learning styles that encourage creativity and innovation. When the emotional conditions for learning are in place, enquiry, critical thinking, problem-solving and dialogue will thrive.

Case Study 1.2

Carole Wheeler, full-time practitioner at an Early Years Centre in a multi-ethnic inner-city setting:

I lacked confidence at the beginning of the course and have needed quite a lot of support to get me to the end. I thought it was going to be easy as I have been on lots of training courses before but this course is more challenging and I struggled at times.

We have got a really strong cohort, it is amazing how over the last two years we have all grown together, and this has been a huge strength. The course has raised my self esteem ten fold; when I started it was quite low but now I am more confident in dealing with other professionals. I want to use the knowledge gained on the course to extend my ability to take the staff and the Centre forward. Now I have the confidence in my own abilities I can go on and be a manager and realise my plans for the future.

Strategies to support returning to study

Every human being has a learning style and every human being has strengths. (Dunn, 1988.)

By the time you reach this section, you will be well on your way. Your new learning journey has begun and you have started to explore your role in developing 'quality provision' for young children and their families. You have thought about what is meant by the term 'quality' and how informed reflection, self-evaluation and dialogue within the context of a supportive learning community can help to drive practice forward. You have hopefully gained some new insights into the emotional needs of all learners and deepened your understanding of learning processes in general. This last section in Chapter 1 will help you to develop practical strategies for coping with the joys and potential pitfalls of returning to study.

E X E R C I S E   1 . 3

Think through your most successful, memorable and enjoyable learning experiences. Were they at school or college, on holiday or travelling, in a club or through a hobby?

EXERCISE 1.3   (CONTINUED)

Why were they successful – what were the significant factors?

- People and relationships?
- Personal choice or interest?
- Inspiration from books, television, video or web-based media?
- First-hand experience?
- Other?

Make a list of the ways in which any of these factors enhanced your learning experience, what do you remember the most, how did you feel and what impact did they have on the image you hold of yourself as a learner?

Think about your own learning style:

Most people are a mixture of visual, auditory and kinaesthetic learners, but this section will help you to consider different strategies that will help you to manage your own learning.

Do you learn best through pictures, diagrams, posters, videos and colour-coding of information? If so you are probably a visual learner. Or do you learn best through discussion, rhymes and raps, music, taped information as an auditory learner? Perhaps are you a kinaesthetic learner, who needs to be active or use objects to understand concepts or visit places to remember facts?

A considerable amount of your time will be spent on independent learning on this course:

- Where will you work? Defining your own space is important and will help you to be organised. Do you need it to be quiet or will you have background music?
- When will you work? If you live with family or friends, discuss and agree with them on these questions. Look at your week and family commitments, and write out a timetable that blocks out your time for study and write it up so everyone can see. Will a year's visual plan on the wall work for you?
- Keep a diary/calendar and mark on it your assignment deadlines. Working backwards from this, break down the tasks that need to be done to complete the assignment and write in earlier deadlines for these. Will colour-coding help?
- Start your reading early. This is the key to success! Do not buy books until you have looked at them in the library or bookshop, as some will appeal to you more than others.
- When you have bought some key texts, use the index to find a topic that really interests you. Set yourself a task to read that section, then tell yourself what it was all about and ask further questions that you want to find out. Return to the passage and make your notes, including details you may not have understood the first time round. You may find this works better with a 'study buddy' – pair up with someone on your course and discuss what you have read.

- Keep a 'reference and reading notebook' in which you write the book reference at the top of the page and the page numbers down the margin when you find a quote or something you think you may need as a reference for your two years of study. You could even write a note to yourself, such as: 'a lot of info here about attachment theory' or the direct quote. Use highlighter pens in your notes. This will save you a lot of time throughout your course.
- Spend time planning your assignments. Use mind-maps, diagrams or lists to help you. Write directly onto the computer screen, starting with the section you feel most confident about. Then you can move, add and delete parts much more easily.

Remember, Claxton's 'Magnificent seven' that are as applicable to children as they are to adults. Are you using them all?

Case Study 1.3

Bridget White, Full-Time Deputy Head at a large city-based Children's Centre:

I enjoyed learning from others ... The modules have covered a wide spectrum and it has been great to have the opportunity to put them into practice. I have definitely become a more avid reader of theory and I am able to use that in practice now. By questioning, observing and analysing I have definitely improved the quality of my practice.

The author wishes to thank Jill Brown, Programme course leader for the Sure Start Sector Endorsed Foundation Degree in Early Childhood Studies at City of Bristol College, who contributed the case studies in the chapter.

STUDY SKILLS AND ICT

Maureen Brookson

Maureen Brookson is a senior lecturer at a large inner city college (Norwich City College) with responsibility for all HND and BA(Hons) in early childhood studies. She is also a researcher in music in the early years, with publications and conference papers disseminating the research nationally and internationally. Maureen is currently undertaking further research in an area of social deprivation.

Aims

To develop understanding of:

☐   and gain an understanding of the ICT tools available to support study
☐   and appreciate the benefits of using these tools for research and professional development.

Many translate information and communication technology (ICT) as being another word for computers. Although computers are a valuable resource to assist your studies, through *researching*, *writing*, *thinking* and *communicating* (see Figure 2.1), there are many other technologies that can help you.

Using computers to present your work

Good presentation of your work is essential. You will probably be given a specification of how your work should be presented. This may include size and type of font and line spacing. Identification will be useful on each page of your work, and this can be typed into the

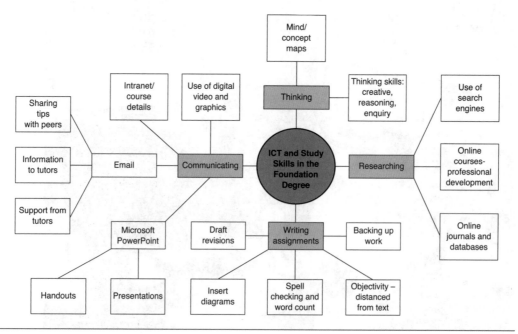

Figure 2.1   *Study skills mind map*

Figure 2.2   *An example of header details*

header or footer of the page. This is the area outside the normal typing space (see Figure 2.2).

By using a computer to present your work, you can make a good impression through the layout, the use of tables, highlighting or italicising text, numbering pages and counting words. Using a computer allows you to make a number of drafts of your work, to edit, move, add and delete text, check spellings and to correct without having to retype your work for each draft. Computers allow you to align your text left or right or to centre it, to indent and to make it stand out by using bullet points.

There are plenty of opportunities to be creative, for example by inserting symbols and pictures and video images. Information can be quickly sorted by using databases and spreadsheets, and complex statistics can be presented with ease. Most courses will offer ICT training and advice, with some preliminary courses with names like 'Computing for the terrified', so lack of experience need be no bar to their use. Laptops and personal digital assistants (PDA)) are invaluable for use by dyslexic students in lectures.

Computers can help you to store information by creating files which should be named as soon as they are opened to ensure they can be easily found again. Just as with the old filing cabinet, folders can be created to put files into for further ease of access. Drafts can be saved with revision numbers included on the work, or in the file name.

Backing up your work is essential. Computers are still temperamental at times, and through power surges, hardware breakdowns and viruses, work can be easily lost. Most computers now have CD/DVD rewriters which will enable the saving of work onto a CD or DVD. These are becoming cheaper. Other devices such as memory sticks which are used in the same way as a floppy disks are now widely available. Printing out a hard copy is good protection, and many find it easier to read print rather than on screen.

Using the Internet for research

The Internet is a tool for good or evil, but used wisely can infinitely enhance your research. There are a number of search engines; many using different ways of searching for information. Some search on 'keywords', such as www.google.co.uk, and others search using questions. www.ask.co.uk is one of the most well-known search engines that work in this way.

Much time is lost through ineffective search techniques. Most search engines have an advanced search facility, or a page of tips which will give better quality results. One of these techniques is to put speech marks around words that need to be found together. For instance, to find the words of a poem, by putting them in speech marks will make the search look only for instances of that text together in the given order.

Your learner support centre will give help in effective use of the Internet to access journals and databases, as with such a wealth of information, research is made more accessible. Check with your library to see if access to some of the databases and journals is available to you from your home computer.

Using computers to support your thinking skills

Mind-mapping or concept-mapping to enable thoughts to be organised can be useful tools for students. There are many software packages that help with this process. Some are available to buy, but many have free trials available on the Internet (see www.inspiration.com). These mind-maps can be created using a drawing package, but specialist software makes it much simpler. Thinking skills are an important part of the National Curriculum, grouped under the headings *information-processing skills*, *reasoning skills*, *enquiry skills*, *creative thinking skills* and *evaluation skills*. Using ICT to support thinking skills will enable you to think about the relationship between ideas, make connections, present and re-present ideas and information in a variety of different forms which can easily and quickly be manipulated and changed. 'It is therefore an essential option in any teacher's toolkit of choices for developing thinking and understanding' (Higgins and Packard, 2004: 151).

Using computers for communication

For professional presentations, there are many software applications to help. The most well-known is Microsoft PowerPoint which is very accessible and enables you to produce slides. These can be used to present a subject, but will also allow you to print out high-quality handouts for your lecturer and peers. Try not to get too carried away and cause 'death by PowerPoint'. Microsoft PowerPoint has the ability to integrate sound, video and animation, but many people try to use all of the facilities within one presentation, with bullet points flying in and pirouetting on the screen. Simplicity is the key, plus sound research, of course! A simple 'house style' using the same backgrounds, colours, fonts and the same minimal animations make for a professional presentation. It is your work that is important, and your communication can be lost in the mechanics of the software. You want your audience to remember your message, not how you had an audience clapping at the end!

As an adult returner, communication between yourself and your tutors is of extreme importance. Check to see if you have access to your college emails from home. Some colleges have an intranet where tutors can put handouts, notices and so on for up-to-date communications with students. This also makes possible staying in touch with your peers and sharing ideas, questions and anxieties. It is reassuring to get feedback quickly from your lecturers on drafts of work without the need for face to face meetings. This is particularly a boon for part-time and distance students.

Other applications

We forget that skills easily learnt at home can be transferred to our college work to enhance what we produce. We use photos and videos to record and communicate, and these can be used to document project work. Be careful to ensure that the correct permissions are acquired if you intend to use children as the source of these photos. Use of digital still and video cameras will bring your work to life, and analogue photos can be scanned into your work. Confidentiality is a real issue here, so always check the current conventions.

Last words

Before undertaking any training it is essential that you complete an audit of your own skills to find out where your strengths and weaknesses lie. By doing this you will find that you can build on your own skills and increase your personal confidence in these areas as well as developing your knowledge of ICT. You will then find that you can apply these newly learnt skills to your own practice in the classroom.

EXERCISE 2.1

Using the following audit grid, complete an evaluation of your strengths and weaknesses.

Skill	Proficient
Use Word Processors And General Computer Skills	
Open Files	
Save Files	
Save Copies Of Files With New File Names	
Save Files As New Type	
Create Text	

(Continued)

EXERCISE 2.1 (CONTINUED)

Format Text (Bold, Italic, Underline, Change Size etc)	
Use Print Preview	
Print Documents	
Cut Text Or Objects	
Copy Text Or Objects	
Paste Text Or Objects	
Use Print Screen	
Use Find And Replace	
Create Headers And Footers	
Add Or Remove Buttons On Toolbar	
Create Columns	
Add Page Numbers	
Use Tables	
Track Changes	
Use Spell Checker	
Use Thesaurus	
Insert Clip Art/Photos	
Resize Pictures	
Create Spreadsheets	
Add Text And Numbers	
Select Cells	
Add Numbers With Autosum	

EXERCISE 2.1 (CONTINUED)

Use Formulae	
Replicate Formulae	
Use Drag And Drop	
Resize Columns etc	
Print Options – Print Selection, Fit To One Page etc	
Insert New Rows And Columns	
Format Cells – Change Alignment, Font Size, etc	
Merge Cells	
Wrap Text	
Format Decimal Places	
Sort Data	
Filter Data	
Use Absolute Cell References	
Print Workbooks	
Print Selections	
'Fit To One Page' Function	
Use 'If' Functions	
Create Charts	
Print Charts	
Use Databases	
Create A New Database	
Use Tables	

(Continued)

EXERCISE 2.1 (CONTINUED)

Find And Sort Records	
Print Tables	
Create Simple Queries	
Filter Data	
Use Forms	
Use Reports	
Mail Labels	
Presentations	
Create A Presentation	
Add Text To Slides	
Sort Slides	
Animate Text	
Animate Objects	
Print Slides	
Print Handouts	
Add Notes	
Add Backgrounds Or Themes	
Use The Master Slide	
Add Charts	
Record Sounds	
Add Video	

EXERCISE 2.1   (CONTINUED)

Emailing	
Write Email	
Send Email	
Forward Emails	
Reply To Emails	
Sort Emails Into Folders	
Sort Emails	
Add Attachments	
Find Emails Or Content	
Use The Address Book	
Use Personal Distribution Lists	
Send Copy Emails (CC) and Blind Copy Emails (BCC)	
Internet	
Use Search Engines	
Use Search Terms '–', '+' 'And' (Specific For Each Search Engine)	
Save Web Pages	
Images	
Multimedia	
Use Digital Cameras	
Save Photos	
Edit Photos	

(Continued)

EXERCISE 2.1 (CONTINUED)

Scan Photos	
Use Video	
Edit Video	
Use Digital Projector	
Use Whiteboards	

Source: adapted from South Devon College skills audit, see ferl.becta website.

Further reading

Bessant, A. (2003) *Learning to use Office XP*. Oxford: Heinemann.

Coombes, H. (2001) *Research Using IT*. Basingstoke: Palgrave Macmillan.

Cottrell, S. (2003) *The Study Skills Handbook*. 2nd edition. Basingstoke: Palgrave Macmillan.

Wempen, F. (2004) *PowerPoint: Advanced Presentation Techniques*. Indiannapolis, IN: Wiley Publishing.

www. becta.org.uk

www.standards.dfes.gov.uk/thinking skills

The author would like to thank Alison Schwier for her ICT support in this chapter

USING ICT TO SUPPORT CHILDREN'S DEVELOPMENT AND LEARNING

Ruth Pimentel

Ruth Pimentel has worked in a variety of schools and settings and has inspected nursery provision across the country. She also provided qualified teacher support to Foundation Stage settings and then moved on to co-ordinate the team of early years mentors with Cambridgeshire Care and Education Partnership. Ruth is National Director for the Foundation Stage strand of the Primary National Strategy. For many years Ruth has been influential in considering the role of ICT to support children's learning.

Aims

To develop understanding of:

☐ and consider how a range of information communication technology resources can be used to support children's development and learning

☐ and gain an understanding of the role of the practitioner in using information and communication technology as a tool to support children's development and learning.

Children's use of ICT

Children are surrounded by ICT in their immediate environments. Increasingly, new technologies support, influence and shape the lives that we lead, and are also an integral part of the experiences of even our youngest children. Technology is something children are going to grow up with, learn about and master, and use as a tool to increase their understanding in all areas of development and learning. Technology is increasingly a part of their lives at home and in the wider environment, and children are being exposed to very sophisticated technologies from a young age. We are all able to tell tales of children being more confident at programming the video recorder than we are, and we have to ask ourselves why this is. The answer is probably because of the attitude that our youngest children have to exploring, problem-solving and investigating equipment to see how they can make it work for them, particularly if there is a strong motivation to succeed.

For the purposes of work with our youngest children, ICT encompasses a whole range of technology, from sophisticated hardware such as computers and interactive whiteboards, to electronic toys and games, walkie-talkies, remote-controlled toys and a vast range of imitation role-play equipment with realistic features. Many activities in the early years revolve around children developing an understanding of their environment. Children should be encouraged to use a wide range of technologies to explore, observe, problem-solve, predict, discuss and consider. Information and communication technology resources can provide tools for using these skills as well as being examined in their own right. Technology allows children to engage positively in imaginative, active learning. It can motivate, provide practice, reassure, build confidence, encourage children to persist in taking the next steps and build their self-esteem.

Here are some examples of the range of experiences that can be offered:

- The use of a digital camera can encourage children to reflect on past experiences, observe details, share personal likes/dislikes, sequence events, record and share a significant event.
- A programmable toy can be used to develop a range of skills. Children learn that pressing buttons causes an action, that they can control the action, left, right,forwards, backwards

and that the numbers of presses equals number of moves. Critically, a programmable toy can put the child at the centre of the learning process as they learn how to programme a toy to perform a particular action.

- An overhead projector introduces children to shadows and patterns, while also being a motivating tool to display and share learning.

- Walkie-talkies can encourage children's use of language, and they can use this equipment to share experiences, connect ideas, explain what is happening and recall and relive past experiences.

- Metal detectors can help children identify differences in materials – particularly useful for encouraging children to explore the outdoor environment.

- Musical mats or keyboards can encourage moving to a rhythm and creating patterns with sound.

- Cassette recorders can encourage children to listen to and retell stories and there's nothing like a karaoke machine to encourage children in their singing!

- An interactive whiteboard brings a new dimension to a learning environment. It immediately captures children's attention by the impact of the images, the colour and the control that it gives children. As a very motivating tool children can use it independently to 'paint', 'draw' and 'explore' environments. An interactive whiteboard is particularly effective for sharing experiences; for example small groups of children can all collaborate and, as importantly, can all be a part of an activity.

- Computers can be added to role-play areas to reflect their use in day-to-day living, or used around the setting for children in many different ways. Software can bring in different environments for children to explore that would be impossible to gain experience of otherwise. With a computer, other applications become possible: access to the Internet and its widening range of resources for learning, web cams for seeing themselves and their activities through, digital microscopes to investigate with and children's digital camcorders to use for their own recording. In particular well-chosen computer software can support children's learning by providing an alternative tool, for example software that encourages children to use a vast range of colours and tools to 'paint' can provide a vehicle for children's creativity that may not be achieved through traditional painting activities.

- Information and communication technology is particularly enabling for children with special educational needs; it can provide access to experiences that might be hard for some children to access through any other means and thereby aid children's learning and development. It is also highly motivating, can help build children's confidence in their abilities and is an excellent focus for social interaction.

- Information and communication technology equipment added to role-play reflects the real world, builds on children's experiences and allows them opportunities to understand how, why, when and where different forms of technology are used in everyday life. Environments such as a shop, café or office can be set up in role-play areas, making use of ICT to record and access information with a real purpose in mind.

All children can benefit from learning with and about ICT. We need to provide equitable access to all ICT equipment and ensure that we are being creative and critical in our thinking about ICT resources. In order to reflect and celebrate the true diversity and richness of cultures and religions in our society and include all children, regardless of race or gender, we will need to be mindful and resourceful in our provision. We will need to select resources with care, and observe, record, assess and intervene to help children extend their learning, solve problems and express themselves.

EXERCISE 3.1

Spend time considering the environment that is provided for children in a setting. Does the range of equipment reflect children's experiences of their world? For example, the role play area – does this have mobile telephones, fax machines, keyboard and computer monitors?

Observe children in a well-resourced role-play area and note the learning that takes place through the use of ICT; for example how they make use of a range of technologies to develop their language skills, to solve problems or to interact with others.

Gabriella and Frances were playing in the role-play shop and using a range of technologies to support their play. The mobile phone was used to order food, ring friends and to ring 999. This was used as a tool to communicate as they used language to imagine and re-create roles and experiences. They were also making use of the till to total up the bill and to swipe the credit card, gaining an understanding about the everyday uses for mathematics.

Some next steps for these children would be to extend these experiences through provision of other communication devices, for example walkie-talkies. These could be used to encourage dialogue between other groups of children. It would also be worthwhile to take the children to visit a shop and encourage them to look at the technologies that are being used.

EXERCISE 3.2

Observe children in a well-resourced ICT environment, that is, where they have access to a range of technologies such as programmable toys, electronic equipment and computer access. Observe how children's learning is supported using these technologies.

The children were highly motivated to be part of an outdoor activity using a robust remote-controlled toy. They were excited and interested and ready to work within the group to take their turn and to share fairly. They listened carefully to the instructions about using the remote control. They handled the control carefully, looking and checking that pushing the buttons was moving the car. They were working to gain greater mastery over the control. The open area gives the children an ideal environment to gain increasing control over the remote. They listened to directional vocabulary and saw the meaning of this vocabulary in context and were interested in the cause and effect of the remote control, and the open environment allowed them to freely explore this. The programmable toy supported the children's learning about spatial relationships; Carlos moves his legs out of the way of the car coming towards him.

Some next steps for this group would be to allow further opportunities to develop control of the vehicle by using large construction equipment to make a course. Once they have mastered controlling the vehicle then the children could be extended into using the language to describe a journey or the path of the vehicle.

Making effective use of ICT as a practitioner

The role of adults in supporting children's development and learning is critical, and ICT has an important role in this. One of the most valuable developments has been the use of digital images. Computers are an excellent tool for adults to use in their own work and, together with digital cameras and camcorders, can be used to great effect to communicate with parents and the community.

The use of digital cameras (and video cameras) is expanding quickly in early childhood settings because of the opportunity it provides to capture children's learning, and share it with the children, with parents, carers and other professionals. These images not only provide opportunities for instant feedback, but can also provide a wonderful opportunity to document children's learning over time. One of the main benefits is encouraging dialogue with parents – children and practitioners can capture activities and experiences throughout the day that can be shared with parents and carers when they arrive to collect the children. This immediately provides a link between the setting and the parents and carers as the children describes the context to the activity and this becomes a shared experience. It can also prevent the 'what have you done today' dialogue! This can also be an added benefit to support the anxious parent or carer – a photograph of a contented child can be more convincing than just the words.

In terms of documenting children's learning, the digital camera can provide a range of images which together tell a story of the development and learning of each child. In particular, this can be used to show participation in activities, the progression within an activity and to capture some of the learning process that the child has been involved in. Through the use of ICT images children can see themselves as capable and confident learners, children and adults together can reflect on the learning, and this contributes to a developing self-esteem and self-belief while also supporting them to build effective relationships with those who live and work with them.

EXERCISE 3.3

Developing skills in using digital images is a valuable exercise to support your work. Once you have mastered the art of taking photos, storing and printing them, spend time reflecting on a range of images focused on one particular child. How have these images been used to capture the development and learning of that child, what value has it added to the partnership with parents? Share your thoughts with a colleague and use this opportunity to plan the next steps in this child's learning.

As Jordan's keyworker Ricardo noticed, through his own observations and also from the photos of Jordan, that many of his activities showed him engaged in solitary activity in a limited range of areas of the indoor environment. After discussion with other practitioners the next steps in his learning were planned. Ricardo planned to spend time playing alongside Jordan and encouraging other children to also become involved in activities. Small group activities were organised that focused on activities that Jordan enjoyed but organised in other areas of the learning environment, including the outdoor area. Photographs were taken that showed Jordan at play alongside others and these were used as a focus for discussion with Jordan and others. Over time the keyworker noticed the developing confidence of Jordan to play alongside others and to explore new areas of the environment. These developments were documented and shared with the parents.

Information and communication technology can also support your role as an effective practitioner by using it to produce:

- professional-looking newsletters and notices
- labels and captions
- support material for parents and carers
- lists of children's names for administrative purposes
- planning pro formas and documentation of children's development and learning.

Information and communications technology has a lot to offer an early childhood setting as a sophisticated tool for the children and the adults. As we are confronted with new and exciting technologies one thing to keep in mind is how can this be used to support children's development and learning? What value does it add to the range of experiences that are offered to children? It is important it does not become an end in itself but has its value in providing exciting, motivating and challenging experiences for children and adults.

Further reading

More than computers – Information and Communication Technology in the Early Years by Iram Siraj-Blatchford and John Siraj-Blatchford (2003).
This book identifies principles of good practice for developmentally appropriate information and communication technology for children. It explores why it is important for children to be confident with ICT. It identifies how practitioners and parents can support children's development in this area, and looks at the issues which should be considered for a healthy, balanced approach to this aspect of the modern world. Available from Early Education at www.early-education.org.uk/1orderpublications.htm

Supporting Information and Communications Technology in the Early Years by John Siraj-Blatchford and David Whitebread, Open University Press (ISBN 0-335-20943-2).
This book helps readers to understand how very young children (from birth to 6) develop an early awareness, and subsequently develop their knowledge, skills and understanding of information and communication technologies.(www.openup.co.uk).

Early Education: Young Children and Technology.
As part of the Learning Together series, Early Education have produced a leaflet on young children and technology for parents, students and practitioners. This can be downloaded from the website at www.early-education.org.uk If you would like a single paper copy of each of the learning together leaflets, send a stamped addressed envelope (C5 or A4) with two first class stamps to Early Education, 136 Cavell Street, London E1 2JA.

Learning and Teaching Using ICT: Example Materials for the Foundation Stage.
This CD-ROM is now available to support practitioners in their understanding of using ICT in the Foundation Stage. This has been developed as part of the Primary National Strategy's aim to enhance learning and teaching using ICT. The CD-ROM consists of a set of video clips and supporting documentation, an outline of how ICT can be used as a tool to support children's learning across the Foundation Stage and a series of helpful 'How to … ' sheets. The CD-ROM is available from Prolog (0845 6022260), ref: DFES 0384-2004 GCDI.

Picture This: Digital and Instant Photography Activities for Early Childhood Learning by Susan Entz and Sher Lyn Galarza. Corwin Press (ISBN 0-8039-6887-6).
This book shows how you can put children at the centre of the learning process using a camera and simple computer equipment.

WORKING WITH CHILDREN

MEETING INDIVIDUAL NEEDS

Vicky Hutchin

Vicky Hutchin, Regional Adviser for the Foundation Stage in the DfES National Strategies, has worked first in playgroups and then as an early years teacher and advisory teacher. She has written three books, published by Hodder & Stoughton, on effective early years practice, especially observation and assessment.

Aims

To develop understanding of:

☐ and consider why it is important to meet children's individual needs
☐ and consider the essential role of observation in working with young children, 0–6 yrs
☐ and consider the special significance of observing play, with reference to some theories about the role of play in child development
☐ and examine some of the practical skills necessary for an effective observation/assessment/planning cycle.

To ensure children are confident, happy and engaged in learning, their individual needs must be met. This may sound simple, but it is a highly complex task, requiring practitioners to be constantly alert and responsive. As one experienced nursery teacher put it: 'It's about seeing something happen with a child. You need to think about what is happening then suddenly you start to understand what is going on and you begin to work out how you can intervene appropriately to support the child.'

The importance of meeting individual needs is well established in recent guidelines for early childhood practitioners. The English *Curriculum Guidance for the Foundation Stage* (CGFS) states that we should 'ensure that all children feel included, secure and valued' and 'treat children as individuals' (CGFS, 2000: 11); the underpinning principles of *Birth to Three Matters* (Sure Start, 2002: 4) assert that: 'schedules and routines must flow with the child's needs'. These principles are incorporated into the framework for services for children birth to five, Early Years Foundation Stage, 2006. Similar points are reiterated, for example, in the Scottish document *Birth to Three: Supporting our Youngest Children* (LT Scotland, 2005). But none of this is possible unless practitioners tune into children through observing them, interacting with them and listening to what their parents/carers have to say about them. Key questions need to be answered:

- How does this child respond in different situations?
- What sort of things interest and absorb her/him?
- In what situations does she/he show most confidence?
- What does she/he appear to find challenging and/or frustrating?

And most important of all, in the light of what we know about this child:

- What can we do to further her/his development and learning?

In very broad terms children develop along a similar path as they mature. But the order and time span in which 'developmental milestones' are achieved may differ considerably from child to child. As noted in *Birth to Three Matters* 'growth and development are less predictable for some children than for others' (DfES, 2002: 14).

Tuning into children

Each child responds differently to events, the environment and situations. A few close observations of children will reveal this. Joshua is now 4 years and 9 months old. Observations in his record folder have been collected since he first began nursery school five terms ago and judging by the number which involve play with cars or trucks, this type of play has been a major interest for him for some considerable time. Many of these observations show how cars and trucks have led him to experiment and solve problems. Here are two observations from his record:

> Joshua and friends were in the sandpit. They were calling out 'HELP! HELP!' Their trucks were stuck in a big hole they had dug, just like in 'The Big Red Bus' story.

> A car was caught in a tree. Joshua had told me about it and then went to try and rescue it. He tried throwing things at it; he tried a stick to poke. Nothing worked. Then he thought how to get higher and went and got a big heavy metal A frame (climbing frame) and pulled it under the tree. He climbed up so that he could reach the high branches and rescued the little car.

Observations of Hettie, who is of a similar age to Joshua, show her involvement in quite different sorts of play from Joshua, especially fantasy play.

> Hettie sets up homes and encampments at every opportunity. Even when we go out to the adventure playground, Hettie is to be found sometimes alone, sometimes with others, arranging her homes and camps. Today she had a picnic in the garden. She explained that she keeps all her food in the house. 'My mum and dad have died so I do all the work.' She was busy with her domestic chores and told me that she had to look after her five brothers all by herself. 'Mud in the house!' she cried and she set about sweeping vigorously.

What interests a child at any particular time can be deeply significant to her/him, a burning concern or passion. It cannot be ignored: it is the starting point for supporting a child's learning and development. 'Whenever I think about children's differences, my sense of the excitement of teaching mounts. Without the uniqueness of each child, teaching would be a dull repetitive exercise' (Paley, 1990: 47). Vivian Gussin Paley, who wrote this statement, has written extensively about young children's learning. Her books are built on real examples taken from tape transcripts she made daily of the children with whom she worked in Chicago, USA. The books are full of deep insights into how children develop their ideas, concepts and competence in very individual ways, through imagination and relationships.

The role of observation in Early Years practice

One of the underpinning principles of the English CGFS states that 'practitioners must be able to observe and respond appropriately to children' (CGFS, 2000: 11). The importance of observation across the age range is strengthened in the Early Years Foundation Stage (2006).

Observing is also seen as a key aspect of the practitioner's role working with children up to 3 in *Birth to Three: Supporting Our Youngest Children* in Scotland: 'Being tuned in to the child means … being closely observant, attentive and responsive' (LT Scotland, 2005: 27).

Margaret Edgington points out that 'Observation has traditionally been a feature of effective early years practice' (Edgington, 2004: 148), but she is concerned that all too often assumptions are made about children, rather than using observation, resulting in inappropriate learning experiences being presented, thus running 'the risk of switching children off from learning' (ibid.: 147). There is ample backing from recent research about the importance of observation. The REPEY research project (Siraj-Blatchford et al., 2002) examined the small group of early years settings, highlighted through the EPPE project 1997–2003 (Sylva et al., 2004) in which children made the greatest progress. One of the key findings of the REPEY research (Siraj-Blatchford et al., 2002) states that: 'The more knowledge the adult has of the child, the better matched their support and the more effective the subsequent learning.' Two other sources of information are vital in order to tune in to children. These are talking with parents/carers and communicating with the children themselves.

Talking with parents/carers

Parents/carers know their children intimately. For practitioners, therefore, building a close, trusting and reciprocal relationship with parents needs to begin before a child starts in a setting. This ongoing relationship can be started in many ways, such as home visits, parents' meetings and visits to the setting. These events are invaluable in helping staff to get to know the children. There are several sources of useful questions to ask parents about their child (see, for example, Hutchin, 1999: 66, or Edgington, 2004: 160). There are also some excellent projects aimed at building closer partnerships with parents to promote a deeper understanding by both practitioners and parents of children's development (see, for example, 'Involving Parents in Their Children's Learning', Research, Development and Training Base, Pen Green Centre, 2000, and DfES, 2005).

The role of parents in the process of assessment and planning has been strengthened in England through the introduction of the Foundation Stage Profile in 2003. This is the first statutory assessment of children's learning which takes place when a child reaches the end of the Foundation Stage. There is *an expectation* that parents will be involved in a continuing dialogue about their child's development: 'practitioners should involve parents from the time when the children arrive in the setting … working with them to gain a shared picture of their children' (QCA, 2003: 102).

Development and learning is bound to be hindered for the child if the care and support a child receives in the setting is inconsistent with what happens at home. Scepticism from practitioners about the information they gather from parents sometimes occurs because parents may see their child very differently from how she/he is perceived in the setting. As Hutchin (2003: 66) suggests 'this is precisely the point: to build a full picture of the child, an idea of what the child is doing at home is invaluable. Parents and principal carers do know their child better than anyone else ever could.'

Finding out from the children themselves

'Tuning in' must involve communicating directly with the child. Often the child's interpretation of an event may be quite different from that of the adults involved. Reading the wonderful books by Vivian Gussin Paley will help students to see how wrong our interpretations can sometimes be (see, for example, Paley, 1988: 36–7).

Gathering information from the children about themselves requires careful thought and planning. Young children will have varying degrees of competence in language and communication skills. Many children will be learning English as an additional language, some will already have competence in more than one other language and some will have specific language difficulties. *Listening to Young Children: The Mosaic Approach* by Clark and Moss (2001) describes a research project on collecting children's views about their settings, from age 2 upwards. The project used many different techniques to elicit their views, such as getting them to take photographs of the people, spaces and things which were important to them. The research showed that, as well as talking with children in their preferred medium, such as English, home language, signing or picture exchange, for example, using several techniques (a 'mosaic') is the best way to achieve an in-depth understanding of the child's perspective. However, asking children about themselves in a group may result in the children giving answers similar to each other. It is best to talk to them individually or in very small groups where they feel most at home and comfortable.

The what and how of observing

The purpose of observing is to assess children's achievements and needs, in order to ensure that planning and provision is appropriate. To be effective it requires practitioners to develop skills in:

- observing
- writing observations
- analysing what they have observed and making assessments
- deciding what to do next as a result of what was seen.

The skill of observing

An observation needs to describe as accurately as possible what was seen and/or heard. Knowledge of child development is important: what are you likely to see? The following aspects of development may be of greatest importance:

- emotional and social
- dispositions and attitudes (for example curiosity, confidence, independence, enthusiasm and persistence)

- physical skills
- communication skills
- cognitive development – how the child is making connections, demonstrating creativity, exploring and investigating.

However, keeping an open mind to other possibilities which might be evident is important. For example, observing a 3- or 4-year-old child in a small group of children in the home corner, the practitioner might intend to observe how the child relates to others. In the course of the observation she/he may also notice how the child:

- makes connections between real-life experiences and fantasy play – often in unexpected ways (cognitive and creative)
- shows confidence, enthusiasm and independence (dispositions)
- sequences an event such as cooking (cognitive)
- dresses and undresses with dressing up clothes (physical)
- writes a message on the telephone pad in own emergent writing (communication skills and cognitive)
- explains how something worked to another child (communication and cognitive)
- develops the storyline for the play in collaboration with another child (creative and social).

In the space of a 3-minute observation, a great deal of information about the child's all – round development can be gathered.

Different types of observations

Children need to be observed in different situations and contexts to arrive at a holistic picture of their development. Some observations need to be planned and others are just collected in the course of a normal day. The method of observation will depend on what else the practitioner is actually doing at the time, and different situations require different observation techniques. For example, there are:

- *Participant observations* – when practitioners are involved in play or an activity with the child
- *'Catch as you can' notes/observations* – something the practitioner noticed but was not involved in
- *Planned, focused observations* – when practitioner stands back to observe, tracking a child in an independently chosen activity or play, for a few minutes. These are *narrative* observations, recounting of what happens.

The planned, 'focused' observation needs to be planned into the daily timetable, so that the observer is not interrupted while observing. It requires the practictioner to observe closely over several minutes, writing or videoing what the child is doing. Usually 4–5 minutes of observation time is quite enough, but time is needed to analyse the observation as well. It is essential that the child is observed in a play situation, or at least involved in independent self-chosen activities. Why?

Play gives opportunities for self-expression and creativity, opportunities to collaborate and negotiate with others, to practise newly acquired skills as well as to try out some not yet fully acquired. Vygotsky (1978: 102) believed that in play children operate at their highest level, 'beyond his average age, above his daily behaviour; in play it is as though he were a head taller than himself'.

As Susan Isaacs puts it: 'The most fertile means of education is the child's spontaneous play ... It provides the normal means of growth in manipulative skill and imaginative expression, in discovery, thought and reasoning' (Isaacs, 1935: 40). And as Vivian Gussin Paley has stated more recently: 'fantasy play is the glue that binds together all other pursuits', it 'provides the nourishing habitat for the growth of cognitive, narrative and social connectivity in young children' (Paley, 2004: 8).

A breadth of evidence is likely to come from a planned, focused observation of play, which is not easily gathered in other ways. Narrative observations of this type should take place on each child at regular intervals, at least once every two to three months, depending on the age of the child and speed at which changes are developing.

What to write in an observation

The amount and type of detail needed during an observation depends on how well the child is already known to the observer. Generally, unless carrying out a narrative observation, the practitioner should look out for things which seem significant: something new or different. Below is a typical example of a 'catch as you can' observation. Through this snippet on 2-year-old Matilda, written as the practitioner played with her, we get a real insight into her curiosity about herself and life in general.

> Matilda is standing next to me in the home corner. She suddenly informs me: I'm growing bigger ... I'm growing bigger and bigger but I can't feel myself growing.

Suzzanne, the practitioner, analysed her observation, noting how Matilda is puzzled by her growth and she added a point for planning: 'Revisit "self" books with her in book corner and add some of these to home corner.'

Knowing what to look for

Although it is easiest to notice visible skills, if these are over emphasised, evidence of the child's developing dispositions, attitudes and emotional development which can be of greatest significance may be missed. In her book *Learning Stories: Assessment in Early Childhood*

Settings (2001), Margaret Carr, working in New Zealand, discusses a new approach to assessing children's learning, based on observations. The assessment of children's *dispositions* is central to this approach. Carr calls these observations 'Learning Stories'. They are narrative observations which document the child's learning in greater depth than one-off observations. 'Learning Stories can capture the complexity of the child's learning and development ... integrate the social with the cognitive and the affective ... and incorporate the child's voice' (ibid.: 95). They may be built up from a sequence of observations which show how a child is solving problems and grappling with new skills and ideas, and often include photographic evidence. Many early childhood centres and nursery schools and classes in Britain now use this approach to recording observation.

Here is Matilda again, still aged 2. This observation is like a Learning Story and consists of photographs as well as the written observation:

Matilda tells me she'd like to make a flag. I tell her I don't know how to do it – does she?

Matilda: 'I think we need a stick.'
Me: 'We don't have any sticks.'
Matilda: 'Maybe we could use a brush.' She fetches one from the sink. 'We could put this paper on here.'
Me: 'How shall we stick it?'
Matilda: 'Maybe with a little bit of glue. We could then stick it together.'

The practitioner, Suzzanne then adds her analysis and assessment:

Matilda shows she is able to make suggestions for how to make things and then design independently with little help from an adult.

Analysing observations and making assessments

Analysing an observation means questioning the evidence.

* What does this tell us about this child's learning and development?
* What areas or aspects of learning and development are evident?
* What can we do next to support this child's development? (That is, what are the implications for planning?)

Sometimes the analysis may require a few moments' thinking time or a quick discussion with other team members at the end of the session. With experience, the process becomes easier to do immediately after the observation. When observing play, it can be helpful to have some assessment questions to hand. The questions below are linked to specific Foundation Stage areas of learning but could be adapted for younger children. Similar questions for each area or aspect of learning could be devised.

Assessing a Child In Play or Child-Initiated Activities: Some Useful Assessment Questions

Personal, social and emotional development

Dispositions and attitudes: who initiated the play/activity? Did the child introduce new ideas – if so, what? Did the child select or create any 'props' to use – if so, how? How involved was the child – did she/he show persistence/determination? How confident did the child seem?

Social development: was there any new evidence of building relationships, negotiating skills, sharing and co-operating with others? Was there evidence of respect for others and growing cultural awareness?

Emotional development: how did the child express feelings and/or respond to the feelings of others? Was there evidence of growing control over own behaviour – if so, how was this shown?

Communication, language and literacy

What type of language was in evidence? For example: talking about present, past or future events; sustaining a conversation with adult or child; using language to express imaginary or real ideas; using language to create or add to a storyline; using language to question or clarify thoughts. Note which language or form of communication was used.

(*Source:* Hutchin, 2003)

How observation informs assessment *for* learning

Every observation is likely to have some implications for planning: first, with regard to the individual child and, secondly, for the staff and setting – perhaps changing a routine or introducing something new. A set of questions to consider when asking 'what next for this child?' might be:

- What can we do to extend this child's skills or understanding in relation to what has been observed?
- What activities, learning opportunities or resources should we provide?
- How will staff be involved?

For the setting and staff possible questions might be:

- What do we need to change or develop to build on this child's interests?
- Can all children access the full range of learning opportunities we provide?

The processes described so far in this chapter have been those of formative assessment, *informing* future planning for the children concerned. A term which has become increasingly prevalent in primary and secondary education for a certain type of formative assessment is 'assessment *for* learning'. It is formative assessment which fully involves children and practitioners together in deciding 'where the learners are in their learning, where they need to go and how best to get there' (DfES, 2004b: 10). For primary school children (Year 1 upwards) it means sharing learning goals with the children, helping children to recognise what they are aiming for, involving children in assessing themselves as well as group assessment with their peers, giving the children feedback on their learning and helping them to identify their own next steps.

However, for younger children (up to the age of 6 years) assessment *for* learning needs to be quite different from the processes used with older children. As stated in the Foundation Stage Profile training guide: 'Given the open ended and play based nature of many of the learning experiences that children encounter within the foundation stage, it may not always be appropriate to share learning objectives with children before they begin activities' (QCA, 2003: 22).

Below is a good example of analysing observations to make assessments and then devising plans to support the child's future development. The nursery teacher, Glynis, in a nursery school had been concerned about how best to help Hannan, 3 years 8 months for a few weeks. The observations show the difficulties Hannan was having in building relationships with her peers. Hannan was new to learning English when she had first started at nursery a few months earlier.

> *Observation:* Hannan hurt her friend but agreed to bring her inside and see that she was looked after. She bought her some ice to hold on her hurt hand. She then agreed to get a story and tell it to her friend.

> *Analysis:* Hannan is beginning to understand that there are consequences to her actions. She is becoming aware that she needs to make her friends feel better if she has caused their hurt. (PSED: managing conflict, feelings and emotions)

A month later a second observation shows how an event resulted in Glynis feeling more confident in developing an approach which would really help support Hannan deal with conflict and develop her ability to form relationships.

> Hannan really wanted to ride the red bike this morning but another child got it first. She shouted, stamped and cried, then came to me the nearest adult for support. I tried a comforting approach rather than a stern 'matter of fact' one and it worked well. It let her get to grips emotionally with what had happened.

The teacher, Glynis, then went on to describe the approach:

1. Comfort her – open arms to cuddle, concerned expression, bring onto lap.
2. Explore her concerns – what is wrong?

3. Give her the words for her feelings – 'you are disappointed, you are sad and cross because … '
4. Involve others to consolidate the words used – 'Hey look come and see, Hannan is really disappointed/sad/cross. Do you know what happened? … '
5. Sometimes this will be enough, but we may need to help her get involved in something else afterwards.

A great deal of thought, teasing out the best responses, went into this example of planning to meet individual needs. Such depth of thinking is not always needed as much learning is more straightforward. For example, the following two examples are of the same child.

16 September: Hannan brought a photo from home to nursery today and proudly showed it to staff. She talked about who was in the photo but did not describe the event (Hannan is at an early stage of learning English).

Next steps: make a photobook about her and her family with agreed sentences she can tell everyone.

22 September: Hannan was being shopkeeper in the nursery shop today. She told me what was for sale: 'Tomato, banana, orange' but did not offer words for melon, apple, lemon or pear.

Next steps: build up her food vocabulary – invite her to name items on food posters and lunch choices.

Sharing observations and giving children feedback

Wherever possible all practitioners should discuss the learning with the children, giving them feedback and identifying next steps, when appropriate, without interrupting their play. This is part of the 'assessment *for* learning' process. The children's records used in the examples in this chapter were presented so that they can be shared at any time with children. They are in the rooms, accessible to children, parents and staff. The observations are kept together with photographs of the children *in action* and samples such as drawings or other art work.

A key finding in the REPEY research (Siraj-Blatchford et al., 2002) was that settings where children made most progress tended to give children feedback on their learning during the learning activity or event. The research calls this process 'focused, formative feedback' to children. It takes place moment by moment as practitioners and children interact together but it is not usually recorded in written observations.

How observation informs assessment *of* learning

Although the most important type of assessment is assessment for learning, from time to time *summative assessment* is useful. The reviews most settings and schools do for parents on a regular basis and at transition times are summative assessments. They enable staff and parents to discuss the child's progress and development together. The Foundation Stage Profile is the statutory summative assessment for children at the end of the Foundation Stage (QCA, 2003).

Summative assessment in the early years must be based on the observations which practitioners and parents have made over time. This means reviewing records, noting any gaps (for example an area or aspect of learning) and making a more general assessment on the child's progress and development, then deciding, with parents and the child, what might be the next steps to support further learning and development. If every observation has been analysed already and points for planning have been suggested, then the summative assessment will be easy to collate. The process ensures that the planning points from each observation, not already addressed, are brought together, ready to feed into what is planned. This is an early years 'target setting' process, more accurately called in the early years context 'learning priorities'. They need to be:

- individual, geared to the child's specific needs
- achievable
- relevant to the child's interests and learning styles
- as far as possible, set with parent and child involvement.

Joycie is in her second term at nursery school. Reviews (summative assessments) are carried out termly. This school has a form with two simple headings:

1. Summary of observations.
2. Next steps.

Here is her review.

Summary of observations

- Accesses collage and workshop well.
- Beginning to mark make and write her name.
- Skilful and creative communicator, able to tell others clearly how to do things.
- Often complains of being tired, especially when asked to tidy up or try a new activity – may mean she is unsure of what to do or how to approach it.

Next steps

- Make an 'I can' book to give her confidence in herself as a learner and ideas as to what things she can do next.
- Structure tidy up tasks for her to ensure success – short goals, obvious tasks, perhaps place her in charge of a younger helper.

These points do not rest in the review section of a child's folder – they are shared with all staff, discussed at a staff planning meeting and built into the normal planning for the children. The school that Joycie attends takes this part of their work very seriously, organising regular reviews of every child's records as well as evaluating how the day went for the children and the staff at the end of every day.

The following term Joycie's review includes these comments:

Summary of observations

- Often helpful to adults and children.
- Much busier now – gets lots done.

In conclusion

Meeting children's individual needs is a complex process, but it is at the heart of the role of the early years practitioner. It must be based on observing children in action and teasing out evidence about the child's development, learning and overall dispositions. For many early years practitioners it is the joy of observing children and the challenge this presents as they try to understand the child and figure out what to do next to support the child which is the most exciting part of the work. It is not the assessment itself which is important, but what we do with what we know. As Pascal and Bertram (in Fisher, 1999: 92) tell us: 'We live in an audited society where what is measurable is seen as significant. We need to ensure that what we are measuring truly matters and that we are not simply focusing on those things that are easily measured.'

EXERCISE 4.1

Carry out a planned, focused observation on a child in your setting in play or a self chosen activity. Use the assessment questions on (page 37 in this chapter) to help you analyse the observation, then make some suggestions for future planning based on what you have seen. The learning priorities bullet points on page 40 may help you with the planning. If possible, ask a colleague to observe the same child with you, then analyse together what you have written.

EXERCISE 4.2

Group activity: ask participants to take part in a turn-taking board game together. After 5–7 minutes of the game ask them to decide what types of skills, dispositions and attitudes as well as knowledge could have been observed by someone watching the game. What would they prioritise in importance? Compare this with the list of possible aspects of development to look for on pages 33–4.

EXERCISE 4.3

Discuss with colleagues in your workplace the arrangements you have for sharing records with parents and children, as well as regularly reviewing records. How does it compare with the points raised in this chapter – are there any points for development agreed by the group?

With thanks to the children, staff and parents at Maxilla Nursery School and Maxilla Nursery Centre.

Further reading

Bartholomew, L. and Bruce, T. (1993), *Getting to Know You*. London: Hodder & Stoughton Educational.
Chapter 2 has a very useful account of the importance of observation in the study of child development as well as for educational purposes.

QCA (2003), *Building the Foundation Stage Profile: Training Materials*.

QCA (2005) *Observing Children – Building the Profile: Training Materials*. Ref. QCA/05/1569
A CD-ROM of the above title is also available, ref. QCA/04/1304 as is a video, *Building Foundation Stage Profile.*

Seeing Steps in Children's Learning (2005) QCA/05/1546.
This is a booklet and DVD illustrating the learning journeys of five children in early years settings, with commentaries which make links to the CGFS stepping stones and early learning goals.

QCA materials are available from QCA Orderline 08700 60 60 15.
The following publications, published by the DfES in conjunction with the Primary National Strategy are available free of charge. They are available from Prolog, tel: 0845 60 222 60:

Foundation Stage Parents: Partners in Learning (2005) (folder) DfES 1210-2005G.

Celebrating Young Children and those who live and work with them (2005) DfES 1211-2005.
This DVD contains very useful footage about 12 children in the Foundation Stage in different early years settings. It includes interviews with their parents and the practitioners who work with them and provides ideal material on the topic of 'meeting individual needs'.

Excellence & Enjoyment in Primary Years Containing Learning and Teaching – Professional Development Materials (2004) DfES 0519-2004 CDI.

EPPE and REPEY: Summary reports of these two research papers are available as downloadable PDF files from various sources, for example: www.ioe.ac.uk/cdl/eppe/pdfs/eppe_brief 2503.pdf and www.surestart. gov.uk/_doc/0-B51527.pdf

THEORY, PRACTICE AND CONTEXT

Tina Bruce

Tina Bruce is Honorary Visiting Professor at Roehampton University, where she originally trained (when it was the Froebel Educational Institute) as a teacher for the Primary phase. She is a trained teacher of children with hearing impairments. She is a widely published author in books, articles and journals, with an international reputation. She was awarded International Woman Scholar in Education by Virginia Commonwealth University and has worked with the British Council in Egypt and New Zealand.

Aim

To develop understanding of:

☐ how to locate yourself in your practice.

Pioneers who continue to influence current practice

When you meet another practitioner who works with young children, you will inevitably size them up to get a sense of the way they work, and their approach to children and their families.

Everyone has personal theories about how children develop and learn, but they do not always realise they have. This is fine for those who are not working with children in a professional capacity, but it is not fine if they are. In many countries the opening remarks between practitioners meeting for the first time will be along the lines of, 'Who influences your practice?'

To work with children in a professional role, it is important to have a sense of your professional identity, and to be able to locate yourself so that your practice is consistent, and has an inner logic, so that it does not simply follow educational fashion, flitting from one trend to the next. It ensures that your practice does not get stuck in a rut, and that you do not just do what the people you work with do without thinking through the implications and discussing your practice together.

In this book you will find references to different approaches, some of them in other countries. Examples would be the Reggio Emilia approach in Italy, or the framework of the Te Whariki curriculum in New Zealand. However, it is important to make links and connections between these and the journey of educational practice with children and families in the first seven years of life in England, in order to locate what is happening in ways which help you to develop your practice thoughtfully, as you work with colleagues and discuss with them.

With the introduction of statutory schooling for children from the age of 5 years in England from 1872, the main influence on the education of most children in schools was that of Samuel Wilderspin. Classrooms were arranged with tiers of children who could be taught by rote, sitting still in large groups. Teachers were usually men, as women were considered too frail for the job of disciplining such large groups and standing before them to deliver lessons and supervise children as they carried out follow-up tasks, writing on slates. The aim was to produce children competent enough to read, write and be sufficiently numerate to be useful in working at everyday jobs. This was a utilitarian approach to education, and the influence lingers.

More privileged children were increasingly educated at home by women who, as mothers, were allowed by their husbands to undertake training to learn about the approach of the German pioneer, Friedrich Froebel (1782–1852) to children's learning. Sometimes children were taught in home-based groups, which took the Froebelian name of kinder-gartens. Children were taught to read, write and be numerate within the framework of a broadly based introduction to literature and poetry, and to mathematics including pattern and relationships, shapes and size, with a rich education in the arts (song, dance, visual arts, both two and three dimensional) and natural science through learning to study nature in the garden. For these mothers, confined by the social conventions of middle-class women of their day to working in the home, this gave them the opportunity to become highly professional, and highly trained teachers, accredited by the National Froebel Foundation.

Gradually, through the influence of Froebelians such as Margaret McMillan (the god-mother of medical inspections in school, the school meals service in the early 1900s, and nursery schools which included classes for parents and worked in multi-agency ways with health professionals), the Froebelian approach began to exert its influence on elementary schools in the mainstream of education, and continues to do so today in the core docu-ments of the Early Years Foundation Stage: *Birth to Three Matters* (DfES, 2002) and *Curriculum Guidance for the Foundation Stage* (CGFS, 2000), which will be embedded in the 'Early Years Foundation Stage' from 2008.

Further reading

Bruce, T. (2005) *Early Childhood Education.* 3rd edition. London: Hodder Arnold. Foreword and Background.

Bruce, T. (2004) *Developing Learning in Childhood.* London: Paul Chapman Publishing. Chapter 2.

THE LEARNING ENVIRONMENT: CREATING A LEARNING ENVIRONMENT INDOORS AND OUTDOORS

Marion Dowling

Marion Dowling has an international reputation as an early years specialist. She is author of a number of books, including *Young Children's Personal, Social and Emotional Development*, and is President of Early Education, a national charity that supports young children and all adults who live and work with them.

Aims

To develop understanding of:

☐ how to see the historic influences on current practice in setting up learning environments indoors and outdoors

☐ and see how these connect with current research and theories.

The learning environment has been rightly described as the third teacher but it is important to remember that the environment is not an end in itself. We can look at settings in identical accommodation with similar equipment but the quality of provision and learning is very different. The crucial factor is what we do with what we have. The indoor and outdoor environments should complement rather than duplicate each other. When we understand what experiences children should have, we can then determine where the provision is best located.

I am taking the learning environment to include:

- the planned allocation of physical space
- the use of display
- the selection and storage of material resources.

All the decisions we make about these aspects of our work will give out strong messages about children learning, and the messages will derive from our beliefs, values and principles.

Knowledge of child development and informed observations of groups and individuals lead us to recognise the best environmental conditions for learning. Children will learn well when they:

- feel confident and in harmony with their environment
- repeat, re-enforce and elaborate on early patterns of activity
- are with others
- use language as a learning tool
- become agents in their own learning
- want to do so.

Children will learn well when they feel confident and in harmony with their environment

Indoors

Until children feel welcome and become familiar with a setting, they will be ill at ease. Are there pictorial signposts that young children can decipher? Is it easy for them to hang up their coats and are their coat pegs visible to them during the day (their coat may be a reas-suring memory that home still exists!)? Are spaces designed and practitioners deployed to enable less secure children to work in small groups and have easy access to an adult at all times? Children are affirmed when they see images of themselves and their families: dis-play can include family photographs; enlarged photographs of individual children can be used to create personalised jigsaws; mirrors allow children to see themselves when involved in different activities.

Rudolph Steiner settings pay particular attention to providing a harmonious environ-ment which allows each child to develop in his or her own way and time. Franz Jaffke (1996) a Steiner educator, claims that the aim is to 'carefully select the impressions which confront and surround the children'. We see this reflected in a Steiner setting, which is both simple and homely. An open space equipped with screens, wooden blocks, a table and lengths of material allow children to transform their world rather than leaving adults to pre-form it.

Outdoors

Outdoor provision can easily lend itself to supporting young children's natural means of learning. Sensory experiences are readily available. Children can observe minibeasts in their natural environment, match leaves of different colours, feel their textures and listen to the sound of their feet crunching on dry leaves. Movement is initially the prime way of learning. Children urgently need to become adept at using their bodies and they want to do so. The *Curriculum Guidance for the Foundation Stage* suggests that provision of an outside space should give scope for children to work and play on a larger scale (CGFS, 2000: 15). This will be embedded in the EYFS from 2008.

When the outdoor area is freely available throughout the session, children will start to use it in their own time and without pressure.

Repeat and elaborate early patterns of activity

Inside

An environment should provide, across the six areas of learning, a rich range of resources which is always available to children. This gives them scope to build on developing inter-ests or schema and to practise and apply what they have learned. In this way children make learning their own. When given time to follow their interests, children start to make con-nections. A layout and organisation of resources which encourages children not only to use a variety of materials within an area, but to combine them, will further strengthen their learning. If children's comments and questions which arise from their play are scribed, dis-played and shared, this makes their thinking visible and helps them to remember.

Outside

Young children's schema (Athey, 1991) are initially linked with movement. In an outside area they can follow interests of transporting, for example, through moving leaves and fir cones by using wheelbarrows. Ropes and pulleys allow exploration of moving things up and down, while using materials to build dens (always a favourite activity) strengthens interests about hiding and enclosures. Wherever possible, children need space to move, make and do things and to develop these interests without disturbing others.

Learn with others

Inside

Of course, children will learn a lot by themselves, but learning expands when they are with others. The environment can strongly facilitate social learning. Warm, inviting spaces invite conversation and conviviality. Interactive displays encourage children to explore and experiment with others. A comfy reading area invites children to share books together.

Outside

Almost 30 years ago Tizard's study of the play of 4-year-olds in pre-school centres found that children from working-class backgrounds opted to spend 75 per cent of their time outside and that here their co-operative play was more evident than indoors (Tizard et al., 1976). Large construction and resources for imaginative play encourage collaborative work, while a friendship bench situated in a quiet area suggests shared conversations.

Become agents in their own learning

A setting which is organised as a workshop can increase opportunities for children to use their initiative.

Inside

There is a need to have a well-ordered layout where children know where each piece of apparatus lives, where there is a space for everything and where it is possible to put things away easily. (I warmed to 4-year-old Luke who, after trying feverishly and unsuccessfully to unscrew an ill-fitting lid on a container, threw it down in disgust, muttering 'why don't things bloody work here?')

Attention to detail when organising resources should make it possible for children to succeed for themselves.

Outside

Children are offered more scope for challenge outside; opportunities to take risks in climbing and balancing, in having more spaces to hide, in experiencing the weather, in building and constructing. Provision of parking bays encourages children to access and return wheeled toys for themselves. Provision of an outside tap or a rain barrel with a tap allows easy access to water. The nature of outside play means that children are more likely to instigate activities for themselves rather than being reliant on the adult.

Want to do so

We can plan the curriculum in detail and have highly organised routines, but we cannot insist that children learn. Both indoor and outdoor environments can tempt children into, or dissuade them from, learning. If we observe young children playing and really listen to them describing what they like to do, this gives us clues about what to provide. Four-year-old Tasmin said that she loved dressing up 'more than anything in my life'. Joe, when asked, simply pointed to the large construction blocks. Children need to know that when they arrive each day there are intriguing and interesting things to experience.

Indoors

The physical environment needs to appeal to children's channels of learning – initially their senses. Spaces should as far as possible be carefully designed to allow for comfort, ease of movement and to be easy on the eye. The following points matter:

- Noise levels – some children are very sensitive to noise and need quiet withdrawal areas.
- Fresh air – the young brain needs oxygen in order to function well.
- Colour – use of different colours can help children to experience and create light and space, calm and stimulus.

It is important to make purchases which allow children to have access to a variety of materials but also to have sufficient resources to allow them the satisfaction of working in depth. Some commercial equipment, particularly for construction, is expensive but may be supplemented with found materials such as cardboard boxes and tubes.

Outside

When given a choice, children often prefer to play outside (Finch, 1999). The environment should give them scope to develop their own interests through a wide range of continuous provision. Even a small area which is planned well should cater for children's differing needs over a period of time. Rather than overcrowding an area with fixed equipment, it is preferable to provide a wheeled trolley with transparent or wire baskets filled with different equipment – items for gardening, small-scale play props with mats, equipment for being minibug detectives.

EXERCISE 6.1

Review your learning environment indoors and outdoors. Consider how well it reflects the six conditions for learning outlined in this section.

PRACTICAL PROJECTS:
BIRTH TO 5 YEARS

Jenny Spratt

Jenny Spratt is Head of Early Years and Childcare Services for Peterborough City Council. She was previously head-teacher of a maintained nursery school in the city and is currently studying on a part-time basis for a PhD.

Aims

To develop understanding of:

☐ ways of tuning into children
☐ ways of observing children's pauses and silences
☐ ways of engaging with theatre and the arts

It is a sunny, warm June morning and children are happily engaged in various activities throughout the nursery garden. One child runs across the play area and under the covered way that provides shade from the sun. He eventually emerges back into the sunshine and runs towards the path that leads around the nursery garden. After a few minutes he runs up to the one of the nursery practitioners and says, 'I have been on the London Underground.'

This chapter considers how observations of children's play can be undertaken at any time – indoors, outdoors and in more unusual situations, such as a visit to a theatre. It is often during situations that we are not expecting, that observations provide the richest moments in children's play. If practitioners are not tuning into the child, these moments are easily missed.

I learnt this years ago, when making the observation quoted above. A video camera was being used to record observations of a child being studied. Rich play had been observed indoors, but when the child took his play into the nursery garden, he appeared to be aimlessly running around in the summer sunshine. At this point I switched off the video camera, but continued observing until I eventually realised, once the child engaged in conversation with the adult, that I almost missed a very rich example of his learning. The child was 'being a London Underground train' and during his apparent aimless running was going in the 'direction of travel' that was needed for his train to arrive at its destination. As the play developed (recorded again on video) the child involved the adult to extend and deepen the play.

The child in this observation (aged 3 years 10 months) used language to signal his play to the adult. She understood and responded accordingly.

However, the signals children give are not always so clear, and practitioners need to be aware that children will use other forms of communication, such as gesture, to engage the adult in their play. This is particularly true of babies and very young children, and as in the observation above, which took place in a busy nursery school environment, practitioners need to be aware of or 'listen' to the 'pauses and silences' of the children.

> Roberto Frabetti, co-founder of La Baracca, Produzioni Teatri, Bologna, Italy, suggests such listening is complex – it means paying attention to what is not said, to the hidden, to the evoked ... the children's eyes and silences go hand in hand and sometimes they open doors to hidden worlds. Most of the time we are not able to see them, and then we lose a good chance to be astonished. (Frabetti, 2005: 64)

Engaging with the arts, and particularly with theatre, for young children provides another perspective to observing young children. 'Theatre often represents what should happen in human relationships. It is about the way that individuals meet and influence each other, sharing memories, projects, with no defence of power or privilege' (Frabetti, 2005: 68).

This is evidenced in the following observation undertaken during a performance or game for babies created by the theatre company 'Oogly Boogly' which shows how non-verbal communication provides the signal to the adult when the child is on the cusp of spoken language.

> The baby, aged fifteen months, sits on his mother's knee inside the Oogly Boogly dome. This is a neutral space and soft music is playing, so that it is not silent.
> The baby feels secure and bangs his foot on the padded floor – it makes a thudding sound.
> The actor, sitting opposite the baby bangs his foot in the same way – mirroring the baby's action.
> The baby bangs his foot again – the actor bangs his foot.
> The baby looks at the actor for a moment and then lifts his foot and pulls his sock off – the actor lifts his foot and pulls his sock off.
> The baby realises that the actor is copying him and that whatever he does, the actor will do. The baby also realises that he is the one in control of the game.

The whole focus of the Oogly Boogly experience is based on observation, and the actors and dancers taking part in the game have spent a long time focusing on how to observe the sounds, postures, facial expressions, eye pointing, gaze, intonation, tone, rhythm and movement of the babies they work with. The Oogly Boogly experience is only for babies aged from 12 to 18 months as they are developing:

- a sense of physical self – embodiment
- a sense of themselves as a thinker – metacognition
- a sense of feelings and management of them – emotional literacy,

and are on the cusp of language. Damasio (2004) suggests a 'nesting principle' where the baby is laying down the foundations for communication and later reading and writing. Frabetti suggests:

> Children react unpredictably, and above all, they are uncatchable and this happens mostly because we cannot use verbal communication with them. This is the phase during which children absorb billions of pieces of information and systems to process them. They begin to understand what language is, and to understand that it is necessary. (2005: 66)

Another important aspect of this observational experience is the space in which the game takes place. The Oogly Boogly 'dome' is an inflatable, padded room, designed by architects of the air, to ensure its originality and safety. It is unusual, in today's busy world, to experience such a neutral environment, but it is one in which both parents/carers and children are able to focus on the game itself.

It provides the adult with the opportunity to observe their own child, probably in a way that they have not been able to do before. Parents and carers who were involved in the Oogly Boogly sessions really appreciated the way in which this space provided a quiet time for them as well as their child, which enabled them to celebrate what their child was doing. One parent commented that observing her child in this way 'made me fall in love with my daughter all over again'. Other parents felt a sense of pride in how they observed what their child was able to do within the game, but they also felt pride in seeing the other seven babies in the session flourish in the same way.

Parents then questioned whether it was a good idea to always put their child in a 'busy' environment – meaning one that contained lots of toys, pictures and constant sound or even taking older children to a busy programme of different activities. They came away from the Oogly Boogly experience wanting to:

- experience it again
- ensure other parents/carers and children were able to experience it
- find time to have 'quiet' times with their children, where they could observe and celebrate the things that they were able to do.

They ultimately described the experience as 'a feeling that we all had and took away – we still feel excited about it – it was a feeling of calmness – a very lovely feeling.'

In October 2004, at the Festival Hall, London, Roberto Frabetti and his sister Valeria Frabetti, presented a play, *The Colours of Water*, for nursery children aged 1–4. The play was made of light, sounds, images and movements, where words fade into the background to accompany the action. This takes the experience of theatre beyond that offered by Oogly Boogly – the children themselves are no longer the performance, they are observing the performance given by the actors. The words that are used in this performance explain the context before the action and sound take over. Frabetti explains, 'Early childhood is a faraway place and theatre can be one of the many ways to try and reach it, because it is a "human" language. It forces human beings to meet each other face to face, showing all kinds of diversities' (2005: 68). The children experiencing 'the colours of water' had a sense of performance, they were absorbed in the story, the action and the sound. They sat with the parent/carer/practitioner, so felt secure, and after the performance were invited to experience the feel of the water and the materials used.

At the same conference at the Festival Hall another group of nursery children, aged between 18 months and 3 years, experienced a different theatrical performance, which like La Baracca, required the children to observe a performance and later respond in their own ways. The performance was *Terre* by the Theatre de la Guimbarde from Belgium, which transformed clay into landscapes, animals and surprising things alongside a musical language composed of the natural rhythm of voice and percussion. During the performance the children sat with familiar adults, so felt secure as they enjoyed the show. Afterwards, in their own time and space, they were able to explore and play in their own world of clay, building upon the observations they had made.

The performances described in this chapter have considered how observation of the pauses and silences that young children display, enable the practitioner to celebrate the child's achievements and reflect upon the way in which to support the next steps in the child's learning. The child in the first observation was engaged in his own play or performance, and he used pauses and silences followed by words to convey his meaning. The adult was key to continuing and extending his play.

The examples taken from Oogly Boogly show how babies on the cusp of language engaged adults in a 'conversation' that they choreographed and led, and how the adults observing them engaged in the pauses and silences with a sense of celebration over what they had experienced.

The performances from La Baracca and Theatre de la Guimbarde showed how children with language were able to observe a performance by being part of an audience, and could then interpret the experience through their own pauses, silences, actions and words. Frabetti concludes that 'nursery children's pauses take our breath away. They are long pauses that make you consider time from a different point of view' (2005: 70).

CHAPTER 8

INTRODUCING CHILD DEVELOPMENT

Tony Bertram and Chris Pascal

Professor Tony Bertram has a Chair in Early Childhood Development (International) at University of Worcester and is also Director of the Centre for Research in Early Childhood, based at the St Thomas Centre, Birmingham. He is President and Co-Founder of the European Early Childhood Education Research Association, His current research is a five-country, cross-national project looking at home/setting transition issues for children and families of the 'newly arrived'.

Professor Christine Pascal OBE is Professor in Early Childhood Education at University of Worcester and Director of the Centre for Research in Early Childhood, based at the St Thomas Centre, Birmingham, specialising in early childhood research and evaluation projects. She is Project Director of the Effective Early Learning (EEL) Project and of the Accounting Early for Life Long Learning (AcE) Project. She is early years specialist adviser to the House of Commons Select Committee.

Aims

To develop understanding of:

- [ ] and gain an introduction to child development in the western tradition
- [ ] this knowledge in action
- [ ] and use the knowledge and ideas to improve your own professional practice.

Introduction

New research and theories about child development are appearing all the time and adding to our understanding about young children's lives. This chapter sets out some of the main ideas, predominantly from western traditions of research and theory, and shows how they help us to work more effectively with young children and their families.

Each section of the chapter sets out some key messages about what we know and understand about child development, and explores how this information can help practitioners and carers interact with children to support their learning. The chapter also provides ideas for putting the key messages into practice and offers some exercises for readers to try out these ideas within their workplace.

How children develop and learn

Key messages

1. *Pre- and post-natal experience is a major determinant in the long-term healthy progress of the child.* The mother's state of health, levels of stress and nutrition during pregnancy play a key part in the healthy development of the foetus and new-born baby. Smoking, alcohol and other substance abuse by the mother, are factors in the low birth weight of babies, and this is linked to long-term health problems in children. Breast-feeding can also offer the child significant health benefits. Research has shown the key part played by health visitors and other supportive practitioners or family members in helping parents and the wider family to prepare for the birth of their child and to support the new-born infant.

2. *The first 60 months of a child's life are critical in determining their future development, with the first four months being the most influential.* Research on brain development and emotional well-being has shown the critical nature of experiences in the first months of a child's life, and in particular, the first four months (Abbott and Moylett, 1997). During this period the architectural structure of the brain's connectivity is being formed. Small babies have an extraordinary range of capabilities, some of which they

will lose before 3 years of age. The early thickets of synaptic connections begin to be pruned when not used and the connecting branches that are used and stimulated become the major pathways for thought. The quality of stimulation and interaction at this time will largely determine the child's capacity to learn in the long term and the associations they will make between learning and pleasure, or between stimulation and emotional well-being. The quality of stimulation, affection and care received by the child during the first five years of life has been shown to shape a child's life chances.

3. *There appear to be developmental phases that all children go through but a child's individual progress is shaped by their experience and culture.* Research has continued to show that developmental psychologists, like Piaget (Piaget and Inhelder, 1969), were right in stating that all children go through a series of developmental phases or stages as they mature and that the rate and timing of these stages are part of our biological and genetic programming. But to understand development we must go beyond biological explanations. Social constructivists like Vygotsky (1978) and Bruner (1960; 1996) have also shown that a child's development and learning is significantly mediated by individual, social and cultural experiences. Social constructivists believe that the culture and society in which children are raised impacts on the pace and nature of development. So development is constructed, in part, by the social environment in which children live. Each child's developmental profile will be unique, and development may be non-linear and uneven.

4. *From birth children are competent and skilful learners, with a wide range of skills that are further shaped by their family and community.* Children are born full of capability, able to communicate, influence and make sense of the world and their experiences within it. Humans are characterised by a strong exploratory drive and curiosity. This capacity is further enhanced and extended in enriching environments and in particular ways by a child's family and community. Relationships, interactions and shared experiences feed this capacity. Children often indicate whether they are bored or involved in an activity, and children who are involved in stimulating, purposeful and meaningful activity will display confirming signals. Cultural diversity adds complexity and richness to our society and it is important that such diversity is acknowledged, valued and incorporated into practitioners' thinking and actions. Parents are valuable partners in ensuring a child's cultural identity is celebrated, reinforced and extended, in sharing information about a child's early experiences and in ensuring a child's capabilities are recognised and built upon.

5. *Children are born with a strong exploratory drive and seek active experiences and play.* From birth, children have a strong exploratory drive through which they experiment, explore, interact with and make sense of their world (Laevers, 1994; Pascal and Bertram, 1997). Young children are essentially active risk-takers and problem-solvers and they require an environment which is full of stimulation, opportunities to stretch themselves to their limits and take risks, to play for extended periods of time, both alone and with adult and child playmates. They also need encouragement to follow

through their self-chosen activities and to be self-organised, persistent, resilient, creative and playful.

6. *Young children learn with and through other people, especially their parents/carers and other children.* As Vygotsky (1978) has shown, development and learning is essentially a social activity. Children learn with and through significant others, who may be a parent or carer, an older child or sibling or other playmates. It is through interactions and collaborative play activity that seeks and solves problems, combined with plenty of supported opportunities to express their meaning-making, that a child develops and learns. Action and interaction are the twin keys to development and learning.

7. *Children's development is hugely affected by their social and emotional well-being.* Children's development and learning is fundamentally influenced by their emotional state (Pascal and Bertram, 1997). A child who has a confident sense of connection with, and attachment to, those around them will thrive. Laevers (1994) has demonstrated that children with strong well-being will be able to open themselves to deep levels of involvement and immersion in their explorations of the world. Whereas a child who lacks social skills and is timid and insecure will miss the joy of experimentation, adventure and shared risk-taking.

EXERCISE 8.1

Exploring the first weeks of a baby's life

1. Make contact with a parent(s) of a child under the age of 3 months and arrange an interview.
2. Discuss and record how the pregnancy progressed and any facts about the child's pre- and post-natal history. Find out how the child developed during the first weeks after birth and any emerging issues that occurred relating to the child's progress. How did the parents deal with these issues, where did they go to for help and advice, and what may have further supported them?
3. Share the information you have gained with a work colleague. Discuss how typical the issues raised are and how additional support may have been provided to the family and child.
4. Consider what your reading says about a child's development in the first few weeks of life and reflect in your journal how this pattern of development fits the baby you have been focusing on.
5. Write a plan of support for this parent and baby for the next six months and state what difference this action might make to both the parent and the child.
6. How will you evaluate the benefits of your planned action?

Feelings, relationships and socio cultural development

Key messages

1. *Children's overall development is fundamentally affected by their relationships and feelings.* There has been a revolution in recent thinking about children's development and we now know that there is a close link between emotions and cognition (Bruner, 1996). Children who experience close, affectionate, loving relationships, and who are emotionally supported, develop better in all areas. Children who do not form strong attachments, have disrupted relationships and experience cold, distant care, especially during the first few months of life, are vulnerable to long-term developmental delay.

2. *Children's sense of self and their ability to form relationships with others is substantially shaped by their early interactions with others.* During the first few weeks of life children form strong bonds with those who care for them. Through the interactions with their carer(s) and other close family and community members, children start to develop a sense of themselves and their particular place in the world (Trevarthen, 2003). They are exploring where they 'fit' and who they are, seeking feedback continually from those around them on their actions and experiences and feelings. Their capacity to connect with others and make relationships is therefore critical if they are to receive the feedback and reinforcement they seek from these early interactions.

3. *The emotional life of the young child underpins the way they explore and make sense of the world.* Children's emotional state has a profound effect on the way they explore and attempt to make sense of their world (Pascal and Bertram, 1997). Children who have poor emotional well-being often respond with timidity, fear and rigidity to new experiences, lacking the open, exploratory state that learning about the world requires. Research has shown that such children can become withdrawn, hesitant and very clingy, in a way that inhibits their exploration. In contrast, children who are secure, attached and confident usually play, and become adventurous, enjoying risk-taking, and having the flexibility that new experiences need. These attitudes, dispositions and feelings will positively shape the way the child faces the unknown and ensure that their curiosity and exploratory drive thrives.

4. *The social and emotional life of the child is culturally embedded.* The way a child feels and expresses emotion, and the nature and shape of their social relationships, will be influenced a good deal by the particular family and community into which they are born. Each family and community has certain values and beliefs (or culture) that shape the way children are dealt with, related to and encouraged to behave. These experiences, in turn, will shape the child's emotional and social life, and the way the child will deal with feelings and relationships. It can sometimes be hard accurately to read the social and emotional signals that children from other cultures communicate.

5. *Children's identities are shaped by the nature of their interactions with different cultures.* In the early months of a child's life, children are forming a sense of themselves and their own identity(ies). In today's global and visual world, a child's sense of self and identity is shaped by a complex range of experiences and interactions with a culturally diverse range of sources. Young children become very adept at cultural brokering, and will draw on all these cultural sources when creating their own identity(ies) and sense of self. They are also capable early on of understanding when to display certain aspects of self, and when to suppress certain aspects. We should not underestimate the hybrid and multiple nature of identity and the choices young children make when constructing a sense of who they are and what constitutes their internal self.

EXERCISE 8.2

Who are the child's 'companions'?

1. Observe a child under the age of 4 over several days and record who are the child's favoured companions (both adults and other children).
2. Record the nature and content of the interactions between the child and her/his companions. What do you think the child is gaining from these companions?
3. Talk to the child's parents and or carers about the child's favoured companions and how these relationships have developed.
4. What does your reading say about 'companionship' or 'friendship' in the early months and years of life? Can you find evidence in your reading of cultural differences in 'companionship' patterns?
5. Reflect on how you might use both child and adult 'companions' to support children's development within an early years centre.

Communication and language development

Key messages

1. *Children are born as gifted communicators.* From birth children are skilful communicators, using a whole range of verbal and non-verbal signals to reach out to, and manipulate, those around them. This capacity to direct others to tend to their needs is vital to a child's survival. The young child is also gifted at orchestrating the communication and effective partners, both adults and children, often follow the child's cues and leads, through imitation and improvisation. This is true of facial and bodily communication cues, as well as vocalisations (Doherty-Sneddon, 2003; Trevarthen, 2003).
2. *There are critical periods for the development of language.* Research on the development of the brain has confirmed the view that there are critical periods for the development of a child's linguistic ability (Chomsky, 1975). Experiences during the first

weeks of a child's life appear to determine the child's capacity to vocalise in certain ways. Young children need lots of opportunity to both hear (listen) and vocalise (speak), and are very receptive to sound. The kinds of vocal patterns that they will be able to achieve are shaped by the vocal patterns they hear and imitate. Rich and extended opportunities for interaction and communication are centrally important in these early months of development.

3. *The development of communication and language is intimately linked to the development of thought.* The capacity of the child to think, to internalise their growing sense of the world, and to extend their understanding through the development of higher order thinking skills, is to a large extent determined by their growing capacity to use and understand language or sign language (Vygotsky, 1978). Young children need to experience and participate in a language-rich environment, and to be encouraged to talk about and reflect on their experiences.

4. *Children have many languages that they use to communicate their thoughts, feelings and understandings about the world.* Children express themselves in many non-verbal ways before they use words (Doherty-Sneddon, 2003). They have many languages to draw on to communicate meaning and their non-verbal languages provide an important window on all aspects of their development and learning. Hand gestures, posture, eye gaze, facial expressions and touch are all key ways that children use to communicate. Understanding these important channels of communication can help parents and practitioners to support children's development and learning. Unfortunately, sometimes these other languages are ignored or misinterpreted with the emphasis largely on the significance of the spoken word.

5. *Children need adults and other children to respond to, and stimulate, their developing communication and language skills.* Children are inherently social beings and seek others to share their world and help in the co-construction of their growing understandings. The importance of interaction and talk within affectionate, caring relationships cannot be overestimated in the development of a child's communication and language skills. The sharing of stories, rhymes, singing and other play activities will provide further stimulus to the child's developing communication and language skills.

EXERCISE 8.3

Making sense of young children's communication

1. Observe a small group (two or three) of young children interacting together.
2. Make a list of the different ways the children use to communicate with each other and note what was the intention of the communication. Include non-verbal and verbal or signed communication in your record.

(Continued)

E X E R C I S E   8 . 3   (C O N T I N U E D)

y and group the kinds of communication strategies you have recorded into various
types, for example, hand gestures, body posture, eye gaze, facial expressions, touch,
vocalisations.

4. Discuss with other practitioners how they interpret children's communications – in particular try to analyse how non-verbal communications are used by practitioners to make
sense of children's experiences and feelings.

5. Read about how new-born babies communicate with the world and reflect on how far
and in what ways these strategies are used by older children?

6. Plan a small group session with young children that encourages them to use a range
of communication strategies with each other and yourself.

7. Evaluate why there is a tendency to focus primarily on verbal communication in many
early years centres and consider how this focus might be extended to better understand
young children's experiences and feelings.

Learning through the senses and direct experience

Key messages

1. *Children are born with a natural curiosity, and a strong exploratory drive.* All children are born with a strong inner exploratory drive that feeds their natural curiousity
and inclination to investigate the world (Laevers, 1994; Pascal and Bertram, 1997). The
inquisitive nature of young children feeds their development and learning, and is a
disposition to be celebrated and encouraged. Challenge, risk-taking and adventure
come naturally to the young child and adults need to ensure these dispositions can
thrive within a secure and safe environment.

2. *All five senses are used in a child's exploration but sight and sound are critical.*
Children draw on all their senses to explore and make sense of the world. Touch,
sight, smell, sound and taste are the conduits of action and experience, and each of
these senses needs stimulation from birth. Research has shown that the senses of
sight and sound develop earliest and need vital stimulation if they are to develop normally. There appears to be a critical period in young children's development when the
capacity for these senses to develop normally is set, and therefore stimulation of these
senses from birth is essential.

3. *Children actively seek stimulation and need first-hand experiences with real
objects and occurrences, and responsive adults or children who both support and
model.* There can be no substitute for first-hand experience and active, self-directed
experiences which flow from the child's own initiatives. Although children do learn

through modelling, demonstration and imitation, offering active, problem-posing and play experiences with real objects within a rich environment will stimulate the child's development far more effectively (Bruce, 2001; Bruner, 1996).

4. *Children need lots of opportunities to be self-directed and should be encouraged to manage their own learning.* Research has shown that children should be given the chance from the earliest age to be self-directing and to take initiatives (Laevers, 1994). Adults can support a child's choices and progress towards self-identified goals. The capacity of children from the earliest age to self-manage and self-evaluate their own learning should be acknowledged and built upon, and where a child finds this difficult further support should be provided as a priority.

E X E R C I S E 8 . 4

Mapping involvement levels in young children

1. Read about Laever's (1994) 'Child involvement scale' and reflect on how this might help you 'tune into' a child's learning processes more effectively.
2. Using Laever's involvement scale, observe two children: (a) engaged in free play; (b) engaged in circle time; (c) engaged in a collaborative activity; and record their involvement levels.
3. Analyse where you found involvement levels were high and where they were low, and reflect on the reasons why these levels were observed.
4. Talk with practitioners and parents and ask them what conditions seem to favour high and low involvement levels in children.
5. Reflect on how the 'Child involvement scale' might be used to evaluate and improve the quality of practice within a centre.

Diversity and inclusion – gender, ethnicity and culture

Key messages

1. *Children are born into a diverse, intercultural society and seek to find their place and identity.* The world into which children are now born is diverse and made up of myriad different cultures and communities. Globalisation and increasing migration means that they are likely to travel and mix with children and families from different cultures and communities. Helping children to have a sense of both individual and collective identity, and also a feeling of connectedness to society as a whole, is an important task for those who care for and educate the young.
2. *All cultures are rich but not all cultures are given equal value in our society and this impacts on children's sense of self and self-worth.* It is important to acknowledge that

while all cultures are rich, society tends to endow some cultures with more value than others. Often, there is an ignorance of other cultures, and this can lead to stereotypes and prejudices developing (Siraj-Blatchford, 1994). Young children are acutely aware of the responses of others towards them, their family and their community as they form their own sense of self-worth and identity.

3. *Gender identity affects a child's progress.* There has been much written to document the differences between boys and girls in various areas of development. It appears that the developmental profiles of even very young children are affected by their gender. However, it is also evident that any biological determinism can be reinforced or challenged by the way boys and girls are treated, particularly in the early years. The feminisation of the early years workforce may be a factor in the superior progress of girls within the existing system. This raises important questions of equity and access for boys in early childhood settings.

4. *All children have the legal right to be treated equally and not suffer discrimination.* The United Nations Convention on Children's Rights, which has been ratified by the UK, gives children from birth important rights and entitlements. The appointment of the first Children's Commissioner for England and Wales in 2005 adds weight to the importance of children's rights. The UK also has strong laws to ensure that all children are treated equally and should not suffer discrimination on the grounds of race or gender. Early childhood practitioners are required by law to provide equal access to their services and to adopt inclusive, anti-discriminatory practice.

EXERCISE 8.5

Looking at diversity

1. Focus on a group of children who attend an early childhood centre and try and map the diversity of cultures that are present in the group.
2. Research the cultures represented in the group and in particular find out about the cultures with which you are less familiar.
3. Talk to a small group of parents from a range of a different cultures about their own childhood experiences and their aspirations for their children.
4. Find out from the practitioners within the centre how they support cultural diversity and difference within their practice.
5. Find out about the legal requirements on equality in public services. Look at an early years centre's policy on equality and diversity and talk with the centre manager about how this is put into practice.
6. Identify what you feel are the key challenges to achieving anti-discriminatory practice within all early childhood centres.

Children with special educational needs and disabilities

Key messages

1. *There is a wide range in the normal development of young children, and we should be cautious of pathologising variations in children's development.* Although it can be helpful to look at expected norms of development for children, recent work has shown that developmental expectations at different ages are also culturally embedded (Bruner, 1996). What can be expected of a 2-year-old in one culture may be very different to a 2-year-old child growing up in another culture. It should also be emphasised that there is a very wide range in the normal development of children and we should be careful about labelling children with developmental delay or precociousness (Bruce, 2001).

2. *Early diagnosis and intervention to support children's special needs can lead to more favourable long-term development.* The early identification of children with special needs and the provision of specialist support have been shown to make a remarkable difference to children's subsequent progress. All early childhood settings are required to have an identified member of staff with responsibility for co-ordinating specialist support for children with particular needs, but all practitioners have an important role to play in identifying a child's needs as early as possible and linking with specialist support where necessary.

3. *All practitioners need to work together with other professionals to ensure a network of support around children with special needs and their families.* Recent legislation requires all agencies and professionals working with young children to co-ordinate their efforts to ensure a 'joined up' network of support for all children, and their families, based on individual needs. Each child and family should have a Lead Professional who is the primary point of contact, and whose role is to identify and coordinate appropriate support. There is also a requirement to share information to ensure a seamless service, to avoid duplication of effort and ensure all children receive the support they need.

4. *Practitioners should ensure their practice is inclusive and anti-discriminatory towards children with special needs.* There is a legal requirement for practitioners to adopt anti-discriminatory practices towards all children and families. Services should be open and accessible for all children, and promote positive and inclusive practice that celebrates diversity and difference (Siraj-Blatchford, 1994). This means practitioners need to understand fully the nature of a child's needs and be aware of their obligations towards meeting these fully and respectfully. Parents too may need particular support in understanding and realising their child's rights.

5. *The pedagogy for children with special needs should mirror that for all children.* Children with special needs have an entitlement to a curriculum or programme that fully meets their needs and ensures access to experiences in all areas of learning. The pedagogy adopted for children with special needs should encourage independence, autonomy and choice, emphasising self-directed and self-managed learning, as

recommended for all children. Practitioners need to provide additional support where necessary, but should not change the nature of learning experiences where this would discriminate against children with special needs (Bruce, 2005).

6. *Settings should ensure resources are accessible and appropriate to support the particular needs of all their children.* Anti-discriminatory practice requires that all resources, including materials, equipment, room layout and staffing, are reviewed regularly to ensure accessibility and appropriateness to the whole range of need within a setting (Siraj-Blatchford, 1994). This may require specialist resources and equipment that are geared to a child's particular needs. Accessing specialist advice is vital when reviewing access to, and equality of, programmes for all children within a setting.

EXERCISE 8.6

How inclusive are we?

1. What does your reading say about the legal requirements to support all children with special educational needs and disabilities?
2. Talk to a centre manager about their views on inclusive practice for children with special educational needs. What do they feel are the key challenges in ensuring inclusive practice works well?
3. Interview a parent of a child with special educational needs and discuss their experience of their child's inclusion in early childhood centres. Who do they deal with and where is their key point of support?
4. Observe a child with special educational needs or a disability within a centre and record how the practitioners involved ensure the child has equal access and entitlement to the experiences on offer.
5. How might you evaluate the inclusiveness of an early years centre for children with special educational needs? What evidence would you use?

The impact of economic poverty on a child's development

Key messages

1. *In England we continue to have unacceptably high levels of child poverty, which has a long-term impact on the life chances of many children.* In comparison with other developed countries, England continues to have high levels of child poverty and the gap between rich and poor persists despite government policies devised to address this. Growing up in poverty has a long-term impact on children's attainment and significantly shapes future life chances (OECD, 2000).

2. *The long-term development of the child is negatively affected by factors related to poverty.* Living in poverty is the single most damaging influence on a child's life and is associated with a range of negative factors connected with development in children. These factors include family stress, strained relationships, poor pre- and post-natal nutrition, poor physical and mental health, inadequate housing, low well-being and low aspirations. The impact of such factors on children's lives can be profound and hard to redress later.

3. *High-quality, integrated, early childhood provision, with a strong educational component can make a difference to children's life chances.* There is robust evidence that providing high-quality, integrated early childhood services can be particularly beneficial to less advantaged families. Combining health and social care services with a strong and early educational focus for children and families can be particularly effective in improving life chances. The development of Children's Centres in all neighbourhoods, where multi-professional teams work collectively for children and families, reflects a more 'joined-up' approach to early childhood services, in an attempt to break cycles of poverty and disadvantage.

Issues of child development

Key messages

1. *Children's development is determined by both biological factors and sociocultural experiences.* Current evidence points to a dynamic and symbiotic relationship between biological or genetically determined patterns of development and socioculturally embedded development. Knowledge about genomes is revolutionising our understanding of genetic endowment and its impact on developmental progress. However, sociocultural studies reveal the significance of life experiences, especially in the very early years of life, in determining the realisation of capabilities and human potential.

2. *There is a rapidly increasing knowledge base about young children's development that is providing important insights for effective practice.* Rapid strides have been made in our knowledge and understanding of human development, and the factors that contribute positively and negatively to healthy progress. These factors provide valuable insights into what constitutes effective practice in the rearing of young children, both in home- and centre-based care. A key factor appears to be the nature of early relationships and interactions.

3. *The child's brain is at its most malleable in the first weeks of life and stimulation is critical at this time.* Brain research shows that during the first weeks of a child's life the brain has immense plasticity and that this is a critical time for shaping the architecture of the brain and the long-term capacity to learn. The brain is at its most impressionable

during this early period of life. Stimulation, both sensory and socially through interaction with others, is hugely important and profoundly shapes a child's potential.

4. *The impact of early experience on a child's developmental profile is profound and provides a critical challenge for practitioners to provide high-quality experiences.* The long-term significance of experiences in the early weeks and months of a child's life provides practitioners with both a challenge and an opportunity. If high-quality, cognitive and affective experiences can be provided for children during these early years, life chances can be improved impressively. This is a huge incentive for practitioners to raise the quality of their services, to ensure maximum impact and outcomes for all children.

5. *Globalisation means that young children are increasingly likely to experience migration, transitions and cross-cultural experiences that will shape their development.* It is important to acknowledge that modern life, and the impact of globalisation, means that migration, transitions and change are endemic in children's and family lives. These experiences can be enormously beneficial for children when handled with sensitivity, empathy and support. They can certainly open doors to new worlds for children whose lives are marred by disadvantage and deprivation of various kinds. But, such experiences can also disrupt, dislocate and disturb children's progress, and practitioners need to respond actively and positively to the reality of children's lives.

6. *Every child's developmental profile is unique although there are universal patterns in human development.* Our ever-increasing knowledge of child development supports the view that although there are universal patterns which may be recognised and used to guide practice, each child's growing journey is unique, shaped by a powerful cocktail of genetic endowment and life experiences which are culturally and socially embedded. This means that practitioners have to be able to respond to children as individuals with a unique and exclusive response to the world into which they are born and are living and growing. The skills required of adults who can respond to all children with insight, affection and expertise cannot be overestimated.

Further reading

Bruce, T. (2005) *Early Childhood Education* 3rd edition. London: Hodder Arnold.
This is a thoroughly practical and well-researched introductory text which shows how current understandings of child development build on from traditional approaches, and may be used to inform early childhood policy and practice during a time of radical reform in the delivery of early childhood services. The book provides a comprehensive overview of past and present understandings and looks ahead to explore how this knowledge of young children's learning and development might be incorporated into an agenda for change. It emphasises the sociocultural context in which children develop, and puts this alongside the biological aspects of child development and learning.

Bruner, J. (1960) *The Process of Education*. Cambridge, MA: Harvard University Press.

Bruner, J. (1996) *The Culture of Education*. Cambridge, MA: Harvard University Press.
Both these texts are rightly recognised as twentieth-century 'classics' and have had a direct impact on policy formation and the thinking and orientation of a wide group of teachers and scholars. In *The Process of Education* (1960) Bruner's view of children as active problem-solvers who are ready from birth to explore 'difficult' subjects challenged many of the accepted canons of educational practice. His later reflections in *The Culture of Education* (1996) show the changes in his thinking since the 1960s. He now places his work within a thorough appreciation of culture, which he sees as shaping the mind.

Oates J. (ed.) (1995) *The Foundations of Child Development*. Oxford: Blackwell.
This is the first in a series of four books that form part of the Open University course, Child Development. They provide a detailed and thorough undergraduate-level introduction to the central concepts, theories, current issues and research evidence in developmental psychology. These books assume no previous knowledge of the field and encourage the reader's active involvement, especially through the use of activities. Examples drawn from case studies, psychological research and practice stimulate critical appreciation of the issues covered. Selected short readings accompany the chapters to present ideas from a variety of sources. A focus on modern developmental theories is complemented by detailed consideration of models of developmental processes. A theme that runs through the book is a concern with the ways in which biological, social and cultural influences interact in development.

Piaget, J. and Inhelder, B. (1969) *The Psychology of the Child*. New York: Basic Books.
This is a seminal text that has profoundly shaped our understanding of child development. The concept of cognitive structure is central to his theory. Cognitive structures or schemas are patterns of physical or mental action that correspond to stages of child development. There are four primary development stages according to Piaget: sensorimotor, pre-operations, concrete operations and formal operations. In the sensorimotor stage (0–2 years), intelligence takes the form of motor actions. Intelligence in the pre-operation period (3–7 years) is intuitive in nature. The cognitive structure during the concrete operational stage (8–11 years) is logical but depends upon concrete referents. In the final stage, formal operations (12–15 years), thinking involves abstractions. Cognitive structures change through the processes of adaptation: assimilation and accommodation. Assimilation involves the interpretation of events in terms of existing cognitive structure whereas accommodation refers to changing the cognitive structure to make sense of the environment. Cognitive development consists of a constant effort to adapt to the environment in terms of assimilation and accommodation. In this sense, Piaget's theory is similar in nature to other constructivist perspectives of learning.

Vygotsky, L.S. (1978) *Mind in Society*. Cambridge, MA: Harvard University Press.
Lev Vygotsky, born in the USSR in 1896, developed the social constructivist theory of learning and development. In this book he proposed that social interaction profoundly influences cognitive development. Central to Vygotsky's theory is his belief that biological and cultural development do not occur in isolation. He argued that the process of development is dependent on social interaction and that social learning actually leads to cognitive development.

UNDERSTANDING SYMBOLIC DEVELOPMENT

Tina Bruce

Tina Bruce is Honorary Visiting Professor at Roehampton University, where she originally trained (when it was the Froebel Educational Institute) as a teacher for the Primary phase. She is a trained teacher of children with hearing impairments. She is a widely published author in books, articles and journals, with an international reputation. She was awarded International Woman Scholar in Education by Virginia Commonwealth University and has worked with the British Council in Egypt and New Zealand.

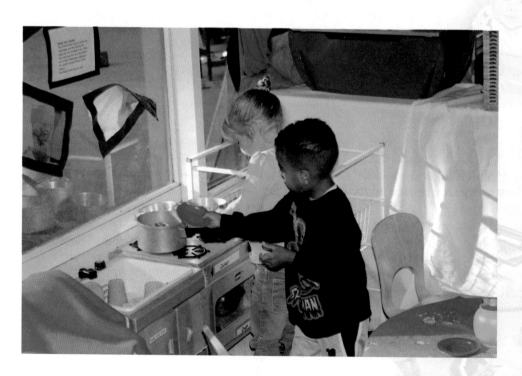

> **Aims**
>
> To develop understanding of:
>
> ☐ how children develop as symbol users, appreciating, recognising and understanding the symbols of others
> ☐ how children develop as symbol-makers, and their creativity
> ☐ how adults can support children to use conventional symbols of the culture with confidence and competence.

What is symbolic development?

A symbol is something which stands for something else. It might be a word, an object or a person or a event. The word dog stands for the real dog. The doll stands for the baby. The child rocking the baby doll stands for the parent of the baby. In some cultures the birthday celebration stands for the day when a person was born.

Symbols help us to operate in the future as well as the past. Symbolic behaviour allows human beings to go beyond the here and now in time and space in ways which other animals do not seem to be able to do.

Symbolic behaviour develops during the period when walking, talking and pretending begin to emerge (DfES, 2002). It takes many forms.

Language/signing

Language, both spoken and signed, is of especial importance in human development (Communicating Matters, 2005). There has been robust debate among psychologists about whether or not language is a separate system from other kinds of representation. This is fascinating to study and tease out, rather like a detective story. However, for practitioners working with young children in the practical setting, the key message is that language/signing is of deep importance in enabling children to begin to operate with more abstract thinking that does not depend on the immediate situation.

In other chapters there has been discussion of the ability of the human brain to use several languages, and to be multi-lingual. In many parts of the world *this is the norm*. If children are brought up to speak three different languages, each with a different root, such as English, Spanish and Hindi, they are likely to be able to learn any language very quickly. It seems to bring a facility for languages. This is because the brain, instead of losing the ability to distinguish sounds and utter spoken sounds across a wide range, has kept using them. Babies who hear Chinese being spoken learn to recognise and speak its sounds. If that same baby hears English being spoken, then the 'r' sound is retained and not lost. Usually Chinese speakers shed the ability to differentiate between and pronounce 'r' through lack of use in that language. In the same way, English speakers usually lose the ability to recognise and say sounds with a rolling 'rrr' unless they grow up hearing people speaking French. (Bruce, 2004a) See Chapter 14 by Marian Whitehead.

EXERCISE 9.1

Talk with a friend or colleague who is not mono-lingual, and make a note of the sounds that are most challenging to say in English. Discuss the implications of being mono-lingual, bi-lingual or multi-lingual for children's symbolic behaviour.

Representing in three and two dimensions

Children do not just scribble. The way adults look at the early marks children make on paper influences the way they value their journey as symbol-makers. John Matthews (2003) suggests that from an early age, children are naturally very interested in marks and movements for their own sake, just as much as they are interested in their symbolic possibilities.

At first children explore mark-making in ways which reflect their movements. Research (Matthews, 2003) suggests that children develop a visual language alongside gesture and language/signing. In this way they develop some powerful strategies as they draw and paint, which help them to co-ordinate what they know about shapes and colours.

They explore and show what they understand and are fascinated as they draw and paint objects. Sometimes they do not use a fixed viewpoint, but show the objects from all sorts of angles and perspectives. At other times they keep to one fixed viewpoint, and at other times they do a bit of each!

This means that it is unwise to think of children's drawings as progressing in fixed stages of development. This is especially so if drawings and paintings by young children are looked at across the world. John Matthews suggests that it is more helpful to think of a dynamic weaving together of dynamic movement and configurative patterns and lines which are continually becoming more complex. These emerge from a small repertoire of marks and gestures which arise out of the baby's and toddler's movements, visual and talked/signed languages.

Children explore and try out objects, look at them from different viewpoints and move them about in different ways. We see this in their construction and wooden blockplay (Gura, (ed.) 1992)

The development of symbolic behaviour in drawing and painting is therefore a coming together of biological and sociocultural development.

EXERCISE 9.2

Observe a child playing with an object. Note how the object is rotated, moved up and down, on top of surfaces and in other ways. Link these movements to the list of topological space concepts below.

Topological space – how things relate in space

In/out, on/off, under/over, near/far, going through,
Next to, in front of,
Behind, lines in relationships (eg parallel) covering

EXERCISE 9.3

Also observe, (as it is unfolding) a spontaneous, child-initiated drawing or painting by the child you have observed playing. Has the child used any topological space concepts?

Nancy Smith (1979) (cited in Matthews, 2003) suggests that although children are becoming aware of letters, numbers and pictures, they need to incorporate them into their play if they are to fully understand them. Then they begin to use them confidently and in conventional writing and mathematical recording, and they develop recognisable conventions of the culture in the way they use symbols as they draw and paint.

The same is true of the way children become symbol-users three-dimensionally. When children make things out of clay, or sand, small-world play scenarios assume roles wearing dressing-up clothes, or dance like a bird, or move like a car, they bring to bear the powerful multi-sensory processes which are visual, full of sounds, touch, movement and gesture. Ideas, feelings and relationships together with physical embodiment all combine to make a wooden blockplay construction of a garage or a bicycle made out of found materials.

EXERCISE 9.4

Do you emphasise children's early writing more than their drawings and paintings? Do you pay attention to the models and constructions they make? Do you distinguish between the child who is exploring a process and the child who is making a product? Think about the following, and discuss these issues with colleagues, keeping in mind the importance of valuing all aspects of two and three dimensional symbol use.

Jody (3 years) is standing at the table (she chooses not to sit) drawing with a thin red felt pen. She makes marks on the large sheet of white paper which are circles, in a row across the middle. She puts dabs/dots next to one of them. She says they are people in the bus queue. She points at the dab, and says, 'The little boy dropped his crisps.'

It is important that Jody can be comfortable while she is concentrating. It is also important that she can choose her materials and her medium. This is a meticulous drawing, and so paint would be difficult. She might have chosen clay, or another medium, but this is her preference on this occasion. Some children have strong preferences for a particular medium. Others like to explore different media. Some of us are specialists and some of us are generalists! Young children need to be offered a wide range of media, and shown the possibilities. This is very different from defining what they must draw, paint or make. They need to be able to develop their own ideas, using their feelings, relationships and physical selves to do so.

Movement and dance

Babies suck, swallow, grasp, release, gaze, track, locate sound, gain postural control, sit, manipulate objects, balance, crawl and, typically, toddle in the first two years. Mollie Davies (2003: 43) says they 'delight those around them by adding new actions which they constantly repeat, vary and combine in different ways'.

During early childhood, children increase the range of actions they can manage and they begin to refine the way they carry them out. They practise and hone their skills over and over again. Have you ever been with a toddler who wanted to climb the stairs all day? This is an important way of becoming confident and competent enough to climb in all sorts of different situations.

Of course, physical movement development is like any other aspect of child development. It is a case of use it or lose it. This is why it is so concerning that so many children spend so much time in pushchairs or car seats. Mollie Davies says that movement is a 'must' in children's lives, and that they have a natural appetite for it.

Just as we saw that in developing as a symbol-user in the two- and three-dimensional, visual arts emerge out of kinaesthetic feedback, so the development of dance arises out of the connections and co-ordinations between movement and the senses. (Jabadao, 2005) We can see that dance shares some resonances with what is involved in the visual arts and, as we shall see, drama, music and stories.

Just as John Matthews stresses the way in which children's feelings and ideas influence the way they paint, draw and make three-dimensional constructions, so Mollie Davies sees dance as supporting children in this. Children can be creators, performers and appreciators of dance from an early age. There are powerful examples of this in Chapter 7 by Jenny Spratt, in which she describes the way in which children aged 12–18 months, on the cusp of developing talking and walking and pretending (DfES, 2002), create emergent dances with adults trained in the 'Oogly Boogly' techniques, who have learnt to follow their ideas and support the process. Penny Greenland, in Chapter 17, gives further important examples of Developmental movement play.

As children develop embodiment (which means they feel comfortable in their own bodies and have a sense of control over their movements, which is intertwined with well-being) they often become involved in dance play. Three and four year olds are especially likely to do so. They often practise these over and over again, so that they can be repeated. These are early examples of choreography. Because they are here and gone, unlike paintings, drawing and models, they are often hardly noticed, let alone recorded.

Movement involves:

- the body
- dynamics – how the body moves
- space – how the body uses and is in the space
- relationships – how the body moves in relation to other people and objects.

E X E R C I S E   9 . 5

Observe a child/children in the garden/playground or indoors. Using the above framework, identify how the child uses his/her body, the dynamics of the movement, the space and relationship aspects of the movement.

Children who move with co-ordination have higher well-being and are therefore more confident and autonomous learners. They are more likely to dare to try and make dances, perform them with their friends and appreciate the dances of others.

Children soon become appreciative of the way in which sensitive adults can help them to shape their dances. Children need to see that there are different parts of the dance that can be linked, such as the two opposites, fast and slow. This means that children are helped if they learn the language and vocabulary of dance. Nature (splashing in puddles), machinery (swings and see-saws), sounds (crashing and humming), percussion instruments, action words (creeping and stamping), poetry, recorded music, dressing-up clothes, all of these provide opportunities for children to become dance-makers (Davies, 2003: 167).

Performance for young children means sharing with others, or self, the dance you have made, and knowing what you did to make the dance repeatable. This is different from improvising. A parallel would be the example of finger painting. This is often an improvisation, but sometimes the child makes something in the paint which is a product and they decide to repeat this.

Performance in early childhood does not mean putting children on the stage before they are able to share their dance and remain involved in it. Sharing with self and familiar adults and children who are important to the children comes before showing the dance to people they do not know well, and who are not important to them. If children are to become symbol-makers in ways which are not superficial, then they need to learn to share their dance-making with deep focus and involvement.

Of course, seeing dances performed by others helps children to become aware of and to appreciate what dance is. Dancing and becoming a dance-maker helps children to link creating and making a dance, performing a dance and appreciating a dance. Seeing theatre performances by groups such as Theatre Rites also helps children to appreciate what drama is.

Singing and making music

So far in this chapter, we have seen the importance of visual, movement, gesture and dance education from babyhood onwards in becoming a symbol-user. We also need to remember that children with disabilities and learning difficulties often develop differently. Music, dance and the visual arts are powerful ways in which some children become symbol-users, because the challenge of putting their ideas into spoken/signed/ written words is removed.

However, we do need to remember that not all children become symbol-users. Some may enjoy dance, music and the visual arts as a means of expression, or as something to appreciate physically through being offered melody, movement and rhythm, rather than becoming a symbol-user or symbol-maker.

Marjorie Ouvry (2004) reminds us that there are five ways to make sounds with instruments, either home-made or commercially produced. These are:

- bang, hit and tap
- shake
- scrape
- blow
- twang and pluck.

She points out that fast and slow refers to the pace/tempo. High and low is about the pitch. Hard and soft sounds relate to the timbre. Music has a pulse, rhythm and pattern. Music has a texture, thick when several make music together, thin for a solo.

EXERCISE 9.6

Observe a child in the garden. Can you identify the child applying any of the ways listed above in which sounds can be produced? Can you comment on the way the child uses pace, pitch, timbre rhythm, pattern and texture? Do you write this sort of observation in your records? If not, will you from now on?

On the one hand, children progress, or are constrained according to biological development. On the other hand, biology is shaped by the relationships children have and the cultural context in which they grow up. Dances, music and the visual arts are sociocultural events. In every culture there are community songs, dances and visual arts which are developed in everyday life. Examples are rap, hip hop, country dances, pop arts. There are also less everyday aspects in most cultures of the world, which require that children (or adults) are directly taught about them, as they cannot just be learned by osmosis and apprenticeship. This applies to dance, music and the visual arts. Children will almost inevitably be introduced to the everyday culture of music, dance and the visual arts. But they will not necessarily be in contact with the canon of dance, music and visual arts which requires someone who knows enough about them to introduce them with understanding and enthusiasm.

E X E R C I S E   9 . 7

Find three pieces of taped music which are regarded as classics, one from Europe, one from Asia and one from Africa. Use the Internet to help you in this.

Play the music, and discuss the different aspects using the above framework to do so. Then do the same with dances. Find some classical dance from Spanish flamenco, ballet, India.

Repeat this with three examples of paintings and three-dimensional art. Which were your favourites? Why do you think this is so?

Imagination and creativity and symbolic behaviour

Peter McKellar (1957) suggests that imagination is the rearrangement of past experience in new and fascinating ways. This is important, because it means that the experiences we offer children are central in developing their imaginative potential, (Duffy, 2005). When we imagine, it is an internal and private process. We create images in our mind of movements we have seen or made, sounds we have heard or made, what we have seen or been shown, tastes and smells we have experienced. Putting these together, blending things, juxtaposing them is what the imagination does.

Because images are internal, it is difficult to know if they are made in the minds of very young children and children who are challenged through disabilities or learning difficulties in using spoken/signed language, but they must be. We know that, typically, babies have an image of their mother by the age of 5 months, because they are disturbed when shown multiple images of her. In order to do this, they have to be able to match the image they have of her in their head with the multiple images they are shown of her.

Children with a rich store of images in their heads, arising from their experiences through the senses and movement, can draw on these as a resource to use when they make dances, drawings, constructions and models, or compose music.

Creativity and being a symbol-maker

Creative development is a process which involves making use of experience stored in the imagination, gathering it together and incubating it. Incubation requires illumination and insight through a dawning on the part of the child/person that this is an idea (becoming aware of what you are thinking is usually referred to as meta-cognition). It is often called the 'ah ha phenomenon'. The next step is the hatching of the creative idea. Of course not all creative ideas hatch successfully, and many just fade away before they become a creation. Creative ideas are about being original, and innovative, and rearranging something so that it is different from the way it was before and making connections.

There is a myth that creativity is only something which occurs in the arts. Nothing could be further from the truth. Creativity is at the heart of science, and the humanities (Bruce, 2004b).

Play and symbol-generating

The development of play is an enormous subject, as are the others in this chapter. It is, however, a particularly sophisticated concept, and elusive, all of which makes it difficult to understand and support children as they develop the power of play for their learning.

The English *Birth to Three Matters* framework (DfES, 2002) has incorporated the 12 features of play (Bruce, 1991) identified as central in the traditional literature, and more recent research. The English core reference document *Curriculum Guidance for the Foundation Stage* (CGFS, 2000) also includes the features within the section on play and throughout. These documents will be embedded in the EYFS from 2008.

The 12 features of play demonstrate the free-flowing nature of children's play from birth onwards, but can also be applied to adult play. The features are inclusive and embrace a diverse approach to play cross-culturally and in relation to children with disabilities and learning difficulties. In other words, this is a birth throughout life approach to play.

The 12 features (Bruce, 1991, updated 2005) are:

1. Children draw upon the first-hand experiences they have had in their play. The richer and deeper the experiences, in the way they bring into action all the senses as well as movement and the kinaesthetic feedback that accompanies it, the more the child's possibilities for rich play develops.
2. In play children make up their own rules. This is different from the rules they learn about in games such as hopscotch or ring dances like 'Here we go round the mulberry bush'.
3. Children make play props from found materials and sometimes from toys, However, it is interesting to note that home-made play props are often the most loved by children in their play, rather than expensive toys. This is because they are more open-ended and flexible to use and offer more opportunities. Toys which are designed to be used narrowly are rather closed in their possibilities, and quickly become boring. They also 'suggest' to children that they ought to use them in particular ways. Of course, children who are experienced and highly developed players ignore these messages, and might use a telephone with a bell as an ambulance in a play scenario. It does not need to cost money to play. Play props making dens under the table, with a drape for the walls, are far more deeply satisfying than expensive toys which are often just status symbols.

4. One of the more crucial features of play is that children must choose to play. They cannot be made to play. It is simply no good trying to timetable play. Children have to move into play in their own way, at their own pace. Play does not happen on demand. Given that it is taking children into one of the highest forms of learning, it is not surprising that play develops when the circumstances, conditions and atmosphere are right.

5. Children rehearse future possibilities when they play. We see this in their role play.

6. Play opens up opportunities to pretend. Pretend play involves the child in becoming an active symbol-user. Children pretend to eat, to sleep and, across the world, food preparation dominates the pretend play of 3-year-olds.

7. Sometimes children play alone. This is in no way inferior to playing alongside or with others. Often, it is a question of not having friends to play with, or not being in the mood to play with others, and instead choosing to play alone. Small-world play, sand play, play on the rocking horse and play with clay are often chosen by children for their solitary play. This kind of play brings opportunities to reflect without having to worry about anybody else's ideas or feelings, so that an idea can be pursued in great depth. Many creative adults spent a great deal of time alone during childhood playing. Beatrix Potter is an example.

8. When children are playing with others they might play in companionship, which means they play in parallel enjoying each other's company, but not wishing to interact directly. They often mirror and imitate each other though. They are very aware of what the others are doing. Alternatively, they might play with other adults/children co-operatively. Often this kind of play is deepest when two children play together co-operatively, but as children become experienced players, they manage to do this with larger groups.

9. It is easier to play in a larger group co-operatively if everyone is clear what the play theme is, for example shops. One child, who emerges as a leader in the play usually makes an announcement to signal to the group the key messages of the play scenario. 'We're going to go shopping in the market. This is the market isn't it?' This enables each and every child participating in the play to develop their own personal play agenda. One child might want to wrap up pretend bread and put it in bags. Another child might want to cut the cheese with the wire cutter. Children usually need more play props which look realistic in early group play. This gives them clarity about what is going on. If they play together often and they know each other well and are tuned into each other's thinking and feelings, they can be free to make their own play props, which might be using a shoe as a pretend iron or telephone.

10. Quality free-flowing play means that children become deeply involved in their play. They will not easily be distracted. They might be involved in pretend play or role play, or they might be playing with materials without imbuing them with symbolic life.

11. When children are involved in their play, they often demonstrate their recent learning. It is as if they are celebrating what they have been learning by applying it in their play. Play is hugely about the application of what has been learnt in a safe environment. You can escape into play in this way, but you can also escape out of it if it becomes too much.

12. Free-flow play helps children to co-ordinate and bring together their learning. It orchestrates their feelings, ideas and relationships with their family, friends and culture. It also develops their physical and embodied self.

Games and becoming a symbol-user

The Opies (1988) observed children as they played games in the street, or participated in ring games in the playground. They found that when the children first began to gather together, they used games that had rules set by people outside their context. These games might be hopscotch or ring games with set actions. As the children played together and became more relaxed and used to each other, they started to change the rules and make them their own, agreed between them only for the duration of their time together before being called in to their homes, or at the end of the school playtime. In other words, the children started with games with set rules, and ended with free-flow play in which they made up their own rules, but these emerged by changing the real rules. In order to do this, you have to understand quite a bit about rules in games.

More recently Marjatta Kalliala (2005) has observed that these street games are rare now, because children do not play in the street as they used to do. This means that the older children no longer teach the younger children, and so these games are fading as an aspect of children's play culture. This is interesting in the light of recent debates in England about the teaching of reading. The main way in which, traditionally, children became phonologically aware and began to make the crucial relationships between letters, their look and sounds, was through rhymes and ring games and actions songs. These traditions in games could be taught in the safe environment of early childhood settings. Many staff are now regularly playing these songs and rhyme games with children, and parents are enjoying taking part too.

In a reception class which was moving away from a curriculum which 'mainly consisted of unconnected adult-initiated activities provided ... to prepare children for key stage 1', (Marsden et al., 2005) staff turned their attention to the way they developed mathematics. Adults introduced board games. Observations revealed that the 5-year-olds knew a great deal about playing board games. Observations also showed that when adults led the games, they were shorter, less complicated and were less fun. When the adults tuned into what the children did and said, the children were able to use what they knew about games to make up their own, which were very creative and of deep quality.

As their teacher, Lesley Hill said, they had become 5-year-old gamesters because she had involved them in 'shared sustained thinking' (Siraj-Blatchford, 2004). The children had available for their use resources which were interesting to them. They felt secure, and they had time for their games.

Stories, poems and storytelling

So often it is easier to understand really difficult ideas if they are presented in a story form. In an earlier part of this chapter, we looked at the powerful learning mechanism for learning that humans develop during very early childhood which is symbolic behaviour. Stories are symbolic and stand for things. They help to make the abstract and intangible concrete and tangible (Woolf and Belloli, 2005).

The ancient forms of stories were told, long before people wrote them down. Children respond readily to being told stories, because of the eye contact, and because it is easier to tune into the audience. It is best to use props. Telling stories is a powerful way of engaging with children as a group. The words can readily be adjusted for the audience, and the story can be paced just right more easily. Children often delight in having a go and telling stories too, free from the feeling that they cannot yet read fluently.

Picture books are also a traditional and time-honoured way of telling stories with great subtlety. Children learn to read the symbolic aspects of the pictures, and delight in talking with others about what they see. Picture books offer children beautiful visual experiences by illustrators, and demonstrate that stories can be told without words, as they can through dance, mime and music.

Poetry and rhyme books, or poetry cards, give children small and manageable chunks of text, easily known by heart, and easy for the child to point at words as the rhyme is chanted and to try approximate reading. Children soon learn what they need to do to land up in the right place, and they begin to look closely at the words, and to remember them because they are in a meaningful context. Poetry and rhyme books are another traditional and highly effective way of offering children a canon of literature, which they often use as a resource for their own symbol-making. Children will piggy-back on to known, loved and favourite texts and use them as a structure for their own stories and rhymes.

Making books and writing

As children begin to develop their own stories, they delight in being able to make books to put them in. In many early childhood settings there are tables set aside for writing, but it is less usual to see book-making as part of these areas. It is well worth the effort of maintaining the resources needed.

There are different ways to make simple books, but these are some of the easiest and so most suitable for children in their early childhood:

- zig zag books
- books which have holes punched on the spine, so that string can be threaded through and tied in a bow or knot – very popular, as children love to hang them on their pegs if they have them
- books that are stapled along the spine, and then covered in sticky tape so that they do not scratch the readers.

Children use their home-made books to experiment with writing, and sometimes spontaneously copy bits of writing that have taken their interest. Children need to find out what writing is, and so they need a print-rich environment. This means they need text they can engage with. This is why they respond to seeing their own name in print, which is often very symbolic in its importance. Their name is not just a piece of text on a name card, it is an aspect of self. Children often pick out their name and say, 'That's me'. They write their name, but not necessarily in a conventional way. Hannah made the H at the end of her name look like a bed, and drew herself sleeping on it.

As we can see in Chapter 14 by Marian Whitehead and Chapter 15 by Maulfry Worthington and Elizabeth Carruthers, if children are permitted to explore print fully, as personal symbols and as conventions to be learnt, the two processes feed off and into each other such that children understand print and numbers, and use these with increasing convention in their attempts to write. This in turn helps the process of learning to read. Having shared sustained conversations about these things deepens the learning (Siraj-Blatchford et al., 2002).

Parents

In this chapter we have looked at some of the important ways in which children develop symbolic behaviour. Sharing what we learn with parents is an important part of working with other people's children. Something as simple as explaining why you are excited about the child's symbolic play, music-making, storying, drawing, painting or three-dimensional construction shows that you value the journey children take in developing as symbol-users and symbol-makers.

This can be further developed by making profiles showing a child's learning journey using the child's symbolic behaviour, through photography and drawings and mark-making for example.

Further reading

You may find it useful to read some practical projects about symbolic development undertaken by teachers and practitioners in their schools and settings in *Early Childhood Practice: The Journal for Multi-Professional Partnerships,* Ormond House Cottage, Ormond Road, Richmond, TWIO 6TH. Some useful articles selected are:

Asquith, T., 'The development of writing in the nursery'.
Vol. 3. No. 1, 2001, pp. 55–56

Long, A., 'Forget about "music" – concentrate on the children'.
Vol. 3, No. 1, 2001, pp. 71–76

Martin, P., 'Developing learning at Waverley School'.
Vol. 6, No. 2, 2004, pp. 29–34

Windebank, R., 'How can I develop Dave's communication, language and literacy skills through a multi-sensory environment with reference to small world and wooden blockplay?'
Vol. 7, No. 1, 2005, pp. 75–82.

CONTINUING THE LEARNING JOURNEY: PRACTICAL PROJECTS IN YEAR 1

Tina Bruce

Tina Bruce is Honorary Visiting Professor at Roehampton University, where she originally trained (when it was the Froebel Educational Institute) as a teacher for the Primary phase. She is a trained teacher of children with hearing impairments. She is a widely published author in books, articles and journals, with an international reputation. She was awarded International Woman Scholar in Education by Virginia Commonwealth University and has worked with the British Council in Egypt and New Zealand.

Aims

To develop understanding of:

☐   theory so that your practice you can tune into where a child is in different aspects of his/her developing learning.

☐   how to support children's interests and needs as part of your assessment for learning, so that you offer them educationally worthwhite experiences.

☐   The importance of beginning where the learner is, and not where you think the learner ought to be.

It is important that children have a positive experience of transition between the Foundation Stage and Key Stage 1. This means that practitioners and teachers need to tune into the children and families they work with, and to work in individual ways with them. One size does not fit all.

Having a principled approach lies at the heart of work with children, together with a shared understanding of how principles are turned into key features of good practice. These (based on DfES, Sure Start and QCA, 2003) are:

- observation-led assessment, informed by knowledge of child development, supports practitioners and teachers in learning from and tuning into the children they work with
- a curriculum which holds meaning and is relevant to young children, ensuring they are interested, enthusiastic and wanting to learn, and that the curriculum is responsive to children's interests and needs
- learning inside and outside as equally important parts of the learning environment
- learning through first-hand experiences
- learning using the senses and movement
- developing play
- cultivating creativity
- sustained, unbroken time for children to work at length and in depth
- encouragement of autonomy, choice and independence, so that children work at their own level, without a ceiling being imposed on the possible outcomes
- partnership with families and carers.

As you read the next section of this chapter, consider and reflect on how many of the bullet points above you are identifying in the following practical projects undertaken by teachers and practitioners in Year 1 classes, as they support a positive transition for children from the Early Years Foundation Stage to Key Stage 1.

Harry is a summer-born boy. On entry to Key Stage 1, he is 5 years and a few days old. Some of the children in his group, born in September, are a year older. The younger a child is, the more difference there is developmentally and experientially. There is not such a great gap between a 14- and 15-year-old. This is important to bear in mind when working with young children. The National Foundation for Educational Research (NFER) longitudinal study alerted educators to the neglected fact that the youngest children in classes were vulnerable throughout their education, as they were constantly having to try and keep up with the older children. Typically, this resulted in under-achievement.

The teacher and teacher assistant (TA) have spent time visiting the children in the reception class (in the Early Years Foundation Stage). They know the names of all the children, and the children have also visited their new classroom.

The staff have made it a priority to plan the first week in the new classroom with the individual interests of the children in mind. In order to work with the interests and needs of the children, they have studied the Foundation Profile of each child, and looked at the observations on which the assessments were made. It has become clear that Harry is fascinated by minibeasts, and has spent considerable time in the outdoor area collecting ants, beetles and spiders and examining them in magnifier pots, and looking them up in books, before returning them to their habitat. This has prompted the staff to make a maths game with these creatures pictured. The children have to collect legs for them, either six or eight depending on whether they are ants and beetles or spiders. Although this is planned with Harry in mind, other children may enjoy this too.

The teacher uses large poetry cards with groups of children. Amandip is acquiring English as an additional language. He enjoys singing and dancing, and using props at group time. He responds well to the manageable chunks of text provided by poetry cards. The staff make a huge outline of a spider out of a cardboard box, with the words of 'Little Miss Muffet' written on it. This is suspended from a rafter. A three-legged stool is placed next to it, and a large rag doll wearing a mob cap and a long dress. At group time the children sing the song, and the props are used to enact the story in a theatrical style. Amandip points to the words with a pointer stick, singing gustily. Although the teacher does introduce the synthetic aspects of phonics, she also uses analytic phonics and the onset and rime types of phonics. She finds, as an experienced teacher, that children respond well to the patterns they quickly see with onset and rime. This is why she uses poetry cards:

Muffet	M (onset)	uffet (rime)
Tuffet	T	uffet

It is not surprising that Harry is attracted to the spider. He wants to know what sort of spider it is. This leads to interesting discussion about the way fictional spiders do not usually bear much resemblance to real ones. He wants to make a real-looking one, and so he goes, after the group time, to the workshop area, taking with him a book of spiders from the book corner. He chooses a crusader spider (which has a large cross pattern on its back). This is quite a large spider, which he has seen in the garden at home, as they are very evident in the autumn in England. He draws it, and then cuts it out, going carefully round the legs. He sticks the picture on a large piece of card, and takes it to show the TA. He wants to hang it up. She asks him if he would like to hang it up to replace the fictional one. He nods. She helps him to do this, using the step ladder under supervision.

At the next story time, Amandip is thrilled with the new spider, and wants the words of "Miss Muffet" to be written on the card. He goes to the box of words the teacher has placed next to the poetry card, and finds 'uffet' and then 'M' and 'T' and pieces them together. He matches all the words to the poem on the card with the fictional spider on it. The teacher suggests that he might like to stick this onto the card Harry has made, but asks Harry's permission first. Harry agrees. It is important that he still feels ownership of his drawing and his making of the card. It is also important that Amandip has opportunities to use initiative and explore texts which are manageable.

The teacher decides that the interest is developing for prop-making as an accompaniment to literacy and literary experiences. She introduces the children to the story boxes developed by Helen Bromley. She acquires shoe boxes from a shoe shop, and makes three into story boxes. She has found across the years that only introducing one example constrains the creativity of children, and they just copy the model given by her. When given several examples, they use these as scaffolding for their own ideas about story-making and writing.

One of the story boxes she makes contains tiny props of the story of the Greek myth, Ariadne. Introducing children to this canon of literature is important as the Greek myths are referenced in many examples of English literature. The children delight in the stories, and come to the group time eagerly. Several begin making them in the workshop area. They make efforts to write the stories too, retelling them in their own words, supported by the TA at the writing table. She introduces a story box each week. Harry is taken with the story about the tarantella dance, and researches tarantula spiders, finding that it is a myth that a bite from this spider causes the bitten person to dance the tarantella until they die. His box is non-fictional. Amandip makes a box of Miss Muffet. He can now write the text himself without support.

When visiting the children before they came to Key Stage 1, the staff found out that Sade loved sewing. Evidently her mother was a keen needlewoman, and her daughter has developed a strong interest too. Sade could manage to make a running stitch and she could oversew, and sew on a button. She chose to make a face for the Man in the Moon. This was a poetry card (Hey diddle, diddle! the cat and the fiddle/the cow jumped over the moon! The little dog laughed! to see such fun/ and the dish ran away with the spoon). This had been introduced in the Foundation Stage. She used buttons for the eyes, and used over-sewing to join pieces of material she cut out for the nose and mouth.

She then made a book (helped by the TA) in which she wrote the words of the rhyme. The teacher had given each child a book in which to write words for their personal dictionary. Sade could manage some words independently, and she looked up some in her dictionary. The TA helped with the others.

Paula has a visual impairment. She has no vision, and has glass eyes. She enjoys developing her story box. Her favourite song is 'In an English country garden' She collects all the objects for this from the trays of the workshop provision. She also goes into the outdoor area with the learning support assistant and gathers bark and twigs and leaves and feathers. The teacher has brought the CD of the song, which is put into the story box. The title of the song is placed in the box in Braille, which she is encouraged to feel and discuss.

The examples outlined are resonant with the key features of good practice in transition from the Early Years Foundation Stage to Key Stage 1. They are also examples of good practice within Key Stage 1. They demonstrate the principles of inclusion outlined in the National Curriculum (DfEE and QCA, 1999). They offer suitable learning opportunities which extend the learning of individual children. The teaching responds to the individual learning needs of children, creating effective learning environments. Paula is helped to overcome potential barriers to her learning.

The careful planning of the curriculum links easily into the programmes of study of Key Stage 1. For example, in English the children are telling stories, and retelling stories and poems and rhymes across the range of the canon of literature. Some are comfortable, familiar and predictable, and others are challenging in terms of length or vocabulary. They are reading aloud and reciting, speaking to different people, while adults are offering detailed explanations and presentations, and helping children to record. There is great emphasis on making plans and investigating, sharing ideas and experiences, commenting and reporting. As the children develop their props for the story boxes or the poetry cards, they move into dramatic roles of the characters, and respond to each other's and the adults' performances. Information and communication technology opportunities are taken up, with audio tapes, and word-processed as well as handwritten versions. Dictionaries and other reference materials are used. The children are helped to link their ideas in sentences and sequences.

It is not the intention in this chapter to chug through every kind of connection with the programmes of study in Key Stage 1, but rather to indicate that there is no conflict between offering children the key features of good practice for the Early Years Foundation Stage and delivering the requirements of Key Stage 1. A few further examples will suffice.

In science, Harry and others were learning to recognise and compare the main external parts of the bodies of animals (minibeasts). In mathematics children were counting. and seeing number patterns in the minibeast game. In design and technology the children were encouraged in focused practical tasks that developed a range of techniques, skills, processes and knowledge. In information and communication technology children worked with poetry cards, making books, story boxes, and CDs, as well as word processing.

When children experience a sense of belonging to a group, and feel a valued member of that community, they open up to learning. Being treated as a respected, unique individual is part of that. In classrooms where the atmosphere is sensitive to children's interest and needs, and to their families and contexts, embracing diversity and inclusion principles, staff find children behave better, take more responsibility for their actions and learning, and are more autonomous and caring of others. These outcomes make working with children deeply satisfying, and present challenges which feel worthwhile.

CHAPTER

11

BIRTH TO THREE

Ann Langston and Lesley Abbott

Ann Langston, who is an early years consultant and writer, is based at Manchester Metropolitan University and was a major contributor to the development of the *Birth to Three Matters* framework.

Lesley Abbott OBE is Professor of Early Childhood Education at Manchester Metropolitan University and Head of the Early Years Research Centre. She has published widely and has directed a number of major research projects including the development of the *Birth to Three Matters* Framework.

Aims

To develop understanding of:

- ☐ how research helps us in thinking about the development of babies and young children
- ☐ and knowledge of how babies and young children are described in the *Birth to Three Matters* framework
- ☐ effective practice with babies and young children in out-of-home settings
- ☐ some of the issues relating to working with parents of babies and young children.

How research helps us in thinking about the development of babies and young children

Have you ever noticed families with young children who are shopping, or sitting in a doctor's waiting room and been interested by the way they interact with one another? I love to baby watch and, while standing in a queue recently, I was very amused to observe a young man trying hard to engage his baby, aged about 8 months, in a little game. He gently ran his finger down her forehead, over her nose and under her chin – obviously wanting to make her smile or laugh. The baby was, I'm sure, quite aware of the rules of this game, and was determined not to reward her father with a smile, no matter how hard he tried to entertain her! Well if you have noticed something like this, you are doing exactly what researchers do when they begin to conduct research into a particular phenomenon, in this case a baby's communication skills.

What does this little story tell us about babies as young as 8 months or so? It shows that babies communicate as much by what they do not do and say as by what they actually do or say! Indeed, it could be argued that before a child communicates with words they communicate through the language of the body. It also helps us to think about babies as capable of making choices and having a sense of their own power in relationships – demonstrating that they do not have to do what somebody else wants them to do. This self-confidence is illustrated by the baby just described, and there is evidence that the research supports to show that this baby girl receives the sort of acceptance that is not dependent on behaviour; in other words, she does not feel impelled to laugh or giggle simply to please her father.

An issue for most practitioners in understanding the contribution of research in thinking about the development of babies and young children is which research to read, which to take notice of, and where, and how, to access the most relevant and useful research, at the same time as understanding its role in their professional lives as they review their practice, hoping to learn more about babies and young children.

Which research to read?

To address the first of these questions, it is important to be aware that research in relation to babies and young children comes from a number of sources including the more traditional areas of psychology, medicine and education along with the newer ones such as psychobiology and neuroscience. This presents the reader with vast amounts of material to make decisions about; fortunately, however, many writers have synthesised and distilled this primary research data into secondary sources giving a broad introduction to subjects such as child development, child health, social and emotional development, brain development and so forth. The annotated further reading section at the end of this chapter provides information about a small number of such texts.

Clearly a valuable starting point in accessing research is identifying a particular interest, which is initially fairly narrow – for example, *finding out why a baby constantly throws out a toy from his or her pram.* Once a subject of interest has been identified, the field is substantially narrowed and the interested reader could, in this example, eliminate from their search children beyond 2 years, since this behaviour is characteristic of the child in the first year or so, described in the *Birth to Three Matters* (DfES, 2002) framework as the broad developmental area: Sitters, Standers and Explorers.

Which research should I take notice of and where and how can I access the most relevant and useful research?

In determining the importance of particular pieces of research it is important to know the source of the information and to be clear about when and why the original material had currency. This is a most important point in relation to the development of the brain, for example, where enormous strides have been made in understanding the working of the brain through the use of a number of technologies including positron emission tomography (PET) scans, magnetic resonance imaging (MRI) scans, functional magnetic resonance imaging (fMRI) scans, as well as other research techniques.

However, if the research had been undertaken by a medicine company, for example, you might wish to confirm that findings were consistent with other research into the same area, because, very occasionally, some research findings may be presented in a biased fashion in order to achieve interest or to encourage people to buy a certain product. While this is rare, it is important to be aware that unscrupulous people do, sometimes, manipulate research data to achieve their own ends.

Another factor to take into account is the time since the research was carried out, because its findings could have been superseded by the introduction of newer research methods. In terms of brain research, this would suggest some textbooks written more than ten years ago may not be up to date. Therefore, the most recent and reliable material would be likely to come from papers from research centres, or perhaps from medical research institutions, where findings have been published following a new discovery of some kind – such as the recent data which has become available through four-dimensional (4D) ultrasound scans used to observe babies in the womb.

If your interest in research is to support your everyday practice with young children you will probably find up-to-date journal articles and books in public libraries, or in materials provided by your employer, or the local Early Years Development and Childcare Partnership (EYDCP). If, however, your research is part of a more sustained piece of study you will no doubt have access to research materials through university and college libraries and to Internet sources, which if they meet the criteria identified above often provide very useful articles and sources of information.

Whatever source of information you choose, you will discover that modern research provides remarkable perspectives on the world of early childhood development. A recent major source of early childhood research was conducted to support the development of the *Birth to Three Matters* framework (DfES, 2002). This review distils much of the often dry, tedious research papers into interesting and entertaining nuggets of useful information. So, for example, it begins an exploration of the complex nature of the growth, development and learning of babies and young children with a story about 9-month old William who, seated with family members at the table, for a meal, took a round slice of bread offered him and 'without any instigation from anyone else, (he) *'began making noises "brm, brm", twisting the bread from side to side, like a steering wheel'*. (David et al., 2003: 14). The research report goes on to show how the everyday stories that families tell, describing babies' and young children's competence, are now borne out by research findings, whereas, in the past, much of what families knew was given little credence because research was based on scientific principles which did not take account of this type of evidence, referred to as anecdotal evidence, provided by people like family members.

So, let us now consider how babies and young children are described in the *Birth to Three Matters* framework (DfES, 2002). Babies and young children are described as *Strong* and *Healthy* children, *Skilful Communicators* and *Competent Learners*. These four *Aspects* are each made up of four *Components*, which help us to understand each part of an Aspect; so for example, *A Strong Child* is made up of the following Components:

- me, myself and I
- being acknowledged and affirmed
- developing self-assurance
- a sense of belonging.

A Strong Child

Central to the idea of a Strong Child is one who has developed a sense of their own identity, like the 8-month-old described at the beginning of this chapter, who felt able to withhold from laughing when her father gently tickled under her chin. At the root of this Aspect is a recognition that children can only become confident, self-assured individuals when their need for closeness to a parent or carer are met, and when their efforts to assert themselves are rewarded by others, leading them to feel a sense of being accepted as part of a family, or other group.

A theory which helps us to understand this Aspect is Attachment Theory, first proposed by John Bowlby (Bowlby 1951; 1953) and later expanded in terms of Patterns of Attachment by Mary Ainsworth (Ainsworth et al., 1978) in relation to the baby's use of its mother (or carer) as a secure base from which the baby is able to explore the world. This will be discussed later in this chapter.

Bowlby argued that in order for healthy (mental) growth: 'the infant and young child should experience a warm, intimate relationship with his mother (or permanent mother substitute) in which both find satisfaction and enjoyment' (Bowlby, 1951: 13) Unfortunately this led to misunderstandings by some people who thought that Bowlby was saying that *the only* satisfactory relationship a baby could have was with its mother – which of course he was not saying at all – as indicated by the statement in brackets in the above quote.

Bowlby went on to define attachment behaviour as: 'behaviour that has proximity to an attachment figure as a predictable outcome and whose evolutionary function is protection of the infant from danger' (Bretherton, 1992: 788). Researchers who questioned Bowlby's theory later described how these behaviours become increasingly focused on: 'those primary figures who are responsive to the infant's crying and who engage the infant in social interaction' (Schaffer and Emerson, 1964). This finding confirmed that the primary relationship need not be with the mother, and that it could be with another figure such as the father, a carer or even an older sibling.

The contribution of Mary Ainsworth's work to this and Bowlby's theory was to demonstrate how, once the baby had become attached to a primary caregiver, such as the main carer or, as occurs in out-of-home settings, a key person, the mobile infant uses the attachment figure as a secure base. This is a little like being an explorer who sets up camp and who then goes off to explore the surrounding terrain. Because the explorer (the baby) has established a camp (a strong relationship with the primary caregiver) they feel able to go and come back at will (into the environment) and this is exactly what the baby does when it moves away in order to explore its surroundings, returning from time to time to seek reassurance (Bretherton, 1992).

Effective practice to support babies and young children to be strong

These theories help us in thinking about the ways we can support children to become strong when they are separated from their families for periods in out-of-home settings. While this research emphasised that primary caregivers were of central importance in a young child's life Bowlby himself, later went on to suggest that babies and young children were capable of multiple attachments and could become attached to several important people at the same time. This finding emphasises the important role the key person plays in ensuring the baby or young child feels safe and secure while he or she attends a day-care setting, whether this is for a short or long period of time. At the same time all these theories remind us of the need for the key person, rather than just any person, to be responsive to the child and the important role social interaction between the child and the key person plays in contributing to the child's sense of security. It also tells us that once babies become mobile their investigative and exploratory behaviour is encouraged (or impeded) by the presence (or absence) of this person in their lives.

E X E R C I S E   1 1 . 1

How does your setting support young children to become strong? Think about:

- Routines
- Supporting attachment through the key worker role.

A *Healthy Child* is made up of the following Components:

- emotional well-being
- growing and developing
- keeping safe
- healthy choices.

A Healthy Child

Many facets of the Strong Child have application in thinking about a child that is healthy, since the term healthiness is used in this context to refer to both psychological and physical well-being. To return to the baby described at the beginning of this chapter, who refused to be amused by the behaviour of her father when he tried to tickle under her chin, it is clear that she has a real sense of security because she does not appear to need to go along with her father's agenda since she obviously feels safe in following her own – she does not want to laugh! This may seem something of a conundrum when we realise that the healthy child is described as one who is able to express their feelings. However this Aspect also emphasises another important feature of health, the fact that even very young children are capable of choosing their responses to things, including deciding on their own likes and dislikes, whether these are temporary (she did not want to laugh just at that moment, perhaps?) or permanent (she may never like to wear red shoes).

This Aspect is about what in the past was referred to as *a healthy mind in a healthy body*, but which has the additional prospect that healthiness can be defined in relation to each individual child rather than comparatively, as was once the case. This Aspect encourages us to think about the health of an 8-month-old baby with a hole in the heart, or some other condition, not in comparison with all other 8-month-olds, but in relation to his or her own progress which may show them to be very healthy and progressing well, when their development is reviewed against their earlier progress.

An influential theory about children's holistic development, that is, the way they develop physically, intellectually, linguistically, emotionally and socially, is known as the nature versus nurture debate, which has been widely discussed as a subject for a long time. This debate stems from philosophers such as John Locke in the seventeenth century who believed the child began life as a *tabula rasa*, or 'blank slate' and that his or her experiences in life would influence the way that he or she developed. This school of thought is known as environmental determinism, which supports the view that the environment and what it contains is the greatest determinant of behaviour (and development) in the child. These theories later led to behaviourist learning theories and social learning theories, each of which explains behaviour in terms of conditioning and/or modelling when the child's behaviour is influenced by the responses of others or the behaviour of objects, or by the way he or she observes and repeats what has been seen demonstrated by others. Some of these theories are still current.

The theory of biological determinism, posed by Charles Darwin in the nineteenth century, subsequently the study of human psychology, led to a view that the individual child's development was genetically determined and to the description of universal stages of development, in other words, the birth of what we now know as 'stage theory' (Sherry, 2004). This approach subsequently influenced other theorists, such as Piaget whose work we will examine in more detail later.

Effective practice to support babies and young children to be healthy

How do these theories help us to support children (and their parents) to be healthy, in the terms described in the *Birth to Three Matters* framework? First, they provide us with a way of questioning whether and to what extent we can judge that children's development is determined by their own genetic inheritance or by the influence of the environment – things such as housing, family size and so on. Secondly, they lead us to consider other theories and information which suggest that both nature and nurture have a part to play in children's development, and therefore the way we can think about it.

The *Birth to Three Matters* framework describes the development of a healthy child in terms of the child's own individual progress. It makes clear that children's health includes many elements such as being free from illness, as opposed to having certain conditions that will remain with the individual through life, such as cerebral palsy. It also emphasises the importance of being fit, being happy and being able to adapt and develop throughout one's life (Meggitt, 2001 in David et al., 2003: 108). All these things suggest that when we work with babies and young children we should take account of:

- what parents and other professionals involved in the child's life tell us
- what we observe and know about a particular child, as well as children in general
- current thinking about child development

and use this information to focus on all the factors that contribute to a child's physical and emotional well-being while they are in our care. This approach will ensure that when we observe a child of 20 months who has not yet begun to walk we will be familiar with what the child's parents and/or other professionals have told us, and we will also know that by the time they reach that age the majority of children have already begun to take their first steps. However, the knowledge from all these sources will help us to reach sensible conclusions – either that the child has some developmental delay or that she will, in common with the development of other children in her family, be likely to start walking any day soon!

EXERCISE 11.2

Are all children, including those with particular needs, viewed as healthy children in your setting? How is every child supported to engage in a range of experiences?

A Competent Learner is made up of the following Components:

- making connections
- being imaginative
- being creative
- representing.

A Competent Learner

This Aspect takes as its theme that learning is multidimensional, and that babies are constantly finding out about themselves, other people and the environment through exploratory behaviour. The idea of babies and young children as learners is one that has been considered by many developmental psychologists, especially Jean Piaget (Das Gupta, 1994) whose theories of cognitive development have contributed to our understanding of the ways in which young children learn, think and remember. Piaget's view was that babies and children progress through distinct stages of development as they learn; beginning in the first two years of life with the *sensori-motor* stage, followed by the *pre-operational* stage which occurs between 2 and 7 years; the *concrete operations* stage from 7 to 11 or 12 years, finally reaching the *formal operations* stage in the years leading towards adolescence.

Piaget describes young babies' learning in terms of the senses and movement in the sensori-motor stage as they progress from reflex actions such as sucking and moving their whole bodies, to intentional acts such as pulling a toy out from a box, showing their ability to co-ordinate actions with thinking, and demonstrating mastery over their own bodies. As the baby reaches about 8 months they become capable of co-ordinating actions and are able to solve problems such as seeking out a toy which has been hidden under a cloth. In the second year the young child becomes capable of mental representation, observing and imitating what they have seen or heard, and is now able to think a problem through.

Piaget described sets of actions, as applied to situations, whether these were physical or mental, as schemas. He believed that these patterns of thought led in time, to repetition and incremental learning. This hypothesis was later used by theorists such as Chris Athey to describe the types of schemas babies and young children might develop. Common schemas Athey described include: *connecting* – where a child joins and separates things; *rotational* – where the child is interested in the circular motion of themselves or objects; and *transporting* in which the child moves things from place to place.

Later, when children entered the period of pre-operational thought, Piaget described mental operations as internalised forms of action which result in children being able to order, combine and separate things in the physical world, allowing them to reason about simple problems such as whether to put talcum powder or cream on a doll, or to conclude that it is wiser to wear wellingtons, as opposed to sandals, on a wet day.

Piaget's theory was extended substantially by neo-Piagetians who provided a helpful insight into the ways in which young children's thinking changes as they grow and develop. They challenged Piaget's theories by showing that when children could understand the reason behind why they were being asked to do something they were much more capable than Piaget had believed (Donaldson, 1978; Light et al., 1991).

One example of this, which they highlighted, was referred to by Piaget as a conservation task. To do this, Piaget showed children two identical, tall, narrow beakers with the same amount of liquid in each. He then asked them to observe the liquid being poured from one of the beakers into a shorter, broad beaker. Asked whether there was now less or more liquid in the second beaker the children said there was less because the liquid in the short, broad beaker looked lower than when it was in the tall, thin one.

However, Paul Light (Light et al., 1991), a neo-Piagetian, suggested that if children could see the *reason* for the liquid being poured from one container into another they would be able to conclude that the quantity of liquid remained the same. So he set up an experiment to demonstrate this. In this experiment, children were shown two identical beakers with the same amount of food in them. Then it was pointed out to them, by the experimenter, that one of the beakers was chipped. The experimenter then suggested that they should transfer the contents of the chipped beaker into a fresh, differently shaped container so that the food would not be affected. After the transfer was completed more children stated correctly that the quantity of food in the container remained the same. This showed that when children could see the *purpose* of the change they were able to make better judgements about whether the quantities had changed or not. More recently, experiments have demonstrated that much younger children are capable of higher levels of thinking than Piaget ever believed possible.

One such example is described by some psychologists who found that unlike 14-month-olds, 18-month-old children were able to realise that their own food preferences were different from adults' preferences. The experimenters describe how when shown two bowls – one full of 'delicious Goldfish crackers' and the other full of 'raw broccoli' all the children preferred the crackers. When the experimenter showed the two groups of children that she preferred the broccoli and wanted them to give her some to eat, the 14-month-olds still gave her the crackers because they preferred them, while the 18-month-olds, still preferring the crackers themselves, were able to recognise that the other person might want to eat something they did not like themselves and so gave her the broccoli, as requested (Gopnik et al., 1999: 36).

Another influential theorist, who has contributed extensively to our present understandings of how young children learn, is Lev Vygotsky. Vygotsky (1978) argued that children's development is heavily influenced by both the social context in which it occurs and by the adult's behaviour. He suggested that when children are offered the right sort of help they become capable of further action. This results from being supported in what he described as the zone of proximal development (ZPD) (Das Gupta, 1994). This learning occurs when the child is not fully competent at a given task, perhaps when they are unsure how to fit all the pieces together in a jigsaw and the adult who is more skilled at the task intervenes, either by asking them questions that lead them into new ways of thinking or modelling an action that the child can imitate. This intervention helps the child to achieve new levels of learning. They are then able to both repeat, practise and, at some point, internalise what has been learned, before moving on to develop a new skill or interest. The benefits of working with a more skilled person also translate across to the 'teacher' as well as the learner. So if two children, of different ages and/or abilities, play alongside one another they are *both* likely to gain from the experience – one from explaining and demonstrating an action and the other from watching and listening to what is said or done.

Effective practice to support babies and young children to be competent learners

The usefulness of any theory can be judged by the extent to which it informs our thinking and practice. The theories described here offer helpful insights into the ways that children learn and help us also to understand the factors that influence their learning.

If we consider Piaget's theory for example, it is easy to understand the emphasis he placed on the type of play in which babies use their senses to explore their environment – touching, mouthing and manipulating objects in order to find out about their properties such as how much an object weighs, what it will do, its texture, whether it makes a sound and so on. This theory informs us of the importance of allowing children to find out about new things through using all their senses, and warns us against expecting children to use materials to produce some sort of end product before they have first encountered them at an exploratory and sensory level.

If we return to the work of the neo-Piagetians, described earlier, we can see that their theories suggest that children are capable of understanding complex ideas if they make sense to them. So, they can take on board the idea that things may alter in appearance (the space they fill) without in fact changing mass (the quantity), or they can understand that while they prefer one taste an adult may prefer another, and this highlights for us that both the context and the purpose are important in children's learning. In other words, they work out what each situation is about in order to understand it and act appropriately. This should encourage us to explain carefully to children our reasons for doing things and the reasons why we are asking them to do things.

Vygotsky's theory supports this view and helps us realise the important role adults play in babies' explorations, either when offering the child support in locating objects or by playing with the child in ways that extend their experience – in games such as peek-a-boo or hiding and finding an object. His theories also support the argument for nurseries including, from time to time, sessions for babies and children of mixed ages to be together, when we consider the impact of one child learning from another through explaining or demonstrating a task, modelling an activity or copying a behaviour or activity. Vygotsky has therefore helped us to understand the importance of interaction as a tool for learning and the role that adults (and others) play in supporting children to reach deeper levels of understanding.

EXERCISE 11.3

Monitor interaction in your setting for an afternoon or morning to discover what proportion of time adults spend:

- listening to children
- explaining things to them
- having in-depth conversations with them.

We will now consider the Aspect, *A Skilful Communicator*, which is made up of the following Components:

- being together
- finding a voice
- listening and responding
- making meaning.

A Skilful Communicator

This Aspect focuses on young children's communication, both verbal and non-verbal and emphasises once more the important role adults play in children's development. Many theorists including nativists such as Noam Chomsky, social learning theorists like Bandura, and interactionists such as Vygotsky have contributed to our understanding of how children become language users (Das Gupta, 1994). More recently, neuroscientists conducting research into brain development and processes have also thrown light on this area. The conclusions these theories lead us to are complex, suggesting that children's communication skills depend on a number of factors including the child being:

- encouraged to communicate
- able to hear and distinguish sounds
- ready to learn
- treated as if they are a language user.

When these conditions are fulfilled the child communicates effortlessly and acquires language rapidly. So, how do the theories explain language development in babies and young children? Noam Chomsky, a developmental psychologist, argued that language learning is innate and that the baby's brain is hard-wired for language learning through a language acquisition device (LAD) (Das Gupta, 1994). He suggested that this device allows the baby to absorb, process, and subsequently produce sounds, in the language to which they are most exposed, but relies heavily on the social context, which encourages communication.

Bandura and other social learning theorists (Das Gupta, 1994) argued that in order to produce sounds the baby requires a language model which he or she can imitate, and from whom he or she learns his or her sounds are valued. In this way the baby or young child will repeat and use those sounds that are rewarded by the caregiver's smiles, or praise, and discontinue those which are not rewarded. This theory also emphasises the importance of repetition, practice and consolidation when a baby or young child is learning to speak.

Vygotsky's theories about language highlighted the importance of the relationship between language and thinking, since he believed the two to be interdependent. His view, which is widely respected, is that language is social and communicative, and that through sharing with others in social exchanges children learn to internalise speech, which he called private speech, which in turn forms the basis of thought. The way this occurs is individual but the child learns through the social speech of adults to use what they have heard to direct their own behaviour. So, for example, the child might be asked by the adult what the model insect on the table is and the child might reply that it is a spider. Later the child may then ask himself (or herself) what the object is and repeat the same answer, to himself. As the child continues to play or engage in such interactions the spoken words he or she has heard become internalised as private speech, which directs his or her own behaviour, helping them to plan and organise their behaviour and ideas. This leads, according to Vygotsky, to shifts in the child's cognitive development, that is, their thinking.

More recent evidence from brain research shows us that while at birth the baby's brain has as many neurons as that of an adult's, nerve cells, (or neurons) need to be stimulated in order to form connections between one another.

In the case of language sounds, the connections formed occur as the baby hears language sounds, or phonemes, which are the building blocks of spoken language. When these sounds are heard by the baby, the brain cells in the auditory cortex are stimulated and recognition of sounds occurs, leading later to the baby's ability to distinguish and make sense of sounds, words and verbal communication.

Supporting this view, Gwyneth Doherty-Sneddon (2003), a developmental psychologist, has outlined principles of early child communication which suggest that this relies as much on what the child is conveying through non-verbal messages like eye gaze, facial expressions and hand gestures as on the way in which adults respond to the child's intentions; she suggests that communication is both innate and learned and that the responsiveness of the adult is key in supporting young children's communication.

Further principles for communicating with children have been identified through a project developed on behalf of the DfES at Manchester Metropolitan University, entitled Communicating Matters, which focuses on the importance of adults listening to children and of allowing children uninterrupted time to talk and engage in real conversations.

Effective practice to support babies and young children to be skilful communicators

So, once more it is important to consider the usefulness of theories for thinking about practice. What can we learn from theories about language learning? We know that babies and young children do have a drive to communicate and we now have evidence for this, though we do not yet know where, if at all, Chomsky's LAD can be found in the brain. However, we do know that in order to learn and become skilful communicators babies and young children need skilful adults who observe, watch them and listen to them in order both to make sense of their non-verbal cues and to engage with them in meaningful communication as they learn to become confident language users.

The debate still continues about the relative contributions of nature and nurture in the development of language, and Chomsky's theory concerning the LAD has not been disproved. Similarly, there is strong support for the views of social interactionists such as Vygotsky, who argued that language held the key to thought and that through interactions with sensitive and contingent others, such as parents, teachers and so on, babies and young children would 'learn to use words first to communicate with others, but then begin using words as symbols of thinking' (Doherty-Sneddon, 2003). There is also good evidence to suggest that social learning theory has its place in providing the child with models of communication, since the way in which children communicate both verbally and non-verbally, partially, though not entirely, reflects the styles and nature of communication which surround the child in their main language environment.

EXERCISE 11.4

What features of communication have you observed in babies 0–8 months and in children from 24 to 36 months? How do early skills lead to later skills, in your opinion?

Understanding issues relating to working with parents of babies and young children

All our work with children is only possible because of their parents. They are the people with whom we must learn to work, and who are most important in children's lives. Becoming a parent usually exposes strong emotions – love, joy and happiness, alongside anxiety, fear of failure and, for some people, mainly mothers, depression. So work with all parents should be undertaken with sensitivity, kindness and care. Work with vulnerable parents is more challenging and may require the support of more than one agency.

The vast majority of parents and carers of young children want the very best for their children, parents do things both great and small every day for their children, and the father described at the start of this chapter is no exception, trying as he was to relate to his small daughter. However, the factors that influence parenting styles and interaction with their children are complex and frequently complicated by many factors such as numbers of children in the family; the parents' ages, whether they are teenage parents, first time parents, experienced or confident parents; whether they are in paid employment; their housing; the environment they live in; the support available to them and their own experiences of being a child. Clearly, a discussion of these factors is beyond the remit of this chapter; however, the main message childcare practitioners should take from this is that parenting only looks easy and straightforward from the outside. So, supporting parents of children aged from birth to 3 is extremely important and should be based on mutual respect, helping them to understand and recognise their own skills as parents and to value the skills and competence of their children as strong, healthy people who are also communicators and learners right from birth.

The *Birth to Three Matters* framework (DfES, 2002) is a helpful tool in providing a focus for discussions in this area. We have already considered in this chapter how it offers perspectives on children and their development; however, it will also be important to be familiar with what is described in the framework as the 'broad areas of development' since these are used to describe babies' and children's development in the years between birth and 3. The broad areas can be used to illustrate the ways that babies' and young children's development occurs, often patchily, and happening more rapidly in one area than another. So, for example, it could be used to help a parent recognise that their young child is a healthy child, developing strong bones, teeth and muscles, even though the child may not yet be moving around or sitting unaided, which may be a concern for the parent and may require the involvement of the health visitor, doctor or other health professional. This approach is one that can be taken in relation to every Aspect of the framework, since skilled, observant, childcare practitioners will always be able to note things that show even the youngest or most severely handicapped child to be progressing in some way.

The skills of the childcare practitioner in communicating with parents about every child's development will include being sensitive to parents' emotional anxieties, responsive to them, positive about their child's abilities and honest about their child's needs. The latter will always include the need to share information as required and to seek help and assistance from other professionals including line managers and, at times multidisciplinary teams, drawn from a variety of agencies.

Further reading

Research

A book addressing some of the issues faced when undertaking research on children is *Doing Research with Children and Young People* (2004) by Fraser, S., Lewis, V., Ding, S., Kellett, M. and Robinson, C. (eds), London: Sage/Open University Press. See especially chapter 10, 'Early childhood' by Ann Langston, Lesley Abbott, Vicky Lewis and Mary Kellet.

Understanding children's development and learning

Many useful books address this area but the lively and well-written book *How Babies Think* (1999) by Gopnik, A., Meltzoff, A. and Kuhl, P. (eds) is helpful in conveying information about babies and young children thinking.

Another text which explains and describes many of the theories dealt with in this chapter is *The Foundations of Child Development* (1994) by Oates, J. (ed.) Milton Keynes: Open University Press.

CHAPTER 12

SUPPORTING CHILDREN'S DEVELOPMENT AND LEARNING

Helen Moylett

Helen Moylett works for the Primary National Strategy as a Foundation Stage senior regional adviser. Prior to this she was the head of an early years centre and before that worked as a senior lecturer in early years and primary. Earlier in her career she was a senior advisory teacher, a home school teacher and a class teacher in early years and primary.

Aims

To develop understanding of:

- ☐ the ways in which the aims and principles of the *Curriculum Guidance for the Foundation Stage* should underpin learning and teaching
- ☐ the central role of play and communication in children's social, emotional and academic development and learning
- ☐ the ways in which working with parents can enrich children's learning.

Throughout the chapter reference will be made to the relevant pages in the *Curriculum Guidance for the Foundation Stage* (CGFS, 2000) which will be embedded in the Early Years Foundation Stage from 2008.

Introduction

The *Curriculum Guidance for the Foundation Stage* (CGFS) has been part of the National Curriculum since 2002. It is intended to help practitioners meet the diverse development and learning needs of all children aged 3 to the end of reception.

Practitioners use this guidance to build on the range of different learning experiences children will have had before they begin the foundation stage. Where appropriate they make links with the *Birth to Three Matters* framework (see Abbott and Langston, Chapter 11 in this volume) in order to ensure continuity and ease transitions for children and their families. There are obvious links between the four aspects of *Birth to Three Matters* and the six areas of learning in the CGFS which are made explicit on the CD-ROM in the *Birth to Three Matters* pack.

At the time of writing, the birth to 5 quality framework promised in the ten-year strategy for childcare (DfES, 2004) is being developed. It will make these links between *Birth to Three Matters* and CGFS and their shared principles more explicit, as well as incorporating the National Standards for Daycare (DfES/DWP, 2003). Whatever this eventually looks like, the child-centred approaches to children's learning advocated in both *Birth to Three Matters* and the *Curriculum Guidance for the Foundation Stage* and explored in this chapter will not change.

Children receive their first year of Foundation Stage care and education either at an early years setting or at home or, for many, in a combination of settings. (Page 7 of the CGFS gives some examples.) The vast majority of children will receive the second year of their Foundation Stage care and education in a school reception class. Whatever the setting, children need a high-quality range of experiences to extend their skills, develop their confidence and build on what they already know. In order to provide this high quality, practitioners need to understand the aims and principles underpinning the CGFS.

Aims for the Foundation Stage

These can be found in the CGFS on pages 8, 9 and 10. Clearly the major aim for everyone involved with young children is for those children to make progress in their development and learning. In the section on aims the importance of monitoring children's progress throughout the Foundation Stage is stressed so that their achievements can be celebrated and any difficulties supported both at home and in the setting. This process starts before the child enters the setting with practitioners asking parents and other workers for information. All the way through the Foundation Stage practitioners will be working with parents and carers, and observing and assessing children in order to support and challenge them in moving on in their learning.

The aim is that the Foundation Stage curriculum in any setting should lay the social, emotional, intellectual and physical foundations on which children can build by developing children's learning in six areas:

- personal, social and emotional well-being
- communication, language and literacy
- mathematical development
- knowledge and understanding of the world
- physical development
- creative development.

These areas are further unpacked and explored in this chapter and elsewhere in this volume. However, before any practitioner begins to think about how they are going to work with children and their parents on these six areas, they need to became familiar with the principles on which the whole guidance document is based. In some settings practitioners may not have read the whole document and may be working with lists of the Stepping Stones and Early Learning Goals which come much later in the document and only have a very limited usefulness without knowledge of the principles underpinning them. When practitioners understand these principles they find it much easier to make appropriate decisions for, and with, children.

The principles for early years education

These can be found in the CGFS and will be embedded in the Early Years Foundation Stage. They are drawn from effective practice in early years settings and are based on well-established theories about child development and learning. They link with those in Chapter 10.

Effective education requires both a relevant curriculum and practitioners who understand and are able to implement the curriculum requirements.

Effective education requires practitioners who understand that children develop rapidly during the early years – physically, intellectually, emotionally and socially. Children are entitled to provision that supports and extends knowledge, skills, understanding and confidence, and helps them to overcome any disadvantage.

Practitioners should ensure that all children feel included, secure and valued. They must build positive relationships with parents in order to work effectively with them and their children.

Early years experience should build on what children already know and can do. It should encourage a positive attitude and disposition to learn and aim to prevent early failure.

No child should be excluded or disadvantaged because of ethnicity, culture or religion, home language, family background, special educational needs, disability, gender or ability.

Parents and practitioners should work together in an atmosphere of mutual respect within which children can have security and confidence.

To be effective, an early years curriculum should be carefully structured. In that structure, there should be three strands:

- provision for the different starting points from which children develop their learning, building on what they can already do
- relevant and appropriate content that matches the different levels of young children's needs
- planned and purposeful activity that provides opportunities for teaching and learning, both indoors and outdoors.

There should be opportunities for children to engage in activities planned by adults and also those that they plan or initiate themselves. Children do not make a distinction between 'play' and 'work' and neither should practitioners. Children need time to become engrossed, work in depth and complete activities.

Practitioners must be able to observe and respond appropriately to children, informed by a knowledge of how children develop and learn and a clear understanding of possible next steps in their development and learning.

Well-planned, purposeful activity and appropriate intervention by practitioners will engage children in the learning process and help them make progress in their learning.

For children to have rich and stimulating experiences, the learning environment should be well planned and well organised. It provides the structure for teaching within which children explore, experiment, plan and make decisions for themselves, thus enabling them to learn, develop and make good progress.

EXERCISE 12.1 PART A

Having read the principles carefully, read the case study below and consider the following questions:

- Which of the principles can you see in action?
- What sort of preparation and planning do you think the staff had engaged in before the walk happened?
- What do you think the children might have learned in terms of the six areas of learning listed above in the paragraph on the aims for the Foundations Stage?
- How do you think the children's learning might have been recorded?
- How might parents have been involved?

Case Study 12.1. Bear hunt

The 3- and 4-year-old children in an early years centre had listened to and acted out the story of 'The Bear Hunt'. This had led to map-making and child-initiated den-making and exploratory play inside and outdoors. The staff took this further by initiating a group problem-solving activity involving bears.

In a small group the children were told that one of the teddy bears had been on a walk to find his mum. The group were given laminated photos of the teddy at various stages of his walk, for example sitting against a street sign, outside a house, next to a phone box. Each child had one photo and it was explained that it was important to look carefully at it and then check as they walked to see when they came to the place their photo was taken. Matching, sequencing and careful observation skills were required as well as co-operation between group members. To help them they took it in turns to carry the teddy and whenever anyone thought they had found the place their photo, or someone else's, was taken they placed the teddy to re-create the photo scenario. This was a way of checking and led to discussion about the area and the creation of a story about why the teddy acted as he did and how he felt at various times, for example tired, sad because he could not find his mum, scared when he came to the house that had giant-sized concrete 'footprints' as a path to the front door.

All the time the children were encouraged to look carefully at the local area and recall where they had been and, as the photos to be matched got fewer, to predict which scene would be next using their existing knowledge of the area. There was also consolidation of previous work on road safety. When the circular route eventually led them back to the centre, they found the teddy's mum waiting in reception and very pleased to see him. This led to some discussion about what to do if you lose your parent or carer and the fact that it would not be appropriate to go wandering around outside the centre on your own.

This activity was accessed by all children. Those with language and/or communication difficulties or who had English as an additional language could use the visual cues provided both by the photos and the area itself to help them join in. Skills learnt in other areas were practised and, on their return, some of the children initiated drawing maps and writing notes for others. Others made their own teddy trail in the centre's outdoor area. Others returned to acting out the bear hunt story with fresh enthusiasm and tried out different twists in the narrative.

EXERCISE 12.1 PART B

You will probably have found many of the principles in action in this example of everyday activity in an early years setting. You may also have related the principles you found and the actions of the children and adults on the bear hunt to some of the theories explored earlier in this volume.

EXERCISE 12.1 PART B (CONTINUED)

- How, for instance, do you think the adults might have been scaffolding the children's learning in ways both Bruner and Donaldson describe?
- How might the children's learning during this activity be seen to be influenced by the ideas of Piaget and Vygotsky around active learning and interaction with more knowledgeable peers?

EXERCISE 12.1 PART C

- Observe an activity at your workplace and write a narrative observation. Afterwards refer to the principles and note which ones you have seen in action.
- What proportion of the time spent on the activity was adult-led?
- Did the children have opportunities to build on or consolidate what they learned?
- What are the messages for future practice?

All the principles are equally important and the case study illustrates the delicate balance between well-planned adult-directed activity, the time children need for what the EPPE project (Sylva et al., 2004) has called 'sustained shared thinking' and the time they need to develop their own play. The teddy hunt described, built on, and was subsequently expanded into, more child-initiated activity where children could take what they had done and make it their own. As Hendy and Toon (2001: 76) so eloquently put it : 'Drama can be used to speak the silence of stories, or to change the direction of stories or to create alternative endings.' Children's stories and how they relate to the Foundation Stage curriculum will be returned to later in this chapter. Before that we focus on the most powerful players in children's lives – their parents.

Working with parents

> Parents are children's first and most enduring educators. When parents and practitioners work together in early years settings, the results have a positive impact on the child's development and learning. Therefore each setting should seek to develop an effective partnership with parents. (CGFS: 9)

We are all competent learners from birth and it is usually our parents who give us the confidence to keep learning and stretch the boundaries of our understanding. Most parents are very interested in their children's progress as they become more independent and join groups of other children in the Foundation Stage. Early years practitioners are also interested in children's progress, so on the face of it this should be an easy partnership to establish. We know from research evidence that successful relationships between parents and educators can have long-lasting and beneficial effects on children's learning and well-being. (Desforges, 2003; Evangelou et al., 2005).

The CGFS states: 'A successful partnership needs a two-way flow of information, knowledge and expertise.' It then goes on to suggest ways in which this two-way flow may be achieved. As well as these practical suggestions, four of the principles explored above are particularly relevant:

- Practitioners should ensure that all children feel included, secure and valued. They must build positive relationships with parents in order to work effectively with them and their children.
- Early years experience should build on what children already know and can do. It should encourage a positive attitude and disposition to learn and aim to prevent early failure.
- No child should be excluded or disadvantaged because of ethnicity, culture or religion, home language, family background, special educational needs, disability, gender or ability.
- Parents and practitioners should work together in an atmosphere of mutual respect within which children can have security and confidence.

We can see these principles in action in the following case study taken from the CGFS (page 12).

Case Study 12.2

At a nursery, the children start to visit with their parents as babies or toddlers. By offering childcare and group work with and apart from children, practitioners help parents develop skills that support them and their children. They encourage parents to share their knowledge and views of their child's development, and to raise any concerns.

The setting has a multi-lingual practitioner who relates with families from a range of ethnic and cultural traditions. She ensures that families know about the services available and is a link between the families, key staff and other agencies. The practitioners ensure that the displays and resources reflect children's home and community experience.

Before admission at age 3, a practitioner visits the family and child at home to get to know them. The family is given information in an accessible format about the way sessions are organised that outlines how different activities contribute to the curriculum.

The parent is encouraged to stay with the child as part of the process of transition between home and the group wherever possible, and arrangements are flexible to accommodate the needs of working parents.

(Continued)

Throughout the family's association with the setting, the key practitioner, parent and child talk regularly to check how well they are all adjusting to the arrangements for settling in, learning and teaching. She makes sure that the family or child's particular interests and experiences, such as the birth of a new baby, are used in planning work with the child.

When the child transfers to primary school, the practitioner ensures that the parent knows how to select a school and how the transition will work. She meets the parent to prepare the final record of the child's progress and attainment. She liaises with the receiving school and the family so that everyone is kept fully informed.

This case study touches on admissions where inclusion begins. The first contact parents have with a setting sets the tone for all future contact. It may be easier for some groups to access provision than others. Edgington (1998: 59) points out that, where places are in short supply, staff decisions about which groups they prioritise are important. If, for instance one operates on a purely first come first served basis, parents who are unfamiliar with, or unable to cope with, the procedures will be excluded. She goes on to say that 'Offering as far as possible, equal access to nursery education is a start but is not enough in itself', and discusses the need to examine attitudes and values around equal opportunities. The Children Act 1989, which applies to all settings, lays down the legal duty to take into account children's racial, religious, cultural and linguistic backgrounds. At this point you might want to consider your setting's admissions policy and how it operates to help children and parents feel included from day one.

Once children, parents and other members of the community get into your setting how welcome do they feel? Some questions to consider:

- Do the resources and displays represent the ethnic, cultural and social diversity in society or are they giving messages that white, middle-class, able-bodied, heterosexual, two-parent families are what is expected?
- How welcoming are you to fathers and other male carers?
- Do you open up lots of opportunities for informal talk with parents and carers?
- Do parents and carers understand your policies on important areas like learning and teaching, inclusion and behaviour? Have they been involved in drawing them up?
- Do you provide workshops and other sessions on the curriculum, for example play, early literacy?
- Do you run family learning courses or other opportunities for parents to access learning and continue to college and elsewhere if appropriate?
- Do parents contribute to children's profiles? Do they regularly review their children's progress with you?
- Do you really listen to and value what they say?

- Have you got an effective transition policy in place that means you have visited the home or other setting before the children come in and that you have good links with the children's next class or setting?
- If a child comes in with special educational needs have you already made links with any health or social care professionals involved, as well as the parents?

You may have worked through that list and felt confident that your setting does all of these things. However, all successful work with parents and carers is much more than just doing particular activities. Two settings could give similar answers to the questions listed above and yet one could be much more successful in inspiring parents and gaining their support than the other. The difference would probably lie in the attitudes of staff and their ability to de-centre and see the world from another's point of view – we always find it easier to empathise with those who are like ourselves. Part of the professional duty of educators is to see the world through the eyes of others (both parents and children) in order to understand, support and extend their learning. This is an area where training and professional development can help practitioners to reflect on some of the issues around their work. However, it is interesting that, when local authorities were recently asked to audit the training and development offered to practitioners using the Key Elements of Effective Practice (KEEP) evaluation tool, working with parents was an area where relatively few training and professional development opportunities were being offered.

Exercise 12.2 asks you to reflect on how you show parents you value them in your workplace.

EXERCISE 12.2

Read these two short extracts from Pugh et al. (1994: 40 and 65).

WANTED: A responsible person, Male or female, to undertake a life-long project. Candidates should be totally committed, willing to work up to 24 hours daily, including weekends during the initial 16 year period. Occasional holidays possible, but may be cancelled at no notice. Knowledge of health care, nutrition, psychology, child development, household management and the education system essential. Necessary skills: stress management and conflict resolution, negotiation and problem solving, communication and listening, budgeting and time management, decision making, ability to set boundaries and priorities as well as providing loving support. Necessary qualities: energy, tolerance, patience, good self-esteem, self-confidence and a sense of humour. No training or experience needed. No salary but very rewarding work for the right person.

There were times before I had my own children when I was already advising other people how to bring up theirs. I thought it was all really quite straightforward. Those people who came to see me were in a mess. They weren't normal parents like we would be. And then we had children. And we were in a mess as well. (Paediatrician quoted in Sokolov and Hutton, 1998)

> ## EXERCISE 12.2 (CONTINUED)
>
> - Look at the documentation provided for parents in your workplace – does it explicitly recognise and value the hard job they are engaged in?
> - Think of any interactions you or colleagues have had with parents recently where you have explicitly valued their role as parents.
> - For the next week briefly log all your interactions with parents, for example greeting parents in the morning and at the end of the day, writing in a home/setting journal, talking about a child's progress. Note which interactions you felt were most positive and why.
> - Reflect on your log (preferably with a colleague) and note three actions you could take to improve your practice.

One of the areas that practitioners sometimes complain about is that parents do not value play – they think that children should be 'working' and do not understand that the distinction between play and work is misleading, as much evidence suggests that children do their really deep learning when playing. This parental misunderstanding is sometimes used as a justification for providing inappropriate activities like worksheets for very young children because they can take them home and prove that work has been done. However, consider which of these activities children are more likely to remember – the experience of watching real frogs, playing with plastic frogs, plants, wood and water in a builder's tray, singing and acting out five little speckled frogs, playing their own stories about frogs, or colouring in an adult-drawn picture on a worksheet?

Parents only have their own experiences of education to draw on when developing expectations of practitioners. It is the professional duty of settings to help parents understand the educational value of play, as without it children cannot learn and develop emotionally, socially, cognitively and physically.

Play

The CGFS principle which has most to say about play returns to the balance between adult-led and child-initiated activities which featured in Case study 12.1 and stresses the need for time:

> There should be opportunities for children to engage in activities planned by adults and also those that they plan or initiate themselves. Children do not make a distinction between 'play' and 'work' and neither should practitioners. Children need time to become engrossed, work in depth and complete activities.

The CGFS (page 25) goes on to explain why this is so important for young children. If we deny them play we deny them deep learning:

Well-planned play, both indoors and outdoors, is a key way in which young children learn with enjoyment and challenge. In playing, they behave in different ways: sometimes their play will be boisterous, sometimes they will describe and discuss what they are doing, sometimes they will be quiet and reflective as they play.

The role of the practitioner is crucial in:

- planning and resourcing a challenging environment;
- supporting children's learning through planned play activity;
- extending and supporting children's spontaneous play;
- extending and developing children's language and communication in their play.

Through play, in a secure environment with effective adult support, children can:

- explore, develop and represent learning experiences that help them make sense of the world;
- practise and build up ideas, concepts and skills;
- learn how to control impulses and understand the need for rules;
- be alone, be alongside others or cooperate as they talk or rehearse their feelings;
- take risks and make mistakes;
- think creatively and imaginatively;
- communicate with others as they investigate or solve problems;
- express fears or relive anxious experiences in controlled and safe situations.

In other words, play underpins all learning; indeed, Bruce (2001: 128) claims it is the highest form of learning in early childhood. Piaget (1951: 167) claimed that 'Play is a form of thought'.

Whitebread (2003: 10) explains the experiments that Bruner and others undertook in 1984 around children's problem-solving skills. Typically in these experiments one group of children was given the opportunity to play with the objects involved and the other group were taught how to use them in ways that would help them solve the problem. When they were actually given the problem, similar numbers of children in each group solved it but, of the unsuccessful children, it was those in the taught group who gave up more quickly and exhibited less perseverance and inventiveness than the 'players' who got nearer to the solution. As Whitebread observes 'the children who played were learning far more generalisable skills, and far more positive attitudes to problem solving. They were, indeed learning how to learn'. So what are the implications of this research and other theories about the importance of play for practice in working with young children in the Foundation Stage?

Clearly play has to be given pride of place in any early years provision. The overwhelming majority of early years practitioners would probably agree with what the CGFS says about supporting children's play, however, we often find children's play challenging. How many of the following questions, for instance, can you answer yes to?

- Have you ever looked over at a group of children playing and asked them from a distance to be quiet or to stop being silly; for example, 'Can you be a bit quieter please, we're trying to work on this table'?
- Have you ever joined a group of children at play and sensed that you are not welcome?
- Have you ever uttered words like 'That's a hairdryer, Jack, not a gun' or 'If I see any more guns being made in that Mobilo it's going away'?
- Do you sometimes feel uncomfortable with superhero play?

We will come back to these challenges, but it might be useful to bear in mind your answers to those questions as you read the 12 features of play that Bruce (2001) has developed from her many years of observing, teaching and playing with young children (See Chapter 9):

1. In their play, children use the first-hand experiences they have in life.
2. Children make up rules as they play, and so keep control of their play.
3. Children make play props.
4. Children choose to play. They cannot be made to play.
5. Children rehearse the future in their role play.
6. Children pretend when they play.
7. Children play alone sometimes.
8. Children and/or adults play together, in parallel, associatively or co-operatively in pairs or groups.
9. Each player has a personal play agenda, although they may not be aware of this.
10. Children playing will be deeply involved, and difficult to distract from their deep learning. Children at play wallow in their learning.
11. Children try out their most recent learning, skills and competencies when they play. They seem to celebrate what they know.
12. Children at play co-ordinate their ideas and feelings, and make sense of relationships with their family, friends and culture. When play is co-ordinated it flows along in a sustained way. It is called free-flow play. (Developed from Bruce, 1991; 1996)

EXERCISE 12.3: DEN-MAKING

If you and the children are used to making dens, observe either the making of a new den or the play in an existing one – taking photos would be useful as well as some narrative observation.

If you have never done it before in your setting or it is relatively unusual, make a den with a small group of children either inside or outdoors with anything that is available, for example large cardboard boxes, a clotheshorse, blankets, sticks, planks, branches; it does not matter as long as you create a small space to hide in, squash into, call home, leave and return to – whatever the play demands. Observe and note down what the children do and say.

Use the 12 features of play to analyse your observations. Which ones were present? What does your analysis tell you about the children's learning? What did the observations tell you about children's needs in terms of space and time for play? If den-making was relatively unusual in your setting what might be the next steps for you and the children? Was there anything challenging for you as a practitioner in doing this exercise? Were you aware of any differences in the play of boys and girls?

The next scenario, or something similar, may have happened in your setting.

It's a lovely sunny day. You are sitting outside under a tree reading a story to a group of attentive girls when suddenly the peace is shattered by a group of boys running around and around the tree shouting loudly and waving sticks. You gather that they are 'Power Rangers' on a mission and then they are off to another tree to do the same thing there. After a few minutes they run back to their den, disappear inside for a few seconds and then come out again to run around shouting.

This brings us back to the questions posed earlier about aspects of children's play we might find challenging. Holland (2003: 21) claims that most of our negative attention is directed at the noisy play usually associated with boys and involving war, weapon and superhero play. She provides a list of the many ways in which practitioners may say 'no' to this sort of active play

You know we don't play like that at nursery:

because we don't want any of you to be hurt;
because we don't want you to hurt each other;
because we don't want you to even pretend to hurt each other;
because we don't want you to disturb the other children;
because you are here to learn;
because guns hurt people;
because it's noisy;
because we want you to do a nice painting for mummy;
because you boys would never do anything else;
because it isn't nice;
because I don't like it;
because I said so.

There is not space in this chapter to further explore the gender issues illustrated here, but it might be productive to think about the messages girls and boys are receiving about their play in your setting at a time when they are constructing their ideas of maleness and femaleness. Do you attempt to keep out references to television programmes and films you do not approve of, for instance? Are parents made to feel that popular culture is not welcome?

Many practitioners are now finding that if boys are allowed to play out the stories and themes that interest them, and understand that normal rules about safety apply, they feel more valued and, consequently, seem to talk more about what they are doing with other children and with practitioners. As Paley, who has spent many years engaging in children's stories and the way in which they play out their ideas, wryly observed as long ago as 1984:

If I have not yet learned to love Darth Vader, I have at least made some useful discoveries while watching him at play. As I interrupt less, it becomes clear that boys' play is serious drama, not morbid mischief. Its rhythms and images are often discordant to me, but I must try to make sense of a style that, after all, belongs to half the population of the classroom. (p. xii)

In her book on fantasy play entitled *A Child's Work* Paley reiterates the importance of children's stories and the ways in which they play out ideas in them from peers, family, practitioners, books and television 'from play into story and back into more play' (2004: xii). Observing and recording the children thus engaged has enabled Paley to value the deep connections between play and analytical thinking.

To return to the passage about the importance of play from the CGFS, quoted at the beginning of this section, are you sure that children in your setting have access to learning activities that will allow them to engage in learning in the ways listed there?

Learning and teaching

> Nearly everything in my training as a teacher led me to believe that the questions were supposed to come from me. (Paley, 2004: 16)

It is evident that a simple input/output model which suggests that children learn what we teach them is untenable, although many of us were trained, like Paley, to believe in our power as transmitters of knowledge rather than co-constructors of meaning. All the CGFS principles relate to effective learning and teaching. On page 20 the CGFS explains the approach to children's learning evident throughout the document:

> Learning for young children is a rewarding and enjoyable experience in which they explore, investigate, discover, create, practise, rehearse, repeat, revise and consolidate their developing knowledge, skills, understanding and attitudes. During the foundation stage, many of these aspects of learning are brought together effectively through playing and talking.

On the same page an example is given of the need for practitioners to be flexible if children are to be able to engage in the process of learning and be satisfied with what they have achieved.

> ... a child climbing in the garden sees a spider. She recalls seeing a book about spiders and goes indoors to find it. She shows a friend the picture and then takes him outdoors to find the real spider, which is now spinning a web. The two children return indoors to the painting easel and paint spiders. They become interested in making web patterns with many different coloured lines. Finally, they cover their paintings with a single colour and use their fingers to 'draw' spiders in the wet paint. This whole process has taken some 40 minutes of concentrated, focused and sustained activity, which the children describe in detail to their group and key practitioner at the end of the session.

Practitioners, whether they have a formal teaching qualification or not, teach children in many ways. The CGFS tells us (page 22) that teaching means systematically helping children to learn so that they make connections and reflect on what they have already learned and move forward. It includes planning the indoor and outdoor learning environment, modelling positive behaviours, direct teaching of skills and knowledge, facilitating children teaching each other, and interacting with and supporting children in a way that supports positive attitudes to learning.

The spider incident was clearly a significant learning experience for those two children. The practitioner's role may seem relatively insignificant but in fact she has provided the book, the space and the time. She has also maintained interest and observed what has happened. The setting is also clearly committed to the use of indoors and out-doors, the free flow of children between them and children having first-hand experiences on which to build their learning.

Observation and assessment of children's learning gives insight into their interests, achievements and possible difficulties in their learning from which next steps can be planned. It also helps ensure early identification of special educational needs and particular abilities. It is only through careful observation that practitioners can understand where children are and how to move them on. Practitioners need to share assessment information to group children for particular activities and interests and to ensure that the curriculum meets the needs of all children. Assessment information can also help identify areas for improvement in terms of organisation and resources as well as any professional development needed for practitioners.

Parents are vital partners in this assessment process. If, when their parents come to collect them, the children and the practitioner tell them about the spider and the process they went through, parents may be able to contribute other relevant information as well as being able to celebrate their children's learning. Or, if this is not possible, photos in the children's pro-files may be a focus for discussion with parents at another time. Sharing of information between the setting and home ensures that appropriate targets are set for children and that parents and practitioners can continue to work together to teach the children.

In the Foundation Stage children are working towards achieving the early learning goals in all six areas of learning listed earlier in this chapter. The six areas help practitioners to plan the learning environment and experiences offered to the children. They are a frame-work for the curriculum. But that does not mean that the children's learning is neatly divided up into areas.

The CGFS (page 26) gives an example of an experience that provides children with opportunities to develop a number of competencies, skills and concepts across several areas of learning:

> … children building with blocks may cooperate in carrying the heavy and large blocks, nego-tiate the best place to put them, compare the weight and dimensions of different blocks and act out an imaginary scene. Therefore, they may be developing language, mathematical, phys-ical, personal and social competencies through this one activity.

Case study 12.1, earlier in this chapter, was another example of children engaging in several areas of learning. Which areas of learning did the two children engaged with the spider work in? Effective learners whether aged 4 or 40 make connections across areas of learning all the time. The focus for practitioners in Foundation Stage must be on effective learning based on play not on trying to 'deliver' a series of knowledge bases.

The early learning goals establish expectations for most children to reach by the end of the Foundation Stage but are not a curriculum in themselves. The Foundation Stage Profile, which must be completed by practitioners for each child, is a summative statement of their achievement in relation to the early learning goals at the end of their reception year. It rests on the assumption that practitioners build up their assessment throughout the year from the close observation of ongoing learning and teaching.

Pages 28 to 127 of the CGFS set out the main features of each area of learning and the 'stepping stones' of progress towards the early learning goals in each area. These stepping stones identify developing knowledge, skills and understanding children need if they are to achieve the early learning goals. Alongside these are examples of what children might do at different stages as well as ideas for what the practitioner might usefully do to support and extend children's learning. All these ideas and examples, as well as the stepping stones and early learning goals, are support for practitioners in putting the principles for early years education into practice. They will help practitioners to support and challenge young children in being confident learners. As Roberts (2002: 141) says: 'Children who have learned from their important adults to value their own genuine efforts and achievements are more likely to believe they *can* learn, and so to learn successfully … not only as they start school, but throughout school and for the rest of their lives.'

Personal, social and emotional development and communication

Personal, social and emotional development (PSED) and communication should underpin the whole Foundation Stage curriculum. If children have positive dispositions and attitudes to learning, self-confidence and self-esteem, are able to make relationships with others, are able to control their own behaviour, look after themselves and treat others with respect and communicate effectively, they will have firm foundations on which to build their learning. They will also be more likely to show their confidence across all areas of learning.

EXERCISE 12.4

1. Time sampling : choose a child in your class or group that you feel you know less well than others. Observe her/him for four 5-minute periods across the day – choose times that are convenient, it does not matter what they are doing. You must not be distracted and must spend each of the 5-minute periods concentrating on that child.
2. Note down what the child does and who he/she communicates with. Do not make judgements as to motives, or attempt to analyse what is happening; just record at this stage.
3. Analyse your observations with a colleague if possible – what do they tell you about the child's dispositions to learning? *Prompts:* is the child independent and curious, willing to take risks, involved in activities, persistent when things go wrong? Do some activities or areas in the setting seem to be more attractive to her/him than others?

(Continued)

EXERCISE 12.4 (CONTINUED)

Did you observe any particular schemas the child seemed to be working with? (See Further Reading for information on schemas.) Does the child communicate freely with others asking questions and offering opinions or only respond when spoken to or communicated with? Did you observe anything unexpected?

4. What will you do next with this child? Why?
    (Some practitioners may feel that they know all the children equally well, but there are usually some children who, for various reasons, do not demand as much attention as others. This would also be a useful exercise to do with a child you think you know very well. All children surprise us when we observe them closely. It would also be useful to do this exercise several times.)

5. Read the sections in the CGFS on personal social and emotional development (pp. 28–31) and communication language and literacy (pp. 44–7). Are there any resources or opportunities that could be improved in your setting in order to support learning and teaching in these areas?

6. Discuss your observations of children and your analysis of resources and opportunities with colleagues and draw up an action plan for improvement. It should include a timescale for action and strategies for evaluating its success. (Repeat observations could be appropriate here.)

Trevarthen (1998: 97) argues that a 3-year-old is 'a socially aware person who is capable of making and keeping friends and of negotiating interesting co-operations and tests of understandings with a wide range of acquaintances'. This statement is undoubtedly true, but how many children find social life in the setting difficult? You may have found that your own observations for Exercise 12.4 or for other purposes have recorded some of these difficulties for some children. There are some comparatively simple things that practitioners can do to help children become more socially adept between the ages of 3 and 5.

As Brooker and Broadbent (2003: 33) observe:

For all children, even the most confident, entering a pre-school setting is more than a step into a new world, full of promise; it is a step away from the familiar world of home and carries with it innumerable anxieties which may revive memories of the child's earliest experiences. Literally from birth, children have undergone the pain of separation and loss. Most will have come to terms with temporary absences and feelings of grief … Nevertheless, the dawning realisation that this new stage in their lives means something different … is something that many children understandably resist. The 'self' which for many children has developed gradually, separating in tiny steps from others who surround and enfold it, now has to take on an independent identity, mirrored in the eyes and actions of a whole new company of 'significant others'.

This separation needs to be built on by practitioners to help children to 'belong' in the setting. Children going into reception class in a primary school at the age of 4 may have similar anxieties, particularly if they have not been to a pre-school setting.

Fostering a sense of belonging is important for the development of self-concept. Putting photos of children on their pegs and in their 'home base' or classroom and asking children to bring in photos of their families and homes will give children the chance to talk about these and recognise that they belong to several groups – that they belong in the setting as well as at home. Children will feel that they belong in an environment where they can predict the shape of the day and its routines, and where they are given responsibility for planning the environment, serving food, tidying up and so on.

Children who feel they belong are more likely to have high self-esteem. Children need praise and recognition for their efforts and achievements but practitioners need to be aware of how often they use phrases such as 'good girl', 'well done' and 'lovely' without any explanation or detail about what they are praising. Roberts (2002: 106) argues that 'the use of strategies such as habitual empty praise, gold stars, smiley stickers and meaningless statements are more likely to feed children's self pre-occupation and narcissism than to help them form a genuine sense of their own worth'. Consider how much more effective a statement like this would be in developing a child's self-esteem: 'Well done, Shabana, it's the first time you've climbed that high, we must tell your mum later. I'm going to write it down so we don't forget.' By speaking to the child like this the practitioner is showing genuine interest in the achievement, acknowledging that mum needs to know and modelling courtesy and attentiveness in communication. It is this modelling of appropriate behaviour that will help many children to modify their own behaviour in socially acceptable ways. Practitioners' use of communication and language can reinforce PSED, as this extract from the CGFS (p. 30) illustrates:

> Many young children rely on gesture and facial and body language to initiate interaction and express their feelings. These strands continue to be important in achieving successful social communication and emotional development and need to be developed alongside the necessary language. Practitioners should know about and be able to respond to different forms of body language, for example in many cultures casting the eyes down is respectful and should not be interpreted as defiant or sullen. Practitioners can promote interactions by acting as a catalyst and then withdrawing. For example, the practitioner, on being offered pitta bread in the home corner says it is more tasty when it is warm and asks if it could be heated up. The child then negotiates with another who is already at the cooker and begins to discuss the cakes that are in the oven and whether there is room for the pitta bread too. Initiating interactions and entering conversations are sophisticated skills which require knowledge of social codes and conventional phrases such as 'Excuse me' and 'May I tell you about?' Practitioners also need to help children by offering the vocabulary with which to articulate their feelings in a wide range of contexts, to practise resolving conflict, make choices and decisions, see situations from another's point of view and form relationships. Using open-ended questions such as, 'How ... ?', 'Why ... ?' and 'What will happen if ... ?' provides children with an environment that encourages exploration and will set any learning outcome in the context of being part of a problem solving process rather than as success and failure.

In the CGFS, communication is bracketed with language and literacy. This is because the ability to communicate and use language underpins the development of the skills necessary for reading and writing. Language and literacy are explored in other chapters in this volume. Here we are looking at communication.

We are all born learners and communicators, whatever the limits of our physical ability. As can be seen in the extract above, as language develops, non-verbal communication may become less important, but it still remains an important form of communication. For some children who have difficulty speaking, non-verbal communication, such as signing, may be their main form of communication throughout life.

It is important to value all the forms of communication children bring with them into the setting and to accept that some children may make their feelings known by not speaking or by wanting to listen at first. An issue to consider is how much you use non-verbal communication to empathise with children – your smiles, frowns and body language, as well as the physical contact you make with them are giving them messages all the time about their worth to you, the boundaries you set and whether you understand their feelings. They also pick up messages about how you view their families from the way in which you talk with their parents and carers.

In 1984 Tizard and Hughes published research which showed how similar the language experiences of working-class and middle-class children at home with their mothers were, and how quickly well meaning staff disempowered the working-class children when they went to nursery school and then lowered their expectations of them. The second edition of their book was published in 2002 because the issues it raises are still relevant. Working-class and poor children still underachieve and are less healthy (Sylva et al., 2004; Wilkinson, 2005).

EXERCISE 12.5

1. How do the children, parents and visitors in your setting know what is happening and where things are? Are there photo cues for those who find listening hard, who are bi-lingual or who have forgotten what was said? If you have children who sign, can everybody communicate with them?
2. Think about the parents and children you find it hardest to have a conversation with. Why is this? Do you think they find it hard to communicate with you? What steps could you take to make communication easier for the child, the parent and yourself?

Conclusion

In Reggio Emilia in Italy the educators talk about the 'hundred languages of children'. Providing a broad and rich curriculum based on the principles for early years education, which follows the child's interests, is play based and, where practitioners use observation as their main form of assessment, will help children use some of those languages.

No way. The hundred is there

The child
is made of one hundred.
The child has
a hundred languages
a hundred hands
a hundred thoughts
a hundred ways of thinking
of playing, of speaking.
A hundred always a hundred
ways of listening
of marvelling, of loving
a hundred joys
for singing and understanding
a hundred worlds
to discover
a hundred worlds
to invent
a hundred worlds to dream.
The child has
a hundred languages
(and a hundred hundred hundred more)
but they steal ninety nine.
The school and the culture
separate the head from the body.
They tell the child:
to think without hands
to do without head
to listen and not to speak
to understand without joy
to love and to marvel
only at Easter and Christmas.
They tell the child:
to discover the world already there
and of the hundred
they steal ninety-nine.
They tell the child:
that work and play
reality and fantasy
science and imagination
sky and earth
reason and dream
are things
that do not belong together.

And thus they tell the child
that the hundred is not there.
The child says:
no way. The hundred is there.

(Loris Malaguzzi, 1996: 3, translated by Lella Gandini)
From the catalogue of the Exhibition 'The Hundred Languages of Children', © Preschools and Infant – toddlers centers – Instituzione of the Municipality of Reggio Emilia, Italy, published by Reggio Children, 1996.

Further reading

Bruce, T. (2001) *Learning through Play: Babies, Toddlers and the Foundation Years*. London: Hodder & Stoughton.
A very accessible book which looks at play in children's lives and how adults can support it. It is full of beautiful sequences of photographs which are analysed to help adults understand what is happening. It refers to the stepping stones and early learning goals of CGFS.

Nutbrown, C. (1999) *Threads of Thinking: Young Children Learning and the Role of Early Education*. 2nd edition. London: Paul Chapman Publishing.
If you are interested in schemas this book is easy to read and is packed full of examples of children being active dynamic learners. It helps practitioners to reflect on children's patterns of repeatable behaviour out of which concepts grow (schemas). It also illustrates how this involves children in making connections across traditional subject areas and how practitioners can support this.

Paley, V. (2004) *A Child's Work*. Chicago, IL: University of Chicago Press.
This book is pure inspiration. It is a short easy read on one level; on another it makes one reflect deeply about the implications of the children's responses to having their stories valued.

Primary National Strategy (2005) *Parents: Partners in Learning*. Nottingham: DfES Publications.
A folder with leaflets outlining the learning stories of seven local authority projects involving parents in sharing curriculum knowledge and developing partnerships.

Rich, D., Casanova, D., Dixon., A, Drummond, M.J., Durrant, A. and Myer, C. (2005) *First Hand Experience, What Matters to Children*. Woodbridge, Suffolk: Rich Learning Opportunities.
This book is an alphabet of first-hand experiences. The text for each letter has been designed as a springboard for multi-sensory experience. It is not a conventional book and is all the richer for that.

Whitebread, D. (ed.) (2003) *Teaching and Learning in the Early Years*. 2nd edition. London: Routledge.
This book provides excellent summaries of research about how children learn. It also deals with classroom management and organisation, and then includes a section on play and language followed by chapters on other curriculum areas. All the writers take a child-centred approach.

CHAPTER

13

DIVERSITY AND INCLUSION

Tina Bruce

Tina Bruce is Honorary Visiting Professor at Roehampton University, where she originally trained (when it was the Froebel Educational Institute) as a teacher for the Primary phase. She is a trained teacher of children with hearing impairments. She is a widely published author in books, articles and journals, with an international reputation. She was awarded International Woman Scholar in Education by Virginia Commonwealth University and has worked with the British Council in Egypt and New Zealand.

Aims

To develop understanding of:

☐ some of the challenges in relation to embedding principles of diversity and inclusion in practice
☐ strategies which support the process
☐ children and adults as unique individuals, and recognise that approaches based on the premise that one size fits all undermine the principles of diversity and inclusion in destructive ways.

There is a tendency to separate the terms diversity and inclusion, such that diversity is used to address issues surrounding culture, while inclusion is interpreted as including children with special educational needs and disabilities. It is more useful if the two words are used together. This is why this chapter is titled in the way it is, and the title is mirrored in reverse in Chapter 20. Julie Jennings (2002) and Tina Hyder (2005) see diversity and inclusion as inextricably linked.

Diversity

Diversity helps us to think about and embrace the wide range of people in the world, and specifically in the UK today. Bronfenbrenner (1979) pioneered a very tangible way of expressing this with circles, so that the child first becomes aware of family/carers and the immediate circle of neighbours and community in everyday life. Gradually these circles ripple outwards, so that the child is steadily and increasingly influenced by the wider community, and the culture and atmosphere of society on a broader scale. Trans-global issues also impact, and as children grow up they are either helped to be aware of these or not encouraged to think beyond their own communities.

According to John Elkington, (personal communication, 2005) it is useful to approach a concept such as diversity, using three circles. One circle represents the past, one the present and one the future. He suggests that there are variations in the way different countries in the world bring these three aspects into relationship with each other.

1. *Past*: for example, in Europe, colonial pasts still impact hugely on the present, and this influences the way people think about a future and the next steps that should be taken. Historically there were famous scientists and engineers, and this masks the fact that there is now comparatively little active scientific research at present in the UK, with few children studying science in the later stages of school.

2. *Present*: Elkington suggests that in the USA there is less emphasis on the past, and very little emphasis on the long-term implications of recent actions for the future. The present is the dominant influence, and the focus is on doing what is needed now.

3. *Future*: in China the main emphasis is on the future, with a huge education programme now to train scientists and engineers who can also be creative thinkers, so as to equip the country for an unknown and fast-changing future.

Inclusion

Inclusion helps us to think about how we can come together in a diverse world, and particularly in our local community, despite being so different from each other (Orr, 2003). We need to search for ways of doing this which do not trample on each other's diverse traditions, but which show that we value and respect each other. Valuing and respecting a person because they are a fellow human being does not necessarily mean agreeing with them, and disagreements do not necessarily mean lacking respect or undervaluing someone.

In the chapter on leadership (Chapter 28), Lesley Benson, has written a section on how we can work as a team when we have to work out our areas of disagreement and find ways forward. Where we do not agree with others (and this will surely be the case as some aspects of all cultures will be unacceptable to others) we need to find ways of having robust discussions, and forging agreements so that children and adults feel safe, valued and respected, and that the agreements made are acceptable to everyone in that community (such as a school or early childhood setting).

One alternative is to develop a separate development system with communities of different cultures and faiths having their own schools. (e.g. Christians or Muslims) Separate schools are usually promoted by those who have a faith in a revelationary god, rather than free thinkers. Those who belong to the Ethical Society, or Humanists, also have strong value systems which guide their lives.

Another alternative is to take a relativist view, which promotes all cultural views as equal. Such an approach does not address some of the difficult issues. For example, there is a crucial difference between an arranged marriage with the agreement of all parties and a forced marriage.

Valuing a multi-cultural approach means valuing all cultures in society. Many children from the majority ethnic group, as well as minority ethnic groups, need to know the traditional English dances and songs, poetry, costume, literature or architecture. This is encouraged in Wales, Scotland and Northern Ireland, where heritage teaching of the culture (e.g. dances, songs and stories) is enshrined in the National Curricula. It is important to be proud of being part of a multi-cultural England, which includes being knowledgeable about the culture and traditions of the country in which you live.

Grandparents often express their sadness that their grandchildren no longer speak, for example, Punjabi or Polish at home, and so find conversations with their grandparents difficult, but it is also often the case that children half know the two languages of home and school English (Whitehead, 2003). This impacts on their thinking. It means they are constrained in their ability to fully participate in either their home community or their school/early childhood setting community (Baker, 2000).

Challenges

We can see how difficult many of these issues are, but also that it is of fundamental importance to keep trying to tease them out, working hard to think our way through issues in discussions during which people feel safe and valued Siraj Blatchford (1999). In a modern contest, having a sense of belonging to a community, in the early childhood setting or school, is very complex. It is about finding where agreements can be made and celebrating these, while addressing the difficult areas of disagreement and deciding what to do about them (Brown, 1998). The word hegemony is useful. It is about power relationships. It is vital that early childhood settings and school communities lead the process, but it is also essential that they do not dictate to or bully parents and carers in the community.

In the final part of this chapter, we shall explore principled ways of embracing diversity and inclusion, and taking forward the important work to be done.

It is important that there are national policies which address the issues of diversity and inclusion. A policy is the starting point of a principled approach. A policy needs to be a living document which is continually referred back to and acted upon. It also needs to be regularly reviewed. It is an important way of monitoring and evaluating how diversity and inclusion are being valued on a daily and constant basis.

It is easy for a policy to turn into a list containing separated and different aspects of diversity and inclusion which are not connected to each other. At the beginning of the chapter, it was pointed out that inclusion is often seen as addressing issues of disability and special educational needs, while diversity is seen to be concerned with issues of ethnicity, creed, language and culture. A good policy document links all aspects together through a principled approach.

In the document *A Policy for Excellence* the authors state: 'Policy-making may perhaps appear to have the potential of raising "difficult" issues that would be easier left alone. Nevertheless, for those committed to equality, the process of policy development will itself be helpful and provide a supporting framework within which to work' (EYTARN, 2001: p. 4).

Getting together is important, so that everyone feels they can have their say and that what is agreed means that everyone feels a sense of ownership in it. Naturally this takes longer than the head/manager writing a document and then implementing it. However, in the long term it will be time saved because everyone, governors, trustees, staff, those linked with the setting or based there in a multi-agency role, local authority staff linked to the setting/school, parents/carers and children too, will want to implement it, not just the head/manager.

The *Every Child Matters* framework to be incorporated in English law emphasises the importance of listening to children and valuing their thoughts and feelings. Penny Lancaster, based at Coram Family, has developed training for staff in this (with DfES funding) through the 'Listening to Children' initiative which won the Charity Award in 2005.

EXERCISE 13.1

In the setting/school where you work, look at the policy document for diversity and inclusion. This may be titled Equality or Anti-discrimination Policy.

How easy was it to find? When was it last reviewed? What are the main principles it espouses? Who was involved in writing it? Discuss the document with colleagues. How is the document used to monitor and evaluate practice? How can you use this document to develop your practice? Name three action points that you will implement as a result of reading it and discussing it.

It is almost inevitable that some families/carers will not agree with some aspects of the work with children. For example, recently, headteachers have reported that parents have complained that their children dislike the healthy eating policy introduced to tackle the issues of poor health in children. At one level, it is an invasion of a family life. It forces children eating in school or the setting to eat in the way dictated by a government initiative. There are reports that children are being taken to the shop by parents to buy crisps and sweets to fill them up after they have refused to eat any lunch in the setting/school.

This example raises all the issues in demonstrating how there can be barriers and difficulties in implementing a policy of diversity with inclusion at its heart.

New policies take time to embed

If a vocal minority resist healthy eating, should the setting/school/government persist? The argument could be made that democracy is supposed to be about giving the people what they want rather than ensuring that everyone's rights are considered, and that there should be social justice. Children have the right to healthy food. Adults are in a position to choose whether or not to eat healthy food, unless there is economic poverty. Fruit and vegetables and high-quality proteins are expensive. Children should be offered these and not penalised because there is poverty.

The argument for persisting with a healthy diet is that, biologically, children develop better health long term, think better and get more out of life because they have more energy and zing, and they behave better if they do not have a poor diet.

However, different cultures have very different foods. Studies show that children and adults find strange food difficult and tend to refuse it. In order to meet the biological needs and rights of children, it is therefore necessary to do so in ways which are socio culturally sensitive.

At one Extended Primary Services School in London, there has been a policy in place prior to the government's healthy food initiative. Children do not bring packed lunches to school. There are flowers on the table and tablecloths. Staff are carefully trained and enjoy eating with the children, engaging in fascinating conversations. The atmosphere is more like a busy restaurant. Children have a wide choice of food. They can have salad, freshly cooked vegetables, a vegetarian option and the food is carefully chosen to be attractive across a range of cultures.

A considerable minority of parents were not happy with the change, and complained to the head. There were robust discussions, and the parents were invited to join the lunch times. They found there were things there that they enjoyed eating and that their children were beginning to go back for second helpings. They no longer felt forced into something strange and new. Instead, they felt they were listened to and that their views were genuinely respected. They became supportive of the policy, and began to ask for classes to learn to cook some of the dishes with their children. This was arranged.

Just as there are issues for diversity and inclusion in relation to ethnicity, creed and culture in eating, so there are issues for children with special educational needs, disabilities and allergies.

If Ian eats dairy products, it triggers eczema. But he still needs to be able to make some choices about what he eats, just as other children do. There needs to be discussion so that he learns to avoid these foods without an adult doing this for him. He needs, therefore, to be taught which are dairy products and what will happen if he eats them. Once he understands that milk, butter, yogourt and cheese are from the cow, goat or sheep, he will be able to decide which of the other choices he would like. There might be rice and dall, pasta with a tomato sauce or potatoes, meat and vegetables, or fish cakes and salad and fruit.

The same principles apply to a child like Emma, who has diabetes. For Luke, who has complex needs the issue of choice is a challenge. He eats with the other children, sitting in his wheelchair, and is tube fed by his carer. He appreciates being with them, and participating, with a sense of belonging.

Another issue arises when English is an additional language for a child. It is difficult for a child to say they do not like or do not want a food. It is very helpful to children if they can be given food vocabulary as they point or shake their head. In some settings now, children serve themselves vegetables and salad and water to drink from bowls and jugs at the table. Small jugs are essential so that they are not too heavy for a small child to lift.

EXERCISE 13.2

Observe a mealtime in the setting/school where you work. Make observations of a child with:

- an allergy/disability
- English as an additional language
- a child brought up in a religion with dietary laws
- a child who is new to the school/setting.

How does the child participate? How do staff support the child so that mealtime is an enjoyable experience, eating with friends and engaging in fascinating conversations?

Staff need genuinely to embrace the principles and spirit of diversity and inclusion

Training is the key element here. Professional development supports practitioners in the process of reflecting on practice, and becoming more informed about the research and theories and attitudes which impact on practice. People are often unaware of what they think, or of the things that influence them. Training helps practitioners to become more *aware* of what they know, and how that knowledge needs to be based on evidence if they are to work effectively, morally and ethically with other people's children. This process is called meta-cognition. It means becoming aware of your own thinking, and reflecting on it. Practitioners who work at being reflective practitioners throughout their working lives are better able to embrace the need to change, modify as well as actively reaffirm the way they approach issues of all kinds, but especially principled practice in relation to diversity and inclusion.

Being informed with a good understanding of child development

Every practitioner working with young children needs a sound and thorough training in child development. Part of this is to understand how language/languages develop. This becomes essential when working with children who have English as an additional language.

Children have a great facility for language in the first five years, but this is especially so in the first three years. Children understand what is said to them before they can speak the language themselves. Understanding comes before talking and fluency takes time to be established. The long period of listening before speaking can last for several months. It is sometimes called the 'silent period'.

If a child has learnt one language, which is used at home, they will find it relatively easy to learn another language. This is especially so if they are free to use their home language outside the home. (Communicating Matters, DfES, 2005)

Languages tend to develop in clusters. For this reason, it is important to assess whether a child speaks fluently in their home language, particularly if that child is very slow to learn any English in the setting/school. There may be a hearing impairment. Low incident disabilities such as hearing and visual impairments are often missed if English is an additional language. The same is true of the child who has a learning difficulty. Because the child does not speak English, it is assumed he/she speaks the home language, but language may not be developing in the usual way in either language.

Naturally, a child who has experienced trauma, perhaps because the family has become separated in a war, may be slow to speak while healing, which is a slow and painful process.

Most children with English as an additional language become fairly fluent within two years. It seems to take longer to become a fluent writer in English though, and this needs to be borne in mind, especially when working with children in Key Stage 1 and beyond.

There is a tendency only to use one word or short phrases rather than normal sentences with children developing English as an additional language. This is not helpful for the child, who is then deprived of a language-rich environment. It does help to speak slowly and clearly. It also helps to emphasise key words. 'Have you found your *hat?*'

Song, rhyme and dance are very helpful when learning an additional language, or indeed a first language. As Adam Ockelford (1996: 13) points out, 'Music can inform and enrich living and learning throughout the day'. For example, a simple song about the days of the weeks helps children to learn this vocabulary more easily than saying the words.

It is important for children to feel part of things. Encouraging them to sit and chat with children who speak English as their first language, and teaching each other words is very satisfying for everyone, staff and children alike.

Parents appreciate having books (made with the children) to take home, with photographs of cooking, building with wooden blocks, making things out of clay, sharing books in the home language and in English. These are often read over and over again, and become treasured possessions.

Significant markers In the journey for children with English as an additional language

- Beginner – the child is silent or uses little English even if encouraged to do so.
- Developing – the child begins to talk in English, and joins in with the group, understanding quite well.
- Functional – as well as talking with increasing confidence in English, the child begins to join in with mark-making on paper, demonstrating he/she is becoming an emergent writer or write simple words in either the home language with the script appropriate, or in English. There are real challenges here, for example for an Urdu speaker or a child writing in Chinese or Arabic, and the contrasting directions and different scripts of the languages on paper.

EXERCISE 13.3

Observe a child who is mono-lingual. Note their language in a conversation with another child, and with an adult one to one, and in a group context. Observe a child with English as an additional language, and repeat the task. Observe a child who is a balanced bi-lingual speaker of English and another language, and repeat the exercise.

Where, when and how did you find a greater likelihood of shared, sustained conversations? What are the implications? What supports the child in developing English and maintaining the home language?

It is easy to give up when a situation seems impossible to solve

Whilst it is important not to be over-idealistic and unrealistic about what can be achieved in the short term, we need to be very practical and look at what can be done now. However, it is very important to hang on to principles, because these guide the vision we have of how we want things to be in the long term. In Chapter 5 'Theory, practice and content' we saw that the principled approach of the pioneers was interpreted very practically, and in diverse ways, and that there was an impact on practice which is still exerting steady influence in the UK today.

In this chapter, we have related these principles to diversity and inclusion. In Chapter 20, written by Tina Hyder and Julie Jennings, you will be able to read more about inclusion and diversity with a view to how the principles which are important in the years from birth to 5 years become nested in the years when children attend primary school. These two chapters, 13 and 20, build on the principles of diversity and inclusion enshrined in the *Birth to Three Matters* framework and the *Curriculum Guidance for the Foundation Stage* you read about in Chapter 12 by Helen Moylett and will be central within the Early Years Foundation Stage. The key message is that when we treat children as unique individuals, we work in the spirit of diversity and inclusion.

Further reading

Hyder, T. (2005) *War, Conflict and Play*. Maidenhead: Open University Press. This book will help you to tune into children's feelings in ways which help them to heal and learn after experiencing trauma.

Jennings, J. (2002) 'A broad vision and a narrow focus'. *Early Childhood Practice: the Journal for Multi-Professional Partnerships*, vol. 4, No 1 2002, pp. 50–60.

Ockleford, A. (1996) *All Join In! A Framework for making music with children and young people who are visually impaired and having learning difficulties*. London: RNIB. This is a very good book full of simple songs, and a CD-ROM with music to support practioners. It would help all children, not just those with visual impairments.

THE FOUNDATION STAGE

COMMUNICATION, LANGUAGE AND LITERACY

Marian Whitehead

Marian Whitehead, formerly Senior Lecturer at Goldsmiths College, is a language and early years consultant, a journal editor and the author of several standard texts on language and literacy development in early childhood.

Aims

To develop understanding of:

- ☐ and help readers/student gain a deeper understanding of the communication skills of babies and young children.
- ☐ and ensure that readers/student understand the broad pattern of language development and be able to implement a range of professional good practices to support children's language development.
- ☐ and enable readers/students to gain a professional understanding of the nature of literacy and of its emergence in early childhood.
- ☐ and promote understand of a wide range of good practices that nurture early literacy development.

Language: understanding young children communicating and using language

Communication

Case Study

I am visiting the recently opened baby rooms of a large Children's Centre and notice a toddler (18 months) standing by the transparent barrier that divides the rooms from the main nursery. He is with his key worker and gazing with obvious concentration into the nursery. I am told that James is 'waiting for his special friend the cleaner'. Suddenly his body tenses, he smiles and extends his right arm, fist clenched but index finger extended, pointing at the cleaner entering the main nursery doors that are a considerable distance from the baby area. Later, returning through the nursery, I meet James and his special friend vacuuming the carpets in companionable silence.

This observation reminds us that very young children are learning communication skills and language as part of their daily lives and social contacts, and using sensitive observations and appropriate gestures to express their needs, feelings and experiences. The incident demonstrates how tuned in toddlers are to what is happening around them, to familiar routines and the activities of significant adults.

The Foundation Stage of education in England starts at 3 years, but no child first starts learning to communicate and use language at 3 years. Communication starts at birth, long before verbal language develops, and is the real foundation on which language and literacy develop. If we observe babies closely we can see how they begin to communicate with their regular carers and this gives us some clues about the development of communication, signing and language.

- *Listening* – babies are always listening and can hear in the womb. They prefer human voices to noise and soon recognise their carers' voices and will turn towards them and be comforted by them. Babies who are born deaf still communicate but rely on other senses, such as, sight, touch and smell. Signing systems can be adapted for babies and there is an increasing interest in using a few signs for everyday events and objects with hearing infants. This will certainly enhance the use of familiar gestures that babies and toddlers, like James in the case study, learn in a particular community.

- *Looking* – eye contact is very important in the non-verbal stages of communication and language development, and actually remains a crucial part of how we all manage our talk and conversations with other people. Newborns are fascinated by eyes and spend considerable periods of time gazing into the eyes of their carers. They can make eye contact when they are feeling sociable and will drop their gaze to end a 'conversation'. Babies with impaired vision react to voices, touch and smell, and those with impaired hearing rely on eye contact, facial expressions, touch, gestures and signs.

- *Making faces* – the use by carers of exaggerated facial expressions when interacting with babies and toddlers appears to be a 'natural' response to the fact that their young partner does not fully understand many of the words used in a conversation. All this drama holds a child's attention and helps her to focus on the shared topic of the conversation. The over-acting skill remains with us all and can still be seen when adults wish to be very funny or attract the attention of a big audience! (Observations in pubs are useful at this point!)

- *Getting excited* – babies respond with what we might call 'whole body excitement' to the attention and the talk of adults. The energy pulses through babies' bodies as they wave their arms, open and shut their hands, kick their legs and wriggle their toes. They may not have words yet, but babies can make many sounds, such as, grunts, squeals, hiccups, cries and gurgles. All these are important preparations for rhythmic babbling and the first words. Once conventional words develop, the excitement lessens, but it can still be found in dance, drama, music-making and rituals in all cultures.

- *Talk to me* – it is as simple as that! If we want to give babies and young children the best possible start as communicators and talkers we must talk with them, not at them. It is the amount of ordinary everyday talk – about activities and people – that is shared with infants and children that makes all the difference to their later literacy and general success in school. The other crucial factor is sharing songs, rhymes and books with babies, but that is another story for a later section of this chapter.

Words and talk

Infants' first words emerge out of the caring relationships and the communications they have shared with adults (and older children) and their inclusion in a linguistic culture where everything is negotiated through non-verbal communications, spoken words and written texts.

Babbling

The rhythmic sounds of babbling are shaped and influenced by the languages used with and around young children. Babies quickly develop particular sounds as signs for favourite people, objects and events ('ba' for 'bath', perhaps). These personal pre-words get taken up by adults as meaningful labels and are repeated back to the child in the appropriate context. Spontaneous babbling is a way of practising the specific sound patterns of a language, or languages, and also strengthens an infant's control of the lips, tongue, palate and breathing – all essential for articulating words.

First words

Real first words have the following characteristics:

- They are used spontaneously.
- They are used consistently for the same objects or events.
- They are identified by children's carers.

So, first words are not simply imitated 'parrot-fashion'; they are meaningful and transferred to similar circumstances and contexts, and children's carers are the 'experts' who recognise first words because they have full knowledge of the child's experiences and the situations in which meaningful words emerge.

Word combinations and grammar

Once young children start putting words together in unique two- and three-word combinations we have solid evidence that they are thinking for themselves, and have some powerful understanding about how languages work. As they struggle to share their meanings and insights about their worlds with us we hear such wonderful communications as,

'door uppy' (open the door)
'all-gone Sammy' (Sammy, the cat, has jumped out of the window).

This ability to combine words together so that they communicate specific meanings is grammar and reminds us that very young talkers are thinkers as well as communicators. In fact, they are getting to grips with the three main aspects of grammar:

- the organisation and pattern of sounds (phonology)
- the meaningful combination of words (syntax)
- the meanings of words and groups of words (semantics).

From this point on young linguists get better at doing all these things: they pronounce words more accurately, they learn more words for things (vocabulary), they get better at talking with many people and they gain greater experience of life.

Good practice

This brief review of communication and language development has implications for families and practitioners:

- The highest priority must be given to communication and talk.
- We must ensure that our own use of language is meaningful and appropriate.
- We must understand and respect the significance of all the languages that children and families use.
- We must support the ongoing language development of young children by providing, people to play with, talk to and learn from; environments that are cosy, as well as stimulating and challenging; shared activities like chatting, singing, dancing, walking, paddling, eating, cooking, bathing, dressing and shopping, and so on.

Literacy: understanding literacy – writing and reading

Case study

We are waiting for the school bus to pick up 7-year-old Dylan when his younger brother Mattias, just 5 years old, notices a temporary road sign that has been set up by the roadside. It is a large triangular easel-like structure, nearly 2 metres high, and bears the words 'ROAD WORKS ½ MILE' in luminous orange. Mattias stands very close to the sign and just stares at it in silence for three to four minutes. He turns to me and says very quietly, 'It's "M" for Mattias'.

Defining literacy

It is usual to think of literacy as *the ability to write and read*, although even this apparently straightforward definition covers up complications such as how effectively and evenly these skills are acquired and exercised, or in how many languages, and so on.

Early years practitioners also need to understand the developmental aspect of literacy and this is usually referred to as *emergent literacy.* The complex skills of writing and reading emerge out of children's earliest communications, talking, drawing, encounters with stories and books, and interest in everyday print in the environment.

Modern research also draws our attention to the fact that literacy is an important kind of *social activity or practice* and is part of the way that we get things done in a society (Pahl and Rowsell, 2005). It now includes areas like visual literacy (understanding images and pictures), community literacies (how literacy is used in different language and cultural groups) and techno-literacy (the ability to participate in the world of electronic communications, for example).

Revisiting the case study

At the time of the observation Mattias was just 5 years old and living in the USA in a British/American household. If he had been resident in England he would still have been in the Reception year of the Foundation Stage. As we look back at Mattias and his encounter with a road sign, we can see that it includes all the aspects of literacy mentioned above. It is an example of a young boy's *emergent literacy*, but Mattias can also pick out the important first initial of his name, even in a strange context. We can see that he is *starting to read*. Furthermore, he is very interested in new print in his environment and beginning to understand the *social practices* connected with public signs and warnings.

As Makin and Whitehead (2004: 12–13) point out:

Most experts agree that young children's early literacy is best supported when they:

- have opportunities to learn about the many ways in which literacy is a part of their society;
- are read to frequently;
- have many opportunities to develop their oral language;
- know and enjoy songs and rhymes;
- learn to recognise environmental print such as logos and shop signs;
- develop knowledge of the mechanics of print, for example, that you read from left to right and top to bottom in English;
- have opportunities to play with letters and the sounds they make;
- visit the library often.

Writing

In the Foundation Stage (from 3 to the end of the Reception year) it is essential to create positive, enjoyable and meaningful associations with writing and ensure open access to the widest possible range of materials, tools and technologies for drawing, mark-making and writing.

It is also important to introduce as many examples of writing from the environment as possible, including seeking them out on walks and outdoor investigations and encouraging the children to collect their own examples of print, so that they can read it, display it and play with it.

The real basics of early writing include:

- a powerful human drive to communicate and share meanings and messages
- an equally powerful drive to make marks
- exposure to all kinds of print
- opportunities to watch older children and adults writing, printing and sending messages
- opportunities to investigate, use, and play with many different markers, brushes, paints, water, surfaces, malleable materials, printing devices and computer programs.

This carefully planned exposure to printed materials and people who write and read for communication, information and pleasure will inspire young children to become real writers and readers – not passive fillers-in of worksheets and copiers of writing patterns! They will begin to ask the crucial questions about literacy and print:

- What does this print 'say'?
- What is it for?
- How do you do it?

Reading

In the Foundation Stage (3 to the end of the Reception year) the fundamentals of early reading are established by:

- listening to stories told, as well as read from books, by adults/older children
- sharing books with caring adults for mutual pleasure
- finding out how picture books work by combining images and words
- enjoying a wide range of quality books, factual as well as fictional, and having time and opportunities to reread favourites again and again – and again
- using story props like soft toys, puppets, pictures, storysacks and relevant objects to support retellings of, and variations on, favourite stories and books.

These are the foundations of early reading and enable young children to get *the big picture* about how books and narratives work, how written language sounds and what kinds of things readers have to do. Close investigations of interesting words and chunks of print are possible when adults share readings with individuals and very small groups. This introduces children to *the little black marks* that have to be looked at closely in early reading and it is helpful to draw attention to important names (Bernard), exciting words (CRASH!) and words that have the same initial letters as the children's names ('m' for miles/'m' for Mattias). Adults should draw attention to repeated phrases and encourage 'joining in' as they occur. It is helpful to emphasise rhyming words and ask children to suggest other similar rhymes. Songs and poetry are really important in their own right but they also support early *phonological awareness* of this kind.

Good practice

This brief review of literacy in the years from 3 to the end of the Reception year (the Foundation Stage) has implications for good practice in homes and group settings:

- We must ensure that children have easy access to the materials for mark-making, drawing and writing.
- We must ensure that children see other people reading and writing for real purposes.
- We must invite the children to read and write with us and encourage them to put their own words to books and stories and add their own marks to lists, letters, and so on, or find relevant letters on the computer keyboard.
- We should create special places indoors and outside where children can read in comfort and find all the materials they need for marking and writing.
- We should build up, and constantly add to, large collections of the print and texts we use in our daily lives and various language communities.
- We can create role-play areas that are 'print-rich' by filling them with all the appropriate print, documents and writing materials (for example, market stalls, hairdressers,

doctors' surgeries, post offices, garages, construction sites, garden centres, home areas, and so on.

- We can ask the children to 'sign in' every day on large sheets of paper, or a chalkboard.
- We can show the children simple techniques for making their own books, for example using folded, sewn or stapled paper. These books can be personal records filled with drawings, 'messages', cut-out pictures, photos and contributions from home.
- We must provide a varied collection of quality books that include such categories as traditional tales, picture books, rhymes and poetry, factual books, animal stories, family stories, and so on.
- We should supplement the book collection with audio-taped stories, relevant play materials and story props of all kinds.

Finally, remember that literacy can go outside! Set up a collection of mark-making and writing materials on a trolley that can be wheeled outside. Do the same with a collection of books, maps and other everyday print and documents.

Make sure that the children have simple clipboards and pencils for writing while 'on the move'. Improvise sheltered dens for reading and talking by using shrubs, trees, windbreaks, big umbrellas, cushions and blankets. Identify some walls, fences and hard ground surfaces for chalking and water painting. Create little individual postboxes and scatter them around so that adults and children can leave messages and 'treasures' for each other.

E X E R C I S E   1 4 . 1

- Choose an area of role play (for example a construction site; a garden centre; a café).
- Make it 'print rich' with as many appropriate literacy materials and tools as you can.
- Observe the children's play, communications and interactions for at least 20 minutes, focusing on children's (and adult's) activities, gestures, eye contact, talk, mark-making, writing, reading, and so on.
- Share your observations with colleagues in the setting, other students and children's families, if possible.
- Think about your observation, and write it up with added comments and reflections based on your discussions, thinking and reading.
- What comes next? Add a list of ideas for new provision and appropriate pedagogical strategies to extend the children's play, communication, language and learning.

Further reading

Makin, L. and Whitehead, M. (2004) *How to Develop Children's Early Literacy: A Guide for Professional Carers and Educators.* London: Paul Chapman Publishing.

This is a very readable and practical book that addresses current issues relating to early literacy development from birth to 5. It is of particular interest to non-teacher professionals and parents.

Whitehead, M.R. (2002) 'Dylan's routes to literacy: the first three years with picture books', *Journal of Early Childhood Literacy*, 2(3): 269–89.

This article is a case study of one little boy's encounters with picture books shared with his family, from his birth to 3. There are many fascinating insights into a young child's emotional, social, linguistic and literary development in this account.

Whitehead, M.R. (2002) *Developing Language and Literacy with Young Children.* 2nd edition. London: Paul Chapman Publishing.

This very readable book looks at language development from birth to 8 and is of interest to carers, parents and teachers. There are major chapters on early communication, young bi-linguals, stories, narrative and play and the emergence of literacy.

MATHEMATICAL DEVELOPMENT

Maulfry Worthington and Elizabeth Carruthers

Maulfry Worthington is engaged in doctoral research on children's mathematical graphics and is an Early Years Consultant. She has lectured in Early Years pedagogy and Primary mathematics and was a National Numeracy Strategy Consultant.

Elizabeth Carruthers is Headteacher of Redcliffe Children's Centre, Bristol. She has worked as a National Numeracy Strategy Consultant and as an Early Years Advisor. Her research interests are the pedagogy of children's mathematical graphics and early number.

Aims

To develop understanding of:

- the potential of every child's mathematical thinking and link this to your teaching of mathematics to young children
- children's mathematical development and provide suggestions to support this development
- and link the above to the *Curriculum Guidance for the Foundation Stage* (CGFS) (CGFS, 2000) and National Numeracy Strategy framework (and in future the EYFS)

Children are born into a mathematical world. Their earliest interactions are mathematical as they explore the spaces, shapes and patterns of their world. At home children develop the ability to tune into the mathematics of their home environment which will be meaningful to them.

> Every day Lorraine's mum comes home at 3.00 p.m. Lorraine (aged 3 years) shouts to her daddy, 'It's 3 o'clock and mummy's here'. Lorraine helps her dad set the table and he asks her 'Do we have enough plates because James is coming tonight for dinner?' The family sits down to watch television and Lorraine finds the number '4' on the remote control to locate her favourite programme.

From this brief synopsis we can see that Lorraine has used time, spoken the number three in the right context and was involved in a genuine mathematical conversation which could have led to calculation. She has also recognised the numeral 4 and understands the function of this number in the context of a television channel.

It is important therefore for practitioners to build on this meaningful home context which has been a positive start to the child's understanding of the world. Perhaps the most important principle of a good Foundation Stage mathematical curriculum is not to view mathematics as right or wrong but to see *every* child as a mathematician who is willing to take risks and try out new thinking.

> Effective teaching requires: Practitioners who help children to see themselves as mathematicians, and develop positive attitudes and dispositions towards their learning. (CGFS, 2000: 71)

**Mathematical development (Curriculum Guidance for
the Foundation Stage, 2000)**

The stepping stones of the CGFS merge into the key objectives for Reception of the
framework of the National Numeracy Strategy. There are three aspects of the mathematics section of the CGFS and they are:

- numbers as labels and for counting
- calculating
- space and shape and measures.

The key objectives of the framework of the National Numeracy Strategy are:

- Say and use the numbers in order in familiar contexts.
- Count reliably up to ten everyday objects.
- Recognise numerals 1 to 9.
- Use language such as more or less, greater or smaller, heavier or lighter, to compare
  two numbers or quantities.
- In practical activities and discussion, begin to use the vocabulary involved in adding
  and subtracting.
- Find one more or one less, than a number from one to ten.
- Begin to relate addition to combining two groups of objects, and subtraction to 'taking
  away'.
- Talk about, recognise and re-create simple patterns.
- Use language such as circle or bigger to describe the shape and size of solids and flat
  shapes.
- Use everyday words to describe position.
- Use developing mathematical ideas and methods to solve practical problems.

Mathematical schemas

In your observations of children's play you will often see children engaged in specific
schemas (chapter 12; Worthington and Carruthers, 2003; Athey, 1990; Nutbrown 1994;
Bruce, 2005). Most schemas are mathematical: for example *rotation*, *vertical* and *horizontal* schemas. Mathematical concepts are often explored as a result of a schematic interest.

If we support and enrich the schematic mathematical potential of young children then we
open out the mathematics curriculum to match the child's interests in mathematics.

Danny often plays with the toy cars and uses a cardboard box as a garage. He pushes
the cars up the sides and into the corners of the box. The Foundation staff have also
observed that Danny plays with the boats and pushes them under the water around the
water tray and into every part of the water tray.

The nursery staff have observed that Danny is in a *containing* schema and the mathematical concepts he is exploring in his play through this schema are perimeter, angle, vertex, cube, cuboid, edge and inside.

Children's number development

Just as children engage in the mathematics of space, shape and pattern, they also become aware of measurement and numbers. Numbers and measurement are an integral part of all mathematical areas. Shape, for example, can be measured in terms of number of degrees in angles. Time and measurement of length and width both use numbers. Children tuning into mathematics are naturally aware of this connection, for example:

> Molly is in the role-play area. She picks up a string and puts it around Tina's waist and says 'You're 17. I'm going to make you a dress'.

Molly is re-enacting a situation at home when her mother makes clothes for the family, and has substituted string for a measuring tape. She has chosen a number she has heard to fit the situation and is exploring the mathematical area of measurement. Children do not see mathematics as a discrete subject but as an integral part of their world. Practitioners need to build on this open view of mathematics by illuminating the mathematics in all the 'areas of learning'.

Early calculation

Even before children have a complete grasp of the counting sequence they will begin to extend their understanding of counting and quantities and use language such as 'more' and phrases such as 'she has the same as me'. Early calculation includes:

- counting
- comparing objects, towards subtraction. 'I have two and you have three, you have one more than me'
- combining objects, towards addition. Shabana put two balls from one basket to a basket with three balls and she counted '1, 2, 3, 4, 5'
- sharing, towards division. Tom had some strawberries and shared them out in his group ('one to you and one to you')
- adding groups of the same number of objects, towards multiplication. Adrian collected two play hoops each from three children. He counted 1, 2, 1, 2, 1, 2 as he put them in the box. When they were all in he counted '1, 2, 3, 4, 5, 6 altogether'.

Children moving towards more abstract calculations will not necessarily count objects in front of them, they will also count and calculate objects they cannot see or things they hear, for example bells, claps and musical beats. It is also important to note that young children can subitise up to three objects. This means, for example, that they can look at three apples and know that there are three without counting them.

Play, learning and mathematics

Child-initiated play provides a wonderful context for children's learning (Bruce, 2004a). Foundation settings offer potentially rich environments where children can build on their earlier informal experiences of mathematics at home and in the community.

> Carl was building a 'car-park' with small wooden bricks. He lined up cars (*ordering* and *space*); provided parking bays and made a gateway (*estimating*).
>
> Next he made 'parking tickets' (see p. 152), a '£50' sign for a car that was for sale, 'No parking' and 'Closed' signs. Carl talked about car repairs and sales and was able to recognise which of two prices was the cheaper. He showed a great deal of knowledge about registration plates and repairs.

We can see how Carl drew heavily on personal knowledge about vehicles and car parks from his father who drove a lorry. These self-initiated activities also gave him opportunities to use large numbers in meaningful ways. The social context of play with others allowed a great deal of learning through talk.

Every play area indoors and out offers opportunities for mathematics: the mathematics children learn in areas such as role play, in sand, block play or through making something with junk materials can enrich their understanding.

Graphics area (mark-making)

Young children do not think about learning in separate 'subjects'. Your graphics area will also support mathematical marks if you add mathematical resources including:

- real money
- number lines
- clocks
- stamps
- tape measures
- lottery tickets
- raffle tickets
- calculators.

You can further encourage children by providing a low-level display board for them to use.

Play offers rich opportunities for mathematics. As Marion Dowling emphasises in Chapter 6, it is not the resources alone that support creative mathematical thinking. Children need:

- freedom to make genuine choices
- opportunities to initiate their own ideas
- extended periods of time to play and talk
- adults who recognise the mathematics in children's play and are interested in children's own ideas.

Mark-making and mathematics

Playing and exploring mathematics in practical ways helps children make sense of mathematics. However, to understand 'written' mathematics at a deep level, children need to explore their thinking through their own marks with different media and blank paper. We term mathematical mark-making, *mathematical graphics* (Worthington and Carruthers, 2003).

Common *forms* of mathematical marks – the types of personal marks children *choose* to use

- *Dynamic* – lively marks suggesting action.
- *Pictographic* – pictures of something the child sees.
- *Iconic* – one mark or item for each thing counted.
- *Written* – letters or words (early, 'emergent' writing).
- *Symbolic* – standard numerals, or symbols such as '+' and '='.

The forms of marks that children choose to use are not the mathematics itself (see Figure 15.2 for the development of written number).

Children make marks within their play, as the parking tickets (Figure 15.1) that Carl made while playing car parks show. He read these as '40p, 40p, 50p, 70p, 80p, 90p'. Role play is a rich context for writing and also offers abundant scope for mathematical graphics. Paper and pens in every play area and in a basket or bucket outside can also support mathematical graphics.

Occasionally children will use mathematical graphics within an adult-led group:

Adult-led mathematical graphics

The *Curriculum Guidance for the Foundation Stage* emphasises that adults ask children 'to "*put something down on paper*" about what they have done or found out' (CGFS, 2000: 71). This leaves the decision of how to represent, to the child.

Figure 15.1   *Carl's 'parking tickets' (Carruthers and Worthington, 2006)*

Figure 15.2   focuses on quantities, numerals and the beginnings of calculations which support all aspects of mathematics. Number is connected to all mathematical areas.

Between 3 and 5 years of age, a child's mathematical graphics will develop from 'scribble-like' marks which 'may not be easy for someone else to interpret, but (which) form an important stage in developing fluency' (QCA, 1999: 12). Children need time to explore written number in their own ways and in contexts that make real sense to them. Moving between their informal and more standard ways of 'written' mathematics helps children to bridge the gap (Carruthers and Worthington, 2006). Current understanding is part of a continuing process.

Referring to Figure 15.2

- This figure represents the beginnings of children's own written number and quantities.
- Children do not all follow the same paths in their development.
- The different dimensions in this figure are not 'stages' to be taught.

Figure 21.2 in Chapter 21 shows how calculations develop from early written number to standard calculations with larger numbers.

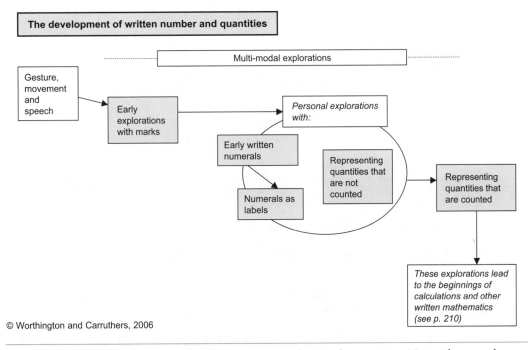

Figure 15.2 *The development of early written number and quantities (Carruthers and Worthington, 2006)*

The adult's role

Practitioners can support children's number and mathematical development in two key ways.

1. Understanding the child's development in a positive way through recognising that:

    (a) children are actively engaging with all aspects of mathematics at home before they come to the pre-school and school settings
    (b) partnership with parents in discussing the child's mathematics at home as well as at school is vital
    (c) children use number language and counting in a variety of ways, through everyday experiences
    (d) their early mathematical graphics will support all aspects of children's written mathematics in Key Stage 1
    (e) children come to the Foundation Stage with a willingness to build on their previous mathematical knowledge.

2. Planning opportunities for adult-directed and child-initiated learning through:

    (a) making observations of children in play and in adult-directed group times, and use these observations to inform planning and record-keeping
    (b) providing a balance of mathematical experiences, both inside and outside

(c) counting in a variety of ways for a variety of purposes
(d) weaving mathematics through the day
(e) combining areas of mathematics together, especially with number
(f) setting open challenges and problems
(g) encouraging children's own mathematical problems
(h) modelling mathematical vocabulary
(i) providing a stimulating mathematical environment
(j) helping children make connections with all areas of learning and the real world.

EXERCISE 15.1

In your setting and with one or more colleagues:

1 Observations: observe a child in a play area (inside or out), and note down any mathematical play and talk:

(a) What aspect of mathematics is the child exploring?
(b) How could you support the child's mathematical interest?

2 Understanding: using the observation you made, discuss what this tells you about the child's mathematical interests.

(a) Did you see evidence of the child's current schemas within their play?
(b) Collect several samples of mathematical graphics from one child and annotate them. Look at the positive things that they show. See if together you can identify what *form* of mathematical marks the child has chosen (see p. 211) and what aspect of written number they have explored (Figure 15.2 p. 153).

3 The curriculum

- Refer to the guidance for the Foundation Stage (CGFS, 2000) and identify the 'stepping stones' within your observations.
- Look at the *Curriculum Guidance for the Foundation Stage*: what opportunities are there for children to explore mathematics across all curriculum areas?
- How does your practice support children's creative approaches to mathematics? (See CGFS, 2000: 118.)
- For adults in Foundation Stage 2, look at an objective from the Numeracy framework (1999) and consider how you might provide for this through adult-directed and child-initiated opportunities and throughout the day

Write what you discovered from your observations. How has your reading informed what you did? How does this link to the Foundation Stage document?

CHAPTER 16

KNOWLEDGE AND UNDERSTANDING

Katrina Foley

Katrina Foley trained in Scotland as a primary and nursery teacher. She has been head of Southway Early Childhood Centre since 1989. Southway serves Bedfordshire as a centre for the dissemination of good Early Childhood practice as well as providing a variety of services for under 5s, including care and education.

Aims

To develop understanding of:

☐ supporting children's developing knowledge and understanding of nature
☐ supporting children's knowledge, understanding and participation in meaningful cultural events through daily life experiences
☐ supporting children in developing strategies and skills to participate in ICT and design and technology

In Knowledge and Understanding of the World 'children are developing the crucial knowledge, skills and understanding that help them to make sense of the world. This forms the foundation for later work in science, design and technology, history, geography and ICT.' (*Curriculum Guidance for the Foundation Stage*, 2000: 82)

According to the curriculum guidance in order 'to give all children the best opportunities for developing knowledge and understanding effectively' [they need] 'activities based on first-hand experiences' which includes 'an environment with a wide range of activities indoors and outdoors that stimulate' their 'interest and curiosity' (CGFS, 2000: 82).

At Southway Early Childhood Centre we have identified a range of experiences, 'The key experiences' (Southway Early Childhood Centre, 1996), in order to develop children's language, thought, concentration, as well as their autonomy and learning skills. Each of the key experiences contains elements of all of the six areas of learning in the Foundation Stage. The children have free access to these experiences throughout the session as choice, decision-making and the development of rational personal autonomy are key features of our curriculum. At Southway we feel that all children need a variety of rich and stimulating activities which give them opportunities to explore, experiment and create, allow for continual progression and are open ended. Above all, they need the time and space to explore the experiences offered. The way in which the day is structured and the access to materials and experiences given is, for us, as important as the experiences themselves. Uninterrupted time coupled with concentration and motivation creates a chance to really engage and develop an interest in self-chosen tasks.

In a nursery setting, the garden is a major part of the children's learning environment and should therefore be as accessible to them as the indoor environment. The garden allows children to observe and appreciate weather and seasonal changes at first hand. Understanding that we need to put on a coat if it is cold, or sun cream and a hat in summer, is developed naturally through use of the garden. Collecting leaves and cones for gluing and creating encourages the children's understanding of the seasons, for example cones, conkers and leaves in autumn, fruits and flowers in summer. It provides opportunities for close examination of natural objects and an exploration of the similarities and differences between similar objects, for example leaves. A pond and some carefully placed stones can provide children with the chance to observe a variety of wildlife in its natural habitat rather than in a tank in the classroom. It is very important, particularly for inner-city children, as this increases children's knowledge and understanding of these life cycles and development much more fully, for example, understanding that tiny frogs can jump out of a pond and hide in long grass for a substantial amount of time is a very different experience to observing these in a tank in the centre. Magnifying glasses need to be readily available in the garden area to encourage children to observe minibeasts and natural objects closely.

Much of the learning that takes place in the garden cannot take place in the same way indoors. Seasonal tasks such as sweeping leaves and clearing weeds can be undertaken regularly and help children to understand the passing seasons. Opportunities to grow vegetables and follow the growing cycle from beginning to end while caring for their plants, deepens children's knowledge of living things generally. Through using the outdoor area purposefully we can provide a range of high-quality first-hand experiences, including growing things, observing minibeasts and having a variety of activities for physical development.

Children at Southway regularly make green tomato chutney, vegetable soup and herb scones from produce grown in the garden. Cooking helps children to identify and closely observe the effects of the changing seasons in a different way from experiencing seasonal weather changes in the garden. Our children regularly use seasonal fruits and cutting, chopping, rolling, manipulating and combining, allowing them to fully explore and discuss the properties of the different fruits and vegetables. Shopping for those ingredients that cannot be home grown helps children to learn about their local community, the function of different types of shops and the use of money and the idea of receiving change. On return to the centre, making a simple display with the children of all of the ingredients and utensils to be used well in advance of the cooking activity introduces the experience, and helps to promote children's language giving them a far better appreciation of the experience to come.

At Southway we use cooking to sensitise our children to the changing seasons and to develop their understanding of a variety of concepts such as changes of state and the celebration of festivals which forms a key part of our approach to the development of Knowledge and Understanding of the World. We feel that this gives them a sense of security and the beginnings of an appreciation of the natural order of events which occur throughout the year (during autumn children make bread and apple pies.) Celebrations of festivals linked to cooking can often involve our parents, who feel confident working with the children on this experience.

The nursery centre has a cooking corner which is available to children on a daily basis. Children can choose to cook individually or as part of a group. Every day we provide our 'crispie'-making (this was developed by lecturers at Moray House as a cooking experience which very young children can do independently with minimal supervision). Each child makes one crispie per day and takes it home. The crispie is never eaten in the nursery. Crispie-making involves ideas of chocolate melting when heated, changes of state when materials are combined, and how a candle extinguishes when air is excluded (nuclear physics).

At least once a week adults plan to cook a seasonal dish such as herb scones, ice cream, chappatis, and so on. Many new ingredients and utensils will be introduced to the children at cooking as well as the more scientific ideas of dissolving, melting, changes of state and the question of what happens to things when heated or cooled.

At Christmas the children who wish to can make their own individual Christmas cake. This experience goes on for many weeks and provides a very good basis for discussion and talk about every aspect of Christmas.

Initially the children and the practitioner use the recipe book to make a list of all of the ingredients required for the cake. Amounts are checked and decisions are made about what to buy. A small group of children will then shop for these at our local supermarket, paying for their purchases and starting to understand concepts of using money and receiving change.

On return, a display of everything to be used, both ingredients and utensils, is made.

Display is a very important teaching tool for encapsulating an experience for the children. It enables the adult to introduce the experience within an immediate, meaningful situation and the children to recap and revisit what has taken place after the event. It is important to make display an integral part of the children's learning experience which they can explore and use to deepen their understanding.

We display all the utensils and ingredients to be used in the cooking, as well as displaying the recipe book and a picture of the cooked product. So, for example, when we make Christmas cakes, we display the lined cake tin, a bowl and spoon, the wire tray for cooling, as well as flour, eggs, currants, cherries, marzipan, spices, and so on. This allows for talk, discussion and clarification of any issues. Children can smell spices, taste marzipan, examine a cake tin, and so on. The display gives everyone the chance to look, touch, taste, smell and discuss. Many new materials are introduced to the children through this experience.

Where possible we use traditional equipment which children may not have seen before; when making marmalade we use and display a traditional preserving pan. It is important that children understand the utensils that are used and how they function, and that they are given the opportunity to taste, smell and feel and name the ingredients. In this way they really become familiar with everything and deepen their understanding of the process and enhance their learning.

The display supports the children's learning before, during and after the cooking. Making Christmas cakes takes several weeks and, so once these are cooked, a cake is placed on the display. As the cooking progresses and the cakes are marzipanned, iced and decorated the cake display reflects these stages to allow the children to really note this sequence of events. By displaying only the materials used in any particular cooking experience we keep the display simple and easy for the children to understand.

Each child who chooses to, participates in each stage of the cake-making. Initially they draw round their tin, cut out their drawing and line their own tin. The cake is then mixed by the children and cooked, unwrapped, marzipanned and, finally, the children make their icing and decorate their cakes with candles and coloured balls before taking them home to share with family. Each stage takes about a week, cakes are displayed at each stage, for example the lined tin, the fruit cake, the marzipanned cake, and so on. Children note these stages and start to understand and appreciate the sequence of events. Often our older children can remember last Christmas in the nursery and talk about the next stage of cake making or what happened last year. Changes of state, heating and cooling are all a natural part of this experience. Other experiences such as crispie-making introduce the children to dissolving and melting in a natural relevant way, as well as developing independent skills.

The celebration of festivals is an important part of developing children's understanding of the richness and diversity which exists in our society today through its many different cultures. At Southway we are extremely proud of the many cultures and traditions represented in the nursery. Parents who have first-hand knowledge of these festivals help us to celebrate, often wearing traditional dress and perhaps involving children, who choose to, in the wearing of different clothes, cooking and sharing traditional dishes with the school community. Displays relevant to each festival are made with the group to encourage them to discuss and reflect what is taking place, for example at Divali, the festival of light, divas and torches and pictures of fireworks are displayed. Southway Early Childhood Centre is located in an Asian community.

Home language is highly valued and members of staff who have English as an additional language regularly speak in their home language. It is important to ensure stories are read in their home language to all children who choose to listen, as English-speaking children can then develop an understanding of common languages.

Books and artefacts from other cultures are visible throughout all areas of the centre, for example Asian cooking pots in the home corner, the architecture of Morocco in the block area. All of this helps to develop the understanding of the whole of the centre's community and raises the status of other cultures by encouraging children, parents and carers to understand and view positively the cultures of others. (See also Chapters 13 and 20.)

Each child is also encouraged to celebrate a more personal festival, such as his/her birthday, by making their own cake and sharing it with the group. They can remember their last birthday and talk about their own birthday and those of friends and other family members.

These events can be recorded on laptops for children to remember from year to year both by adults and by children themselves. Increasingly ICT is becoming an integral part of everyone's life. The Nursery Curriculum needs to provide children with real experiences which reflect the world around them, but which also provide a quality experience which will catch their interest, leading to talk, discussion and co-operation with others within the group.

We therefore decided to develop our own individualised, relevant ICT rather than rely on commercial programmes, many of which present rather abstract and isolated ideas. Photographs of all our children, involved in a favourite activity, were made available on disc for them to access so that they could see their own friends as well as themselves. Each child who wished, dictated their own sentence to the practitioner to go with their picture. This year's children will also be able to see children from last year who have now left, to encourage them to reflect on past events and experiences. Class books made with the children were also made available on the laptop as well as in the book corner.

A number of digital cameras are available at Southway and children are encouraged to record events through taking their own photographs on digital cameras and downloading these onto the computer before printing them out (see also Chapter 3). A good example of how this worked was when a child was upset one morning at the beginning of the school day. The practitioner encouraged her to take a photograph of her mother and younger brother and print it out. The child then kept this during the morning to access whenever she wanted. Later in the day, she and the practitioner made a book about her family. Another child, having taken many photographs at school, borrowed her father's digital camera at home, took some photographs of her pet rabbit and then Dad helped her to email these to school. Many children do not have access to a digital camera and links between home and school can be further developed through dedicating one or two cameras for home use, allowing children to use these with parents and bring the results into school to print out. The digital camera allows children to see the photographs before printing and encourages them to develop a critical understanding of their own work.

Although we still use our large computer, the use of laptops, which are easily placed throughout our classroom and which can be set up by some of the more experienced children themselves, has helped us to introduce ICT to the classroom more comprehensively.

At the heart of problem-solving are woodwork, sewing and gluing. How do I join these two pieces of wood together? Do I stick this box to that one and how do I join these two pieces of material? These are all problems which are engaged in naturally within these areas of experience. These areas also provide opportunities for children to begin to make their own design plans. This occurs over time when they have access to these areas on a regular basis without time limitation. Children concentrate, persevere and carry out their plans surprisingly often when they are given the time and space to do so.

Sewing, woodwork and gluing are key areas for development particularly in relation to children's thinking and problem-solving abilities, providing the opportunity to make one's own design plan and try to achieve it. Bruce (2004b) points out that it is not the result in these areas of experience that is important, but the thinking that takes place for the child while participating in the experience.

The role of the adult is to support and encourage children to achieve their plan without taking over and imposing their own ideas and values. Our observations suggest that usually it is the children who have accessed these areas over a long period of time who are able to make the most sophisticated plans. At all times our focus is on the child and not on the end product. The child who visits the sewing corner for the first time and makes one stitch has achieved a great deal through experimenting with a new experience, first, through using unfamiliar tools and secondly, by starting to understand how a needle and thread works. His work is as valuable as that of the child who has been sewing for a long time and has just made a bag for the first time.

The use of needles, hammers, saws and knives ensures that children learn quite early on to select the appropriate tools for a task and use these safely and appropriately. Experiences such as woodwork, cookery and sewing are always well supervised by the adults and each area has a set of simple rules which children must follow. All these are necessary to ensure the children's safety and enjoyment.

The use of tools develops children's confidence, motivation and concentration. The development of their practical independent learning skills enhances their self-esteem and their willingness to try things out. These skills also allow them to involve themselves in many areas of experience without being dependent on adults.

Direct teaching of how and when to switch off the burner and wash up, how to hold and carry scissors, use a saw and hammer safely and replace needles in the appropriate pin cushion is a vital part of the adult's role and the children's learning. The development of these autonomous skills enables them to concentrate on exploring and develops a willingness to try things out, to 'take risks' in a secure environment and to learn to solve problems in a variety of ways.

Opportunities to 'teach' these skills to younger children joining the nursery further enhances confidence and self-esteem, both vital prerequisites for learning.

The role of the adult in developing children's knowledge and understanding of the world is that of sensitive enabler and partner. The provision of fully resourced rich areas of experience which are replenished regularly, and of opportunities for children to talk, discuss and ask questions, are all important aspects of the adult role. It may be that we need to provide other things, some felt to make *Cat in the Hat*, some fastenings for a bag, some wheels for a car. We can also provide for children's continuing interest next day.

Bruce (2005) suggests we observe, support and extend model of teaching. Through observing what the child does, listening to what he/she says and offering suggestions, we are able to extend the learning possibilities for the children. Visits to the local art gallery, market, vet, or museum can be planned by the adult to extend learning. Above all, the role of the adult is to get children to understand that many things are possible within a flexible setting. Our role is to create the conditions where children understand that it is possible to make almost anything happen. For example, one day in the nursery the children were interested in a shop that was in the other class and they constantly visited it. I pointed out they could have a shop in our class if they wanted. They made a cash register as there was no money to buy one and some (real) money was provided. I asked them what kind of shop it was to be. They wanted a food shop. We made some cakes and biscuits. As there was no other space we set the shop up in my office! Later in the term they asked if it could become a jewellery shop, a shoe shop, a fruit shop. The interest lasted for a whole term. Parents became involved too, bringing in things for the shop. After this the children understood that they could use the adult to make things happen. Children are very receptive and understand quickly what the adult will provide and allow, and we need to ensure that we are flexible and receptive enough to maximise children's learning to its fullest potential.

PHYSICAL DEVELOPMENT

Penny Greenland

Penny Greenland MBE is Director of JABADAO, the National Centre for Movement, Learning and Health, where she leads research, training and practical programmes in education and health settings.

Aims

To develop understanding of:

☐ and practice in relation to key aspects of physical development
☐ how to help children to engage with and develop movement patterns deemed to be significant in prompting physical development which also promotes later learning
☐ how to encourage children to make their own risk assessments, thus keeping them and others safe.

Sukjinder is lying upside-down under a table at the side of the room with his feet pushing upwards on the underside. Chelsea is lying tummy down over a big bolster cushion, singing to herself, and gently pushing with her toes so that she rocks slowly to and fro. Ben and Royston are locked in a vice-like grip in the centre of the room, pulling and tugging at each other as they roll around the floor, grinning madly and grunting as they go. Chenai is being led solemnly round the room on a 'lead', crawling dog-like between the other children, woofing and growling by turn as they pass. And Bobby is turning slow circles in the corner, arms held wide, head tilted this way then that, before he comes to rest with his head wedged against the wall.

Children's fine and gross motor development, their awareness of their body, and their pleasure and confidence in being a physical creature is underpinned by the whole-hearted, full-bodied movement play that most freely indulge in amid everything else they do. Within this spontaneous flow of movement are some quite specific movement activities that prompt the brain and the nervous system to develop in ways that will lay foundations for future learning, health and well-being. Fortunately, babies and young children – given good health and the right opportunities – are biologically driven to seek out, and create, the experiences they need (see also Chapters 8 and 11). They have an in-built capacity to devise just the right game for their particular stage of development, and an endless capacity to invent new ways of addressing the key issues: where do I begin and end, where this body part is in relation to that, how much force is too much force, how do I fit into the space around, what does it feel like to be a body? Unfortunately, many aspects of contemporary culture get in the way of this most basic learning, but in the Physical Development area of the curriculum we have the opportunity to make sure that children do have the opportunities they need.

Piaget recognised that a child's ability to understand the world around, to communicate with others, and to establish a strong sense of self is grounded in the early sensory and motor experiences available to them. Sensory motor learning is the ability to take in, sort out, process and make use of information from the world around us. Information is gathered from the senses – taste (gustatory sense), smell (olfactory sense), sound (auditory sense), sight (visual sense) and touch (tactile sense). But there are also two other senses intimately connected to movement that we tend to take for granted and often ignore, but which are key to young children's development. These are the sense of the position of our body parts in relation to one another (proprioceptive sense) and the sense of movement and relationship to the ground (vestibular sense). These provide key reference points for our sense of self, and our relationship to the external environment.

With poor foundations for proprioception a child might find it hard to co-ordinate their movements. They might feel ill at ease in their 'skin' or be compelled to wriggle, fidget and be constantly on the move to get a better feel of themself. The vestibular sense is unique in that it has no sensation of its own, but provides us with the capacity to function within the force of gravity, to know which way is up, (even when we tilt our head), and provides the central reference point for all spatial awareness. An under-developed vestibular sense might result in poor balance, fear and dislike of movement, a drive to spin excessively, or an uncomfortable relationship to the external environment. Since the vestibular system is connected to our emotional development, under-development might also compromise emotional stability.

It is active involvement and exploration through movement play that enables a child to become a more mature, efficient organiser of sensory information – providing the foundations for all future learning. During the early years, therefore, movement is food for the developing system and the opportunities we provide comprise the diet. For healthy eating, 'five fruit and veg' per day are recommended. For a healthy movement diet these are recommended:

- Floor play: on backs and on tummies, young children need to spend time in contact with the floor exploring their moving, sensing bodies.
- Belly crawling: the first self-determined travelling movement that supports a strong sense of the centre of the body whilst in motion.
- Crawling: the activity through which children first combine balance and travelling.
- Push, pull, stretch, hang and slide: through which children prompt enhanced feedback of their felt, or proprioceptive, sense and build the felt sense of self.
- Spinning, tipping, tilting, falling: through which children build their vestibular sense, their upright balance, their sense of space and their primary external relationship – with the ground beneath their feet (Greenland, 2005: 32).

The first three activities also specifically support the development of postural alignment and full articulation of the joints as they take the body from the curled up 'C' shape of the baby in the womb, to the 'S' shape of spine in upright posture.

The key role for practitioners is to create a learning environment in which children can take the lead in finding activities and games that precisely fulfil their sensory needs, both indoors and outdoors. This means thinking about how a setting supports movement within every activity, looking at the spaces and resources provided, and the balance between adult-led and child-led opportunities on offer.

Parklands Children's Centre in Leeds changed the way they laid out 'table top activities'.

We have removed tables in the nursery environment. We had quite a few in the paint area, in the creative area, in the mark making area, in the tactile area, but all those resources are now on the floor … so the children are getting down on the floor and having tummy time while they get on with other things … We feel that the resources work better on the floor. It has been a really positive thing to do. (Greenland, 2005: 159)

Goosehill Nursery, Morpeth, have set up a Movement Corner where children can choose to move when and how they want. This lets them know that their spontaneous movement play – the way they are in their body – is valued alongside all the other kinds of activity provided and ensures that children can respond to their own particular sensory drives. The staff find that the Movement Corner supports learning across the whole curriculum, not just Physical Development.

Yesterday I had time in the movement corner and I had a checklist and I was just ticking off the things the children were doing which related to the Foundation Stage for their records. It links into so many aspects of development. (Greenland, 2005: 149)

Sure Start Elland have changed the way they support movement aiming to provide spaces and resources that stimulate appropriate activities, rather than organising adult-led groups.

We have been observing much more what the children are doing and letting them lead the activities rather than saying, 'Come on, let's do this now'. One day we just taped a big piece of bubble wrap down and the children were beside themselves, they thought it was wonderful. They rolled and they jumped and put their hands on it and wiggled about … It gave them permission to move and they were off … (Greenland, 2005: 125)

Sukjinder, Ben, Royston and the other children mentioned at the start of this chapter attend a nursery in Peterborough where the practitioners have ensured that children can move freely indoors as well as out. Several times a week they have a movement afternoon and one room is available, as part of the continuous provision throughout the nursery, just for spontaneous movement play. Children move freely between leaping, bounding, crawling and rolling in here, and the activities in other rooms. Surprisingly perhaps, children find it very easy to change from, high-spirited rough and tumble one minute, to quiet, contemplative sand play the next.

In any setting, children's natural drive to spin and tip, push and pull, can override their sense of caution. Being on hand to keep them safe is an important adult role, therefore, as is supporting their developing ability to assess risk, and act appropriately. Even very young children can do this.

Children are doing their own risk assessment, keeping themselves safe and keeping others around them safe. To witness that in children under three years old is terrific (Parklands CC). (Greenland, 2005: 169)

When it comes to Physical Development children are the experts. If adults ensure that the opportunities they provide play to this very considerable strength, activities that support physical development will not only build strong, flexible and happy bodies, but also play a central role in building foundations for all other future learning as well.

EXERCISE 17.1

Observation

Set out to notice ways that adults unwittingly shut down children's natural drive to engage in spontaneous movement play. Discuss your findings with the team and think about ways you could value this aspect of children's learning even more.

Observe a child over a week and work out what you think their current sensory energy drives are. How can you support them to follow these drives? What activities or resources would help them?

EXERCISE 17.2

Child-led activities

Create a movement corner in your setting with clear guidelines for its use – numbers, use of music, resources available, and so on. (Some movement corners comprise the space covered by one gym mat; others set aside a room or part of a room.) Observe children using it and record what they choose to do. Revise guidelines and the support you offer in the light of what you see.

EXERCISE 17.3

Everyday changes

What simple changes could you make to the everyday activities in your setting that would support more back and tummy play, belly crawling, crawling, spinning/tipping/tilting and push/pull/stretch/hang activities?

EXERCISE 17.4

Adult-led support

Review the games you already organise (for example, What's the Time, Mrs Wolf?) and think of ways that you could adapt these to incorporate more floor-based movement. Try them out and see how children respond. Ask children to invent games of their own and try them out with them.

Further reading

Goddard Blyth, S. (2004) *The Well Balanced Child Movement and Early Learning*. Hawthorne Press. Chapter 2, 'Balance'.

Greenland, P. (2000) *Hopping Home Backwards: Body Intelligence and Movement Play*. JABADAO publication: Leeds. Chapter 5 'Movement play and the Foundation Stage curriculum'.

Sensory Integration Network (2003) *Sensory Integration Information Booklet*. A resource for parents and therapists, SI Network UK and Ireland, Blackrock, Co. Dublin, Ireland.

CHAPTER 18

CREATIVE DEVELOPMENT

Tina Bruce

Tina Bruce is Honorary Visiting Professor at Roehampton University, where she originally trained (when it was the Froebel Educational Institute) as a teacher for the Primary phase. She is a trained teacher of children with hearing impairments. She is a widely published author in books, articles and journals, with an international reputation. She was awarded International Woman Scholar in Education by Virginia Commonwealth University and has worked with the British Council in Egypt and New Zealand.

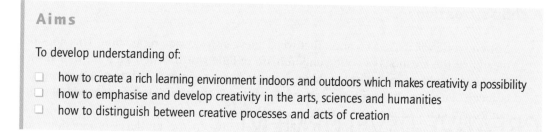

Aims

To develop understanding of:

☐ how to create a rich learning environment indoors and outdoors which makes creativity a possibility
☐ how to emphasise and develop creativity in the arts, sciences and humanities
☐ how to distinguish between creative processes and acts of creation

The links between creativity and childhood play are of central importance for the development and learning of young children. This is because childhood play encourages flexible, imaginative thinking. It gives a mechanism through which children can try out, experiment and apply what they have been learning in ways which are safe physically, emotionally, socially and intellectually. It supports children as they problem-solve and reflect, reason and think through how they feel in different situations, their relationships with others, and it helps them to clarify their thinking and develop ideas.

It is important to distinguish between creative processes and acts of creation. There is often confusion between the two. The processes involved in creation do not necessarily develop into the final making of a creation. Often, for young children, the process is enough. When the creative process does lead into a creation, this can take the form of an idea, theory, model, construction, drawing, painting, dance choreography, musical composition, mathematical pattern, story or poem, to suggest just a few possibilities.

The processes of creative development are:

- the gathering of thoughts, ideas, feelings and relationships
- and simmering them, usually at a subconscious level
- which gradually, or sometimes suddenly (the eureka phenomenon) becomes clear
- and is then hatched out as a creation.

Creative processes are not confined to a minority of the human population. They are part of being human. However, creative development is often constrained, and even stamped out before children reach middle childhood. This is why children need rich learning environments, indoors and outdoors, which support and develop their creativity (Bruce, 2004)

Time and opportunity to be creative

Creative development depends on a balance between child-initiated and adult-led situations. Children need opportunities to use clay, paint, mark-make, dance, make music, play in the home corner, garden and construct in their own way in their own time, and to make choices and decisions.

They need to be able to mull things over, which is not possible in an over-timetabled day.

A child's creation

Not everyone will make a creation that will achieve a worldwide reputation. This does not mean that the creations of young children are of little worth. When they are valued they encourage children to reach their highest levels of achievement, and they bring deep satisfaction. Enjoying and achieving are part of the *Every Child Matters* agenda and are embedded in the Childcare Act 2006.

It is important to understand the difference between the low-level productions still found in some settings and the high-quality creations in others. An example of a low-level production would be when every child is given a template of a butterfly and expected to decorate it with different colours of screwed-up tissue paper. This is a very low-level activity. It is sometime described as busy work. It simply occupies children. The rationale for it is often that 'the parents expect their children to have something to take home to prove they have spent their time usefully'. In fact, once parents see the difference between these low-level, adult-led and controlled activities and the high standards, achievements and satisfaction of a child's own creation, they support and appreciate the latter fully. An example of a child making a creation would be the clay model of the tree in the garden made by 4-year-old Jan. It was her idea to make the tree, and she has put tiny silver balls on it to represent that it is the tree in the song, 'I had a little nut tree, and nothing would it bear, but a silver nutmeg and a golden pear'.

It does not look very tree-like. It is just a tall lump of clay, with silver balls stuck in it, but the idea has emerged for Jan from songs she knows, trees she knows, such that she has mulled this over, and simmered the thoughts until it has become clear, using the clay, that this reflecting is turning into a creation. In this case creative processes have developed into an act of creation.

Barriers to creativity

There are many ways to encourage creativity, as suggested so far. However, since creativity is a vulnerable aspect of a child's development, it is useful to consider barriers which constrain its development.

The screwed-up tissue paper syndrome

The example of the butterfly demonstrates this. The children were given an outline of a stereotypical butterfly, and could choose from pink, blue and yellow screwed up tissue paper, and they filled in the outline by gluing in the colours of paper they wanted.

This contrasts with Harry whose father loves butterflies. He has learnt from his Dad what a cabbage white, peacock and yellow brimstone look like, and has seen them when on holiday in the countryside. He makes models of these using junk model material, and adds one which has green and blue stripes. He says this is from Africa. He is mixing real and imaginary butterflies. This is a creation of his making. The screwed-up tissue paper was the adult's idea and the child is participating in a factory production line to carry out the adult's idea. The children might be permitted to 'personalise' the butterfly with their own pattern, but this is of low level compared with the creative thinking of Harry. He can select the materials he needs and finds appropriate at the well thought through and always available 'workshop' area of the classroom.

The colouring-in curriculum

The use of templates and outlines actively undermines the possibilities for children to draw and paint. A 3-year-old, together with the other children in her group, was given a cut-out template of a hedgehog. The children were presented with dry spaghetti bits, and required to put the spikes on the hedgehog. The adult did not find out if the children had ever seen one. Katie drew a hedgehog on her template, using a circle and drawing spikes around it. It was as if, her mother commented, Katie was oblivious to the outline of the template and simply used the paper to draw her own creation of a hedgehog. Not all children are confident enough to do this. Most would do as the adult asked. But Katie's mother understood the difference between low-level production-line art and high-quality, enjoyable child creations.

Arts and crafts, and performing arts

It is important to be aware that crafts are skills to be taught to children. They blossom in the middle years of childhood. Basket-making, weaving, wood-turning, learning techniques of different kinds of paint and so on are ancient traditions handed down in different cultures in different ways. There are definite techniques to learn, such as how to make a thumb pot, or a coil pot. This is not to be confused with creativity. Both go side by side. One helps the other along. Knowing how to use scissors helps a child to make the paper scenario collage. It is best, when working with young children, to teach these techniques in embedded ways on an as-needed basis.

It is the same with dance, music and drama. Children who make their own stories, dances and music are usually the ones who are told plenty of stories, and encouraged to act them out and to play such that they make their own stories. They hear a diverse range of music and participate in making it, but also have freedom to make their own. They see others dance, and are eager to try out and learn some of the steps, but they also have opportunities to dance to their own ideas.

Creations are about the arts, humanities and the sciences

It is a misconception to see creative development as linked only to the arts. Creative scientists, humanitarians and artists have much to offer the world. Children develop and learn at high levels when their creativity is supported and extended.

CHAPTER

19

SUPPORTING CHILDREN'S DEVELOPMENT AND LEARNING

Kathy Goouch

Kathy Goouch is a Senior Lecturer in Education at Canterbury Christ Church University. Kathy enjoys teaching, researching and writing in the fields of early years education and literacy. She is co-author of *Birth to Three Matters: A Review of the Literature* and *Creativity and Writing: Developing Voice and Verve in the Classroom*.

Aims

To develop understanding of:

☐ and examine the functions and requirements of the Key Stage 1 curriculum and consider how transition between the Foundation Stage and Key Stage 1 can be appropriately supported

☐ and explore the possibility of creating an effective curriculum to satisfy national standards while meeting young children's developmental and learning needs in the early years at school

☐ and identify key principles in relation to learning and teaching at the early stages of formal education.

In previous sections, important principles in relation to children's learning have been identified and the significance of key people who care about them as individuals and seek to nurture their development has been emphasised. In the field of early childhood, it is particularly exciting that researchers and policy-makers have worked together to examine closely what babies and young children know and understand, how they think and learn, from birth to 3. We are now beginning to closely connect this knowledge with developing understandings of children's learning needs from 3 to 5, the period now described as the Foundation Stage years. Professionals working with children have a key role in acknowledging the importance of continuity in children's learning journeys and of supporting children through transitions and this new 'bottom up' approach seems to be essential if we are to be more effective at affectively engaging young learners through their primary years of schooling.

The 'shape' of the National Curriculum

It is interesting to remember that before the introduction of the National Curriculum, in 1988, children were simply identified in schools as 'infants' up to the age of 7 or 'juniors' up to the age of 11. This may reflect how we viewed children during their primary years at school in those times, with 'infancy' defined as the early state of development. It is important to consider the terms we use to describe or label in this way because how children and childhood are constructed and understood, our understandings of what constitutes education and our core values as teachers, all contribute to the pedagogical choices we make and therefore what we put in place for children to experience in school and in society generally.

Changes in education policy over the past 15 years have created a distinct linear construction to primary education, which is now accepted as defined in Key Stages, setting out both what is to be taught and the standards of performance in subject areas that children are expected to achieve at each stage. Combined with the statutory requirements of the National Curriculum (DfEE, 1989, revised 1999), the Literacy and Numeracy Strategies (DfEE, 1998) and the Primary Strategy (DfES, 2003) provide step-by-step guidance on the subject information to be provided to children during each term and year of their primary school life. In each subject section of the National Curriculum, a summary is given of 'the things that children *will* learn' (my italics) (DfEE/QCA, 1999: 26). The language used by the Secretary of State to introduce the revised National Curriculum in 1999 is significant. He described intentions to 'raise standards', a constant challenge to primary teachers whose lives sometimes seem to have been dominated by realms of policy initiatives to drive up standards; he promised to provide a 'clear, full and statutory entitlement to learning' and talked of a curriculum 'robust enough to define and defend the core of knowledge and cultural experience which is the entitlement of every pupil' (DfEE/QCA, 1999: 3). Of course, what constitutes 'the core of knowledge' and whose 'cultural experiences' are to be defended are questions that are often asked and challenge teachers in their interpretations of the primary curriculum.

In contrast, while we were busily defining and describing a national curriculum based on a linear model through which children would be taken and tested, in New Zealand in 1991/92 the curriculum was based upon the metaphor of a woven mat 'for all to stand on' (Carr and May, 2000: 59). Carr and May describe their curriculum as more like a 'spider web or weaving' than an imposed set of stages or steps or a 'flight of stairs' and suggest that 'knowledge and understanding for young children is like a tapestry of increasing complexity and richness' (Carr and May, 2000: 60).

However, in England, from statutory school age, children are faced with a prescriptive curriculum, staged in discrete subjects and with attainment targets against which children are tested until the end of formal schooling. Governments have traditionally compared and contrasted education attainments drawn from test results of children here in the UK with those in other countries around the world, using the argument that we need to provide an education service that will enable future generations to compete in global economies and markets. Addressing the question of what are the 'global imperatives' (Alexander, 2000) that challenge governments to focus upon standards and targets and require attendance to either old 'basics' (literacy and numeracy) or new 'basics' (science and information technology) may cause us to 'forget about other notions of what it means to be educated' (Alexander, 2000: 44, 45). We currently have a school curriculum that appears to be predominantly influenced by instrumental notions of the purpose of education. But, defining education and understanding and how it connects to school learning may be the most effective way of creating bridges between current national and international, economically driven requirements and our understandings of how children grow, develop, think and learn in the early stages of their lives.

Pring argues that to be educated is 'to be in possession of those understandings, knowledge, skills and dispositions whereby one makes sense of the world' (Pring, 2004: 27) and he continues his definition by insisting that it is not the making sense of notions of the world 'inherited' from others but rather being given 'access to the ideas, and thus the tools, through which the learner's own distinctive personal development might actively take place' (Pring, 2004: 27). Here, then, is a definition of education that combines the importance of children developing skills with the significance of children also being involved in world-making and individual ideas and practices. And so, although educational ideologies dominant at this moment in history are sometimes described as instrumental in nature, they coexist, albeit sometimes uncomfortably, with a frequently articulated philosophy that speaks of learner identity, world-making, freedom and choice. A question raised by Pring, 'the place of learning: monastery or marketplace?', may be unnecessarily alarmist or it may be a key prompt in any examination of primary practice.

The Key Stage 1 Challenge

Children who join Key Stage 1 in the first year of statutory schooling may be as little as a month or so older than children in the final year of the Foundation Stage in the Reception year. And yet they will often be moving from a context constructed to facilitate play, choice and autonomy in learning, a child-focused setting, to a classroom based on a subject-led curriculum, determined and led by the teacher. This transition from a learning environment where the child may be the agent of their own learning to one where the teacher is agent, interpreter and dominant driver of each day's agenda for learning can be a challenge for such young children and their teachers, who have been given a 'single pedagogical formula' to implement (BERA Early Years Special Interest Group, 2003: 11). Dahlburg attempts to meet this challenge with the suggestion that teachers adopt the idea of 'walking on two legs' (Dahlburg et al., 1999: 139). In her explanation of this, Dahlburg suggests that traditions cannot simply be cast off but nor must teachers despair during a process of change towards the 'construction rather than the reproduction of knowledge' (ibid.: 56). 'Walking on two legs' could represent several different dichotomies: the challenge of traditions alongside progressive and evolving ideas and practice; policy and political dictats alongside teacher interpretation and initiative; or teacher as technician alongside teacher as artist. It is also pedagogically significant that, however the two legs are defined, pressures of accountability prevail in the current education climate. It is for this reason that some teachers appear to bow to bureaucratic pressures to teach only that which is most easily measurable. These professional dilemmas, compounded by an objectives-led curriculum, can be overcome with professional support and frequent opportunities for professional dialogue between those engaged in policy, research and practice. Significant progress is also possible with impending changes in public assessment procedures at the end of Key Stage 1, thus relieving pressures on individuals to measure their performance as teachers by test results.

The principle focus currently is that children are moving from a Foundation Stage influenced by more holistic views of how children can be supported and encouraged to think and learn, led by children and their interests, to a subject-centred series of staged primary years. However, an effective Key Stage 1 curriculum should be able to provide a bridge between these to encompass both skills development and broader opportunities for development of personal identity, self-esteem and potentials for continued and sustained learning. These should not be seen as conflicting aims, nor should a bridge be conceived as a compromise, but rather as skills viewed as means to learning ends and therefore essential for learners, and authentic purposes and contexts for learning offered as vehicles for skills development. These are the sound principles on which particularly the final year of the

Foundation Stage is based, and opportunities to continue to extend, challenge and support children in engaging, open-ended and carefully resourced opportunities should be part of the subsequent stages of children's primary schooling.

If the principles on which sound early years education is based in the Foundation Stage are clear, how is it possible to create any bridges between this and what has already been described as prescriptive, staged or stepped, objectives-led in a subject-focused, teacher-directed curriculum? Even if teachers are able to 'walk on two legs', how are they to support children as learners in transitions from contexts where process and progress are noticed rather than attainment and performance measured against externally imposed levels and standards?

Teachers and children together

In the very earliest years of children's learning, caring people, family members and others with loving relationships with the child have positive influences on development and learning. This continues to be true as children enter early childhood settings and then primary school. The most significant element in children's learning at school is the teacher, or other skilled adults. In the internationally acclaimed Reggio Emilia pre-schools, pedagogues and researchers refer to the 'pedagogy of relationships' (Edwards et al., 1998). They describe how children, in the company of gifted teachers, become more effective in the pursuit of their enquiries. And, significantly, one of the key findings from the Effective Provision of Pre-school Education (EPPE) Project (Sylva et al., 2004) refers to the quality of adult–child interactions as they engage in 'shared thinking'. Researchers and practitioners in the early years of education are united in that they do not use the term 'teaching' synonymously with 'instruction'. They refer to teachers as co-constructors, co-players and guided participators. Of course, the authenticity of such roles must depend on the authenticity of the learning context or enquiry. If children are provided with real situations to understand, real problems to solve and real decisions to make, and real relationships to explore, then predetermined answers will not be readily available to teachers and they too can be involved in shared explorations, co-constructions and examinations of contexts, resources and relationships, with integrity. This becomes much more difficult, if not impossible, if children are only given textbook questions and exercise book solutions to work with.

Role play, physical construction, exploration of natural materials, storying, puzzling and investigations will all take on different meanings for 3- and 4-year-olds than in classes of 5-, 6- and 7-year-olds. Therefore, the kind of guidance, challenge and support provided by teachers will also take a different shape. For example, a gifted teacher observed working with a young class halfway through their Reception year had been reading traditional tales about dragons and princes; the children had been immersed in these stories for a week or two. During one session their teacher let them loose after revisiting a tale involving the slaying of a dragon. The children noisily and excitedly jumped to their feet. They galloped away and she hailed them with questions as they sped past her: What's the name of your horse? Is he getting tired or is he still full of energy? That dragon looks fierce – do you need the help of a friend to capture him? What tricks are you going to use? Shall we creep quietly close to him? The children chattered, laughed, sang and chanted refrains they had learned as they constructed stories around imaginary dragons. In another classroom, of another gifted teacher who was working with Year 6 children, drama was also taking place. The children were in the middle of writing an extended story over a period of weeks. At the beginning of the Literacy Hour, a section of one child's story was projected onto the screen and read to the class. The author had used a number of elements already discussed by the class in previous sessions and was at the stage of solving a problem. Two characters had entered a room at night, the main character was awakened by a noise. The class were asked to consider whether these characters had good or ill intent and to decide what ensued. In groups of three, a way of working they were accustomed to, the children took on role. Again, this involved movement and action – desks and chairs were not used. Their teacher moved among them with questions, suggestions, sometimes surprise but consistently with interest. In both examples, the relationship between the teacher and the children in her care was mutually one of trust and respect. In both examples, the children were given problems to solve which had no simple, single or right answer. In both examples the expectations of the teacher were high and the levels of support offered were equally high. In both examples, all of the children were engaged in deep learning opportunities. In both examples the teachers appeared not to be 'technicians' but to be 'artists', creating and engaging in creative practices alongside the children (Grainger et al., 2005).

If teachers of children at Key Stage 1, and beyond, can become comfortable with the idea of being a 'learning partner' (Brooker, 2002), as in the examples above, then yet another bridge can be constructed between sound Foundation Stage practice and the next phase of learning in Year 1. Such gifted teachers are not to be *found* (Barsotti, 2004). When discussing the success of the early childhood settings in Reggio Emilia, Malaguzzi claimed that 'the gifted teacher is shaped only by working together with children and other adults, by building together, making mistakes together, correcting, revisiting and reflecting on work that has been done' (Barsotti, 2004: 13). Although the idea of experience 'shaping' teachers is not a new one, nor is the idea of teachers learning from children and more experienced colleagues, giving voice and status to this kind of learning unusual. However, during the last few years and certainly since the challenge of working out new practices with the introduction of the Strategies, it has become more and more common among colleagues working at Key Stages 1, and 2, to collaborate, team and peer teach and evaluate together, often in year group teams. Working in teams, of course, is common practice for those working with younger children.

Interactions between child and adult matter in relation to effective learning, and the kinds of interaction, the nature of such interactions, is significant. In the early years, frequent mention is made of teachers becoming 'co-players' or 'co-constructors', often with the child initiating and leading action and play, suggesting a more equal and reciprocal relationship between teacher and learner. In the later years of school this relationship changes rather dramatically as power, decision-making, agendas for learning are all often the domain of the teacher alone. These kinds of shifting power relations can also be the cause of difficulties in transition between the phases. It could also be argued that the more successful school learners at Key Stage 1 are also those children that quickly learn compliance and the game of second-guessing the teacher's intentions, the game of becoming successful at school 'tasks'. Institutionalised behaviour soon becomes mainstream and those deviating become a problem However, inter- subjectivity and reciprocity are also life and learning skills that need to be nourished and nurtured to survive, and so opportunities need to be contrived to encourage such development.

Thus, effective teachers, at whatever phase they are working, successfully apply their knowledge and understanding of the individual child they are encountering, the 'situation' of the child (that is, their culture, community and context), children's development and stages of learning, the context in which the encounter is taking place and the next stage of learning for the child (that is, the zone of proximal development, Vygotsky, 1978). This kind of seamless application of deep understanding, that appears to be spontaneous and unplanned, has been described as 'intuitive' practice. Intuitive practitioners are those who effectively combine 'explicit knowledge' and 'implicit know-how' (Atkinson and Claxton, 2000: 3). In the early years of education, teachers and other adults working with them capitalise on 'teachable moments' (David and Goouch, 2001) in natural and intuitive ways as co-players or co-constructors of stories. This kind of practice has often been likened to the way that parents respond to children as they learn in authentic contexts at home. It is interesting to note here that, anecdotally, there are many, many examples of people who claim in adulthood to have learned in childhood from significant teachers with whom they connected or who worked to help them make connections with their learning. In life as adults, we claim to learn from those who 'matter' to us and who we often describe as our 'mentors'. Understanding the relationships between effective teachers and learners will support all teachers in developing their practice. Strong and informed interactions, framed by sound intentions built into reflective practices that are responsive to learners' needs and intentions, seem to provide the key to learning. In a project recently carried out by researchers and teachers together to understand creativity and creative practices in teaching writing, several attributes were found to be common among creative and successful teachers from Foundation Stage to Key Stage 2. All such teachers appeared to:

- take risks and know that they are doing so
- be flexible during teaching and to be responsive to children and the opportunities that arise
- trust and demonstrate trust by giving children space for their interests and identity and respect the outcomes
- be independent professionals and demonstrate a degree of autonomy and to value this in others
- model artisitic endeavour (Grainger et al., 2005).

Creative teachers, it seems, are those who provide the kinds of contexts, opportunities and space for learning that are familiar to children during the last year of the Foundation Stage. For young children, transition to the classes of such teachers in Year 1 will be much smoother as a result of this kind of practice.

Play

Learning through play is a complex business; teaching, with play as the central focus is equally complex. There is plenty of evidence now that children, from birth, are eager and curious learners who can initiate play, imitate others, investigate in a self-determined way, sustain interest in people, events and activities over long periods of time and develop effective communicative acts. Research into play has long taught us the complexities of play and the sophistication of young players. Many early years practitioners have now learned that play is self-determined and that it has no predetermined or fixed outcomes and it is therefore distinct from activities directed by teachers or adults. These activities, although perhaps playful in content and context, serve a fixed preset agenda or set of adult intentions. Function and fantasy sit comfortably side by side in children's play as they re-rehearse their lived lives and reconstruct events that have happened to them and co-construct imaginings. In subtle and highly complicated ways children at play are building on their own learning and taking on the task of sorting out their lives, making new sense of what surrounds them. They usually exceed our expectations and astound us with their achievements while at play; they become 'a head taller than themselves' (Vygotsky, 1978: 102). Children play with language, roles, power structures and relationships and, in doing so, they find their own place among others, their identity and their sense of self-worth. These discoveries are not part of single events; they exist as part of a life journey and need to continue, in carefully supported ways, throughout school life and beyond. It is not sufficient, therefore, to relegate opportunities as important in children's lives as this to short bursts of 'golden time' or as a reward which is withdrawn for those young children who are unable to comply easily to imposed systems and structures of work and behaviour. Opportunities for play are essential for all of us, but paramount for young children in their discoveries of their world, their culture and their unique and developing sense of self. This is just as important for children who have been 5 years of age for a little while as it is for children who are not quite 5 years old.

Managing play, while accounting for national targets and standards, is a real challenge for teachers in Year 1 classes. It involves 'walking on two legs'. In practice, those teachers who are used to observing children at play are better equipped to account for children's learning through play. A teacher who now works in a Year 1 class said that, once she had realised that she was 'allowed' to take early years practices into Key Stage 1, she felt a new sense of freedom. Observations for her were the backbone of her practice and through these she felt that she could give a full account of her children's learning and their progress. Her own 'feeling' for good practice, carried from the Foundation Stage into Year 1, had been confirmed by new local initiatives and guidance from specialist teams. In the first term of Year 1, in this class at least, children found themselves immersed in play contexts. Indeed, in support of this teacher, not only is a clear statement made insisting that there should be 'a sensitive transition from the Foundation Stage to Key Stage One' but some of the highly positive recommendations from the Education and Employment Committee's report on the Early Years (2000–01: xviii) combine both Reception and Year 1, as in their recommendation for an adult to child ratio of no more than 15:1. Also in this report a clear statement is made that the age of school entry is less important than the kind of curriculum and teaching young children encounter when they enter statutory schooling. They recommend that the 'nature of the experience' should be appropriate to the age and stage of development of the child (Education and Employment Committee, 2000–01). The rhetoric surrounding 'teaching', 'learning' and 'play' occurs in abundance, although it is sometimes conflicting and often contentious. However, it is children themselves, their interests and engagement in learning that represent the true measure of success and of effective practices. Governments can make policy, inspectors can enforce it and tests can be put in place to measure, perhaps simply, children's performance in tests. But it is 'only children themselves (who) can make sense, understand and learn' (Pollard, 2004: 294). Engaging and enticing children into learning spaces is infinitely more successful than coercing them and thus causing disaffection and disillusionment. Play, play contexts and teachers who value play are seductive.

Spaces for learning

Our view of children, childhood, education and the purposes for schooling all influence the learning spaces defined in our classrooms. Learning spaces and pedagogy are intricately entwined. There appears to be a distinct difference between learning environments that shape and lead children's opportunities and experiences and environments that are shaped and influenced by children and their intentions. Each classroom reflects the aims and values of teachers; no environment in which teachers and children spend their working lives can be said to be neutral. Children themselves, on the cusp of entering what they perceived as a new world, often talk freely about transition. One group of 5-year-olds talked of classrooms in Year 1 having 'lots and lots, hundreds and hundreds of tables, and chairs', vastly different from their own classroom with few tables but much playing space. In the Reception year, the process of learning predominates; in many Year 1 classes it is performance and product that take centre stage, and the design and definition of space reflects this choice.

The built environment certainly often reflects a view of what is to be expected to be experienced inside. The austere nature of Victorian school buildings, with windows too high to distract, represent a view of how children were expected to be taught, with apparently straightforward transmission of knowledge and rote learning as the core element. Physical spaces though can be changed, adapted and owned by teachers and learners together, if commitment to change exists. Understandings of how architecture influences and is influenced by our understandings of childhood and learning has been a major area of reflection in the Reggio Emilia contexts (Vecchi, 2004: 18), but constructions of effective spaces for learning are about more than the physical constructions. They refer also to conceptual spaces. In order for children to enjoy successful and enabling transitions from the earliest stages of schooling through into Key Stage 1, the tightly packed, subject-based, objectives-led curriculum needs to be redefined to provide adequate spaces for children to continue to play, develop ideas, imagine and dream, to find pleasure in words and fantasy worlds, to make choices and decisions, and to shape roles, contexts, opportunities and spaces for themselves and their friends; and to do this in the company of informed and deeply knowledgeable adult experts.

In his writing at the turn of the twentieth century, Dewey talked about 'arrangements for learning'. He said that 'large numbers can be treated passively' but that 'the moment that children act they individualize themselves; they cease to be a mass and become the intensely distinctive beings that we are acquainted with out of school'. He continues to challenge us by maintaining that 'if everything is on a "listening" basis, you can have uniformity of material and method' (Dewey, 1899: 33). His descriptions of 'the old education: its passivity of attitude, its mechanical massing of children, its uniformity of curriculum and method' sound worryingly familiar more than 100 years later! The dangers of compliance and conformity have also been noticed by the QCA, who now recommend new criteria for creative thinking and behaviour across Key Stages. They list the 'signs to look for and promote: questioning and challenging, making connections and seeing relationships, envisaging what might be, playing with ideas, keeping options open, representing ideas in a variety of ways and evaluating effects of ideas and actions' (QCA, 2002). This offers a major source of support for teachers at Key Stage 1 who may be struggling to account for principled and appropriate practice for young children.

Children's voices

One of the fears that young children own up to, in relation to transition to Year 1, is that 'you aren't allowed to talk much'. Space and time for talk is also an element that teachers in Year 1 feel equally concerned about. They talk about needing room for appropriate activities for young children and about the need to acquire more appropriate resources. Matthew, who is 5 now and about to move to Year 1, was slightly worried that they might not have toys in his new class, but Polly thought they would have 'special kinds of toys' and Tim felt that he knew you got 'lots of toys, even Mobillo'. Esther was confident. She knew that when she started in Reception 'we couldn't do grown up things' and now 'cos we're older we know things'. Esther felt sure that when she got to Year 1 she would 'get gooder at balancing' and Emily, thoughtfully, wondered 'if we're going to have a longer PE lesson'. This group of young-five-year-olds were generally excited at the prospect of transition, slightly concerned at the number of toys that would be available to them, keen for new experiences – 'the big playground' and 'the big climbing frame', slightly disconcerted by the thought of homework but generally comforted by the great thought of being with friends they had grown up with.

Another strong inference from this group of children's conversations in relation to transition was that they trusted the system, they knew how it worked and they felt safe in their school. One reason for this may be that their school's policy included paying attention to periods of transition. Individual teachers used opportunities to send children on messages to other classes, particularly those who they felt were slightly insecure, to take registers to the office, to have short sessions in the 'big playground', to occasionally join in with school assemblies and to engage the children in conversation about transition as it grew nearer. The school as a whole encouraged an ethos of care and support between the oldest and youngest children with regular visits between classes and public praise for those witnessed demonstrating empathy and sensitivity to others. Clearly, the youngest children benefited enormously from this established ethos, and the older children's sense of responsibility and sense of community also thrived in this atmosphere.

World views

It is important for all those involved in working with children to look around the world at other systems, structures, policies and practices for many reasons: in order to understand how other cultures and communities view and care for children; to enable ideas for practice to be discussed and shared; to create a 'prism', as in the Stockholm Project (Dahlburg et al., 1999) through which to view and better understand one's own practice; to create cross-cultural and cross-national relationships. There is , though, an inherent danger of becoming enamoured of a 'model' which is apparently successful elsewhere and transporting it home to overlay or replace or sit alongside existing practice. Travels, which can be either actual or conceptual, are useful if they provide food for reflection and when they can be used to inform teachers with sound existing principles and strong practices.

In the context of transition and age-related practice, it is useful to consider the research-informed educational practice from other places. It has often been said that other European practice is more appropriate than that of the UK in the early years, as children are not required to enter formal educational contexts until the age of 6, and sometimes 7. Certainly many researchers have found that practice here is still generally too formal for young children and that, in countries where children are learning in informal contexts for longer, academic attainment is very high (David et al., 2000; Mills and Mills, 1998). In these European contexts, priority is given to social, emotional and physical development rather than the performance of cognitive-related skills. For example, pencil and paper activities might be considered developmentally inappropriate for children whose fine motor skills were not refined. Equally, sitting still for long periods of concentrated time would also not be viable in such settings, but rather physical engagement, activities involving singing and dancing together in groups would be more evident. In these contexts attention would be given to the rhythms of childhood, the need for movement and rest. Following this kind of kindergarten experience, children are then immersed in formal learning, using what may be described as a 'traditional' pedagogy, at an age of 6 or 7 when they are considered to be ready for instruction. The comparison would be that while children here in the UK are engaging in quite formal tasks, seated at tables and often for long periods of time, their peers in central Europe and in Scandanavian countries will be at play in school or kindergarten.

In New Zealand's recent history, clear aims have been created for young children's education with the introduction of Te Whariki, a curriculum framework to address the needs of three age groups: infants, toddlers and the young child. There is much to be celebrated in this curriculum which encompasses four key principles:

- empowerment – the early childhood curriculum empowers the child to learn and grow
- holistic development – the early childhood curriculum reflects the holistic way children learn and grow
- family and community – the wider world of family and community is an integral part of the early childhood curriculum
- relationships – children learn through responsive and reciprocal relationships with people places and things.

Te Whariki promotes the idea that children will be supported through a 'developmental continuum of learning and growing' and also acknowledges the fact that individual children grow and learn in different ways and at different paces (Carr and May, 2000: 56).

However, in New Zealand too, transition from this radical and holistic curriculum to a subject-centred school curriculum at 5 is also a concern for teachers. Carr and May described the challenges of evaluation and assessment of a curriculum model 'that sees learning as the development of more complex and useful understandings, knowledge and skills attached to cultural and purposeful contexts rather than as a staircase of individually acquired skills' (Carr and May, 2000: 67). It seems that, as in the UK, it is accounting for children's learning to external bodies that causes some teachers to look beyond the complexity of play for simple measures to assess simple tasks.

The requirements of assessment and accountability at Key Stages 1 and 2 here in England have historically had a heavily downward impact on the curriculum being offered in the first year of statutory schooling. It seems clear that, universally, governments and policy-makers, communities and individuals need to come together to decide what are the purposes of education and schooling. It is only then that this thorny issue of accountability and measures of success can truly be addressed. Until that time, sadly, teachers' aims and values become entangled with their drive to meet externally imposed standards and to fulfil the role defined for them by society at this moment in history. Seamless transitions, then, are impossible to achieve while the intentions and agendas of those involved are radically different as a result of evaluation and assessment procedures. The politics of education tends to influence the management of practice.

Competent children, confident teachers

In the Reggio Emilia early childhood settings of Northern Italy they describe all children as 'rich', they carefully document and discuss children's learning, pay close attention to the environment provided for young learners and promote high-quality interactions between children and with adults. This approach to teaching and learning for children up to the age of 6 has attracted the attention of the international community and is celebrated widely. Embedded in Reggio practice is their deep knowledge of children, drawn from *noticing* them and their achievements. Children are described as 'possessing many resources at birth and with an extraordinary potential … a child (has) the independent means to build up to its own thought processes, ideas, questioning and attempts at answers; with a high level of ability to observe things and to reconstruct them in their entirety' (Barsotti, 2004: 13). Both noticing and listening to children are key features of practice in the pre-schools and it is evidence from this that causes teachers to celebrate children and their achievements At this age such achievements are not measured against national scales or standards but applauded for their own worth. Because of this, it becomes easier to look for success than to expose gaps or deficits in children's learning progress. It is clear from the Reggio model, too, that children are more important than a curriculum.

Children are designed to learn (David et al., 2003). They are curious from birth and keen to solve 'puzzles' in their environment. With young children, it sometimes seems that as adults we only have to release the potential of resources and opportunities, to let children loose, for them to rush forward in development and learning. But teachers have to re-learn how to trust young learners rather than put all of their trust in a subject-led curriculum and it is this attitude of trust and respect and celebration of children that will enhance learning potentials. Understanding and engaging with learning and learners during all phases of schooling is an essential requirement. Effective education, even when enshrined in schooling, is therefore essentially human in nature.

Extraordinary responsibility lies with teachers. To be effective in working with young children as they journey from carefully tended contexts in the Foundation Stage towards becoming independent and competent learners within the statutory structure of the National Curriculum, requires inordinate skill combined with confidence in children as learners and a principled understanding of an appropriate pedagogy. Trusting children to learn rather than trusting systems to teach requires almost a leap of faith for teachers at Key Stage 1, many of whom have themselves been taught in rigid and arid settings and styles. Talk and interactions around play are powerful tools in a teacher's 'kit bag' of resources. Skill is also required to weave together opportunities for guided participation in children's activities, while respecting independent thought and creative practices. Joining together with children in their learning journeys is always more successful than managing behaviour in a system of coercion and imposition of tasks. Respect for children as individuals is also a key 'tool'. We may have high ideals in relation to choice and independence, but for some children anxiety may be as big a constraint on learning as close prescription of tasks. Children often need huge amounts of time to become accustomed to teacher expectations and ways of working. They also need huge amounts of time to browse, to think, to decide and choose as well as time to watch other children. Time, though, is a precious commodity in Key Stage 1 classrooms and sometimes children and their teachers say they feel as if they are on a conveyor belt whizzing through subject departments and grabbing at small chunks of information as they pass! Teachers too need time to watch children, to reflect and to make decisions and, although this may sometimes feel as if it is not sufficiently active a role to take, it is crucial in order to make sound judgements and to plan appropriately.

Vygosky (1978) had clear and high expectations of play as a vehicle for learning as opposed to 'meaningless' teacher-led tasks. If children, in classrooms, are allowed the freedom to initiate and pursue activities based upon their own interests then teachers 'win' time and are freed to develop other aspects of their role. Researchers' conclusions are most frequently drawn from watching and listening to children. In the Reggio early childhood settings teachers are expected to be researchers, to listen to and understand the intentions of children in order better to equip them to learn. This is the true meaning of assessment and it is through such simply defined practice that children's achievements can be celebrated and plans made for progression.

Informed changes in policy and practice

Historically, in England at least, education policy has jumped around in favour of and against maintained nursery school and early childhood provision, in favour and against a preset curriculum, in favour of and against whole-class, small-group or individual teaching styles. Change has been a fact of life in schools for decades now. Politicians recognise the fundamental role that education plays in shaping society. Published aims for education have become in recent years even more noticeably at the forefront of political agendas. Energetic drives for improved standards of performance, particularly in literacy and numeracy, have confronted teachers. An urge for subject knowledge and assessment against levels of attainment has overwhelmed the curriculum for primary-aged children and this has had a top-down impact on the youngest children in schools.

Principled change is welcome and, with all the information now in the public domain from research and practice with children, we are in a better position than ever before to establish what are this society's underpinning aims for education, to be achieved by all professionals working with children and young people. Such clear and essential ambitions seem achievable. A new, central government document, *Every Child Matters* (DfES, 2005b), contains a 'Common Core of Skills and Knowledge' which will resonate with early years practitioners, reflecting their own existing core of knowledge, and sit comfortably alongside principled curriculum aims contained in, for example, New Zealand's Te Whariki. The six key components outlined in this document are:

- effective communication and engagement with children, young people, their families and carers
- child and young person development
- safeguarding and promoting the welfare of the child
- supporting transitions
- multi-agency working
- sharing information.

Such a powerfully framed document could herald a new beginning of a more principled age for schools as this core of professionalism is developed from principled beginnings through to work with young people and adolescents. It is only when we have clearly defined aims for education in this country, principles that hold true throughout all children's learning journeys in school, and assessment practices that teach children about success rather than failure and celebrate daily achievements rather than collect snapshots, that continuity through key stages can be assured. In this new world of care and education for children across phases and stages, teachers will teach rather than deliver a curriculum, become artists rather than technicians and will journey with children as they learn rather than coerce from the sidelines.

E X E R C I S E   1 9 . 1

One of the key skills emphasised in this chapter has been that of 'noticing' children in order to understand development. The role of the teacher has also been described as fundamental to children's learning. In order to understand how children's thinking develops over time and the kinds of opportunities for learning that children of this transition age are given, students should:

EXERCISE 19.1   (CONTINUED)

1. Observe children who are independently 'making marks' in the Foundation Stage and then identify *independent* 'mark-making' or writing opportunities in a Year 1 class.
2. Observe and record the amount of time that children in a Reception class spend in whole-class groups at a 'listening' activity, when they may be required to sit still, either on the carpet or at tables. Compare this with the amount of time spent similarly in whole-class activities in a Key Stage 1 class.
3. Observe closely the activities of teachers. Identify how much time is spent with children at 'paper and pencil' actitivities at tables and how much time is spent with children as a 'co-player' with physical resources Make these observations in both Reception and Year 1 classes.
4. Create an opportunity to talk to a teacher in a Year 1 class about how she views her teaching role and how it might compare with a teacher of Reception-aged children.
5. Create two time-sampling grids. Record on them the list of activities that children are involved in during one day in a Reception class and then in a Year 1 class. Next to the list, record how much time children are given for each activity. Finally, try to note your view of how 'engaged' children are in each of their activities. You may want to include any evidence from what the children say or do to support this.

Further reading

Early Years Research: Pedagogy, Curriculum and Adult Roles, Training and Professionalism, by members of the British Educational Research Association Early Years Special Interest Group (2003) Nottingham: BERA.

This publication is a scholarly review of research carried out in relation to the three areas of pedagogy, curriculum and adult roles. The team responded to two key questions they had identified as particularly significant:

- What do we know about how young children engage with curricula in educational settings?
- What do we know about how adults promote young children's learning in educational settings?

The text is divided into three sections and presents 'best evidence' about the three focus areas and concludes with some key insights drawn from the research. Although the authors warn that this is not a comprehensive review of all research in the field and has not included policy research, the conclusions are wide-ranging and immensely useful. For example, drawing on research from neurophysiology, the authors conclude that 'learning changes the structure of the young brain' and 'brain growth and development is influenced positively by positive emotional support' (page 42). Other conclusions refer to the effect of disparity between home and school cultures and practice and the need for improved training.

Some key recommendations are made at the end of the review and these include the need for research concerning the arts and creativity in young children, physical development, ecological models, the development of identity, pedagogy in ECEC for children from birth to 3 and policy research.

This seems to be an essential text for all professionals in the field of ECEC.

Early Childhood Services, Theory, Policy and Practice, edited by Helen Penn (2000), Buckingham: Open University Press.

In this edited book, Helen Penn has focused upon six important questions or themes, which are, briefly:

- How do young children learn?
- What should young children be learning?
- Where should young children learn?
- Who should help them to learn?
- What contribution can children make to the plans that are made for them?
- How does practice change or develop?

However, the most interesting feature of this book is that Helen's contributors provide a global view in response to this brief, with representatives from Canada, Germany, New Zealand, Sweden, Spain and Finland as well as the UK. Indeed, the first chapter is by Martin Woodhead who makes a compelling case for a 'global perspective on early childhood'. The chapter by Margaret Carr and Helen May offers a clear introduction to the creation, launch and practice of Te Whariki, providing the underpinning principles expressed in Maori and in English. Discussion of the wider political context in New Zealand is also offered, along with a range of references to broader study. It is, of course, interesting to those of us working in the UK to hear Carr and May's concern in relation to transition between early childhood programmes and school at age 5. This chapter alone would make Penn's book essential reading.

Starting School – Young Children Learning Cultures, by Liz Brooker (2003), Buckingham: Open University press.

This is a sensitively written book, portraying the complex nature of children's journey from home to school in urban Britain. Brooker faces issues of values and culture head on, beginning with her own challenges as an ethnographic researcher and the processes involved in understanding the transition for children, parents and carers and practitioners.

The text details the story of 16 4-year-old children who all began at the same school, in the same Reception class in 'a poor and rather rundown inner urban neighbourhood'. Brooker tackles thorny issues, including ideas concerning 'social capital', 'family socialization', 'instructional discourse' and 'invisible pedagogies', while the effects of language and communication thread their way throughout the text.

The conclusions challenge practitioners to engage in research, action research, to become more effective in supporting children and their families at school. It also makes what I consider to be a key recommendation: that teachers relinquish 'power' over parents and children. She suggests that hierarchical relationships should be replaced by 'relationships of exchange and cooperation' and that 'multiple forms of communication (should) occur: between home and school, parent and teacher, teacher and child' in order that culture sharing can be achieved. These are inspirational aims, in a highly accessible text which binds theory closely to the stories of the children.

The Intuitive Practitioner, on the Value of Not Always Knowing What One Is Doing, edited by Terry Atkinson and Guy Claxton (2000), Buckingham: Open University Press.

This book is challenging, discussing as it does ideas about the behaviour of professionals and puzzling about the nature of and relationship between what we know and what we do and say. 'Intuition' is defined and considered by a range of contributors who write about their perspectives on intuition: intuition and initial teacher education, intuition and continuing professional development, and intuition and assessment.

I believe that this book is particularly important in the current political climate when there is deep concern that matters of pedagogy are now being very closely proscribed, although learning in schools is essentially a human activity requiring close personal interactions. The authors of this book ask us hard questions about objectivity, choice and autonomy, the nature of knowledge, the management of education, assessment and responsibility. These are all elements of professionalism that deserve very careful consideration by those working in education who need to deconstruct, as the authors in this book attempt to, 'the ways in which explicit knowledge and implicit 'know-how', reason and intuition, are braided together in professional contexts'.

The School and Society, by John Dewey (1899), Chicago, IL: the University of Chicago Press.
It is interesting that more than 100 years ago, John Dewey was writing significant texts detailing many of the same concerns that we grapple with now. He discusses in this work the school in relation to society, social class, the psychology of education and Froebel's educational principles, themes threading through many professional courses in this twenty-first century. Dewey's thoughts about play are particularly relevant. He describes free play as 'the interplay of all the child's powers, thoughts and physical movements ... embodying, in a satisfying form, his own images and interests'. To talk about play as 'the psychological attitude of the child, not his outward performance' challenges many of the misconceptions that arise today, in classrooms, in relation to the value of play and the physical and conceptual spaces 'allowed' for play and the allocation of limited time to play.
Although Dewey was writing in a different time and space, this text is worth hunting for, if only to remind us that many of the principles of education are timeless and some of the practicalities haunt us still, as in his story of how he had to hunt for furniture for school that was not designed just 'for listening'!

CHAPTER 20

INCLUSION AND DIVERSITY

Tina Hyder and Julie Jennings

Tina Hyder has managed early years services in inner London and is a former senior lecturer in Early Childhood Studies at London Metropolitan University.

Julie Jennings is a trained teacher who has specialised in the care, development and learning of children with special educational needs and disabled children. She is also a Froebel-trained early childhood teacher. She is currently the National Development Officer: Early Years for the Royal National Institute of the Blind.

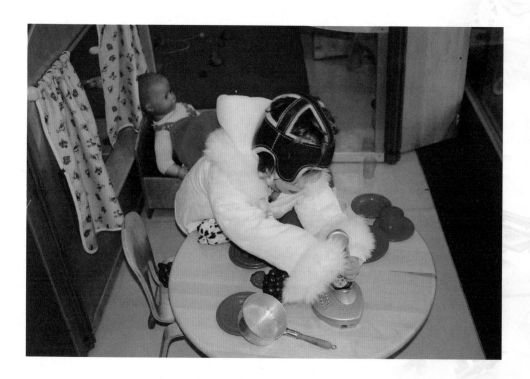

Aims

To develop understanding of:

- [ ] and gain an overview of the principles and policy context of inclusion
- [ ] and understand how inclusive practice can support teaching, learning and assessment with specific groups of children (boys and girls; children from minority religious, ethnic and cultural groups; children who are new to learning English and children with special educational needs and disabled children)
- [ ] and identify the main elements of a framework for inclusion.

Inclusion
The action of including; the fact or condition of being included; an instance of this:

Inclusive
Including, enclosing, comprehending ... characterised by including or taking in as opposed to excluding or leaving out. (*The Shorter Oxford English Dictionary*, vol. 1, 1983)

Settings that are committed to inclusive and anti-discriminatory practice are staffed by people who are sensitive, empathetic, flexible and knowledgeable – staff who constantly examine their own attitudes and are aware of how these influence their assumptions about children and their families. (Brown, 2001: 6)

Introduction

The broad concept of inclusion is one that the majority of people working with young children will instinctively agree with: that every child matters and should have a chance to flourish within a wider educational community. Nevertheless, in many instances, inclusion for all may be an aspiration rather than an immediately achievable goal.

Not all children fit easily into early years classrooms. Furthermore, how pupils are included, and the groups of children who are the focus of inclusion will vary. Inclusion is interpreted and practised in many different ways. There is, however, a set of unifying principles emerging from the inclusion of different groups of children, such as those with disabilities and those who are new to the English language, and this can be drawn upon to ensure that all settings have in place a framework for inclusive practice for all.

This chapter will focus on ways to promote and sustain educational environments that work for all children and families. By focusing on those groups of children who sometimes miss out, the premise of the chapter is that if we get it right for children who are in danger of not being fully included, we will get it right for everyone.

What is inclusion?

The most basic definition of inclusion as applied to the early years of school is about children being present within services. Many people would describe this as integration – not true inclusion. It is still the case that not all children are able to gain access to the education system. For example, some disabled children, despite inclusion being a key principle in current educational policy, are still not able to take up a place in their local school. They and their parents may be deterred by suggestions that they would be happier elsewhere. Equally, Gypsy and Traveller children may not be encouraged to take up school places as school authorities judge that the disruption of pupils being present temporarily is too great.

But inclusive practice does not stop once children are actually in school. Within early years school settings good inclusive practice is about promoting the right to development for each child; meaning, for example, that the impacts of limiting expectations must be actively countered. Just being in the classroom is not sufficient; each child should be able to achieve his/her best. Some children will be quietly present but not fully involved – rarely noticed, little trouble – but not really participating. Other children will be noisily uncomfortable and unhappy, not enjoying or achieving and making the lives of others miserable. There is a huge spectrum of experience between these two extremes.

The best inclusive practice aims to build on existing good practice to create educational environments within which all children can develop and learn. It takes account of varying individual capacities and temperaments; of wider pressures and expectations in society, and the different family backgrounds and belief systems within which children grow up.

A scale of inclusion might be described as follows:

1. Being present (integration).
2. The promotion of the rights and capacities of the individual child, whose potential may be hampered by limited expectations or because of wider social factors such as discrimination.
3. A setting where every child (and adult) is recognised in their diversity and is valued and supported to fulfil their potential through full participation.

Which children are not included?

The Office for Standards in Education (OFSTED, 2000) identifies the following groups of children who are at risk of not being fully included and who are therefore at risk of underachieving:

- both girls and boys
- minority ethnic and faith groups
- travellers, asylum-seekers and refugees
- pupils who need support to learn English as an additional language
- pupils with special educational needs

- children who are gifted and talented
- children who are looked after by the local authority
- sick children, young carers and those whose families are under extreme stress.

Being a member of one of the above groups does not, of course, automatically mean that children will not be included. There are various reasons why children are not included – for instance, children's varying intellectual, physical, emotional and social capacities and experiences will mean that they sometimes learn at different rates and in different ways. Equally, discrimination, stereotyping and reduced expectations mean that some children will not enjoy the same opportunities as others.

Wider policy framework

The government's policy paper, *Every Child Matters* (QCA, DfES, 2005b) and the Children Act 2004 set out a policy framework that aims to ensure that every child is able to:

- be healthy
- enjoy and achieve
- stay safe
- make a positive contribution
- achieve economic well-being.

One of its primary aims is to ensure that all services for children 0–19 work together to narrow the gap between pupils who may be disadvantaged and their peers. Early years and schools settings can contribute to this through the strengthening of links between services for children, and by becoming centres in the community where people come together and begin to break down the barriers of exclusion that so many groups face.

In this way inclusion is not just about what early years settings and schools do internally. It is also a principle that extends to the institution as part of the community.

Inclusion in the National Curriculum – strong foundations

Inclusion is one of four national standards identified in the National Curriculum, and in greater detail requires:

- teaching to respond to pupils' individual needs
- suitable learning challenges to be established
- overcoming of barriers to assessment and learning.

When starting Key Stage 1 children will have varying capacities and differing experiences of the early years. It is important to build upon the flexible and supportive ethos of the Foundation Stage to ensure a smooth transition into Key Stage 1. The Foundation Stage

Profile should provide an insight both into children's strengths and areas that require additional focus.

What are the features of good practice developed in the Foundation Stage that contribute towards an inclusive setting at Key Stage 1? The following examples will illustrate good practice for four groups of children.

Inclusion for girls and boys

Context

> Children's gender influences every aspect of their development, from their values, beliefs, language, emotion, imagination, cognition and style of communication to their involvement in physical activities, use of space and social relations. (McNaughton, 1996: 53)

Different expectations of how a boy or a girl should behave still impact on children's abilities to benefit fully from all that is on offer in the early years of school.

Most obviously, some boys may be drawn to activities that promote specific capacities at the expense of others, for example, motor skills rather than engagement with activities promoting literacy. Some girls may appear to thrive in the school community but never be challenged to extend their physical or spatial skills and abilities.

Principles

The first principle when working to ensure the full inclusion of girls and boys in all aspects of learning is to be aware of the impact of gender stereotyping. This requires the use of systematic monitoring and observation of classroom interactions, expectations and the wider curriculum. It also requires educators to be aware of the different stages of gender development through which children progress.

Around the ages of 5 to 7 years, many children will be quite rigid in their beliefs about what is appropriate for each sex. Some children will be adamant that particular activities or behaviours are suitable for males only (driving lorries, being firefighters) while others are only suitable for females (being a nurse, looking after babies).

It is important to support children through this rigid period of gender development, offering a different picture of the world where men and women, girls and boys can develop skills and interests that are not limited by gender stereotyping. The key principle here is that, while boys and girls may be different, their learning and development should not be limited by that difference.

Implications for development, learning and teaching

Because we are all subject to the impact of gender stereotyping it is very important to stand back and examine objectively how this works. For instance, perceptions often do not reflect reality. A common assumption is that girls talk more than boys – research suggests that in fact boys dominate communication in a group.

This is illustrated by research findings from an experiment where teachers watched a video of children in the classroom; both male and female teachers reported that girls were more talkative whereas, in reality, boys had spent three times as long talking (cited in Hyder and Kenway, 1995: 13).

Nevertheless, the underachievement of some groups of boys, particularly in later school life, continues to be of concern. It can be argued that the roots of such underachievement can be traced back to the early years of schooling, when early teaching practices do not always engage boys, precisely because of the gendered nature of early education (where the vast majority of adults in the settings are female).

As research suggests: 'Reading and the associated behaviour of sitting quietly or becoming absorbed in a book can also be understood as gender marked behaviour' (Barrs (1993), cited in Lloyd, 2000: 9). Barrs goes on to say: 'Teaching a boy to become a reader, and to remain a reader, involves helping him to develop a reading identity that offers him a way of being a male, and which at the same time encourages him to develop a personal response – possibly at risk of being different.'

How to ensure the inclusion of boys and girls? Monitor your setting, noting down:

- Which activities appeal to boys and girls?
- The content of group dynamics – who sets the agenda? Are girls or boys excluded from particular activities because of gender stereotyping, for example boys can't dress up or girls can't play football?
- Child and adult interactions – are gender stereotypes reinforced or challenged? Are girls praised for being helpful and boys for being strong?
- Materials and resources – are they free from gender bias?
- What more can you do to challenge gender inequality?

Effective practice: working with others

It is important that all parents and carers work together to challenge the pressures that may force children to adopt particular roles and behaviours. Children may receive conflicting messages from home and school about what is appropriate for them to do and say. However, an important starting point with all parents is that whatever the beliefs of parents the majority will want their child to be treated as an individual not a stereotype.

Challenges and dilemmas

One of the biggest challenges remaining in the education of young children in respect of gender is the lack of men in childcare and education. According to a new report from the Equal Opportunities Commission (2005) there is an untapped pool of men who express an interest in working with younger children. Ensuring that men and women are seen in nurturing roles must benefit boys and girls. Children actively construct their gender identities; the presence of more appropriately qualified and trained men in the early years will counter the cycle of boys not choosing caring roles in later life owing to the lack of such role models in their earlier years.

Inclusion of children from minority ethnic, religious and cultural groups

Context

The recommendations of the report into the death of Stephen Lawrence highlighted the need for inclusive education as a means to eradicate racism (MacPherson, 1999). The subsequent Race Relations Amendment Act 2000 sets out the duty of schools and other educational establishments to promote race equality and to show 'due regard to the need to eliminate unlawful racial discrimination and promote equality of opportunity and good relations between persons of different racial groups'.

Research demonstrates that the roots of racism and discrimination can be found in early childhood (Brown, 2001). As children grow up, attitudes towards difference can harden into stereotyping and prejudice. Schools have a role in promoting diversity and community cohesion, from a starting point of each child feeling that their respective cultural, ethnic and religious backgrounds is respected; they can then be actively encouraged to respect others.

Just as young children aged 5 to 7 are developing gender awareness, they are also developing a growing awareness of ethnic, cultural and religious identity, of self and others. Children will be very aware of who is like them and who is different. They will also be conscious of the different status allocated or attributed to various communities in the UK. The self-esteem of the individual child may be affected by how the outside world seems to respond to their social identity.

Key principles

A key principle when working on issues of ethnic, religious and cultural difference is to promote a sense of belonging. Being Black, or from a minority ethnic community or a minority faith group can mean that children are not always fully included. Such discrimination can operate even when children have been born and raised in the UK. Educational underachievement is a particular concern for some communities, with racism and discrimination being key contributing factors.

An important further principle is respect for the rights of others, as set out for example in the European Convention of Human Rights (ECHR), which forms the basis of the British Human Rights Act. The ECHR guarantees freedom of thought, conscience and religion, freedom of expression and the right to respect for family and private life.

It also makes it clear that these rights are not absolute, but can be limited by law, particularly where that is necessary to protect the public, or to protect the rights and freedoms of others. It therefore sets a useful framework for promoting diversity and inclusion.

Implications for development, learning and teaching

Schools must have a race equality policy that is linked to an action plan. Equally, school places must be open and fairly administered for pupils from all communities and backgrounds. Additionally, schools also have a specific duty to monitor and assess how their policies affect ethnic minority pupils, staff and parents.

It is essential that practitioners have the highest possible expectations of all pupils, particularly those from minority groups.

Respect for a wide range of cultural, ethnic and religious backgrounds can be demonstrated through the use of assemblies and displays. Parents and members of the wider community can also be invited to support literacy and other curriculum activities – thus bringing diversity into the classroom.

It is equally important that such activities take place in schools where the school population is largely homogeneous. In some instances school will provide the only source of accurate information about the lives of people different from the children themselves.

Assessment for learning

It is important to notice if children from varying ethnic, religious and cultural groups are achieving differentially. This means that data must be gathered and analysed for specific groups of pupils – thus enabling trends to be assessed. If concerns are raised, it is also important to introduce initiatives that focus on raising the attainment of specific groups.

Working with others

Forging effective links between school and home is one of the best ways to ensure that diversity is valued and that there is a match of expectations between the home and setting.

Staff from different minority groups are essential if inclusion is to be a reality in schools.

Challenges and dilemmas

At the time of writing the climate of increased tension following bomb attacks in London underlines how important it is that children feel they are not being blamed for who they are. Religious, ethnic and cultural intolerance could very easily become the common response to extremism. However, in order to ensure that exclusion and alienation do not become worse, schools have an increasingly important role in promoting inclusion and a sense of belonging.

A useful practical checklist has been set out by Jane Lane (2005) is summarised below: Belonging means:

- setting up a policy for equality with effective analysis and evaluation mechanisms. It includes removing any barriers to participation and belonging
- continually challenging stereotypes and assumptions
- talking regularly and openly about equality principles
- reflecting on existing practice
- continually being alert and assessing whether everyone involved really feels they belong
- positively engendering an ethos of hope and optimism for the future
- working together with family members, children and staff so that everyone 'owns' the principles of belonging.

Inclusion for new arrivals and children acquiring English as a second language

Context

Children generally arrive in Key Stage 1 as competent linguists – what they may not be able to do is to speak English. Children who arrive with no or little exposure to spoken and written English may face tough challenges. However, it is likely that they are already fluent in one or more spoken languages and may also be very competent early readers and writers.

Children newly arrived in the country as asylum-seekers or refugees will of course often be coping not only with a new language, but with a completely new life that has been forced upon them.

Key principles

Language is a key to identity, and therefore all children need to be competent in the language(s) of home. At the same time English provides a route into inclusion in the wider society and is the entitlement of all children who are born and live in the UK.

Within Key Stage 1 it is essential that children who are acquiring English as an additional language are provided with opportunities to maintain their home languages, as this will contribute towards a sense of self-esteem and competence. At the same time it is essential to structure children's opportunities to acquire both spoken and written English.

Implications for development, learning and teaching

Children in the early stages of acquiring a new language may be silent at first. This does not mean they are not participating – instead, they are likely to be watching and listening, gaining the confidence they need to start communicating. There will be considerable variation between learners, and it is important that practitioners are familiar with the stages of additional language learning and do not confuse them with signs of developmental delay.

Again, to ensure inclusion it is important for practitioners to think carefully about the ways pupils are grouped, to ensure that children are exposed to fluent exchanges in English from the earliest opportunity. It is these informal exchanges with peers, and the desire to communicate, that will provide the underpinning impetus for language learning.

Reading and writing activities can extend spoken activities, and as usual it is important to recognise that children will arrive with a range of learning styles. Flexibility in the delivery of teaching by adapting schemes of work and using different ways to deliver the standard teaching outcomes is an effective strategy to meet the needs of the individual learner.

Assessment for learning

Teachers can consider a range of strategies for ensuring that newly arrived pupils understand the goals they are pursuing and how they can take a full part in assessing their learning. These include:

- allowing time for pupils to adjust and become familiar with the structure and pace of lessons
- providing positive and constructive feedback
- considering class groupings carefully to enable pupils to work together collaboratively and to talk about learning
- providing opportunities for peer feedback
- ensuring learning objectives are explained clearly through visual supports
- providing key visuals and displays that illustrate the process of tasks and the steps to take

- including opportunities for pupils to build on existing knowledge
- providing opportunities for pupils to use their first-language skills for reflection and self-assessment (QCA, 2005).

Working with others

Good induction in the early stages of children's arrival in school should provide you with information from carers and parents about children's capacities and past experiences. It should also enable you to integrate features of a child's previous cultural experiences into the curriculum. You will also be able to establish parental expectations of the school system and at the same time be able to convey the values and requirements of the school to parents.

Bi-lingual staff are a huge asset when working with bi-lingual communities, and can be key to a good induction. Otherwise it may be possible for other parents to support and interpret for newly arrived families as necessary.

Challenges and dilemmas

Children who arrive as asylum-seekers and refugees will vary tremendously, but it is likely that they will share common experiences of change, loss and, even, trauma. Children may have lived under siege, in hiding, been witness or subject to terrible acts of violence and will have endured difficult journeys to safety.

While the routine of an early years school setting may provide safety and reassurance, for some children the impacts of their experiences will be so profound that the structure and expectations of school will be confusing and threatening.

There is a danger of children such as these becoming excluded from the school community very quickly. But it is important not to underestimate children's resilience, especially if the ethos of the setting enables the child to feel valued. Activities that enable children to express their feelings, whether through art, music or drama, are particularly valuable.

Inclusion of children with special educational needs and disabilities

The context of inclusion

There is a legal basis to meeting the special educational needs (SEN) of children. The 1996 Education Act, which is still current but has been amended by the SEN and Disability Act (HMSO, 2001), sets out the duties that local authorities have in relation to children whose needs require special educational provision to be made for them. Section 312 defines this as: 'for children of two or over, educational provision which is additional to, or otherwise different from, the educational provision made generally for children of their age in schools maintained by the LEA, other than special schools, in the area'.

The SEN Code of Practice (DfES, 2001) offers practical guidance on how to identify and meet the needs of children with SEN.

Like much legislation, these frameworks are needed when children's rights are being tested and this is mainly in relation to their right to be included alongside their peers in a mainstream setting and join in learning experiences in a collaborative way that sets the course for the rest of their lives.

Key principles

So what are the key principles that support children's development and learning when they have a special educational need or impairment? Ruth Wilson describes one critical feature as: 'Young children with disabilities are viewed as active learners who are capable of constructing their own knowledge in environments offering alternative ways to explore and experience the world around them' (Wilson, 1998: 25).

You will bring your own experiences and knowledge to the children you are working with, so start from what you know. But you may meet children where you feel less sure of what you know: children who need alternative ways to learn, ways that are 'additional or different'.

Implications for development, learning and teaching

An understanding of child development, of how children learn, is essential for any practitioner working with children. The care, development and learning of children with specific requirements should be encompassed within the learning and teaching frameworks set out for all children: curriculum, organisation, and match of learning and teaching styles.

There is no real evidence to suggest that the pathway of development for children with specific impairments is substantially and qualitatively different, but the sequence and rate of progress along the pathway may vary, and some of the behaviours children show us may differ from what we anticipate. Mason suggests that:

> the big mistake people are making is to think that all development follows a straight line. In fact, close association with children with disabilities or learning difficulties indicates that development is more like a 'fan' of different levels of development in specific areas which is constantly changing, not just with age, but with experience, stimulation, opportunity and practice. (Mason in Mason and Davies, 1993: 10)

An understanding of the particular needs of the child and the potential risks that may arise from specific impairments will help you to reflect on why children learn in particular ways, and how you can support them in this.

Assessment for learning

Assessing children's needs is about everyday practice. It involves understanding the child, from observations and other information, and understanding the implications of the disability. Brahm Norwich (1996) has written about SEN in the context of related needs:

- Of individual needs arising from characteristics different from all others: what makes a child unique?
- Of exceptional needs arising from characteristics shared by some: what are the potential developmental risks of the SEN or disability, such as a visual impairment or autism?

- Of common needs arising from characteristics shared by all: how do children develop and learn most effectively?

This approach to assessment is interactive, not simplistic. It takes us back to the definition of SEN: what is it that is additional to or otherwise different from what would be effective practice for all children? This will vary from child to child, but gives us the core of effective practice that is our sounding board.

One definition of inclusion states that 'inclusion is a process of identifying, understanding and breaking down the barriers to participation and belonging' (Early Childhood Forum, 2003).

This approach to assessment will help us, as practitioners, to identify both social and physical barriers to participation and belonging. Wilson states that a major goal of inclusion is to 'remove or side-step the barriers to learning' that children face (Wilson, 1998: 1). We may need to enable children to do things that they would not be able to do on their own. If a child cannot tie shoe laces, we can use velcro straps. If a child cannot communicate using speech, a speech therapist can help us to find alternative ways, for instance by using signs or symbols.

Effective practice: involving parents and other professionals

Planning for an inclusive environment requires teamwork. Children with SEN and disabled children are often more dependent on significant adults to develop learning opportunities that minimise the potential developmental risks associated with the impairment.

Many parents will, over the years, have built up skills for working with practitioners: if their child has been identified with a SEN or impairment at birth, their experience of professionals – who can offer something extra to them and their child – will be shaped through countless encounters. This may be your first time of working with a young child with SEN. But you are not on your own:

- Parents can be a great source of information on their child.
- Your setting will have policies and procedures in place for SEN.
- You will have access to a special educational needs co-ordinator (SENCO) who can offer guidance.
- There are specialist support services who can support and advise.

Challenges and dilemmas

The fact that this book still needs a section on special educational needs is a dilemma: 'disability can disappear positively only when it is accepted completely as part of normality . . . we have quite a way to go before that happens' (Mackay, 2002: 162). Some practitioners still feel a lack of confidence when working with children with identified additional requirements, those who follow an alternative pathway in learning.

Working with a disabled child requires equal value to be given to building relationships with responsive adults, and to developing strategies for supporting and extending learning experiences by providing a challenging and stimulating environment, both social and physical. This means that the process of inclusion for children with SEN and disabled children depends on attitudes as well as on systems of provision. Maria Robinson reminds us of the feelings we bring to our relationships with children who have SEN: 'beliefs about and towards them, whether physical, social or emotional'. She describes these as 'filters for our thinking' (Robinson, 2003: 178).

Children with SEN and disabled children may challenge our accepted ways of thinking and working because they have greater need for creative and sensitive support: our challenge is to reflect on the processes that make learning a positive meaningful experience for each child in a way that is truly individualised and personalised.

Points to consider:

- What do I know about how this child learns?
- What does the setting already have in place to support me and the child?
- Are there any potential barriers to inclusion in the setting?
- How could these be addressed?
- How do I involve parents in their child's learning?
- How do I involve the child?
- What specialist support services could help?
- How can we all work together?

Key features of inclusive educational settings

- Clear leadership and commitment to diversity and equality for all children, families and staff.
- Participation as an integral feature of children's experiences; where each child has an opportunity to be heard, and to hear, respect and understand the perspective of others.
- Working effectively with parents and communities as an integral part of the running of the school.
- Viewing children as individuals and as whole people.
- Finding opportunities within the curriculum to draw on the life experiences of boys and girls, and to recognise linguistic, religious, cultural and ethnic differences and differences in ability and aptitude.
- There are the highest expectations for every child, tracked through good monitoring systems that record the progress of each pupil and set targets for improvement if needed.
- Where respect for difference whether on the grounds of (dis)ability, gender and ethnicity and so on is encouraged, and bullying and discrimination actively dealt with.
- Where change is welcome when it works to overcome barriers to inclusion (adapted from Centre for Studies on Inclusive Education, 2005).

Conclusion

For true inclusive practice, the focus is not on moulding the individual child to fit the setting, but instead is on the setting being responsive in its ethos and practices to the needs of every child – thus reinforcing the fact that every child really does matter. As the definition of 'inclusive' at the beginning of the chapter suggests, part of the act of being inclusive is that of comprehending or understanding. If we are to create inclusive services for all children the first step is that of understanding the varying lives, experiences, identities and aspirations of the children and families we work with.

EXERCISE 20.1

Analyse how your setting promotes inclusion and anti-discriminatory practice taking into account:

- strategies for supporting individual children
- working with parents
- whole-school policies and practices.

Which areas of inclusive practice (as identified in the chapter) does your setting address well? Which areas require more work and why?

Further reading

Brown, B. (2001) *Combatting discrimination: Personal dolls in action*. Stoke-on-Trent: Trentham Books.

Brown, B. (2004) *Celebrating Diversity: inclusion in practice*. (Video and Support book) Persona Doll London: Training.

Jones, C. A. (2004) *Supporting Inclusion in the Early Years*. Maidenhead: Open University Press.

Reid, G. (2005) *Learning Styles and Inclusion*. London: Paul Chapman Publishing.

Hyder, T. (2005) *War, Conflict and Play*. Maidenhead: Open University Press.

Wall, K. (2003) *Special Needs and Early Years: A Practitioner's Guide*. London: Paul Chapman Publishing.

KEY STAGE 1 MATHEMATICS

Maulfry Worthington and Elizabeth Carruthers

Maulfry Worthington is engaged in doctoral research on children's mathematical graphics and is an Early Years Consultant. She has lectured in Early Years pedagogy and Primary mathematics and was a National Numeracy Strategy Consultant.

Elizabeth Carruthers is Headteacher of Redcliffe Children's Centre, Bristol. She has worked as a National Numeracy Strategy Consultant and as an Early Years Advisor. Her research interests are the pedagogy of children's mathematical graphics and early number.

Aims

To develop understanding of:

☐ developing a learning environment to support child-initiated play
☐ showing the development of children's written calculations
☐ emphasising that *using and applying mathematics* is at the heart of children's mathematics.
☐ the importance of learning mathematics from Foundation to Key Stage 1

The Primary Strategy emphasises that schools need 'to take a fresh look at their curriculum' and 'think about how they would like to develop and enrich the experience they offer children' (DfES, 2003: 12). The NFER study (2005) concluded that children in Year 1 were subjected to an inappropriate approach to the curriculum in which mathematics lessons included extended periods sitting on the carpet. When children enter Key Stage 1 (KS1) it is important that their experiences in Foundation should be continued in Year 1, providing a seamless transition. The mathematics will continue to be exploratory and exciting: the difference in KS1 will be that the children will be introduced to increasingly more complex mathematical thinking.

The recent National Assessment Authority (NAA) document *Continuing the Learning Journey* (2005) stresses the importance of continuity between the Foundation Stage and Key Stage 1. It recognises the significance of building on previous teaching and learning experiences. The play-based environment that promotes independence and challenge for children to engage successfully in mathematics should be evident in the Year 1 and Year 2 classes as children transfer to Key Stage 1.

Key Stage 1 framework for mathematics

Year 1	Year 2
Count reliably at least 20 objects	Count, read, write and order whole numbers to at least 100, know what each digit represents (including 0 as a place holder)
Count on and back in ones from any small number, and in tens from and back to zero	Describe and extend simple number sequences (including odd/even numbers, counting on or back in ones or tens from any two-digit number and so on)

(Continued)

(Continued)

Year 1	Year 2
Read, write and order numbers from 0 to at least 20; understand and use the vocabulary of comparing and ordering these numbers Within the range of 0 to 30, say the number that is 1 or 10 more or less than any given number	
Understand the operation of addition, and of subtraction (as 'take away' or 'difference'), and use the related vocabulary	Understand that subtraction is the inverse of addition; state the subtraction corresponding to a given addition and vice versa, and multiplication as repeated addition
Know by heart all pairs of numbers with a total of ten	Know by heart all addition and subtraction facts for each number to at least ten
Use mental strategies to solve simple problems	Use knowledge that addition can be done in any order to do mental calculations more efficiently
Compare two lengths, masses or capacities by direct comparison	Estimate, measure and compare lengths, masses and capacities, using standard units Read a simple scale to the nearest labelled division, including using a ruler to draw and measure lines to the nearest centimetre Understand the operation of multiplication as repeated addition or as describing an array Know and use halving as the inverse of doubling
Suggest suitable standard, or uniform non-standard units and measuring equipment to estimate, then measure, a length, mass or capacity	Suggest suitable units and equipment for such measurements Know by heart facts for the two and ten multiplication tables Use mathematical vocabulary to describe position, direction and movement

(Continued)

Year 1	Year 2
	Choose and use appropriate operations and efficient calculation strategies to solve problems, explaining how the problem was solved
Use everyday language to describe familiar three-dimensional (3D) and two-dimensional (2D) shapes	Use mathematical names for common 2D and 3D shapes; sort shapes and describe some of their features

Learning environments

Children of 6–8 years will benefit as much from opportunities for child-initiated play as younger children, and continuity is supported by providing a learning environment appropriate to their development. They can continue to learn through a range of items such as blocks, natural materials, sand and junk resources that provide opportunities for open-ended investigations.

In one mixed-age class of Reception and Year 1 a box of resources supported children's writing and mathematics in role play and was known by the children as the 'office' box. (Figure 21.1)

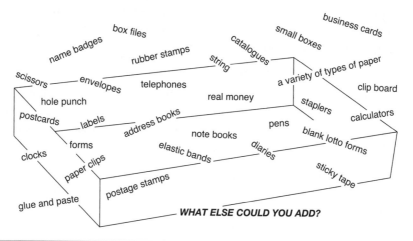

Figure 21.1   *Office box*

Areas that can have particular impact on children's mathematical thinking are the graphics area (see p. 150) and art, and design and technology areas. When children can pursue their own interests in these areas supported by a range of resources – mathematical; writing and art media; technological tools and junk resources – they often engage in a surprising amount of mathematical thinking.

Providing children the time to develop their understanding in open-ended ways enables them to further explore and consolidate aspects of the mathematics they have covered in adult-directed lessons in personally meaningful ways, and contributes to a 'spiral' of learning (Moyles, 1989: 16).

Threading mathematics through the day in a Year 2 class

This Year 2 day starts with an open question written on the board for parents and children to discuss and draw.

Can you design an interesting shape that has a right angle and invent a name for it?

Interesting discussions ensue among the children and parents. Some parents and children discuss what a right angle is. Some laugh at the shapes drawn and others admire the inventiveness of the names of the shapes drawn. As the parents leave and the register is taken, the teacher starts her mathmatics lesson on right angles, beginning with the wonderful drawings that have been invented. The children sit for no longer than 20 minutes and then work in flexible groupings to investigate angles in the outdoor area of the school.

After the lesson the theme of right angles is continued throughout the day. Children become aware of the right angles in the blocks as they freely play with this idea and invent buildings with right angles. In the graphics area the teacher has made sure that protractors and rulers are available so that children can continue their thinking on this subject. The children become interested in the idea that the corners of the classroom are right angles. In the afternoon the teacher writes a statement on the board for all the children to think about, picking up on their previous idea of corners.

Every corner is a right angle. Is this true or false?

The children think about this question for the rest of the week and give examples and explanations of why and why not. For example, Jessica brings in a triangle she made at home for the board with her explanation. Jason brings his boomerang. He argues that right angles can fly.

Some of the key points from this Year 2 class example are that:

- parental involvement is encouraged
- child-initiated learning continues to be valued in Year 2
- children's own ideas are encouraged and accepted
- teaching is based on the National Numeracy Strategy (NNS) (QCA, DfES, 1999) objectives but teachers keep the child's interests and ideas in view

- mathematics is inclusive and all children can be successful
- open questions include everybody
- there are always exciting challenges and problems to solve.

The development of written calculations at Key Stage 1

As children pass through Key Stage 1, just as in the Foundation Stage, they are encouraged to think about mathematics through their mental strategies and their own mathematical graphics. Children's own written methods gradually become more standardised and, in some cases, they move between standard symbolic and previously used forms of marks. This helps them make the transition and feel secure with their earlier ways of working, as they work towards more efficient methods. Problem-solving with larger numbers is encouraged and, when the children are really challenged, they use their own ways and methods to work out the mathematical problems. (See Figure 21.2.)

The 99 times table

A class of Year 2 children were given the challenge of working out the 99 times table. The teacher had begun the lesson with a discussion about different ways to multiply. The children came up with several suggestions including arrays and repeated addition. The children knew the 2, 5 and 10 times tables and some knew the 9 times table. The teacher then asked them if they could do the 99 times table. The class found this amusing and laughed. The teacher then asked them if they could do the 100 times table and started to chant it. The children immediately saw this as quite an easy pattern. They were then asked if they could use their knowledge of the 100 times table to work out the 99 times table. Several discussions went on with the teacher and the children. The children then, using the knowledge they had and paper and pencils, tried to work out the 99 times table.

Alison chose two times 99 and then wrote, after much crossing out '99 + 99 = 20098' (Figure 21.3, p. 211). Although the answer is 198 Alison was on the right track since she had subtracted 2 from 100. She had used her knowledge of 100 to write '20098' which was very logical. Alison went on to choose '99 × 5'. At first she used the iconic method of writing a stroke 99 times enclosed in a ring and then proceeded to carry on with this method for the other four lots of 99. Alison found this method difficult with such large numbers because she often lost count.

In discussion with Alison the teacher asked her if there was anything else she could put down to show 99. She seemed to be perplexed, so the teacher suggested, 'think about repeated addition.' This seemed to be a 'eureka' moment for Alison because she had made the connection between making 99 strokes (tallies) and substituting that form for the symbol. Alison had moved through the iconic to the symbolic response which was much

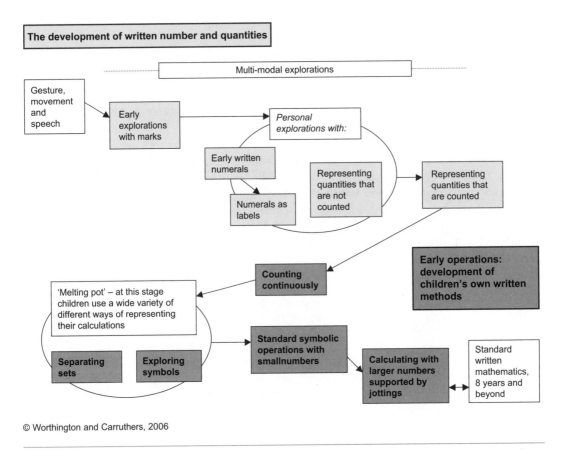

Figure 21.2   *Taxonomy – tracing the development of children's mathematical graphics, from birth to 8 years*

more efficient and less error prone. She had also moved from representing quantities that she counted to using standard symbolic operations. She used repeated addition for 99 and for 100 and was able to subtract the amount needed to come to her final amount.

Using and applying mathematics

Young children are amazingly talented, learning at rates they will never later exceed. They need challenging opportunities to develop their thinking at deep levels. Pound proposes that thinking mathematically 'involves much more than mathematics. It depends upon a playful, reflective and respected start to learning' (1999: 106). Children also need to take risks with their approaches to mathematics, to be adaptive, make decisions and communicate their thinking.

This strand of the National Curriculum is at the heart of mathematics and concerns the *processes* involved in mathematics, rather than purely the content. Children need to be able to:

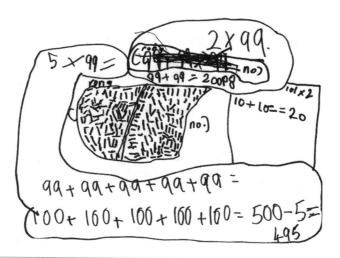

Figure 21.3 *Multiplying larger numbers – Alison (7 years 4 months)*

- try different mental approaches, develop their own strategies for solving problems and check their results
- represent, use and interpret mathematical symbols and communicate their thinking
- choose the most appropriate way of working out calculations
- discuss their work, use mathematical language, explain their written methods and give reasons.

Mathematics will make much more sense to children if they can solve problems and work on calculations within contexts that are real to them.

A Reception/Year 1 class travelled by train to visit a town some miles away. The train was very crowded on the return journey, and back at school Aaron commented 'I bet there's a million seats on the train'. After several suggestions from the children about how they might find out, Aaron phoned the station to ask: there had been 75 seats in each carriage, and seven carriages on the train.

Subsequently a group of children chose their own ways to work on Aaron's question. Several children drew shapes or other iconic marks to represent the seats in 1 carriage: some drew seats or people. Two girls set out a row of scallop shells on the floor and put pairs of bricks in each, exploring repeated addition (early multiplication). Frances drew 76 'seats' within a carriage: she recounted and finding that she had one too many, crossed one out. After pondering how she might represent all seven carriages on the train, she decided to use the photocopier and made six copies to create her train of '7 × 75'.

The investigation had been very real to the children because they had experienced it at first hand and all had been able to choose their own ways to tackle the problem.

Children talking; talking with children

Learning is a social activity and children need to be able to discuss what they are thinking and doing with other children and with adults. Talking helps children build new understanding and extend their vocabulary. Individual explanations about how they worked something out mentally, in a practical context or on paper, can also help other children and develop confidence.

'Open' questions such as 'how did you work it out?' can enable children to speculate, share ideas, justify and to go further in their understanding of mathematics.

Examples of 'enabling' questions:

- This looks interesting …
- How did you work it out?
- Tell us what you were thinking here …
- Does anyone have a different idea?
- What could you try next?
- Is there another way?
- Are you sure?

We hope that this section on mathematics has helped readers to take a fresh look at mathematics in Key Stage 1, working within the ethos of the Primary Strategy document, *Excellence and Enjoyment* (DfES, 2003).

EXERCISE 21.1

Observation

Select objectives from the numeracy strategy appropriate to your situation and plan two lessons, one inside and one outside using the outdoor environment as part of the lesson. Observe the children in both lessons.

Discuss both observations with a colleague and compare them, looking at children's mathematical interests and language and the resources they used. Was there anything that particularly surprised you?

E X E R C I S E   2 1 . 2

Understanding

Collect as at least six pieces of children's mathematical graphics (from both adult-led and child-initiated sessions) over a period of a month. You will need to note down what the child said and did, and the context of each piece.

Analyse these samples using Figure 21.3 on p. 211.

- What do they tell you about the child's development?
- How will you support the child's next steps?

CHAPTER 22

SCIENCE AT KEY STAGE 1

Chris Macro

Chris Macro is a freelance trainer for science and technology with a focus on the early years. She was formerly a senior lecturer at Edge Hill College.

Aims

To develop understanding of:

☐ the need for children to explore, observe and reflect on what they have noticed in order to learn science and to become scientific
☐ and consider the part the adult plays when the children are learning science.
☐ and become familiar with the requirements of the National Curriculum for Science at Key Stage 1.

When children are learning about their world in the Foundation Stage they are involved in experiences which encourage them to explore using all their senses; they have problems to solve and decisions to make and they talk to adults and children about what they have noticed. They do all this using familiar contexts and materials; things which they find inside and outside their settings and their homes. As they move into Key Stage 1 they continue to do all of this. They continue to find science fascinating and deeply enjoyable, and the transition should not be noticed by the children. At the beginning of Key Stage 1 much of their science learning will be through play-based activities.

However, when planning, the teacher has to take account of the requirements of the programmes of study as set out in the National Curriculum. There are four programmes of study, which give brief outlines of what should be taught, and attainment targets, which include level descriptions to illustrate to the teacher what skills and knowledge children might demonstrate at particular levels. At the end of Key Stage 1 the teachers in a school make judgements about children's performance in science and this information is part of the statutory assessment. There are no formal tests in science at Key Stage 1.

The programmes of study can be found in 'The National Curriculum: a handbook for Primary teachers in England, Key Stages 1 and 2' (DfEE, 1999), but briefly they are as follows:

Science 2   *Life Processes and Living Things*

- Children learn about the differences between living and non-living things.
- They learn about animals; how and where they live, what they eat, how they reproduce their young.
- They also look at themselves and their friends and observe the differences.
- They learn about the parts of the human body and the body parts of other animals.
- They learn about plants and the conditions which they need to grow. They study their local environment.
- They learn to treat animals sensitively.

Science 3   *Materials and their Properties*

- Children sort objects by the characteristics of the properties of the material from which they were made.

- They handle different materials and observe how they are used.
- They test materials for properties such as hardness, strength, squishiness, stretchiness and transparency and, in the context of cooking, they heat materials such as chocolate and butter.
- They watch ice melting and blow bubbles. Perhaps they might test the effectiveness of different bubble mixtures or consider where we might put ice in order to slow down the melting process.

Science 4 *Physical Processes*

- Children learn which appliances use electricity. They experiment with switches and learn how to make a bulb light using wires and cells, and they experiment with motors and buzzers in simple circuits.
- They investigate rolling, sliding, pushing, and pulling, and consider ways in which they can make objects move more quickly or slow down.
- They learn that there are many different types of sound. They learn about the sources of sound and explore ways in which they can muffle sound. They find out how the sound which reaches your ear seems fainter as you move away from the source.
- They learn about light and learn that when there is no light it is dark.
- They identify light sources.

These three programmes of study describe contexts which are used, not only for children to develop knowledge and understanding, but also as a basis for developing science skills. These skills are described in:

Science 1 *Scientific Enquiry*

- Children observe objects and materials and ask questions.
- They are encouraged to consider how to collect evidence to answer the questions.
- They make simple measurements to collect data and they use this data to help them to interpret the evidence. They are encouraged to give their ideas about what they have noticed.
- They think about how to make their tests fair.
- They are encouraged to say what they think might happen when they test their ideas and to record their results in a variety of ways.
- They have to evaluate their work and consider how they might improve their testing procedures.

To help teachers with planning science at Key Stage 1, the Qualifications and Curriculum Authority have produced schemes of work (see their website, www.qca.org.uk) which show how all the programmes of study can be taught. Many teachers in Key Stage 1 use these units and some adapt them to suit the needs of the children in their classes. Increasingly, teachers prefer to use their own ideas but find that the learning outcomes which are provided for each learning experience form a useful aide-mémoire for planning.

Learning science

Whether you are 6 or 60 you learn science in the same way. When a 60-year-old lights up a lamp using a cell and wire for the first time she is just as excited as a 6-year-old would be. She has carried out a practical activity and now she knows how to do it. She wants to go on doing similar things because she has been successful. However, she will not remember how to do the same thing two years later if she has not practised in the meantime. This would be because she has had hands on practical activity without *thinking* about *why* the bulb had lit. It is important for teachers to encourage children to *think* and *talk* about their ideas. They need to have some understanding about the phenomena which they observe. This could be a bulb lighting up, sugar dissolving, shadows forming or cars slowing down when they roll onto a carpet from a hard floor. It does not matter if the ideas which they have are incorrect. A skilful teacher can help a child to re-examine his ideas by providing further examples of practical activity and talk. What does matter is that the teacher fosters a climate in the class- room where children are encouraged to voice their ideas and raise their own questions for testing. The teachers also have to ask children to make links between new experiences and those which have gone before. If a child is melting chocolate and observing how the heat source makes the chocolate runny, they could perhaps be encouraged to make links between this experience and one which happened months earlier when they were considering in which place their ice blocks melted quickly. It is by building a series of practical explorations and investigations into their planning, and linking these to what they observe interests indi- vidual children, that teachers can help children to learn scientific ideas.

Developing science skills

In order to learn science ideas, scientists have to use their scientific skills. They collect evi- dence to test out ideas. These scientists could be in a Year 1 classroom or in a research labo- ratory, but, in order to become scientific, you need certain skills. You need to be able to use scientific instruments and to take accurate measurements, and to become skilled in observa- tion and analysing what you see. You have to be creative and to think about interesting ques- tions to investigate, and you have to be a good thinker to interpret the evidence. Good teachers of science work hard in order to help children to develop these skills. They help chil- dren to learn how to measure. They might start off using sand timers to measure how long it takes for their car to roll across a measured distance. They might use string to measure the slime trail left by a snail on black paper; they might use small interlocking cubes to measure distances or they might use plastic strips to measure the diameter of their ice balloon. However, by the end of Key Stage 1 most children will be using standard measures.

They will also be using instruments to enhance observations. The small illuminated micro- scopes which magnify up to 30 times are useful for placing directly onto leaves, fabrics or other materials. Folding magnifiers with a fixed focal length are perfect for young children, who often find that a handheld lens is difficult to use; and large plastic collecting boxes and viewers are ideal for looking at living things. Computer microscopes are also used in Key Stage 1.

Asking questions and finding answers

The National Curriculum programme of study for Science 1 suggests that at Key Stage 1 children should 'ask questions and decide how to find answers to them'. Many teachers do not find this easy, perhaps because they have not had inspirational science teaching them-selves, and very often they decide what investigations the children are going to do. After all this is much easier. The resources can all be at hand if you are quite certain what is going to be investigated. But if this is done all the time it will not help the children to engage with the scientific process, which involves helping children to become aware of their own sci-entific questions, and then to learn how to investigate their question. Of course, there are times when the teacher will choose to tell the children what to do in order to help the chil-dren to develop and learn a particular concept but, if we want children to ask questions and think about how to answer them, then we need to give them plenty of opportunity. It is only by having periods of experience and play with objects, living things and materials that children can begin to become aware of, form and ask questions.

Consider this scenario:

A teacher wants her Year 2 class to learn about forces and to develop the skills of asking ques-tions and planning tests to find the answers. She gives each group of three children three toy cars and asks them to experiment with the cars in order to find out as much as possible about how they move. They push the cars on the carpet and on the hard floor and after a period of time the children all return to the teacher. They sit on cushions, chairs or, if they wish, the car-pet and tell her about what they have seen. They talk about how the size of the 'push' affects how the car moves. Some groups have three identical cars and they talk about how they did not all travel at the same speed. Some notice that their small cars seem to go faster than their larger cars and some notice that the flat cars move more quickly than the others. One boy sug-gests that this is because the air goes over the car more quickly. The children are given the opportunity to explain why they think these things are happening and they come up with ideas to test. They think that certain things might make a difference to how cars move. The teacher lists these on the whiteboard.

What might make a difference to how our cars move?
Weight of the car
The size of the car
The shape of the car
The surface of the floor

The teacher then uses these 'differences' to help the children to frame questions such as 'Does the weight of the car make a difference to how fast it moves?' She then goes on to help them to plan a fair test in order to answer the question.

When planning tests in Key Stage 1, children initially need a great deal of help. Some teachers use planning frames which are differentiated according to the children's needs. They ask questions in order to help children to think about what might happen, what they are going to do and how they might keep the test fair. When, eventually, some children are able to use planning frames for themselves, they are usually asked to evaluate their work and to think about how they might have improved their test. Teachers who tune into what fascinates children as individuals make better use of planning frames than teachers who apply them in a more general way to the group of children they work with.

Of course, the fair test will not be the only type of practical science which children do in Key Stage 1. Goldsworthy et al. (1998) suggest that there are other ways of collecting evidence, such as classifying and identifying living things and materials and making surveys in order to notice patterns and answer questions. Observation is a key to being a good scientist (or teacher, or teaching assistant working with young children). It is important to develop good observation techniques in children too. For instance they might ask: 'Do tall people have a longer reach than small people?' And, when working outside in the garden, they might notice that some plants are taller than others and ask: 'Do plants in the shade grow as big as plants in the sun?' These particular questions can only be answered by making measurements.

Making links with other subjects

Teachers often use a story as a stimulus for science, and plan for some of the writing to have a scientific focus. Children might write letters to soap manufacturers to tell them about the results of their foam test when they tested bars of soap to see which made the most foam. They might write instructions to tell others how to make a bulb light up and they might even write short poems explaining how their chocolate melts. Simple non-fiction books provide children with opportunities to find answers to questions which cannot be answered by practical enquiry. The possibilities are endless and imaginative teachers engage the children in their research by making the context meaningful and exciting, and by knowing what interests and fascinates individual children. After all, a class of children is made up of individuals.

The links with mathematics are obvious. There will be a great deal of measuring in science and the use of graphs, charts and tables enables the children to interrogate and interpret data. Often teachers make links with technology as children make models which they use in their science. One group of Year 2 children made a 'pushing machine' to set their toys cars off down ramps as they were concerned that some people might push harder than others, and others apply the skills and knowledge which they have learned in science to make models which contain lights and motors. A teacher who was planning a teddy bears' picnic made vegetable dyes with her class which were used to colour the cloth napkins. Information and communications technology is used as children work with computer microscopes, tape recorders, digital cameras and simple data handling software.

Health and safety

Most schools have a copy of *Be Safe* which is published by the Association for Science Education (2001). This publication provides advice for primary teachers on the safe use of materials, and there is information about poisonous plants. Teachers must make sure that children are aware of any hazards which they might encounter in their work in science.

Awe and wonder

Our world is an exciting and wonderful place. Children are naturally curious and *wonder why* things happen as well as *wonder at* the amazing things they observe. Learning science gives adults the pleasure of enjoying this awe and wonder with young children, their parents and with colleagues

EXERCISE 22.1

Helping children to ask questions

Work with three or four children. Prepare a collection of materials to make some shakers. Crisp containers are very suitable. The children might fill the shakers with dried peas and lentils, pasta, rice, small paper clips and nails, sand or gravel. Encourage the children to observe the sounds made by the shakers and to compare the differences. Make a note of everything which the children say. Do they observe differences?

Can you help them to turn their observations into questions? For example, does a full container make more sound than a half full container? What happens if we put soft material in the containers? List all the questions and choose one to investigate. Notice which words are used to start the questions.

Read MacFall, D and Macro, C. (2004) 'Working with young children', *Primary Science Review*, 83, May June 2004. Did you use any of the strategies mentioned in this article?

Further reading

Harlen, W., Macro, C., Reed, K. and Schilling, M. (2003) *Making Progress in Primary Science – the Study Book*. London: RoutledgeFalmer.
Modules 1, 3, 4, 5 and 11 would be particularly useful.

Oxfordshire Science Team (2004) *Enjoy Teaching Science Investigations at Key Stage 1*. Oxford: Oxfordshire County Council.

CHAPTER 23

KEY STAGE 1 LITERACY

Marian Whitehead

Marian Whitehead, formerly Senior Lecturer at Goldsmiths College, is a language and early years consultant, a journal editor and the author of several standard texts on language and literacy development in early childhood.

Aims

To develop understanding of:

- [ ] and deepen readers/students understanding of the development of literacy in early childhood, from the Foundation Stage years to Key Stage 1.
- [ ] ensure that readers/students understand the significance of 'the big picture' of literacy development, as well as increasing your knowledge of the nature of written language.
- [ ] enable readers/students todevelop informed and critical insights about phonics and the teaching of reading.
- [ ] and be able to implement a range of good practices that support young children's literacy development.

Part 1 Transition to Key Stage 1

Case study: This is a story from Annabelle Dixon's classroom

... in a mixed-age class of five, six and seven year olds, the children loved playing with a piece of cloth with the letters of the alphabet stitched onto it, each in its own little square space. They would roll the cloth out onto the classroom floor and fetch a box of assorted objects ... All these objects could be associated with several different letters. One challenge for the children was to place each object in an unexpected position: the challenge for me was to guess why ... one day a child came to me after a very few minutes to announce he'd finished. Would I come and guess what he'd done? To my surprise the spaces on the alphabet cloth were all empty except the square for 'e', on which he had heaped, precariously balanced, every single object in the collection. He couldn't wait for me to speak, so pleased was he with his idea. 'Look', he said, opening his arms expansively, 'You see, it's e! E is for everything!' (Rich, et al., 2005: 17)

This child's creative thinking about letters and alphabets is a reminder that literacy is about everything and adults should try not to restrict children's ideas and creativity as they move into the Key Stage 1 curriculum.

The big picture

The big picture in terms of schooling will inevitably involve some changes for children and their families. The buildings may be different and there may be fewer opportunities to play and work in an outside area. The curriculum focus will be more formal and emphasise discrete subjects, and even specific lessons or 'hours'. There will probably be a stronger awareness among practitioners of external assessments and a constant temptation to mask the many individual differences among the children will always exist! However, children do not become different beings over the summer holiday and learning experiences that match their individual needs, abilities and interests must still be planned at Key Stage 1. The literacy curriculum must continue to support children's positive dispositions towards literacy learning, building on the big picture outlined in Chapter 14. This is not the time to allow the formal curriculum of the primary and secondary phases to 'push down' into the early years curriculum; on the contrary, practitioners must promote a 'push up' curriculum that will revitalise the later stages of education. We should always remember that there is a clear government expectation (DfES, 2003) that excellence and enjoyment will be at the heart of the primary strategy!

So what can we do to help children with the transition from Foundation Stage to Key Stage 1 literacy? In the early days we can plan for some key literacy experiences for all the children that:

1. support their positive dispositions towards literacy learning and,
2. build on their own big picture of literacy.

This can be achieved by focusing on some significant areas that might otherwise get overlooked in the rush to cope with tests, targets and tables. Three areas that are worth thinking about and planning for are:

* literacy-enriched play
* individual differences in literacy learning
* partnerships between families and educators in supporting children's early literacy.

These areas have already been mentioned in Chapter 14 but the Key Stage 1 practitioner must continue and extend the experiences of the Foundation Stage.

* *Literacy-enriched play* – this should include provision for the familiar and ever-popular themes like homes, garages, hospitals, shops, restaurants, and so on, but noticeably 'flooded' with literacy materials and activities (calendars, diaries, appointment books, telephone message pads, prescription pads, sticky notes, newspapers, magazines, posters, price tags, menus, signs and notices, bills, receipts). Themes from literature and popular culture can also extend children's interest in literacy

(making superhero posters, books and comics; writing to the authors, and characters, of favourite books and television programmes; making guacamole dip and writing the recipe to take home after reading *Avocado Baby* (Burningham, 1982).

- *Individual differences in literacy learning* – a determination to value what literacy behaviours children demonstrate and observing them closely, can increase our knowledge of how literacy develops in the early years of childhood. This then helps us to make appropriate provision for individual children, as well as being open to any wonderful 'e is for everything' moments!

- *'Emergent writing'* often starts as letters and numerals scattered through pictures; or lists of letters – conventional and invented – on scraps of paper; or a child's attempts to put one or more letters of her name on pictures and other surfaces. Children who have used a computer will have developed considerable alphabetic knowledge as a result of pressing the appropriate keys. This, or lots of experiences with books, often leads to early attempts at spelling words in a semi-phonetic way – 'apl' (apple), 'bk' (book), 'wrk' (work). Writing and reading are two sides of the same coin and each supports and enriches the other.

- *'Emergent reading'* includes all the previous experiences children have had with print and their individual ways of responding to it. One of the best methods for gauging what a child understands about reading is to share a book and note what the child does. Keep detailed notes about the child's behaviour and responses – the following headings may help. *Handling books*: is the book held the right way up; does the child start at the beginning; are the pages turned one by one (right to left for an English text, but remember that home literacy may have introduced different conventions for reading and writing)? What do you know about Arabic, Hebrew or Chinese scripts and conventions? *Visual scanning*: what does the child appear to be 'reading' or looking at as the text is read aloud? Is it the pictures, the print or a combination of both? *Sense of story*: is the child labelling the pictures; or, commenting on what is happening and showing some awareness of a beginning, middle and end, in other words, a story? *Book language*: is the child starting to pick up on bits of literary language found only in books ('One day Chicken Licken went to the woods'; 'Out on the moor the wind whistled and wuthered' – Kelly and Ayto, 2004)? Does this language begin to affect the child's tone of voice and intonation so that she sounds at times more like a 'reader' than a 'talker'? *Reading/decoding*: has the child any strategies for reading some words, and what are they? What does she do about unknown words – skip over them, substitute words that make sense in the context, try to 'sound out' parts of words or name the letters?

- *Partnerships in early literacy learning* – partnerships between families, communities and professional educators are a crucial factor in successful early literacy learning. Children bring quite a few years of experiences with literacy, stories and books with them when they get to Key Stage 1. This may well include several different languages and writing systems, and plenty of everyday kinds of reading and writing in their homes and the wider community. Research also indicates that the sooner babies and toddlers are introduced to books, songs and rhymes the better, and it will soon be the case that all children entering early years classrooms in England will have enjoyed at least one Bookstart pack (Wade and Moore, 2000). So, parents are children's first literacy teachers and professional educators must keep the lines of communication open and explain their approaches to literacy in the classroom. This means responding to any undue pressure from parents to 'get the children reading and spelling correctly' in supportive and positive ways. We have to respect parents' anxieties for their children, but explain clearly and simply the knowledge about language and literacy that our principles are based on (see Makin and Whitehead, 2004: 113–18).

Part 2: Moving on

Finding out more about written language – the little black marks

As children move through Key Stage 1 we should focus our long-term literacy planning on helping them to gain a deeper understanding of the nature of written language. In other words, we are helping them to move on from the big picture in order to investigate and use the fine detail of printed text – the little black marks. Three approaches are of particular importance:

- helping children become authors as well as readers
- helping children investigate conventions of written communication
- understanding the nature and limitations of phonics.

Helping children become authors as well as readers

This is all about showing children that they can be authors themselves and 'publish' in their classroom a range of books that have developed out of their own interests and experiences, actual and imaginary. There is no better way of practising emerging literacy skills than by making a book and becoming confident with the specialised language and conventions of literacy, such as, *pictures, print, text, sentence, word, caption, pages, cover, endpapers, title, author, illustrator, publisher, blurb, reviewer.* The topics chosen by the children can be 'e for everything', ranging from stories new, traditional and revamped, to family histories, accounts of outings or holidays, or detailed studies of dinosaurs, ladybirds, diggers and trucks. Books can be made at home as well as in the classroom and they can range from simple folded paper sheets and 'zig-zags' of concertina-folded card, to sophisticated productions created on a computer. The text can be created with varying amounts of help from adults, but the child's voice should dominate. The illustrations can be children's drawings, photographs, pictures cut out from magazines, or computer graphics.

Helping children investigate conventions of written communication

This involves providing opportunities for children to use and investigate writing as a system of communication. Another significant dimension of writing is its role in supporting thinking. In the Key Stage 1 classroom this means that children should be creating and receiving messages, and making notes and lists. The stimulus for all this written communication can be found in every area of the curriculum and in both the indoor and outdoor learning areas. Make a start by providing message pigeonholes for every child; involve other adults and families in writing to the children; set up real postal correspondents for the class (I write regularly to a kindergarten class in Maryland USA); make lists of favourite food and books, or things to do, collect, buy, and so on, and encourage the writing of brief comments about books, films and television programmes to share.

Investigating alphabets and collecting unusual alphabet books and helping the children create their own eccentric alphabets supports reading, writing and phonic awareness. It also helps children explore the rules and the quirks of conventional English spelling, as does the message-making discussed above. Children should not be discouraged from attempting their own spellings as these approximations actually teach them a great deal about how sounds and the letters of the alphabet are combined into fairly regular patterns. But the best possible support for learning to spell conventionally is reading for pleasure, so never let other curriculum demands reduce the opportunities children have to read and enjoy books. This familiarity with books also provides the right context in which to learn about punctuation. The emphasis in teaching about punctuation should be on the need for written messages to be understandable and organised into meaningful chunks. An excellent way of demonstrating this need is to read aloud familiar bits of texts, but as if they were totally unpunctuated, and let the children 'hear' the problems. This will ensure that all the so-called 'rules' (they are conventions) about capital letters, full stops, question and exclamation marks and commas, make sense to young writers.

Understanding the nature and limitations of phonics

A lot of misunderstandings and fuss surround phonics so it is important to be clear and well informed about the issues. Access to a good reference book can be a great help to the non-specialist teacher of primary English (see Mallett, 2005). The following working definitions are a useful starting point when you are faced with the great debate about phonics:

- *Phonics* – a method for teaching reading that focuses on the correspondence, or relationship, between sounds (phonemes) and letters (graphemes). A phoneme is the smallest unit of sound in a language, but not necessarily a single letter, for example 'ee' in 'bee' is a phoneme.
- *Synthetic phonics* – this approach has received considerable publicity recently, although it is the most traditional. It assumes that simple decoding is all that is required in reading, and teaches children the sounds of the letters of the alphabet and the

44 phonemes of English. Children are taught to sound out the letters in words and 'blend' them together. This does not work when children encounter the many irregular words in a simple English text, for example 'any', 'talk', 'said'.

- *Analytic phonics* – this approach is based on modern linguistic research. Children are taught to look at segments of words and at frequent patterns in sounds and words, by emphasising the beginning sounds of words, called 'onset', and the end phonemes, called 'rimes'. Along with lots of pleasurable play with the alphabet and the sounds of letters (alphabetic awareness), children are helped to enjoy the *alliteration* of same initial sounds in tongue-twisters and the same, or similar, rimes found in words that *rhyme* in songs, poetry and verse.

- *The cure-all* – the one thing that phonics is *not* is a cure-all for every child who has problems learning to read. Indeed, we all get better at using a number of phonic strategies once we can read! Phonological awareness is necessary for learning to write and read but it is not enough. Reading involves several complex processes and simple decoding skills should only be part of a rich language and literacy programme.

Good practice

There are many implications for good practice in literacy teaching at Key Stage 1 that arise from this review, but I have chosen to highlight seven that can get lost in a busy national curriculum.

- Classrooms should be organised as literacy workshops, with constant access to writing, reading and book-making materials. Outdoor learning areas and expeditions into the community should also be literacy-enriched and children should be authors, editors and proofreaders, as well as readers.

- Shared reading should be a regular, possibly daily, event. This is when an adult shares a large book with a group and not only reads the narrative but talks the children through the strategies and decisions a reader makes – picking up on details in print and pictures, responding to book conventions, like punctuation, and pointing out features like alliteration, rhyme, repetition, and so on. Large books are produced especially for this approach, but try to use good non-fiction texts too. *And remember – the narrative comes first*: do not smother it beneath a wealth of detail about ISBN and place of publication!

- Opportunities for children to choose what to read and to read alone must never be forced out of the daily literacy programme by well-intentioned planning for shared reading or the literacy hour. The greatest educational experience we can offer young children is the chance to browse through a pile of books and then get 'lost in a book'.

- Shared writing is very similar to shared reading and gives children the experience of learning about how writers behave. The adult uses a large sheet of paper and a marker pen and initiates a discussion about what to write. She helps the children to shape their spoken contributions into something closer to a written message before writing to their dictation. As this happens the adult writer talks the children through the decisions and issues every writer has to resolve, for example, 'Where do I start?' 'Do I need a capital letter?' 'What does that word start with?' Regular experiences of shared writing help children to see how a text grows, why conventions of spelling and punctuation are important, and why it is essential to rewrite things and redraft until the meaning is absolutely clear.

- Using words about language helps young children to be confident about understanding and using a special vocabulary for genuine purposes. Children and educators should talk comfortably about 'letter', 'sound', 'capital', 'lower case' and 'sentence' in a literacy-focused classroom, and book-making, shared reading and shared writing require the vocabulary of literature and publishing. This is a lively and sensible way of meeting Literacy Strategy and KS1 Language Study requirements that children develop an interest in words and genres.

- Many children in KS1 classrooms will be bi-lingual, or at some stage in the process of acquiring English as an additional language. The approaches to literacy discussed in this section can build on the undoubted asset of being a speaker of more than one language. Play, talk, singing, storytelling, mime and signing can be exciting multi-lingual experiences for children and for professional educators. Children and parents can write and print bi-lingual texts about the children's lives and culture and collect examples of different scripts used in the community. This could be extended to the writing of letters, notes and information about the school so that genuine and mutually helpful multi-language materials emerge out of real needs and are planned for real audiences.

- Drawing is a wonderful reflection of children's thinking and responses, and a very significant early stage of written communication and conventional writing. It should not be pushed out of the early years curriculum by other things because it not only supports early writing development, it is a powerful form of thinking in its own right. The study of children's drawings indicates that it can be a window onto their developing understanding of the world and their relationships to significant people, things and places (Anning and Ring, 2004). Just like literature, children's drawings tell us elaborate stories and should, like literature, be at the heart of the primary curriculum.

EXERCISE 23.1

- Familiarise yourself with the 'seven highlights of good practice' at the end of the Literacy section in this chapter.
- Use them as headings for observation sheets to use in Key Stage 1 classrooms.
- Record under these headings, evidence of the activities and provision for them; children's learning, participation and contributions; teaching strategies used.
- Discuss your observations, whenever possible, with the children, their families and your colleagues.
- Write up your observations, discussions and reflections and analyse why the author considers them to be so significant.

EXERCISE 23.1 (CONTINUED)

Note: Seven highlights of good literacy practice:

- literacy workshops
- shared reading
- lost in a book
- shared writing
- words about language
- a multi-lingual experience
- drawing and thinking.

Further reading

Barratt-Pugh, C. and Rohl, M. (eds) (2000) *Literacy Learning in the Early Years*. Buckingham: Open University Press.
This is a comprehensive guide to our current understanding of literacy development in the early years, with contributions from Australian and UK authors. It combines sound theoretical insights with very practical guidance for practitioners.

Hall, N. and Robinson, A. (2003) *Exploring Writing and Play in the Early Years*. 2nd edition. London: David Fulton.
This very influential book shows how play and literacy can combine to help children understand writing more deeply. It offers detailed advice for setting up effective literacy enriched play situations in the Foundation Stage and into Key Stage 1.

Whitehead, M.R. (2004) *Language and Literacy in the Early Years*. 3rd edition. London: Sage Publications.
This book reflects the research over the past 20 years in the field of language and literacy development, as well as the most recent initiatives in early education. Theory and practice are related in an easily readable style and the book is a useful introduction to linguistics for educators and other professionals.

PROFESSIONAL DEVELOPMENT

WORKING AS A TEACHING ASSISTANT

Maureen Brookson

Maureen Brookson is a senior lecturer at a large inner city college (Norwich City College) with responsibility for all HND and BA(Hons) in early childhood studies. She is also a researcher in music in the early years, with publications and conference papers disseminating the research nationally and internationally. Maureen is currently undertaking further research in an area of social deprivation.

Aims

To develop understanding of:

☐ and gain an understanding of the range of roles and responsibilities of a teaching assistants
☐ and learn ways of supporting children, teachers, the curriculum and the school

What is a teaching assistant?

The term 'teaching assistant' is a generic term for adults who work with children alongside a qualified teacher. Their key role is to help raise educational standards in the classroom by providing support for pupils, teachers and the school. There is an often confusing array of titles attached to this generic term: teaching assistant (TA), learning support assistant (LSA), classroom assistant, special needs assistant, specialist teacher assistant (STA) to support literacy and numeracy in primary, and additional learner support (ALS) for catch-up in primary. There are no set entry requirements but there are a range of nationally recognised qualifications, such as NVQ level 2 or 3, BTEC National Diploma in Child Care and Education, CACHE Certificate and Diploma (formerly NNEB), or the person may be selected because of their experience. There is no national pay scale, and there are regional variations with each local education authority (LEA) setting their own rates based on qualifications and experience (see learndirect website). Recruitment and training is done at a local level by LEAs and individual schools and are often advertised in the local papers. Local employers decide which skills, experience and qualifications are required for the level of support needed. There has been government funding available to contribute to support staff salaries, training and development (see standards website). All those working with children are required by law to have an enhanced Criminal Records Bureau (CRB) check.

Workforce remodelling

This current government initiative has three strands to it. One of the major strands is that teachers will have 10 per cent planning, preparation and assessment (PPA) time, which amounts to 2.5 hours a week, when they will be out of the classroom. This initiative has led to a new role of higher level teaching assistant (HLTA), a level 4 qualification, being created to provide cover during the teacher's PPA time. There is also the idea of a senior higher level teaching assistant (SLTA) with a more managerial role, which would result in three levels, TA, HLTA, SHLTA. The HLTA can be deployed in a number of ways: as cover with the teacher setting the work, or standing in for the teacher and setting his or her own work.

The guidance for HLTA, supporting and delivering learning, states:

To complement the professional work of teachers by taking responsibility for agreed learning activities under an agreed system of supervision. This may involve planning, preparing and delivering learning activities for individuals/groups or short term for whole classes and monitoring pupils and assessing, recording and reporting on pupils' achievement, progress and development. (Annex 1, Summary of Educational 2003 Regulations, see teachernet website)

Specified work related to teaching and learning is to be carried out to assist and support the teacher and is subject to direction and supervision of a teacher.

Support for teaching assistants

National occupational standards for teaching assistants have been available since 2002 and contain units dealing with special educational needs (SEN), literacy, numeracy, ICT and language and are relevant for working with 4–16-year-olds. There are NVQs at levels 2 and 3 based on these standards, and the Teacher Training Agency (TTA) has developed standards and training for HLTAs, and linking these to Qualified Teacher Status (QTS) standards. A wide range of resources, guides and videos are available from the DfES with real-life examples of good practice. The Workforce Agreement Monitoring Group (WAMG) has produced a PPA resource pack to help schools implement phase 3 of the National Agreement, which allows teachers a minimum 10 per cent of their time for PPA from September 2005, and contains guidance for HLTA roles. There is guidance available on *cover supervision* for HLTAs supervising classes in a teacher's absence

Case study: Karen

Karen is a TA in a rural middle school in Norfolk with 450 pupils aged 8–12 years on roll. She achieved the STA award five years ago and has recently completed her HLTA training. She works 17.5 hours a week in the mornings, and during that time works across two year groups with three teachers supporting numeracy. There are eight TAs in the school, only two of whom are full time. There are also four LSAs working one to one with children who have statements. All are encouraged to attend staff meetings if they feel the topic under discussion is of interest to them, and are paid for their overtime. They are welcomed onto committees such as the Well-Being Committee and the Workforce Remodelling Committee to represent their colleagues. Other staff training on issues such as behaviour management and first aid, is arranged on whole-school training days where possible, to ensure full attendance. Teachers at Karen's school have been particularly understanding in offering to be mentors for those taking the HLTA programme, half of whom have completed the training. Decisions about teachers' PPA have yet to be finalised, but the TAs have been reassured by the Head that they will play a valuable role either by providing supervisory cover or by delivering lessons. Karen has recently achieved a BA(Hons) in Early Childhood Studies and has been accepted onto the Graduate Teacher Programme.

There are a number of voices opposing these changes, both parental and professional, saying that it is the job of teachers to teach, and that children should not be left with TAs. There are also worries that subjects like art, music and physical education (PE) will be left to the TAs with the effect of de-skilling teachers. There may also be difficulties of children being confused about the dual roles TAs will have, which could lead to behavioural problems. However, there are also a number of innovative initiatives to implement PPA, for example joining two classes together, or working in a cluster group. As has always been the case, individual schools will come up with their creative ways of implementing this latest government initiative.

Roles and responsibilities

Specific roles and responsibilities will depend on the school and on each individual's qualifications and experience, even within the same school. The role may be *specific* for a pupil, group or subject, or general, which may be with different classes.

Roles may be in the care sector or educational support under a teacher's guidance. The teacher has the overall responsibility for planning and assessing the curriculum. Teaching assistants may support an individual child, a group or the whole class, assisting the class teacher or subject specialist. This requires a TA to be aware of learning objectives, expectations in terms of progress, behaviour and about inclusion of children with SEN. This will require knowledge of Individual Education Plans (IEPs) and Behaviour Support Plans. For a child with an IEP, targets for will be set, teaching strategies to be used, the provision to be put in place with a review date recording outcomes and success and/or exit criteria. There are usually three or four targets for a child in the key areas of communication, literacy, mathematics, aspects of behaviour or physical skills, and these are only intended to record what is different from or additional to the rest of the class. 'An IEP builds on the curriculum that a child with learning difficulties or disabilities is following and is designed to set out strategies being used to meet each child's identified needs' (teachernet website).

EXERCISE 24.1

Make a list of all your roles and responsibilities over the course of a week. Link with a colleague to critique the list and discuss the most effective use of time.

Working as a teaching assistant

Strategies for effective behaviour management

One very important role of the teaching assistant is effective behaviour management (see Rogers, 2003) Here are a few points to consider:

- Keep rules to a minimum, explain the needs for rules and allow children some freedom and control, help them towards a level of self-control.
- Be proactive, use advance planning and preparation, with clarity about the rules.
- Work within a clear framework with clear goals, follow set routines, allow for flexibility and be prepared to alter the activity if children are tired or it proves too difficult.
- Be positive and give praise and encouragement, and be realistic about expectations.
- Think carefully about the environment and how well it supports the activity.
- Be alert to potential and respond to cues, but ignore certain behaviours.
- Be consistent and respond appropriately to each individual, vary techniques.
- Be aware of some specific behaviours such as Attention Deficit Hyperactivity Disorder (ADHD) and autism.
- Remember the importance of praise and encouragement to promote self-esteem, motivation, emotional well-being, positive attitudes and effective communication. Praise is most effective when it provides positive and specific feedback, is sincere and genuine, targets process as well as product, and enables children to appreciate and reflect on their own behaviour or achievement.

EXERCISE 24.2

Mind-map a range of different behaviour management strategies (see Buzan and Buzan, 2003). Observe and record incidents of positive behaviour techniques in your setting and compare their effectiveness with your mind-map.

See Bentham (2006) for an excellent guide to managing behaviour.

Four levels of support

There are four main strands to a teaching assistant's role as support: supporting the children, the teacher, the curriculum and the school.

Ways to support the children

- Respect and value.
- Listen and communicate.
- Encourage independence and autonomy.
- Understand individual needs.
- Enable access.
- Praise, appreciate and value.

There are many practical activities a TA will be involved with: setting up and maintaining the learning environment, looking out for safety of equipment, supervising and supporting children's learning, ensuring they have stowed their personal property appropriately, that their work is kept in the proper place and is finished. They will also have specific tasks in supporting the teacher by ensuring children have understood instructions, transcribing, clarifying, explaining, listening to readers, playing games, directing computer-assisted learning programmes, making teaching resources, reporting on children's progress, and contributing to planning and assessment.

Ways to support the teacher

- Work together to provide a rich, stimulating and safe learning environment.
- Support observation, evaluation, record-keeping and assessment of children.
- Liaise with the teacher to share information about behaviour, progress and difficulties, as well as any information divulged by the child.
- Support the role of parents in children's learning.

Ways to support the curriculum

- Have knowledge and understanding of theories of how children think and learn, how they develop and mature (see Alfrey, 2003).
- Understand the factors that may affect their progress and learning.
- Have knowledge of the complex special needs children may have.
- Be knowledgeable of all statutory documents, such as the *Birth to Three Matters*, the *Curriculum Guidance for the Foundation Stage* (CGFS), the Foundation Stage Profile (FSP), the Birth to Five Framework in the Ten Year Strategy, the National Primary Strategy documents, the National Curriculum, *Excellence and Enjoyment*, and the National Literacy and Numeracy Strategies.
- Use ICT effectively to support learning activities.
- There are many groupings that are effective for different purposes: one to one, pairs, small group and whole class. Utilising a range of groupings allows children opportunities to develop a variety of learning skills: solving problems and differences, learning collaboratively.

Ways to support the school

- Work as part of a team: know the organisational structure and ethos of the school and key school policies, your own roles and responsibilities and those of other team members.
- Contribute to effective team practice and participate in team meetings.
- Attend staff meetings.
- Work in partnership with parents and carers.
- Contribute to assessment and reviews.
- Be aware of and follow all school procedures and policies.

- Recognise and utilise personal skills and knowledge.
- Attend in-service training and remain current in professional practice.
- TAs need to deal swiftly and effectively with behavioural problems, illness and injury, and need to be aware of the school's policies on *each* of these aspects.

Case Study: Claire

Claire began her childcare work with local authority youth groups and play schemes in the early 1990s while her children were young. Her first full employment was in a private day nursery and she began studying for a BTEC National Certificate in early childhood studies. Having decided her aim was to achieve a degree, she became a TA in a city independent school where she worked initially with Reception children and is now in her third year with Year 2 children. The school has 11 TAs, although Claire is the only one in Year 2 supporting five teachers and 77 children. All TAs in the school are expected to attend staff meetings, take a role in planning, attend Inset training and they also have opportunities to attend external training courses funded by the school. Claire's responsibilities have increased in recognition of her increasing experience and qualifications. In areas where her experience has surpassed that of the class teacher, in particular ICT, she now has the role of instructor with all the Year 2 children and is supported by the teachers. A new addition to the curriculum is philosophy, and Claire is working closely with the teacher and finding it extremely interesting and valuable for the children. There are plans for her to introduce philosophy to another class this year and to support a teacher inexperienced in this approach. She is at present completing her dissertation on philosophy in the classroom and is about to apply for a position on the Graduate Teacher Programme or a PGCE.

Safeguarding children and respecting their rights

It is the duty of every adult working with children to be aware of the legal requirements of safeguarding children. There are legal requirements with regard to working with young children, which include the Children Act 2004, the Education Act 2002, the Race Relations Act 1976, Race Relations Amendment Act 2000, the *Special Educational Needs Code of Practice* (2001), the Data Protection Act 1988 and *Every Child Matters* (2005b), and TAs need to have a good level of knowledge of these pieces of legislation.

There are many factors that affect children: genetic, cultural, social and environmental issues. Every child has a right to be respected for who he or she is, and to have an appropriate curriculum designed to meet his or her specific needs, with adults to scaffold and share learning. They have a right to have their social and emotional needs acknowledged and met so they can move freely through the environment and access the full curriculum, to interact effectively with adults and children in their community, and if necessary to modify the environment and curriculum to meet individual needs.

Special educational needs

The Warnock Report on SEN (1978) concluded that up to 20 per cent of children were part of a continuum of special needs related to the child's individual need for support to access the full curriculum. The 1981 Education Act established the principle of integration. The 2001 *SEN Revised Code of Practice* (implemented in 2002) reinforces the right for children with special educational needs to receive education in a mainstream school and calls on schools and LEAs to enable all children the opportunities of inclusive education. It has a more structured, graduated approach and embraces early years education. This has led to a greater need for learning support to provide access to the curriculum. Teaching assistants need to understand concepts of inclusivity and differentiation as an ongoing process. Often, the TA is the one working with children who require extra support to enable the teacher to focus on the majority of the class and thereby provide inclusion for all children. However, it is important, especially in Key Stage 1, to provide ample opportunities for children with an IEP to play as the key way young children learn. The TA may have a role of working with the SENCO and will need to be aware of each child's particular need, how it may affect learning and what support is needed to enable the child full access to a broad and balanced curriculum.

Effective communication

Effective communication is at the heart of effective teaching and learning. Teaching assistants need to learn a number of skills in this area:

- concentrating and listening attentively
- using appropriate non-verbal gestures
- using appropriate vocabulary while extending and providing new words and meanings
- asking open questions
- responding positively and with humour
- being receptive and open to new ideas and other ways of thinking, providing opportunities for meaningful dialogues with other children and adults
- encouraging turn-taking and respect for others' viewpoints.

The key is 'active' listening, not being too quick to jump in with an answer or explanation but giving the child time to formulate their own ideas and questions. There are a number of skills to be learned and refined: initiating and sustaining talk by providing cues, prompts and questions that are appropriate to the task. 'Open' questions allow a variety of responses that help to develop language skills and self-esteem and confidence as children have the opportunity to explore their own feelings and to articulate their own unique way of viewing the world. This sort of dialogue may enable the TA to understand the child's level of knowledge and may help with planning further activities and experiences. Teaching assistants also need to be able to answer children's questions at a level they understand and without taking away their own ability to find out for themselves. Sensitivity is the key. Effective communication requires careful planning of the environment so children have both time and space to communicate effectively. Sitting or crouching next to or opposite a child is preferable to leaning over him or her. In order to access all elements of the curriculum, children need to learn the language of learning, for example, the language needed to understand concepts, to have opportunities to participate in problem-solving and problem-finding and to develop ideas and opinions. The development of children's language and communication is a vital task for all adults who work with children.

Accentuate the positive

Immediate and positive affirmations or rewards are necessary to show that the child is learning and achieving. This requires focusing on the positive aspects of the child's work, the effort involved as well as the achievement. Appreciation and encouragement enable children to grow in confidence and feelings of self-worth, but need to be used judiciously. This means being specific in your appreciation, for example 'I think your use of colour in that painting is really interesting, how did you decide?' This tells the child precisely *what* you like about the painting and also gives the child an opportunity to explore their decision-making process. It may be the practice in your school to give smiley faces, stars or merits. However, these are extrinsic rewards which do not have long-term impact. Writing a positive comment on the child's work, or comments in the child's folder or given to the headteacher to share in school assembly show appreciation and value of a child's efforts.

Learning styles

There has been much research into children's different learning styles. The three most common identified are *visual, auditory* and *kinaesthetic*. Visual learners gain information through observation and reading, and respond to visual aids and are able to visualise ideas and remember visual details. Auditory learners listen carefully and are often talkers and listeners, enjoying discussion, but may be disrupted by noise. Kinaesthetic learners process information through touch and movement. As all children rely on this style, *active learning* is very important as is *learning by doing* (see Rodd, 2001). Children, like adults, may have a lead learning style, but this does not exclude them from using other styles. Adults should also be aware of their own preferred learning style, as often this is the style we prefer to use in teaching.

Play is vitally important

Teaching assistants need to provide interesting, challenging and appropriate play opportunities with varied resources (see Chapter 25). Adults who participate in play, with sensitivity and where appropriate, support children in extending language learning, encourage social interaction, and formulate imaginative and creative ideas.

EXERCISE 24.3

Think about how you support play in your setting. Observe a child or a small group of children at play which is (a) child-led, and (b) adult-initiated. Make a record of what the child or children are learning, and explore appropriate adult interventions in their play.

Emotional intelligence

Understanding the importance of emotional intelligence is fundamental in helping children to learn about their feelings and to understand the feelings of others, in developing their creativity, interpersonal skills, positive self-esteem, emotional strength and confidence, and to feel valued (see Goleman, 1996).

Transitions

Children have a number of transitions in their lives, from nursery to school, from one year group to the next, and from Key Stage 1 to Key Stage 2 for example. All transitions involve change and may involve loss and separation, and children need careful preparation and reassurance to help them remain secure and manage the changes. It is important to talk to children, listen to their fears, read relevant stories and provide opportunities for imaginative play that enable children to express their fears and feelings. It is also helpful to organise visits, provide information, and plan activities for induction.

Managing the learning environment

Teaching assistants will often be expected to provide all the materials and equipment for the day's activities, and maintain the routine of the class, breaks and playtimes as this provides stability and security, and to prepare children and the environment for special events like visitors or outings. There will usually be a timetable posted for the benefit of parents, visitors and staff so everyone is aware of who is responsible for what area of learning. You may be responsible for setting up the room, ensuring fire exits are not obstructed, the room is clean and uncluttered, is welcoming and celebrates the cultural diversity of the community you serve.

Health and safety issues will come under the TA's remit, including: security, hygiene, equipment, emergencies, supervision and storage. It may be your responsibility to use technological equipment and to ensure it is functioning and well maintained, and to keep an inventory of materials and be responsible for ensuring supplies are maintained.

Children also should maintain the environment, so time needs to be allocated to tidying up (a great learning opportunity, especially in mathematical terms) and this means storage needs to be accessible and clearly labelled. This also helps develop confidence and independence as children take control of their own needs. There should also be opportunities for the children to participate in maintaining and developing their environment.

Resources

Newly launched *teachers tv* is intended as a support for all practitioners to help sharing experiences and supporting preparation and research. It is a digital service free of charge and available every day of the year, and it aims to reflect the views of the teaching community. There are debates about current issues in education as well as curriculum-based programmes and professional development. There is also a site specifically for teaching assistants with links of direct relevance plus a free newsletter (see teaching-assistants.co.uk)

Observation and assessment of children

You will have a role in observing and assessing children in a range of activities, and you may have a role in maintaining and updating records. Record-keeping is a very important part of ensuring quality and equality, and has a number of purposes: to monitor progress, learning and attainment, to share information with parents and professionals and to plan effectively for new learning objectives.

Working in partnership

A final, but no less important partnership, is the one between school and home. Effective communication between teachers, TAs, parents and carers is essential for the well-being of children. It takes time and effort to build positive partnerships with families, but they are the building blocks of successful interactions which are of immense benefit to all (see Whalley, 1997 and also Chapter 4 by Vicky Hutchin, Chapter 12 by Helen Moylett and Chapter 28 by Lesley Benson).

Last words

This is an exciting time to be a teaching assistant, with the government providing many excellent resources and with the early years being high on the political agenda. The job is fun, rewarding and tiring, but also a professionally recognised role of fundamental importance to the health and education of our children. As I hear from many of the TAs I teach, 'I just want to make a difference'.

Useful websites

www.dfes.gov.uk
www.dfes.gov.uk/everychildmatters
www.doh.gov.uk (working together to safeguard children)
www.hlta.gov.uk
www.learndirect-advice.co.uk
www.qca.org.uk
www.remodelling.org
www.standards.dfes.gov.uk
www.teaching–assistants.co.uk
www.teachernet.gov.uk
www.teachers.tv
www.tta.gov.uk

Further Reading

Department for Education and Skills (DfES) (2000) *Working with Teaching Assistants: A Good Practice Guide*. London: HMSO. (Also at www.gov.uk/teachingreforms/support.)

Department for Education and Skills (DfES) (2003) *Working with Teaching Assistants in Primary Schools (DfES/0114/2003),* publication line 0845 60 222 60. Also, *Developing the Role of School Support Staff* and *Raising Standards and Tackling Workload: A National Agreement.*

Drake, P., Jacklin, A., Robinson, C. and Thorp, J. (2004) *Becoming a Teaching Assistant*. London: Paul Chapman Publishing.

Kamen, T. (2003) *Teaching Assistant's Handbook*. London: Hodder & Stoughton.

Office for Standards in Education (OFSTED) (2002) *Teaching Assistants in Primary Schools: An Evaluation of the Quality and Impact of their Work*. London: HMI.

Tyrer, R., Gunn, S., Lee, C., Parker, M., Pittman, M. and Townsend, M. (2004) *A Toolkit for the Effective Teaching Assistant*. London: Paul Chapman Publishing

Workforce Agreement Monitoring Group (WAMG) www.remodelling.org.

CHAPTER

25

PLAYWORK

Wendy Russell

Wendy Russell has worked in the playwork sector since 1975 and currently divides her time between being Senior Lecturer in Playwork at the University of Gloucestershire and working as an independent consultant.

Aims

To develop understanding of:

☐ the complexity of play and its centrality in the lives of school-aged children
☐ how playworkers can support children's play
☐ key features of the playwork sector.

This chapter focuses on the elements of playwork that differentiate it from other forms of work with children and young people. It explores theories on the nature and function of school-aged children's play. It then looks at how playworkers can support play, and the tensions that exist in the playworker's job. It finishes with a brief introduction to the playwork sector.

A play episode ...

Have a look at the play scenario below. We will be returning to this as we proceed through the chapter, to help illustrate some of the theories and ideas.

Cherysse (aged 6), Jordan (aged 8) and Ruby (aged 8) are playing on the wide slide. Ruby slides down feet first, swirls around and hangs over the edge of the slide, peering at the bark at very close quarters. Suddenly she jerks away from the bark and squeals loudly and shrilly, 'Aaagghh!! Eeeuugghh! Worm!' 'Where?' says Cherysse, coming down the slide as fast as she can. 'There!' Both girls peer at the worm. Jordan joins them and, finding a small stick, begins to poke the worm. 'Anya! Come here!' shouts Ruby.

Anya, the playworker, comes over and also peers at the worm. She makes interested noises, but says nothing. She listens and watches. After a while, she peels back the large mat at the foot of the slide, to reveal the damp and compacted bark which is teeming with creepy crawlies. Again, the children initially squeal and recoil; again, they return to inspect the creatures at close quarters. More sticks are gathered and more poking ensues. The children dangle worms on sticks in each other's faces, chase each other, throw the worms at each other. Anya goes into the building and comes out with collecting jars, magnifying glasses, plastic spades and rakes. For a while, the game becomes 'see who can collect the most'. Jordan fills his jar with worms, centipedes and earwigs, then watches them crawling and climbing over each other in the confined space, rapt, for some time. Sometimes he shows Anya or asks a question. Ruby dispenses with the stick and picks up worms with her fingers, hunting for the biggest and fattest, continuing to dangle the worms in the faces of

> *(Continued)*
>
> children and adults alike. Cherysse goes back to playing on the slide, calling out on each descent, 'Wiggly wormy, wiggly wormy, wiggly wormy, wiggly wormy, how many have you got now?' This develops into a sing-song ritual.
>
> Eventually, interest in the worms and other creatures subsides, and they are abandoned, together with the equipment, in favour of the next game.

Play is a many-splendoured thing

Anyone who has come into contact with children will recognise this behaviour as play. The squealing, the fascination, the poking, the collecting, the use of worms to scare others, these are all things that children have done across time and across countries (although each country offers its own creatures). What is it that makes this behaviour play?

From this small episode, we might say that play is the way in which children explore the world and their relationship with it; we might say that play is spontaneous, or that it combines many different forms (physical, social, exploratory, sensory, communicative).

Of course, this is only one example of how children play. The early Greek philosophers (who considered that the gods played with humans) classified three forms of play:

- *agon* – games of conflict and competition that represented real wars, such as javelin throwing, archery and other competitive games
- *mimesis* – games of pretence and imitation such as theatre, dance and other forms of symbolic and role play
- *chaos* – games of chance such as dice, cards and other forms of fortune-telling and gambling (Sparioso, 1989).

Since then, there have been a number of classifications of the many different types of play, including one aimed specifically at playworkers (Hughes, 2002) which lists 16 different play types gathered from the literature on play.

The many forms of play and its complexity are reflected in the great difficulty academics have in arriving at a satisfactory all-encompassing definition of this peculiar phenomenon. Each time a defining characteristic of play has been suggested, it has been challenged. For example, many people say that play is fun, but this may not always be the case, particularly if one player's fun is at the expense of someone else, as in teasing. Similarly, play is often described as being voluntary or freely chosen; again, this may not be the case for those for whom belonging to the group and going along with the group leader's wishes is more important than freedom of choice.

Perhaps the one defining characteristic of play is that it is not real, although there is always a relationship with the real world. In the worm scenario, the children play with the worms in a number of different ways: they explore them, and they also use them in playful and symbolic ways to scare each other. The worms are real enough, but their use in the games is at times symbolic of something more dangerous and scary, even perhaps mythological.

Play can be social or solitary, boisterous or contemplative, with or without props, structured or free-flowing. It is more a *way* of doing something rather than a specific activity; for example, there is a big difference between playing at schools and being at school for real.

Within the playwork sector a number of definitions exist, and they all broadly agree that for the purposes of playwork, play is seen as a process that is *freely chosen, personally directed and intrinsically motivated* (that is, children engage in it for its own sake rather than for any specific purpose or end product) (Hughes, 1996: 16). As we have seen, these characteristics can be challenged; however, they serve playworkers well in that they emphasise the purpose of playwork as being to support play according to these characteristics rather than directing, controlling or teaching children.

Play theories

Much of the basis for modern theorising on play stems from what are known as the 'Classic Theories' of play. These theories emerged at the turn of the nineteenth and twentieth centuries and were mostly influenced by theories of evolution being developed by Charles Darwin and others. One example is Karl Groos's Practice Theory, which suggested that play allows children to practise and adapt the skills needed for survival as an adult. Another is Granville Stanley Hall's Recapitulation Theory, which suggested that children play through the evolutionary stages of their human ancestors (Frost et al., 2005).

How might these theories apply to the worms scenario? Practice theorists might say that the children were developing and practising fine motor skills and co-ordination, or learning which creatures might present a threat. The Recapitulationists would say that the children were replaying the foraging behaviour of hunter-gatherers.

Alongside these evolutionary theories were those from philosophy which linked play to creativity and culture (for example, Friedrich von Schiller, cited in Frost et al., 2005). This cultural theme was later explored by the Dutch historian Johann Huizinga (1938, cited in Frost et al., 2005) who saw play as serving social and cultural functions for children and adults alike. This line of study has continued today with children's folklorists and anthropologists. It has been suggested that children have their own cultures that are defined by and through their playing. We can see this in our worms scenario in the song-making, chasing and scaring games that they invent.

Alongside the biological and cultural studies of play were psychoanalytic theories, initially developed by Sigmund Freud in the early twentieth century. Freud saw play as a mechanism through which children could fulfil desires that would ordinarily be socially unacceptable (for example, the small child venting her jealousy on a doll rather than on her newborn baby brother) or to play through events that are frightening or traumatic in some way (Frost et al., 2005). Perhaps the children in the worms scenario are using their play as a way of coming to terms with their fear of slimy and creepy creatures; certainly it took Ruby some time before she could summon up the courage to pick up the worms with her hands.

Towards the middle of the twentieth century interest in child development grew, particularly from developmental psychologists, and the work of people such as Jean Piaget (1951), who linked forms of play to the stages of cognitive development, and Lev Vygotsky (1978), who placed cognitive development within a social context, became highly influential.

Current theorising on play

Contemporary Western theorising on children's play has evolved from these earlier theories. It also reflects the way we think about childhood and children.

Today, play is studied within many academic disciplines across the natural and social sciences (as well as in the arts and literature) including biology, ethology (the study of animals in their natural surroundings), psychology, education, leisure studies, history, philosophy, sociology, folklore and various combinations of these. The playwork sector is also developing its own theorising on play and the role of adults in supporting children's play (Brown, 2003; Hughes, 2001; Sturrock and Else, 2005).

The great play scholar, Brian Sutton-Smith (1997), notes our adult need to show how play is somehow useful or has a purpose. He identifies a number of 'rhetorics' of play: ways of theorising that reflect the interests and biases of particular disciplines.

The progress rhetoric

Perhaps the most familiar of these rhetorics is what Sutton-Smith calls the 'progress rhetoric'. The idea that play helps children learn and develop has become so much a part of our understanding of childhood that we tend to accept it unquestioningly, perhaps to the exclusion of any other theorising about children's play. Children are naturally curious and have an innate propensity to play; using play as an aid to learning can be very effective within early years education settings and has been explored in the core sections of this book (Sections 3, 4, 5 and 6). However, playworkers also need to consider other perspectives on play.

As adults, we no longer experience playing in the same way as children do. Paradoxically, in one sense we know too much to understand empathically the naive explorations, the dead ends, the misunderstandings, the fantastical myths and the quirky interweaving of the real and the not-real that we witness when we watch children at play. We are often tempted to provide the short cut to the adult, rational, 'right' answer, especially if what we see makes us uncomfortable. Often, we interpret symbolic play behaviours literally, and if these do not fit in with our idea of how children should behave, we correct or terminate the playing. For example, we might think that the children should not be cruel to the worms, or that it is not nice to scare each other with them.

Playing is much more than just practising skills that will be needed in later adult life. The children playing with worms might have been learning about minibeasts, but what else was going on here? Have a look back at the scenario now, and consider these questions:

- Why do you think the girls screamed at the worms? Were they really scared? If so, why did they then peer at them so closely?
- Why do you think the children poked the worms with sticks?
- Why did they want to collect them in jars, or throw them at people?
- Why did Cherysse make up a song about collecting worms?

Adaptive variability

The ethologist Robert Fagen (1976) posed the question, if the purpose of play is to learn specific behaviours, why not just learn them?

Sutton-Smith (1997: 224) suggests that play facilitates what he calls 'adaptive variability and adaptive potentiation'. Creativity, spontaneity, inventiveness, redundancy and adaptability are key characteristics of play that help children develop a whole repertoire of broad and adaptive (as opposed to specialised and rigid) responses to situations. In addition, modern brain-imaging technology shows that first-hand experiences such as playing are key to the development of synaptic connections in the brain (Frost et al., 2005).

Fantasy and pretend

The focus on a simple link between play and development also poses questions for the role of fantasy and pretend in children's play. As we saw earlier, Freud thought that such playing could help children gain a sense of control over events in their lives. My discussions with playworkers have provided much anecdotal evidence for this. For example, the scenes on television following the attacks on the World Trade Center in New York in September 2001 gave rise to much tower building and knocking down in children's play in the following weeks. Similarly, following the invasion of Iraq, I was working with a group of playworkers many of whom were running clubs in garrison towns where the children had family members serving in Iraq. There was a marked increase in war play during these times.

These are the kinds of play that can make us feel uncomfortable. If we interpret play behaviour as indicative of future adult behaviour, then we may feel the need to correct or redirect what might appear to be aggressive or violent play. Yet the theorising of the psychoanalysts suggests that there is a purpose to playing through such trauma in order to understand and 'play out' any anxieties.

The therapeutic aspects of play, and the ways in which playworkers can support these, form the basis of work by Gordon Sturrock and Perry Else (2005). They suggest that play is more than energy spent; it is cyclical and involves both the behaviour that we see and processes in the mind of the child that we cannot see. They suggest that children are driven to express deeply symbolic material in their play. It is the completion of the play cycle and the expression of this material that can be therapeutic. Within this understanding of play, playworkers can engage with children at points within the cycle to support the expression of this material. A brief introduction to the concepts of 'psycholudics' (the study of the mind at play) can be found at www.ludemos.co.uk.

In addition, children often use the relatively safe 'frame' of playing to test boundaries and to take risks. Often the consequences of such risk-taking in play are less than they would be in real life, for example, in play fighting (although with physical risk of course the risk of injury is very real). The importance of risk in play is beginning to be recognised, although the professional judgements that playworkers need to take are not straightforward (Play Safety Forum, 2002).

The here and now of childhood

Another consequence of only linking play to development is that it leads us to look on children as adults-in-waiting and allows us to gloss over the here and now of childhood. Childhood is more than a period of waiting and practising before we reach mature, rational and competent adulthood. We should not forget that children are human beings, not only human becomings (Mayall, 2003). If play does nothing else, it makes children better at playing, with all the benefits for friendships in the here and now that that brings, and in learning how to be a child (Sutton-Smith, 1997).

This very brief and superficial run through a number of different ways of theorising play shows just how complex it is. We move on now to consider what all this might mean for playworkers.

What do we mean by 'playwork'?

Playworkers work with school-aged children in their out-of-school time. They work in a number of different dedicated play settings, including:

- adventure playgrounds
- play centres
- out-of-school clubs
- play buses
- holiday playschemes
- breakfast clubs
- hospitals
- schools
- city farms
- parks and streets.

The playworker's primary role is to support children's play. Playworkers do have other aspects to their jobs, of course. For example, they have administrative, teamwork and managerial duties; they need to carry out their work with due regard to the relevant legislation; they need to be aware of their responsibilities regarding health and safety, child protection, equal opportunities, registration and inspection and so on. These aspects of

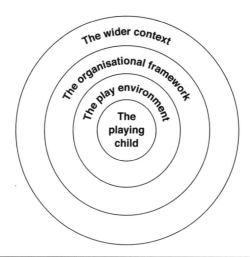

Figure 25.1 *The Manchester circles*

the playworker's job are similar to other work with children and young people, although from the perspective of placing play at the heart of everything they do.

A useful model for illustrating this focus for playwork is one devised as the basis for a quality assurance system for play projects in Manchester (Lester and Russell, 2002). The model is heavily adapted from Bronfenbrenner's (1979) ecological theory of human development. The model consists of four concentric circles (see Figure 25.1)

- the playing child
- the play environment
- the organisational framework
- the wider context.

The first principle of this model is that it is play centred (which is perhaps different from being child centred): the influence from the inner circle (the playing child) on circles two and three is stronger than the influences in the other direction. What this means is that the policies, procedures and practices of the play setting should be founded on a commitment to supporting children's play, rather than children's play being constrained by policies and working practices.

Playwork: not as easy as it sounds

As we have said, the primary role of the playworker is to support children's play. Once we start to think about this, given what we know about play, it is not hard to see that this raises a few problems and contradictions. If the accepted playwork understanding of play is that it is a process that is freely chosen, personally directed and intrinsically motivated (Hughes, 1996) then any involvement from us as adults risks 'adulterating' (Hughes, 2001; Sturrock and Else, 2005) these characteristics and therefore not supporting but constraining play. On the other hand, playworkers are responsible for the physical and emotional safety and security of children in their care, so it is likely that there will be times when we have to intervene to prevent harm. The relationships between playworkers and children are complex: playworkers are adults with all the power and status that this brings; we also have our own beliefs and values and may find some of the ways that children play disturbing or even offensive.

Have a look back at the opening scenario and consider these questions:

- How do you feel about children poking worms with sticks, throwing them at each other, collecting them in jars?
- How might you have responded if you had been the playworker?

In order for children to be able to play, playworkers need to create and maintain an environment that supports this. This is the second of the Manchester circles introduced earlier, which draws on work by Hughes (2001) and is further divided into:

- the physical environment (the layout and landscaping, the equipment and materials, and so on)
- the affective environment (the atmosphere and the feel of the setting, the rules and rituals, etc.)
- the role of the playworker.

Much has been written on the design and maintenance of rich environments for children's play (for example, Hughes, 2001; NPFA et al., 2000; and see Figure 25.2). A key role for playworkers is to try to establish an atmosphere where play is respected, where children expect to be able to play rather than be directed, taught or entertained by adults, or prevented from playing by other children.

A good play setting may sometimes look rather chaotic to an outsider, and may feel so to the playworkers at times as well. Some playworkers find this aspect of the job difficult. Although there is a place in play settings for structured activities, they should form only a small part of the overall picture and often some children will choose not to take part in them, preferring to do whatever comes to mind at that time, or perhaps starting off on the activity and then turning this into some other play experience. Playworkers should accept this and their planning should be flexible and allow for spontaneity and creativity.

What about planning? Often playworkers say that they produce activity programmes, knowing that they are likely to change. Perhaps an alternative approach could be to make the planning of the overall environment (both physical and affective) a conscious and recorded process. Structured activities, together with special events, trips and outings, will have their place in this, and the rationale can still be based on supporting rather than directing children's play. See also Chapters 5, 7, 9, 12 and 18.

Camps, holidays, special trips, outings, yearly or seasonal rituals and celebrations.

Alongside the general resources available to children on a regular basis, there will be other resources and specific activities that are used occasionally or at the spontaneous request of the children.

Planning of the whole physical environment to include design, equipment, resources and materials that stimulate and support a wide range of play experiences. This should include a variety of space and landscapes, outdoor and indoor spaces, wild areas, different heights and textures, a range of flexible materials in abundant supply (including scrap materials), loose parts, natural materials, tools, access to the elements, opportunities for the full range of sensory experiences (sight, sound, touch, smell and taste). Introduction of new parts regularly; frequent modification of the environment by children in their play and by adults in order to support the children's play.

Activities may happen spontaneously, such as playing particular games, or a large group deciding to make something or do something with resources available or provided at the time by the playworkers.

Planning of the affective environment to ensure that children feel respected and that their play is seen as important by the adults and children within the play space. A few, general, flexible, context-bound rules; rites and rituals that help define and develop the culture of the setting, mostly emerging from the children's play but sometimes by the playworkers.

Figure 25.2   *The playwork planning pyramid*

The planning pyramid in Figure 25.2 (Russell, 2004) is adapted from an original from Nottingham Play Forum (1994), using material from Lester and Russell (2002). The base and largest section shows how the general environment is planned to support children's free play; the middle section refers to what might happen frequently but not every day; and the top section describes possible one-off or special events.

Back to the worms again ...

Think back to the opening scenario and consider again the actions of Anya, the playworker. This episode is an example of spontaneous play that emerged, stimulated by something Ruby saw. There was no 'minibeasts' activity on a programme, although the play setting did have the equipment to support the children's exploration. Anya became involved in the activity when invited; her response was to extend the opportunities for the children to explore, but not to direct in any way. It only lasted about 20 minutes before the children lost interest and went on to something else.

This was an activity that was not specifically planned, but the overall physical and affective environment was such that the children were able to follow their own interests in their own way, supported by the playworker.

The playwork sector

Research (SkillsActive, 2004) suggests that there are approximately 100,000 people working in the playwork sector in England, 70 per cent in face-to-face roles and 30 per cent in development, management, training and other facilitative roles. Play Wales, Play Scotland and Play Board Northern Ireland act as co-ordinating organisations in their respective countries. In England, play policy, information and research is co-ordinated by the Children's Play Council, who have also recently launched Play England, initially to provide an infrastructure for the BIG Lottery Fund Children's Play Programme. The SkillsActive Playwork Unit co-ordinates playwork education and training. Playwork has National Occupational Standards at levels 2, 3 and 4 which underpin National Vocational Qualifications and vocationally related qualifications in playwork as well as the sector-endorsed foundation degree. A few universities offer higher education playwork programmes.

Developing your own playwork practice

Reflective practice is a fundamental element of good playwork practice. Three ways to develop your reflective practice are suggested here.

1. Observation: take a step back to observe children playing. In playwork, observation is used to develop playworkers' understanding of play, not to assess an individual child's development or behaviour. Focusing on the range of play types (Hughes, 2002) in which children engage can help you develop your understanding and also make judgements about how successful the setting is in supporting the full range of play types.
2. Understand yourself: notice how you feel emotionally about different children and different ways of playing. It is important to recognise your own reactions as this will influence your playwork style.

3. Critical incidents: critical incident analysis is a well-used tool in reflective practice. A critical incident is one that is particularly significant: sometimes this will be when something goes wrong, sometimes it will be a particularly good moment in a session, or when a particular child plays in a particular way for the first time. Reflect on your emotional and also your behavioural response to the situation. What was good about it? What might you have done better?

In conclusion

In this chapter I have aimed to show that there is more to play than a simple and direct link to development and learning. Children are human beings in their own right, not mere adults-in-waiting, and they engage in play for a number of reasons including building their own social lives as children, therapeutic, cultural and recreational reasons, as well as exploration and understanding. Given the diversity of play, its unpredictability and its centrality in the lives of children, the role of the playworker is complex and sometimes contradictory. Playworkers use their understanding of play to create a physical and affective environment that supports as wide a range of play experiences as possible.

Further reading

Brown, F. (ed.) (2003) *Playwork Theory and Practice*. Buckingham: Open University Press.
An edited text that brings together some of the leading names in playwork to present a theoretical basis and a historical and contemporary context for playwork practice.

Frost, J.L., Wortham, S.C. and Reifel, S. (2005) *Play and Child Development*. 2nd edition. Upper Saddle River, NJ: Pearson Merrill Prentice Hall.
A comprehensive guide to theorising on play and its links to development.

Hughes, B. (2001) *Evolutionary Playwork and Reflective Analytic Practice*. London: Routledge.
An in-depth exploration of one particular approach to playwork, from an author who has extensive experience of face-to-face adventure playground work and also writing on play and playwork.

Hughes, B. (2002) *A Playworker's Taxonomy of Play Types*. 2nd edition. London: PlayLink.
A description of 16 different types of play, drawn from the literature, and how playworkers can recognise and support each type.

National Playing Fields Association (NPFA) Children's Play Council and Play Link (2000) *Best Play: What Play Provision Should do for Children*. London: NPFA.
A useful summary of theorising on play and translating this into effective play provision. Includes eight objectives for play provision and a summary of play types. Available online at www.ncb.org.uk/cpc; click on 'books and reports'.

Sturrock, G. and Else, P. (eds) (2005) *Therapeutic Playwork Readers One (1995–2000) and Two (2000–2005)*. Sheffield: Ludemos Associates.
A collection of papers written on psycholudics (the study of the mind at play) and therapeutic playwork. Includes the seminal 'Colorado Paper' which introduces the concepts of the play cycle and the hierarchy of intervention.

DOING PRACTITIONER RESEARCH

26

Guy Roberts-Holmes

Dr Guy Roberts-Holmes is a Senior Lecturer in the Faculty of Education at Canterbury Christ Church University. His doctoral studies were based upon issues of inclusion and participation in The Gambia, West Africa. His research interests include early childhood educare and research methodologies.

Aims

To develop understanding of:

- [ ] what is meant by practitioner research
- [ ] the importance of reflection
- [ ] and know how to do an action research project.

Sam, a newly qualified Reception class teacher was in the habit of placing reading books on the carpet for the children to look at together before she took the register. One morning as she sat observing the children, she overhead two boys talking together. One said to the other 'We're not girls – so we don't read. We like to play football, don't we'. His friend agreed adding 'yeah I'm not a girl so why should I read?' The boys did not realise that their teacher was listening so the comments were genuine and spontaneous. Sam saw reading as central to school life and was shocked that the children had only just begun their school careers and already they held such negative views about themselves as learners. She wondered how this could be and what could she do to change their attitudes? For Sam this was a critical incident which led to her action research project aimed at improving boys' attitudes to literacy in her Reception class.

What is practitioner research?

Practitioner research is also known as action research because it is centrally concerned with a process of development, change and improvement. Practitioner research is an integral part of your critical professional development (Schon, 1983). With practitioner research you and your setting are the key to the action. Practitioner research involves you asking questions about your past and current practice. What is it in your professional situation that you wish to change and make better? What do you want to improve about your practice? This process of thinking about your practice is known as reflection and is central to the process of practitioner research. At the centre of practitioner research is a desire on your part to change something about your practice in your setting. This ongoing process can be shown in Figure 26.1.

Practitioner research is an ongoing process rather than a one-off event. It involves a constant process of reflecting upon your actions and rethinking your actions in the light of your reflection. One way that practitioners can reflect upon critical incidents such as Sam's, at the beginning of this chapter, is by keeping a journal or diary. Practitioners note down their feelings and thoughts concerning a critical incident. In a trusting space they then share these notes with their critical friend.

This process of critical self-reflection demands a 'safe' space for practitioners (Leeson, 2004). In order to be honest and open about your practice you need to work with a 'critical friend' who can both support and challenge you. A critical friend is somewhat different

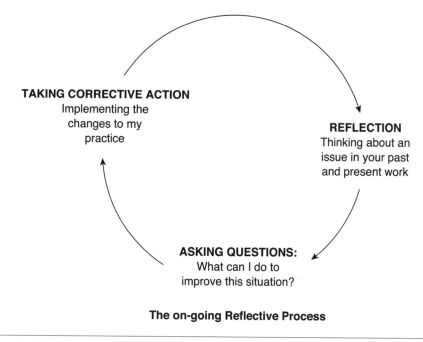

The on-going Reflective Process

Figure 26.1   *The ongoing reflective process*

from your mentor. A mentor by virtue of their experience, knowledge and skills is in a more powerful position than you, but a critical friend ought to be your equal in terms of knowledge and experience. When you talk in such a 'safe' space you and your critical friend can co-reflect what you feel is happening in your context and how to improve the situation. 'Meaningful, reflective conversations can sustain and nourish us. They can raise individual and collective consciousness. Above all else they involve a discussion of values. This is at the heart of the improvement process' (Ghaye and Ghaye, 1998: 122).

E X E R C I S E   2 6 . 1

Think of a recent event or incident which has happened to you at work. Spend a few minutes noting down all the details of the event.

Why are you so interested in this event?
Why did the event occur?

(Continued)

EXERCISE 26.1 (CONTINUED)

How does the event impact upon your personal and professional life?
What does the incident tell you about your values and principles?
What do you want to do about it now?
Are there other ways of thinking about the event?
What is the wider context of the event?

Sit with your critical friend and get them to ask further questions about your story. They might ask the following:

- Can you further clarify the aims of the project?
- What key words could you use to describe your research focus?
- What do you hope to find out?

Reflect upon the conversation you have with your friend and add this to your personal reflective diary.

How will you benefit from doing practitioner research?

There are many potential benefits from carrying out your practitioner research. Practitioners who have carried out action research in their contexts have found the following positive strengths to develop:

- a deeper understanding of their values and principles
- increased professionalism
- improved performance in the classroom
- developed skills and knowledge
- increased theoretical knowledge and engagement
- developed self-respect, power and self-esteem
- increased respect for children
- increased awareness of your potential
- increased awareness of the wider contexts in which you work
- enhancement of collaboration skills with children, parents and colleagues
- increased confidence with research skills.

Practitioner research is enjoyable, rewarding and powerful. It can give you a sense of purpose and a goal to achieve at work. It is sociable in that it demands you collaborate and talk with your colleagues and the children about the research. Self-reflection is part of the process of taking responsibility. The more you take responsibility for your actions the better you feel about yourself, and the more your learn. Action research can become a positive cycle of personal and professional development.

The following list summarises the approximate order which your practitioner research might follow:

- identifying your research topic
- carrying out your literature review
- writing your research questions
- planning the activities with your critical friend
- collecting your data or evidence
- analysing your data
- reflecting on the research's outcomes with your critical friend
- sharing your findings
- developing your research.

Some possible issues to research in your setting

It is important for you to decide what you want to research. This is *your* research project and it is important that it connects with *you* personally and emotionally as well as professionally. You will be spending some considerable time carrying out your research so it is important that you make the right choice of topic for *you*. Perhaps something meaningful happened in your setting some time ago and you have always wanted to find out more about it. Now is your chance.

EXERCISE 26.2

Which of the following research topics interest you? What personal and professional reasons make you interested in this particular topic?

- What is creativity? How can I get the children to be more creative?
- What are the barriers to parental involvement in the life of the school? What strategies can be used to encourage parental involvement?
- What do the children understand about healthy food? What are the influences upon children's eating habits? Does teaching about healthy food make a difference to children's eating habits?
- What is meant by citizenship education? What impact has citizenship education had upon the children's lives?
- How do children form friendships at school? What do children understand by friendship? Do friendship groups change? If so why? How does friendship affect performance at school?
- What is the Italian 'Reggio Emelia' approach to education? How feasible is this approach to my classroom?

How to write your research questions

Your overall research questions are different from the specific field research questions which you might ask in an interview. The overall research questions will guide your study throughout. In the light of your reading, your data and further reflection, you may wish to revisit and refine your research questions.

You need to try to make your research questions specific enough for you to be able to focus upon your area of investigation. Your research questions should also be broad enough to allow you to develop your research in unforeseen ways. Writing your research questions is a bit like Goldilocks tasting the bear's porridge. Some research questions are too broad and therefore not sufficiently focused, achievable or realistic. Other research questions are too specific and therefore might rapidly lose their interest and not allow for the wider context. Still other research questions are just right – they are both sufficiently specific and focused and, at the same time, are broad enough to retain interest and encompass new ideas.

Example: Boys' literacy in the early years

Sam's critical incident reported at the beginning of the chapter led her to ask the following four overall research questions:

What were boys interested in doing in Sam's class?
Which literacy activities were boys involved in at school and at home?
How might some boys' attitudes to reading be improved?
What were the wider issues of boy's engagement at school?

The above research questions are specific, doable and achievable. The questions are also broad enough to be significant and important. They are currently a focus of much government and school thinking. The research is timely and significant and will sustain Sam's interest in her research topic.

EXERCISE 26.3

What is it that you wish to find out more about?
Can you be more specific?
Is the topic doable?
Will there be literature concerning your topic?
Can you write four questions concerning your research area? Try to make a couple of the questions specific, narrow and focused and a couple of the questions broader and more general.

What are the ethical considerations of your research?

There is a range of ethical issues for any piece of research. Ethics are centrally concerned with the attitudes of the researcher (Roberts-Holmes, 2005). An attitude of respect for all the people involved in your research project is essential. You must ensure that the respondents you talk with and interview, both the children and the adults, clearly understand what it is that you want them to do. This is known as *informed consent*. Informed consent refers to the research participants voluntarily agreeing to participate with you based upon complete disclosure of all relevant information (National Children's Bureau, 2000). So you should carefully explain before you interview the children and adults exactly what you want them to do, your expectations and the time it will take. As well as verbally explaining this to the children and adults, you can write it down to read out to them and they can take the information away for their parents/friends. Some children who agree to be involved in research one day, may choose not to participate in it another day. This is frustrating but you need to respect their decision to withdraw from the research at any time.

You must be aware that your research may potentially raise difficulties for the children or the adults, especially if your research is in a sensitive and delicate area. Emotional and personal harm may result inadvertently from you asking questions that cause the respondent to be upset either in the setting or later on. You need to be sensitive to this possibility as you carry out your research. Run through your research and think of any way in which it might inadvertently be upsetting. Sam was aware that some of the boys did not have their Dads living with them so she did not ask directly about male role models that the boys had at home.

You have a responsibility to check out your research with your line managers and/or headteacher before you begin. These people are known as the *gatekeepers*. They are ultimately responsible for the well-being of all children and staff. If they think your research is in anyway problematic, they may make suggestions as to how you can amend your research.

If you are collecting drawings and artwork from the children, you must ask their permission. Perhaps you can scan in the pictures to your work and return the originals to the children. If using the children's photographs, these need to be stored in a secure area and destroyed after a certain length of time.

The National Children's Bureau also draws our attention to the issue of confidentiality in research. The National Children's Bureau (2003: 3) state the following:

> We believe that there must be limits to any guarantee of confidentiality or anonymity in situations where child protection is an issue. Where a child or young person divulges that they or others are at risk of significant harm or where the researcher observes or receives evidence of incidents likely to cause to serious harm, the researcher has a *duty* to take steps to protect the child or other children.

Respondents including children and young people should be told at the outset, and as necessary during the research, that confidentiality cannot be guaranteed if 'difficult' information arises. If, after discussion with the child, the researcher decides it is necessary to inform others – hopefully with the consent of the child – the researcher must ensure that the child has immediate support and is kept fully informed (Masson, 2000: 42).

How to carry out your literature review

In your literature review you can use as many of the following sources of information available:

- the Internet
- radio
- television
- professional magazines
- books
- research journals.

Searching your topic of interest through a powerful search engine such as www.google.com can often lead to a wide range of material. At the end of this chapter there are listed some specific websites that you might find useful. Keep your search specific to your topic area. Your reading may help to reframe and refocus your questions. Do not get bogged down in the detail of the literature. Follow your interests and read what is relevant and interesting to you and your topic area. You will be surprised as to your knowledge in the area already.

The literature that you read should help you to further your understanding of what is already known in your area of interest. As you carry out your literature search you might be wondering to yourself 'what have I got to offer in this area that hasn't already been done?' The answer is that nobody has ever carried out your research questions in your setting before. Everybody has different life experiences and will perceive the same topic in different ways. Your setting and its children are unique and so is your research.

How to answer your research questions

Now that you have decided upon your research questions you are in a position to actually collect the data or evidence. By using a variety of the research methods below you will gain a lot of evidence to answer your research questions. It is important to remember that the quality of the data you collect is more important than the number of ways you collect data. Researchers primarily collect two forms of data. The interpretative researcher will try to get inside individuals and institutions to understand particular situations. They will use qualitative data to attempt to illuminate specific insights and subtleties of human motivations and social interactions. Practitioner research often involves looking to create meanings using rich descriptions and narratives. The practitioner researcher is attempting to professionally develop their expertise through looking closely at specific contexts. Positivist researchers, on the other hand, will gather large amounts of data in order to make generalisations. Quantitative data is collected in order to be measured and represented by numbers (Koshy, 2005).

Some possible methods

- Your literature search – specific legislation and government documents are a source of data.
- Participant and non-participant observations in your setting.
- Interviewing and consulting various stakeholders including colleagues, children, parents and governors.
- Giving the children cameras to take pictures with.
- Questionnairing the stakeholders.
- Using the children's drawings and artwork.

Which of the above research methods lend themselves more towards quantitative data collection and which towards qualitative data collection?

EXERCISE 26.4

Read through your research questions. Under each research question note down exactly what you need to find out in order to answer those questions.

- What methods might be appropriate to collect the information you need to answer those questions?
- What is the timescale for your data collection?
- When will you know that you have collected sufficient material?

Your critical friend is important since they can offer objectivity to the situation and ask questions which you might not have thought of. Together you can discuss the most appropriate methods of collecting the data, talk through the data you do collect and discuss what is significant and relevant to the research questions. As well as helping practically with the research, your critical friend's objectivity is important in ensuring the research's validity (see below). Sam agreed to meet with her critical friend once a week to share and discuss the data.

Observations

One of the best ways of making practitioner observations is known as participant observation. This is where you, the practitioner researcher, are involved with the children in their activities. For example, Sam, who is investigating boys' literacy, decided to bring a range of football magazines and stories to read with the children. She noted the boys' reactions to these stories as she read them. She tape-recorded the discussion at the same time. As soon as she had finished the activity with the boys she noted down how the activity went and what the boys had said. In this way she was both being practitioner and a researcher. As she was participating in the activity she was reflecting upon what she was doing.

Another form of observation is non-participant observation. Sam sat to one side of the class while her critical friend taught the children. Sam made structured observations of the boys. She wrote down everything that the boys actually did over a period of an hour and how many literacy events they were engaged with. On another occasion, with the boys' permission she videoed the boys in the classroom. She later watched and analysed this video with her critical friend.

Listening to children

Recent government legislation such as *Every Child Matters* (DfES, 2005b) and the Children Bill (2004) stipulate that children should be consulted about and involved in decisions that affect them. Children have a right to participate and to be included in your action research in the classroom. Children are sensitive, intelligent and socially competent, and are the experts in understanding their own lives (Langstead, 1994). Children's perspectives can offer tremendous creative insight into your research topic. Children's voices can be expressed in many different creative and artistic ways. Interviews, their artwork and their photos are just some of the ways in which practitioners can listen to children.

> If we, adults, think of children as powerful, they act powerful. If we treat them as powerful, they rise to our expectations. Indeed they can blow the tops of our heads off in terms of what they can do, if we choose to stand aside and let them, and see them in their true colours. (Drummond, 2002: 3)

EXERCISE 26.5

In what ways does your research allow children to surprise and astound you with their abilities, intelligence and social competency?

Giving children cameras to take pictures with is a useful research method to use with children. Sam asked the boys to take pictures of activities they liked doing in the classroom and their favourite spaces both inside and outside the classroom. The boys also took the cameras home and took pictures of their favourite activities at home. The pictures were developed and the boys were able to talk about why they had taken their pictures. With the boys' permission Sam tape-recorded the discussion. Sam learnt a tremendous amount about the boys' interests through this exercise. She was able to see the many opportunities for literacy development in the boys' lives. Similarly Sam asked the boys to draw pictures of what they liked doing at school and at home. She used these pictures as a basis for talking with the boys about their favourite activities. Again she used a tape recorder so as not to miss any of the subtlety or finer points of the boy's comments. It is difficult to have a conversation and write at the same time.

Questionnaires

Finally, Sam wrote a simple open-ended questionnaire which she sent home with the boys for their parents to complete. Included with the questionnaire was a letter explaining the purposes of the research. The questionnaires asked the parents to note down any activities which involved literacy, such as reading, looking at picture books, playing on the computer and reading comics. Who was at home to hear the boys read? Was it other adults and siblings? How often did the boys read? Sam's questionnaire had an unexpected benefit. A mother came in to discuss the questionnaire and wanted to know all about the research. Sam explained why she was carrying out the research and what she had learnt so far. The parent wanted to be more involved and made some observations in the class using the observation schedule. The parent also joined in on several of the weekly discussions with Sam's critical friend. This added further validity to the research.

How to ensure validity of your research

Your research will have greater validity if you have involved your colleagues and listened and included a range of perspectives about the same issue. Sam's research has increased its conviction and validity by including children's, teachers' and parents' voices concerning the same issue. This process is known as methodological triangulation. Triangulation can be achieved through using a range of different research methods, as outlined in the previous section, and a range of different stakeholder voices.

E X E R C I S E   2 6 . 6

In what ways can you ensure that your research is triangulated and valid?

How to analyse the evidence you have collected

Your research project will have created a lot of different forms of evidence. You now have to make sense of this range of material. Look back to your initial research questions and ensure the data you use actually helps to answer those questions. This will help to keep your analysis focused. Look at the evidence you have got and see what it says to you. You must tell the reader what you believe the data extract to be saying – what do you feel the data you have selected contributes to your arguments? During your analysis it is important to use the supporting literature that you have found. This literature can be used to support your findings in your context. It will also show you what is significant about your findings.

The key to your discussion is to tell a story of why you are using the data that you do use. Data cannot simply be left as it is – you must organise it.

- What themes do you think could help you to organise the data?
- What pieces of data fit under which category?
- What are the main arguments running through the whole discussion of your data?

You do not need to use all the interviews and all the children's work. You need to pick out those 'rich and juicy' pieces of the interviews, drawings, paintings and/or photos that really say something that seems important to your research topic. They offer something of interest to the research project. Within the context of the research project they are important and significant pieces of data. It is good to use a range of presentational devices such as graphs, pictures and diagrams. The variety of presenting your material makes it more attractive.

Sharing your key findings and further questions

Now that you have collected all your evidence and organised it into themes it is time to share your action research project with your colleagues. A central aim of sharing your practitioner research is to tell a story which is of interest to other practitioners who may want to learn from it (Koshy, 2005: 123). This process of sharing your findings is also a valuable opportunity for further reflection upon your topic and, thus, your professional development. Some practitioners present their findings to colleagues at staff meetings, conferences and as displays in the local teachers' centre or college. Here are some further ideas about how to share your research with your colleagues:

- narrating the research as a story with your critical friend
- a PowerPoint presentation or use overhead transparencies
- showing the rich pieces of data you have collected including artwork, video footage and the children's photographs
- an A4-sized summary sheet
- a set of open-ended questions which the staff can discuss
- inviting colleagues to discuss ways in which the ideas may be developed and built upon.

This will make your research topic and the ideas come alive for you and your colleagues. You might like to ask any of the parents along who showed particular interest in the research. Some practitioner researchers invite the children to the discussion and get them to share their work.

Sam decided that she would narrate the whole of her action research project with her critical friend in a staff meeting. Sam's evidence confirmed that a key aspect for boys' successful literacy was that the boys must be attracted to the books that they are given to read.

They wanted to read books and comics that featured recent films and Internet games such as *Spiderman, The Incredibles, Batman* and *Lilo and Stitch*. With this new knowledge Sam and her critical friend decided that they would make story sacks based upon these popular films and digital games. Video footage of the boys' disillusionment with literacy before the story sacks and their engaged passionate participation with the material in the story sacks brought the research alive.

Each story sack included the following;

- toys from the film
- soft toys from the film
- masks from the film
- the book of the film
- a comic from the film.

Sam used non-participant and participant observations to note down the impact that these story sacks had upon the boys' attitudes and practices to literacy. Generally the boys did some or all of the following with their story sacks:

- sitting and talking passionately together about the book and the comic
- acting out improvised scenes from the film using the clothes and masks
- taking photos of their improvised story and printing these out
- making a shared book with the photographs.

Copies of the book were made for the boys to decorate, read at school and take home to share with their families. Sam talked about upon how the attitudes to literacy among some of the boys greatly improved as a consequence of using these story sacks. Sam thought this was partly because the boys felt that they had been listened to by Sam and that she had taken their suggestions seriously and had acted upon them to produce the story sacks.

The discussion that developed with her colleagues became much broader than she had imagined was possible. The questions that arose included:

- How are boys perceived within the school system?
- How does this affect teachers' attitudes and assumptions and practices towards boys?
- How might boys' respond to these attitudes and assumptions?
- How can negative cycles be broken?

Colleagues began to reflect upon their own consciously and subconsciously held beliefs, biases and prejudices towards boys. Sam's presentation led to a colleague carrying out an action research project in her classroom. The focus of her research was the interactions she had with the boys in her classroom. Sam and her critical friend continued their interest in story sacks and began to look at the role of storytelling and drama in literacy with both the boys and the girls. In this way Sam continued her process of professional development and the action research spiral.

Further reading

Lancaster, Y. and Broadbent, V. (2003) *Listening to Young Children*. Maidenhead: Open University Press/McGraw-Hill.
This is an innovative and important resource for all early years practitioners who wish to creatively listen to children.

Nutbrown, C. (2002) *Research Studies in Early Childhood Education*. Stoke-on-Trent: Trentham Books.
This useful book written by early years practitioner researchers catalogues and describes fourteen early years action research projects.

Roberts-Holmes, G. (2005) *Doing Your Early Years Research Project: A Step by Step Guide*. London: Sage Publications.
This user-friendly 'how to guide' will take you through the complete process of your research project.

Useful websites

www.standards.dfes.gov.uk/teachers/professional-development – this website provides summaries of the latest research and useful practitioner case studies.
www.teach-tta.org.uk – this website carries practitioner research projects and useful advice for action research.
www.nfer.ac.uk – the National Foundation for Educational Research provides research summaries and has practitioner related projects.
www.ncb.org – the National Children's Bureau website has thorough and detailed guidelines of the ethics of working with children.

CHAPTER 27

EVERY CHILD MATTERS

Sue Owen

Sue Owen is Director of the Early Childhood Unit of the National Children's Bureau, and has worked in early years services since 1968 when she first volunteered in a pre-school playgroup. Her career has covered policy, planning and research in local authorities and voluntary organisations, and she has particular interests in childminding, the early years workforce and quality improvement processes.

Aims

To develop understanding of:

☐ the background to the development of the *Every Child Matters* agenda in current government policy

☐ the content of *Every Child Matters* and its effect on early years policy and strategy initiatives;

☐ and be in a position to consider how *Every Child Matters* affects practice with young children in a range of early childhood settings.

Introduction

> This is the beginning of a long journey, which will present challenges for all of us, but from which we must not flinch. We will be called upon to make common cause across professional boundaries and with reformed structures and services to create the means by which the needs, interests and welfare of children can be better protected and advanced. Underpinning this must be not just the resources but an attitude that reflects the value that our society places on children and childhood. (From the Introduction by the Chief Secretary to the Treasury to *Every Child Matters*; HM Treasury, 2003: 4)

The Green Paper, *Every Child Matters,* was launched on the 8 September 2003 by the Chief Secretary to the Treasury, an important indication that the Treasury, not just the service ministries of Education or Health, was behind this radical re-structuring of services for children. There was also a Foreward by the Prime Minister which hinted at one of the programme's central features, the creation of structures which would ensure service integration:

> we are proposing here a range of measures to reform and improve children's care – crucially, for the first time ever requiring local authorities to bring together in one place under one person services for children, and at the same time suggesting real changes in the way those we ask to do this work carry out their tasks on our and our children's behalf. (HM Treasury, 2003: 1)

The document brought together a number of strands of government work including a cross-cutting review of 'children at risk' which was part of the 2002 Spending Review, the Children and Young People's Unit's consultation on *Building a Strategy for Children and Young People,* which had asked young people themselves about their aspirations, and the government's response to the report of the inquiry by Lord Laming into the abuse and death of Victoria Climbié (DoH and Home Office, 2003). The Laming report detailed the fatal failures of the current structures to save the life of this child, and the government had worked for some time before its publication in order to provide an adequate response (DoH, 2003).

The Green Paper was issued as a consultation paper and responses to it were required by 1 December 2003. Subsequently two more documents have been published: *Every Child Matters: Next Steps* (DfES, 2004d), which provided a report on the consultation responses and an update on related legislation and strategies, and *Every Child Matters: Change for Children* (DfES, 2004a).

It is an ambitious strategy, aiming to do more than make recommendations to local authorities about how to improve their child protection systems. There had been many attempts to do this in the past, but children were still suffering at the hands of adults. *Every Child Matters* aims to reform the entire system of children's services in England, for all children, placing them within an ethos based on children's rights and entitlements and on positive outcomes for children. These are to be planned and delivered by local authorities according to their knowledge of the needs in their areas, but assessed and inspected nationally through performance indicators. It has been called a 'jigsaw' in which all policies for children need to be part of the eventual picture and it is seen as providing a new language of outcomes which all local authorities and the voluntary and private sector now have to speak.

There are five key outcomes which guide the strategy and which arose from the consultation with young people:

- being healthy – enjoying good physical and mental health and living a healthy lifestyle
- staying safe – being protected from harm and neglect, and growing up able to look after themselves
- enjoying and achieving – getting the most out of life and developing broad skills for adulthood
- making a positive contribution – to the community and to society, and not engaging in anti-social or offending behaviour
- economic well-being – overcoming socio-economic disadvantages to achieve their full potential in life.

Although these outcomes are for all children, the focus of the strategy is very firmly on children who are at risk, and the contributing policies and guidance are designed to ensure that local authorities narrow the gap between these children and those who do well.

The content of *Every Child Matters* and its effect on early years services

Every Child Matters: Next Steps was published six months after the Green Paper and outlined the responses which had been made to it and, in turn, the government's own response in the form of a new Children Bill and a programme of other strategies, including a wholesale reform of the children's workforce. The document explains that, although responses to the consultation were broadly favourable, there were some key areas of concern: the need to take a broader view of the services which should be included in the programme (for instance, to make sure that health, the police, schools and the voluntary sector were partners); that there should be more flexibility to enable local needs and circumstances to be taken into account; and the need for extra resources if such an ambitious programme were to be successful.

The main areas of reform included in the Children Bill were:

- embedding the five outcomes as the foundation of services for children and as the basis of partnership working
- the creation of a Children's Commissioner for England
- a requirement for local authorities to make partnership arrangements with other relevant agencies, including the voluntary sector, and reciprocal 'duties to co-operate' on some of those other agencies
- new duties on statutory agencies and those they contract with to have regard to the need to safeguard and promote the welfare of children
- a requirement for all local authorities to create a Local Safeguarding Children Board to replace the non-statutory Area Child Protection Committees
- encouragement for the creation of Children's Trusts and for pooled budgets with which to commission integrated services
- the requirement for local authorities to appoint a Director of Children's Services by 2008 (but with flexibility in how the role is defined)
- a similar requirement to identify a Lead Council Member for Children's Services
- the requirement to produce a Children and Young People's Plan, a single strategic plan for the local authority area which will replace most existing planning requirements
- creation of a new Framework for Inspection of Children's services and Joint Area Reviews of local authorities by two or more inspectorates in order to evaluate the extent to which children's services have been brought together to improve the well-being of children and young people
- provision of a framework for information sharing across agencies to ensure that children and their families can receive support as early as possible.

The wider strategy which was outlined in *Every Child Matters: Next Steps* included some key areas which relate to early years services and it was supported by the Ten Year Strategy for Childcare (HM Treasury et al., 2004) which was published six months later. Overall the government stressed the important role which early years services has to play in *Every Child Matters* and that they should be a priority area within the Children and Young People's Plans. A national outcomes framework against which local authorities would be assessed was also published (and has been updated at various times since) and local authorities are expected to use this as the basis for agreeing local priorities and planning change. Again, it was stated that the early years are extremely important in determining future outcomes and should be central to a local authority's plans to improve outcomes and to narrow the gap between children who do well and those who do not. However, the early years sector was immediately disappointed by this outcomes framework because, within a large and complex chart, the only outcome relating to early childhood provision is that children should be 'ready for school'. The suggested indicator for this is 'level of development reached at the end of the Foundation Stage, including narrowing the gap in the 20% most disadvantaged areas' (DfES, 2004a). The Early Childhood Forum lobbied for a change in wording to: 'Establishing rich foundations from birth for a life of learning, enjoyment and achievement' (McAuliffe, 2005: 23), but this was unsuccessful.

Less controversially, there is a specific emphasis on parenting, 'We need to shift away from associating parenting support with crisis interventions to a more consistent offer of parenting support throughout a child and young person's life' (DfES, 2004d: 26). This is to be supported through a £25 million Parenting Fund focused on the work of the voluntary and community sector and a system of nursery–parent links in 500 communities to introduce very young children to learning and books. The government's existing programme of expansion of early years services is also brought into the fold of *Every Child Matters* and a new project was announced to create Sure Start Children's Centres in the most disadvantaged areas, combining health, family and parenting support and information services with integrated childcare and education for children from birth onwards. A children's centre in every community had long been a campaigning slogan for early years organisations and it seemed as if the government had finally got the message.

Because the term 'integration' is used so loosely in policy discussions, it is worth considering exactly what it covers in this new programme. Sometimes it relates to the co-location of the full range of services which families with young children might need to use, as in 'Integrated services for small children and their families facilitate opportunities for early multi-agency intervention where families are facing difficulties and children might experience risk' (ibid.: 27). There is also the issue of integrating childcare and education within any individual early years setting, a process which has long been promoted by early years organisations but which is still hard to define and realise in practice. The government's initial use of the term 'educare' was not popular and has been dropped, although it is very descriptive of a practice which recognises that there can be no split between care and education for young children. Children's learning happens all the time and it is the responsibility of early years practitioners to be able to support and extend that learning at every point. This has come into sharper focus in these documents because of a proposal to change the way in which the nursery education grant for 3- and 4-year-olds is administered. It has been decided that splitting the hours of 'nursery education' from the rest of what happens in an early years setting makes no sense to children and parents, and creates barriers between practitioners; it also makes for inflexible provision for parents who are trying to juggle their working hours with the available childcare. Consequently, it was decided that the free offer would be extended to more weeks of the year and more hours in the week, and it would be possible for parents to take it at any time which suited them as long as this was spread across three days each week.[1]

Another key area of reform which affects early years services is the creation of a workforce strategy for children's services as a whole. Again, workforce reform has been an important element in the government's approach to services for young children since 1997. However, reforms have been piecemeal and have not always been able to deliver positive change. An example is the attempt to create a graduate-level of qualifications for the sector. A level 4 qualification was added to the list of National Vocational Qualifications as a step towards graduate or teacher trained status but there was a fairly low take-up of this because, at almost the same time, an Early Years sector-endorsed foundation degree was created with a generous package of resources to support workplace-based students. Early Childhood Studies honours degrees had been in existence for some time and they developed a nationally agreed 'practice option' for students who had no practical experience, thus getting over the problem of graduates who might be highly qualified but were not employable within the sector. None of these routes, however, were able to move students into teacher training as easily as had been hoped and foundation degree graduates found that there were few jobs for them in the sector because a career structure and remuneration packages had not developed alongside the new qualifications. Additionally, these higher education qualifications did not appear on the national qualifications framework, which was restricted to vocational qualifications. In all, the situation was confusing for both students and employers, and people were unsure which qualification would help them most in their careers. This was an untenable situation for a low-wage sector in which staff are often investing their own time and money in professional development.

Next Steps announced a consultation document on a pay and workforce strategy which would begin to rationalise this situation for the children's workforce as a whole (DfES, 2004d). The document did, however, place a great deal of emphasis on the early years workforce as being key to the *Every Child Matters* reforms and as being particularly in need of change.

A federated sector Skills Council for Social Care, Children and Young People (SSC) was announced, to cover the whole of the UK and all staff working in social care and with children. A Children, Young People and Families Workforce Development Council (CWDC) would represent England on both this UK SSC and on a UK Children's Workforce Network which would bring together the SSCs for other sectors such as playwork, health and teaching. The CWDC has a strong representation from the early years sector, which comprises a large part of its workforce 'footprint'. This sounds like a complicated structure, but it is designed to deal with a complicated situation. There are numerous agencies representing different workforce and employer interests in different ways in different countries of the UK and in the short term a structure was needed which would allow all these interests to meet together on a basis of equality and to move, in the long term, towards a more rational and planned approach to a children's workforce as a whole.

The workforce consultation took place over the spring and summer of 2005 and included a number of face-to-face consultation events with the early years sector as well as written responses. Before the consultation document was published the word 'pay' was quietly dropped from the title of the strategy, despite (or maybe because of) the fact that the need to improve the pay and conditions of early years workers had featured strongly in early discussions. At the time of writing the final shape of the workforce reform has not been decided but it is expected that a 'graduate qualified early years professional' role will be created for the sector, that more staff, including childminders, will be qualified to level 3, that there will be stronger leadership, management and supervision, and that staff will be able to map and progress careers across an integrated career structure (DfES, 2005c: 25). Local authorities and individual settings will be supported to move staff as quickly as possible into these qualifications via a Transformation Fund of £125 million per year. The CWDC has already embarked on a review of National Occupational Standards across the children's workforce sector, based on a common core of skills and competencies, and leading to a National

Qualifications Framework which will make it clearer and easier for workers to know which qualifications to take and how to move between jobs in the sector. These are all reforms which are long overdue and have been welcomed by the early years sector, even if the detail and the progress and has been the subject of heated debate.

The final document *Every Child Matters: Change for Children* (DfES, 2004a) was published on 1 December 2004 and this time, the Foreword was written jointly by 16 ministers whose departments were responsible for co-ordinating the delivery of services to children, young people and families:

> we are all working together to improve the lives of children, young people and their families. We are determined to make a step-change in the quality, accessibility and coherence of services so that every child and young person is able to fulfil their full potential and those facing particular obstacles are supported to overcome them. (DfES, 2004a: 2)

It introduced the legislative changes in the Children Act 2004, and emphasised that the whole programme of reform was designed 'to shift the focus of services from dealing with the consequences of difficulties in children's lives to preventing things from going wrong in the first place' (ibid.). The transformation is to be effected by local authorities working in partnership with their communities and supported by the government through a programme of change management which includes Local Area Agreements negotiated between central and local government in order to 'achieve a balance between national and local priorities' (DfES, 2004a: 22). Government support is also provided by ten Regional Change Advisers located in the government offices and working alongside new Directors for Children and Learners who will be expected to integrate the regional support which is provided for local authorities as they implement Every Child Matters. This is just one example of how central government is trying to devolve the planning and responsibility for children's services from national to regional and local levels, resulting in a reduction in the number of civil servants in service ministries, fewer hard national targets and more local flexibility in ways of meeting outcomes.

The Ten Year Childcare Strategy

This, and its underpinning legislation the *Childcare Bill,* (DfES, 2005d) is the key early years vehicle for taking forward *Every Child Matters*. It was published in December 2004 as part of the Pre-Budget Report alongside an extension of paid maternity leave, improvements to the childcare element of Working Tax Credit, measures on financial inclusion and measures to improve employment opportunities. Its full title is *Choice for Parents: The Best Start for Children, a Ten Year Strategy for Childcare* (HM Treasury et al., 2004) and this clearly indicates the focus of the strategy, which is on moving children out of poverty via the workforce participation of their parents. Having said this, the strategy also places an emphasis on the needs of vulnerable children whether or not their parents are in the workforce, and on the needs of children from groups who have traditionally not fully benefited from early years services, such as disabled children and children from minority ethnic groups. Its key principles are: Choice, Availability, Quality and Affordability. In essence, the ten year childcare strategy is designed to rationalise, re-design and re-badge the existing early years initiatives so that they fit within the *Every Child Matters* framework. It gives more power to local authorities and stresses investment in the parts which are not currently being reached.

The Childcare Bill underpins the strategy by giving certain duties to local authorities, the most radical being a duty to provide childcare to meet the needs of parents in their areas, assessing the local childcare market to develop a 'realistic and robust' picture of parents' needs for childcare into the future. This duty is to make sure that there is 'sufficient' childcare for children up to the September after they are 14 (16 for disabled children) and it will be fulfilled if the local childcare market allows parents to make a choice about working. However, as mentioned above, there is an emphasis on the needs of parents for whom the market is seen not to have provided in the past – lower-income families and families with disabled children – and local authorities will be expected to have particular regard to their needs. The concept of 'sufficiency' was not defined and local authorities have begun to adopt a variety of ways of measuring this and then planning to meet it, their success and the success of the government's scrutiny of this can only be judged with time. However, the government stressed that making these responsibilities statutory would enshrine them within local authority performance assessment systems and ensure that they were taken seriously.

The Strategy does not just deal with expansion of places, but also with quality, and here there is to be a three-pronged approach. The workforce reform which has been discussed above will provide an improved workforce, better trained and qualified to support young children and their families. There will then be a new single quality framework for all children from birth to the end of the Foundation Stage (the Early Years Foundation Stage) and which will guide the approaches and activities within settings, pulling together the Foundation Stage Guidance and the *Birth to Three Matters* Framework. These will, in turn, be underpinned by the independent registration and inspection framework of OFSTED. This approach would have been met with support from the sector had it not been for two major concerns. The first was a 'simplification' of the registration and inspection framework, which was to effectively remove regulation from non-maintained services for children over 8 and from children using crèches. This was strongly criticised and led to the government rethinking this part of the legislation. The second area concerned quality assurance, or quality improvement processes. The Childcare Bill consultation paper suggested that the government would like to abandon its endorsement of quality assurance (QA) schemes under its Investors in Children programme, and hinted that the three-pronged approach should be sufficient to secure high quality in settings. Again, on this point, there was a strong lobby from both the voluntary sector and local authorities who had made considerable investments of time and money in quality assurance and felt that it was a necessary fourth element in ensuring that quality improvement became part of the ethos of all settings.

The practical effect of these changes on early years services in England will be far reaching and not all the changes can be predicted. For instance, one of the key features of the Strategy is the development of Children's Centres in every community (3,500 are planned by 2010) and the offer of services in Extended Schools (an out-of-school place for all children between the ages of 3 and 14 from 8 a.m. to 6 p.m. each weekday by 2010). The more detailed guidance on these initiatives stresses that services will not necessarily be provided in the centres or schools, nor even by them, especially in less disadvantaged areas, but that they will have a co-ordinating role to ensure that such provision is available. However, the private and voluntary sector is concerned that new strategic managers working within new structures such as Children's Trusts may not understand the role of their services in the mixed economy of the early years sector, resulting in more and more services being provided within the maintained sector, either in schools or Children's Centres.

Another area of concern lies with the workforce reform and the Strategy's expectation that all full day-care settings will be 'professionally' led, that is, by a graduate professional. As mentioned above, this has been welcomed by the sector as a whole, but still leaves private and voluntary providers feeling that they will not be in a position to pay for such changes. The maintained sector is already the employer of choice for many early years workers because of the better pay and conditions it can provide, and this gap could be widened with every new initiative.

The differing histories, structures and philosophies of the various service providers, across the whole range of health, education and social care in the state, voluntary and private sectors makes the aim of integration towards the *Every Child Matters* outcomes a staggering enterprise which, although intellectually possible, provides an enormous practical challenge. The then Minister for Children, Families and Youth, Margaret Hodge, admitted in an interview with the *Guardian* newspaper that the original timetable for reform was too ambitious and that changes of such magnitude would take a long time to be realised and, indeed, her ten year timescale was later reflected in the childcare strategy: 'The cultural change has got to be huge, huge … to become the norm, 10 years' (Brindle, 2004).

The burden of these changes is to ensure that no child can 'slip through' the net of services provided by the variety of agencies, state and voluntary, that work with children. There is an attempt, not the first it must be said, to place children at the centre of the service web and to ensure that service providers work together to meet their needs rather than expecting them to fit into the organisational constraints of each of the many service providers. They appear to be far-reaching changes, but they are aimed primarily at professional activity, structures and organisations, at the way in which adult professionals relate to each other, rather than at changes in our perception and understanding of children and how we relate to them. It remains to be seen whether or not *Every Child Matters* can support early years practitioners to really meet the needs of children.

EXERCISE 27.1

Take the five over-arching *Every Child Matters* outcomes and produce a practical example of how work in your setting, or one you know well, contributes to each outcome.

EXERCISE 27.2

The reform of the children's workforce is a key feature of *Every Child Matters*. Using your own setting or one you know well, consider what changes would need to be made in order to reach the goals for the early years workforce.

Note

1. The 'free offer' of nursery education for 3- and 4-year-olds is to be extended please see page 306 for details.

LEADING AND MANAGING

LEADING AND MANAGING OTHERS

Lesley Benson

Lesley Benson BA(Hons), PGCE, MA gained her degree and had a career in retail management before training to teach at the Froebel Institute, soon becoming a leader in integrated settings. Her MA is in Early Childhood Education and Care, She is an NCSL consultant leader and facilitates on NCSL's Leading from the Middle programme.

Aims

To develop understanding of:

- [ ] challenge and deepen understanding of leading and managing within a values-driven context
- [ ] and consider ways to develop a more inclusive leadership and management approach
- [ ] the significance of individual and collective behaviour in fulfilling a setting's moral purpose.

Leaders need to be managers and managers need to be leaders

Education is in a period of considerable change, with a re-focus on individual need and multi-agency working. Most possible future scenarios (Innovation Unit, 2004) call for a radically different approach to leadership and management from the hierarchical, management-focused model emphasised for most of the twentieth century. There is increasing awareness of leadership as a distinct quality, and that both leadership and management skills are vital to an effective organisation. MacGilchrist et al. (2004) give useful contrasts between the two functions, which also illustrate their interconnectedness (see table 28.1).

I have been surprised in most of my management roles by the strong desire of teams for hierarchy, with the leader as decision-maker, visionary and organiser. I have encountered a push to act in a particular management mode, with eagerness in some for a charismatic leader. Staff have often expected to do things the way 'management' dictate, with communication systems lacking, or so strongly controlled by management that only certain voices are heard. Penn (1997) characterises this desire for hierarchy as an Anglo-American concept, and suggests that in other cultures (she cites Spain and Italy) there has been a co-operative tradition, without a designated leader.

Fullan looked at Collins's work, which identified the most effective industrial leaders as 'a paradoxical blend of personal humility and professional will' (2003: 10). Fullan believes this is the style needed in education leaders, one not characterised by charisma and

Table 28.1   *Distinctions between leadership and management*

Leadership	Management
'Building and maintaining an organisational culture' Schein (1985)	'Building and maintaining an organisational structure' Schein (1985)
'Establishing a mission for the school, giving a sense of direction' Louis and Miles (1992)	'Designing and carrying out plans, getting things done, working effectively with people' Louis and Miles (1992)
'Doing the right thing' Bennis and Nanus (1985)	'Doing things right' Bennis and Nanus (1985)

Source: MacGilchrist et al., 2004: 42, table 3.1

celebrity, but by leaders who contrive to remove their ego from the equation; in short who work against the hierarchical stereotype.

Distributed leadership

Rethinking leadership in this way leads us to a distributed leadership, where an organisation shares leadership (and management) among its members. This links strongly to the theme of inclusion (see Chapter 20), and comes from the principle that all involved can and should contribute, regardless of their role title or their relative position within the power structure. Indeed, distributed leadership calls for a fundemental rethink of the organisation.

Jack and Jordan talk about social capital; 'cultural practices, norms, networks, links, know-how and tradition, through which people conduct informal interactions of all kinds' (1999: 243). Harnessing social capital through a distributed leadership approach will lead to 'an environment in which adults interact as relatively equal members of a community which fosters trust, cooperation and individual initiative, and promotes voluntary organisations for common good' (ibid.: 242). In such a context, we all have leadership and management responsibilities.

Exploring values for working with children and families

In a centralised (prescribed) system, people become defensive, reacting to other people's agendas rather than developing their own collective vision of the way forward. It becomes too easy to take a safe way out, clutching at stereotypical approaches to practice, leadership and management, in a mistaken view that this will get or keep people out of trouble. 'People do what they are told, but they do not take risks and initiatives, do not experiment and are reluctant to participate' (Harrison, 1994: 194).

By contrast, working from principles allows the development of actions and approaches which may not have been detailed within documents, but which nevertheless have validity and power for children, families and practitioners. The National Curriculum, the Curriculum Guidance for the Foundation Stage and the Birth to Three Matters framework all build from governing, underlying principles.

Moral purpose and spiritual intelligence

Fullan's concept of moral purpose is fundamental to the development of a vision based on principles, and to leadership defined as 'doing the right thing'. Fullan identifies five components of leadership (2001: 13):

- moral purpose
- understanding of the change process
- strong relationships
- knowledge building
- coherence making among multiple priorities.

but contends that 'you simply cannot be effective without behaving in a morally purposeful way' (ibid.: 15). This leads to an organisation having a 'values driven' approach, 'a clearly articulated vision underpinned by a core set of values which draw on and relate to the context in which it finds itself' (MacGilchrist et al., 2004: 111).

Moral purpose is a crucial concept in current thinking on leadership. It underpins the leadership programmes of the National College for School Leadership (NCSL), is implicit within recent DfES (2004e) and OFSTED (2005c) documents, and is a driving force behind the major policy shifts within the Every Child Matters agenda (encapsulated in the Children Act 2004).

Gardner's (1993) theory of multiple intelligences (in addition to rational IQ) has been extended by Zohar and Marshall to include spiritual intelligence (SQ):

> the intelligence with which we address and solve problems of meaning and value, the intelligence in which we can place our actions and our lives in a wider, richer, meaning-giving context, the intelligence with which we can assess that one course of action or one life path is more meaningful than another. (2001: 3–4)

This is the intelligence through which moral purpose takes shape, through which we ask the key question 'why are we doing this?' rather than just 'what do we need to do?'

Nevertheless both questions are important. MacGilchrist et al. believe an intelligent school has 'the capacity to mobilise all those within the school to put that *vision into action*. It does this in a *systematic* way which enables the school to connect vision to action and vice versa, in such a way that the whole really is greater than the sum of its parts' (2004: 111, original emphases).

Too rigid a management system prevents flexibility, and ignores individual needs and individuals' capacity to contribute. Yet having no boundaries creates uncertainty and fear of getting it wrong, as people second guess what is expected. This paralyses thought as well as action.

Organisations that lead and manage in competitive and controlling ways waste their human potential. Where these are education settings it is unlikely they can unleash the children's potential. An effective approach to leadership therefore is to develop a clear local vision, founded on a set of principles and moral purpose, shared with the majority of staff, and the wider school community. This is then coupled with clear management systems, which have an underlying and coherent structure, but which leave people free to experiment and innovate. This allows responsiveness to individual need (of the children, their families or staff members). This approach should govern day-to-day business, and the way the organisation conducts itself with members of that organisation.

EXERCISE 28.1

In light of the concept of 'moral purpose' and the theory of spiritual intelligence examine how the vision and principles on parental involvement in your setting show in the practice. You might want to use interviews, questionnaires, examine paperwork (for example policies, evaluations, improvement and action plans) to gather data.

Is there a good match or discrepancies between your setting's vision and principles and what happens in practice?

What steps could you take for improving the match?

You could repeat this exercise to examine how 'moral purpose' and spiritual intelligence show in practice in your setting:

- between staff
- with children
- with the wider community.

Developing a shared vision with colleagues and families

There is a danger if a vision is too strongly driven from one person or small group. People may sign up to the vision thus created, but failure to achieve that vision can cause disengagement. Harrison believes that 'when leaders fail to hold the course and deliver the dreams they have created, the sense of betrayal is actually greater' (1994: 193). This can then paralyse the organisation. We need therefore to challenge the way a vision is created and implemented, taking into account people's different perspectives and experiences.

'Perspective transformation'

Moving towards a more inclusive (distributed) approach is not necessarily a straightforward process. There may be a wish to change the culture, but as developments are showing with workforce reform, staff can be reluctant to take on more responsibility under a distributed leadership model. They may be confident in their own ability (though not always), but reluctant to work beyond what they feel they are properly rewarded for. Officially designated managers and leaders are seen as being paid to take the responsibility, and there are undeniable differentials in pay and conditions within teams. Staff may not be confident or ready to contribute, because of their existing level of knowledge, previous experiences of trying to contribute, or their existing vision of what leadership and management mean.

Individuals within an organisation need to buy into the need for change for any change to be consolidated. Mezirow (1981) describes this as 'perspective transformation', a liberating process through which we become aware of the constraining effects (on ourselves and our relationships) of the structure we are working in, then rethink it in order to change it.

Developing a shared vision does not just cover rational, analytical areas, but emotional responses to vision creation, particularly where that calls for a deeper and more meaningful involvement from individuals. Fullan believes leadership is 'ultimately assessed by the extent to which it awakens people's intrinsic commitment, which is none other than the mobilising of everyone's sense of moral purpose' (2001: 20–21).

Creating an inclusive vision also encompasses the wider community. It is crucial that mechanisms be established to include wider voices, of families and, of course, children, if the vision is to really meet needs.

Listening to young children

It is becoming increasingly acknowledged that children need to be included as stakeholders. They often have very clear views, but are not always helped to express them.

In my current school there was a history of developing children's autonomy, within a secure and respectful environment, but we are now working to further include children's voices in the school's work, looking at all systems to see where we can extend choice, autonomy, expression and influence. Keyworkers are crucial to these processes, as they develop close relationships with individuals, and share that knowledge with the team. We have been surprised by what children tell us when clearly encouraged to, for example via their video recording, questionnaires and ongoing discussions. They have articulated what makes them feel safe, where they prefer not to go and why, what they like doing and why. These explicit approaches have gone alongside our existing observations of children's learning. We have been able to strengthen our vision and improve our practice on the basis of this deeper knowledge.

Involving families

Links with parents have often been characterised by hierarchy, with the professional voice deemed the dominant one, rather than accepting parents as equal partners with unique knowledge of their child's development. Much parenting work starts from the premise that parents need to be taught skills by experts, 'to compensate for their lack of skill and inadequate lifestyles' (Easen et al., 1992: 282). This is a deficit model, leading to the development of compensatory programmes (in pedagogical terms an empiricist approach). Research into children's language development by Wells (1987), Tizard and Hughes (1984) and Shirley Brice Heath (1983) has shown this deficit model to be dangerously inaccurate.

Easen et al. set out a second viewpoint, of parents as consumers, but also offer a third possibility, of a 'participatory approach', where 'a shared relationship is established and information is exchanged' (1992: 283). They call this a 'developmental partnership'.

An example of parental partnership

At my current school we have home-visiting for all new children. The keyworker engages with the child, and the head or deputy records a wide-ranging conversation with the parent or carer about the child's routines, strengths and needs. This gives a strong base for developing work with that child (and ensures settling the child is effective and in partnership with the family). It also establishes our ethos for working with the family. This is extended by subsequent meetings with all parents to jointly assess the child's development, and to plan for future learning through Possible Lines of Development. Parents are encouraged to contribute to their child's Profile Book, which incorporates the child's assessment of their own progress.

In workshops with parents, designed to share our professional approaches and lay them open for discussion and scrutiny, we often learn much about parents' education experiences, what they expect of us, their expectations for their children and for themselves. We emphasise our desire to listen, and acknowledge the often deep awareness parents have of their own child's behaviour. We thus establish a dialogue, for sharing personal and professional knowledge, without claiming either as more important (Athey, 1991). This approach has been very useful in our work with children with special educational needs, as we seek to work alongside parents in understanding and responding to needs. Our Carers and Toddlers group also enables parents to express their concerns and aspirations. Via Children's Centre services we hope to address the wider issues expressed by parents more effectively.

Our approach is underpinned by a commitment to distributed leadership. Our systems aim to develop a greater shared understanding, as through this, joint problem-solving and a shared vision can be developed.

EXERCISE 28.2

Children as leaders and managers

How are children's voices included in the management and leadership of your setting?

Make a series of narrative observations on a child, at different times of the day to include different aspects of the setting's routines. For each observation, analyse how far the child has influence or control over what happens to him or her.

Using an appropriate action plan format, with the team if possible, detail what steps you and/or the team can take to improve this.

Working as a team – exploring issues of being in a team/leading a team

On my first promotion to leading a team, my boss told me not to worry about anything in the first few months except getting the staff team together, that everything else would follow on behind this. This excellent advice contained the point that leadership is an earned act. Leadership should not, however, be about 'trying to engineer learner consent to take the actions favoured by the educator within the new perspective' (Mezirow, 1981: 135) – this would be a retention of a hierarchical approach. It is about developing the team through perspective transformation, through 'systematically examining existing options, building confidence through competence in new roles, acquiring knowledge and skills to implement one's plans and provisionally trying out new roles and relationships' (Mezirow, 1981: 134).

The most effective teams I have encountered have been those where people are valued for their varied range of skills. This is not about labelling people as types (as in Belbin's, 2003, work on teams), or defining skills by people's roles. Rather it is about making effective use of social capital, working and developing from people's strengths. This is supported by the Birth to Three framework principle that 'children [people] learn when they are given appropriate responsibility, allowed to make errors, decisions and choices, and respected as autonomous and competent learners' (2004: 5).

Leadership within the team

As educators it is possible to make the link between an interactionist pedagogy and leadership. Thus teams with distributed leadership will see people as individuals, find out what makes them tick, help them to develop, allow people to make mistakes and to learn from them. Team members will respect difference, but support a search for mutual understanding and consensus. They will be able to acknowledge the passion and anger people can feel, but try to prevent this from becoming destructive. They will try to hold, support and contain others (Roberts, 1995), while knowing how and when to get the support needed for themselves. The founder of John Lewis, Spedan Lewis, urged managers to 'never cease trying to perceive how people do in fact behave under certain rules and practices ... And you may find that by making concessions ... to the human nature of the people in question, you will get results that will be incomparably better'. This becomes the task for all members of a distributed leadership team.

Developing a team using this framework also requires a deeper knowledge of adult learning. Knowles argues that 'adults tend to resist learning under conditions that are incongruent with their self-concept as autonomous individuals' (1970: 56). This also holds for children, so working from an interactionist pedagogy can give a firm foundation for supporting adults. In trying to capture the strengths within a team 'responsibility lies less in giving ready-made answers to pre-determined questions and more in being ingenious in finding better ways to help ... [the team] ... discover the important questions and the answers to them themselves' (Knowles, 1970: 68).

This can be uncomfortable at first, in teams unused to this approach. In developing distributed leadership an important step is 'helping adults construe experience in a way which they may more clearly understand the reasons for their problems and understand the options open to them so that they may assume responsibility for decision making' (Mezirow, 1981: 134–5). This, incidentally, has been one of the powerful approaches to involving parents inherent within England's local Sure Start programmes.

Emotional intelligence

The concept of emotional intelligence is crucial to this approach to teamwork. Like spiritual intelligence, this builds on Gardner's (1993) theory about multiple intelligences and particularly the intrapersonal and interpersonal intelligences.

Gardner defines interpersonal intelligence as 'the ability to understand other people: what motivates them, how they work, how to work cooperatively with them' (1993: 9). He suggests this 'permits a skilled adult to read the intentions and desires – even when these have been hidden – of many other individuals and, potentially, to act upon this knowledge – for example by influencing a group of individuals to behave along desired lines' (ibid.: 240). Clearly Fullan's concept of moral purpose is significant here, as otherwise these skills could be used to manipulate others.

With intrapersonal intelligence, Gardner believes the 'core capacity at work here is access to one's ... range of ... emotions: the capacity instantly to effect discriminations among these feelings and, eventually, to label them ... to draw upon them as a means of understanding and guiding one's behaviour' (1993: 240).

Gardner emphasises the cultural variation of these intelligences, and that they are inter-linked, 'with knowledge of one's own person perennially dependent upon the ability to apply lessons learned from the observation of other people, while knowledge of others draws upon the internal discriminations the individual routinely makes' (1993: 241). Goleman defines this interlinking as emotional intelligence (EQ): 'the capacity for recognizing our own feelings and those of others, for motivating ourselves, and for managing emotions well in ourselves and in our relationships' (1999: 317). He argues that EQ is more important than IQ in the performance of an organisation.

Goleman et al. (2002) set out four domains of emotional intelligence, with 18 competencies. The NCSL (2003) define six of these as 'must-haves' (see Figure 28.1).

MacGilchrist et al. emphasise that managing emotions will increase the EQ of an organisation. They define 'three distinct, but linked skills: Management of emotion, management with emotion, management through emotion' (2004: 131).

Developing these competencies should allow the team to create

a supportive organisation culture in which demands for change and ever-higher performance are balanced by compassion for human frailty ... In such organisations we do not always have to project an image of competence and confidence. We can share our uncertainties and frustrations, and in sharing lighten our individual loads. (Harrison, 1994: 195)

Behaviour policy and beyond

At my current school we have built our behaviour policy on self-regulation, rooted in 'listening to young children' and on supporting children to become aware of their own emotions and what could be motivating others. Staff are supported in understanding their own reactions to situations, and the impact of their own reactions on those situations. We also

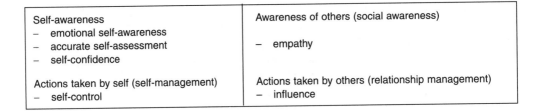

Self-awareness – emotional self-awareness – accurate self-assessment – self-confidence	Awareness of others (social awareness) – empathy
Actions taken by self (self-management) – self-control	Actions taken by others (relationship management) – influence

Figure 28.1 *Emotional intelligence matrix, with 'must-have' competencies (adapted from NCSL, 2003)*

recognise the capacity of different staff to cope with particular behaviours. When allocating key-workers, wherever possible careful matching takes place so that the emotional content of work with children and their families can be managed by keyworkers working to their strengths. Sometimes, however, staff will have children and families they are less comfortable with. They are then encouraged to draw on the collective skills of the team. In these ways, individual and team emotional intelligences are built on, strengthened and developed.

What happens when teams do not agree?

Everyone is likely to have had experience of conflict in groups, within the family or the workplace. It is important to realise that disagreement can be a healthy sign of moving to a more inclusive approach, and part of a dynamic process of development. I am always concerned when working with a new staff group if my comments are greeted with silence or instant agreement. This can indicate a team trapped by hierarchy. How disagreements are tackled, however, will test the effectiveness of a team.

One approach can be to contain conflict, accepting it and holding it for later examination, in a form it can be dealt with (Roberts, 1995). An effective team will perform this defusing role for its members, but will also seek to resolve the problem. For example, a common area of conflict within a team can be the challenge of under-performance. This is not just something identified by external sources or the nominal leader. Teams with a clear vision working within a set of principles can become very unsettled when they perceive individuals not pulling their weight over a period of time. Personal issues may be accepted for a while, but eventually people perceive that something needs to happen.

Of course formal personnel systems may be used, but the organisation's culture can provide a less punitive solution. In a team working towards distributed leadership, the figure-head 'must set the example of himself being open to feedback regarding his performance. He must be skilful in establishing a supportive climate, in which hard-to-accept information about one's performance can be looked at objectively' (Knowles, 1970: 60). This enables issues to be raised calmly and sensitively, in the knowledge that no one is perfect, but that there are effects on the whole team that need to be resolved.

It can seem easy to deal with disagreement by isolating the person, be they a staff member, parent or child. Indeed, management courses sometimes label team members by their behaviour as a means of dealing with them. I find this as unproductive as labelling children as problem or difficult. It de-personalises, takes us away from seeing people as individuals, and can set in train a self-fulfilling prophecy of failure, disengagement or alienation. It also ignores and loses the possible learning inherent in criticism.

It is more productive to try to hear what the person is saying. For example, a parent who constantly complains may be hard to listen to, but will give invaluable insight beyond the staff's perceptions. We could become defensive, hiding behind our professional perspective, effectively 'pulling rank'. Or we could see this information as indicating a need to re-examine practice, and our ability to articulate practice.

There can be tension for teams between wider involvement and a principled approach. Principles may not be common between all stakeholders. They will need to be revisited as more people become involved, but with a constant understanding of what is 'not for sale', and why. Working from principle should allow a team to navigate its way through disagreement or conflict to common practice grounded in agreed theories.

It is also important to remember the significance of laughter. Tensions can be defused by finding the humour in a situation (though not by laughing at anyone) and sharing that perspective in order to move on.

EXERCISE 28.3

Using emotional intelligence in managing team disagreement
  Think about a situation in your setting when there was disagreement in the team.

- What did people (including you) say (exact words?) or do (actions/non-verbal communication)?
- What underlying concerns might people have been expressing?

Using the theory of emotional intelligence, and particularly the emotional intelligence matrix (Figure 28.1), analyse how individuals responded to, reacted to and managed the behaviour of others in the situation.

  Using the principle of distributed leadership, consider what (else) you could have done to support the situation.

  Consider (if possible with the rest of the team) what steps could be taken in your setting to improve the team's capacity to manage disagreement.

  Devise an action plan for putting these steps into action and evaluating their success.

Professional development – human resources

The most fundamental resources available to an organisation are human. This encompasses staff, children and families, all of whom can and must be developed to support the development of others. Thus working with parents via a developmental partnership can enrich staff thinking at least as much as staff can offer to parents. Listening to young children is part of professional development.

MacGilchrist et al. identify a learning organisation as one of the core characteristics of an effective school 'with staff who are willing to be learners and to participate in a staff development programme' (2004: 28). Boyatzis, however, talks about self-directed learning, and points out that people only change when they see the need for change, and that they need support to do so, in what he calls 'psychological safety' (1999: 27). Courses alone are a costly waste when not linked to other approaches. Talking together, evaluating and reflecting on practice, raises the consciousness of team members about their work, and individuals may benefit from deeper discussions.

In an interactionist approach to teaching and learning the knowledge and skills of more experienced children are available to support new or less experienced children. This has twin benefits. It widens possible interactions and learning from others. It also helps the more experienced children become more conscious of what they know. By having to explain to someone else, they lay their own thinking or knowledge out for their own consideration, encouraging what Donaldson (1978) has called a move to 'disembedded' thinking. This approach is equally valid for adults in their professional development.

At my current school all students are given a supervisor to support their learning, but staff seeking to develop their skills are also regularly coached by an appropriate staff member. All staff also have termly personal review meetings with the head, where they can raise any issues (using a social work model of supervision), and focus on future development needs. Monthly Development Mornings, training days, and a Classroom Assistant Training and Development Forum pick up group needs. All these systems are designed to create an atmosphere of critical reflection, within a supportive environment.

Getting organised – developing resources, time space and action plans

There are practical steps that support the approaches described in earlier sections. This takes us into managerial skills, or 'doing things right'.

In a newly constituted team it is unlikely that any of the processes described will happen quickly or easily, since this context is bringing together people with different experiences, beliefs, stages of self-awareness or awareness of others, of different principles even. Even within an established team there may be tensions to resolve, new ways of working to be planned for and new people joining as others leave. Boyatzis usefully reminds us that 'Change itself is not the object. The ideal or desired end result is the object of the change process' (1999: 24).

None of this is easy. MacGilchrist et al. identify some key messages about making improvements: 'Change takes time. A school's capacity for change will vary. Change is complex. Change needs to be well led and managed. Teachers need to be the main agents of change. The pupils need to be the main focus for change' (2004: 34).

The biggest resource need in this is time: ongoing times to meet, discuss and organise, plus a realisation of the time frame within which ongoing work takes place.

Ongoing time

When joining a new setting one of my first actions is to decipher the existing systems for people to meet and talk, as a team, and as individuals. I then examine these with the team, to see how they are working (or not working), and agree what times will be put in place for the future. These times then act as the mechanism through which people can move the organisation forward. This process also needs to examine the wider team, that is parents, children, other agencies and community members. Systems must include everyone if everyone is to exert his/her influence.

Time frames

Time frames can only realistically be agreed when it is clear what is being planned or worked on. Some things can happen quite quickly. Other developments take much longer. If there has been no understanding about principles or vision, this will not always be straightforward or quick to resolve. Team conflicts or disagreements cannot always be easily unpicked. The Every Child Matters agenda (see Chapter 27) requires different organisational cultures to work together and even integrate (for example in Children's Centres or extended schools). Developing a new organisational concept to meet this challenge will be complex, often stressful, and will need a longer time frame than perhaps the government has imagined.

Bazalgette of the Grubb Institute has talked of the 'organisation-in-the-mind', where people were 'working with a mental image of how what they were talking about fitted into their own picture of the organisation … [but where] both had quite different pictures of the organisation in their minds' (2002: 2). This process is almost certainly at work when bringing together different professional cultures, when working in partnerships across organisations, or with parents (for example in their views of education). It is important to understand and accept this, to deal with it explicitly, and to stand firm for realistic time frames with those outside the teams (such as local and national government). There are no quick fixes to this process, even where there is complete commitment to a vision.

Space

The need for space is another crucial factor, appropriate spaces where teams can meet. They need to be large enough to accommodate everyone who needs to be included. They should be comfortable, warm, and welcoming, with appropriate resources for the purpose (for example facilities for refreshments, or audio-visual equipment).

More subtly, spaces need to fit with organisational culture and underlying principles. A meeting held around a high table will have a different quality to one held on low comfortable chairs without a table between participants. Both can be business-like and purposeful, but people will perceive them differently, and the different approaches may be deeply embedded within organisational cultures. Even suggesting a change can cause dissonance for team members. It is important to examine such space issues in the light of underlying principles, to critique the relative merits of different types and layouts of space, in order to agree spaces that meet needs.

Action plans

The use of action plans is well established within organisations, for individuals, groups and the whole organisation. The myriad forms work from some basic structures. They:

- usually define the aim, target or objective to be achieved
- break this down into a set of actions, tasks or steps to be taken
- which have timescales attached for start and completion, define the people involved and the resources needed
- specify how progress towards success will be monitored
- most importantly, will have defined success criteria
- include an indication of who will evaluate, review and report on the success (or otherwise).

Many formats work from SMART targets (small, measurable, achievable, realistic and time-framed). It is important to realise, however, that plans define concrete and human-sized action to bring about often big and far-reaching ambitions. The overall aim becomes achievable through a series of logical, even everyday actions, encapsulated within a written format that can be shared and understood within the team, and examined by others.

The principle of a widely defined and inclusive team is fundamental to organisational action plans. All staff will have a crucial role to play throughout the plan, and should be fully involved in its formulation. Parents, governors or management board members, and children should also be included in this formulation, and may be integral to many of the actions. The majority of outcomes (success criteria) will certainly be directed at children.

Achieving this inclusive approach to action planning is not always easy. Traditionally such plans have been drawn up by a few, usually the 'leaders', then presented to the rest of the team as a work plan. The wider constituency has not been included. The move to self-evaluation within education, as defined by the DfES (2004) and within the new OFSTED framework (2005), will be a strong driver to a more inclusive approach. The process of self-evaluation is examined in Chapter 30, and OFSTED (2004) are explicit about the need to include a very wide constituency in this.

An organisation can build its capacity to include wider perspectives by working with external organisations which have expertise to share. Teams need not be afraid to test their thinking and expand their approaches with the help of other organisations or individuals. Equally, however, they need to make the changes their own, and test anything they incorporate against their own principles.

Establishing, monitoring, reviewing, evaluating and modifying the work of the team

A traditional way of looking at management systems has been to create something, then 'freeze' it, making sure everyone complies with the laid-down approaches and procedures. A more dynamic theory, set out strongly by the National Remodelling Team (NRT, 2003) in relation to workforce reform, sees systems developing via ongoing cycles. Their model also acknowledges the rational, political and emotional components to change. If political and emotional barriers are ignored, no manner of rational solutions will bring about the required change. The NRT believe it must be clear that each dimension is being considered. This is a more flexible approach to change, which draws on the theory of emotional intelligence, and builds on the collective wisdom of a team, utilising its ongoing experience and learning.

An example – developing record-keeping and assessment

When leading an early years setting from status as an under 3 centre back to a full 0–5s setting, I needed to establish with staff the systems for record-keeping and assessment of children.

This involved looking at what was already there, to see what could be built from. As there was very little in place, we discussed in training sessions what *principles* should underpin our approach. Once these were agreed, we looked at a variety of possible systems, tested these against our principles, and *established* the approaches we would adopt.

These were then *monitored*, by me as head, by looking at individual records on a regular basis, with feedback on my monitoring to individuals, and of general points to the teams. (Clearly there could have been further development to include peer monitoring).

We *reviewed* the effectiveness of our collective decisions, enlightened by the monitoring and people's own evaluations of the systems in use. This enabled us to collectively *evaluate* the systems in an open way, and agree any *modifications* needed to make the systems more effective for their purpose. This then established the next version of the system.

In my current school this cycle of establishing, monitoring, regular review, evaluation and modification has become deeper and more effective as staff have grown confident in the authenticity of the process. People are very quick to understand when they are token partners in a process, but make very effective contributions when they feel their input is integral and genuine. Our system has become much more thoughtful and rich as a result of staff's deeper engagement, with improvements based on an awareness of what is happening, as perceived by the team, and as they make efforts to find ways of including parents and children in the cycle.

Staff are also able to articulate their understanding of the purposes of the system to others far more effectively than before. It is no longer something that they merely feel required to do, but something they are committed to because they have agreed the principles that guide the system, and have helped to create, and can critique, the elements that meet the system's purpose.

Monitoring

It should be emphasised that internal monitoring is only one approach. The DfES have made it clear that

> the underlying process which the school employs to identify its strengths and weaknesses is not prescribed. Schools are free to follow any model which gives them the best insights into their improvement priorities. ... The best schools will have simple processes which enable their leaders to measure progress in practical ways through their day-to-day work. (DfES, 2004: 6)

Monitoring falls into several categories:

- Internal monitoring – by management/leadership team, peer monitoring and mentoring. This will usually involve formalised procedures, and may be incorporated in a performance management policy.
- Self-evaluation – this builds on the early years tradition of reflective practice by individual practitioners. It systematises individual, team and whole school evaluation.
- Feedback from the wider community – incorporating parental/family evaluation of the work of the school or setting. This will include a variety of formal and informal mechanisms, and needs to be culturally appropriate in order to engage all members of this wider community.
- External monitoring – this includes OFSTED and local authority representatives. There is little control over the format but the process can be controlled by people's responses to it. Chapter 30 looks at this area in more detail.

Summary

Creating a shared, collective vision, with a wide number of stakeholders, using people's spiritual intelligence, provides a moral purpose for the work of the team. Leadership is distributed or shared among team members, along with the management of work. Social capital is increased as the team is encouraged to transform its perspectives, develop its emotional intelligence and its professional capacity. These processes need space and, crucially, time. Clear, inclusive, systems support often difficult changes, making them human-sized and achievable.

Further reading

Goleman, D., Boyatzis, R. and McKee, A. (2002) *The New Leaders: Transforming the Art of Leadership into the Science of Results* London: Time Warner.
This usefully applies thinking on emotional intelligence to issues of leadership.

MacGilchrist, B., Myers, K. and Reed, J. (2004) *The Intelligent School*. 2nd edition. London: Sage Publications.
A comprehensive examination of the issues of leading and managing in education, with very good referencing to key texts.

MANAGING IN CONTEXT

Jenny Spratt

Jenny Spratt is Head of Early Years and Childcare Services for Peterborough City Council. She was previously head-teacher of a maintained nursery school in the city and is currently studying on a part-time basis for a PhD.

Aims

To develop understanding of:

☐   how to prepare for inspection
☐   how to address self-assessment
☐   how to work with other professionals

The job description for a manager of a Children's Centre, advertised recently, required knowledge of child development, the ability to build and manage a budget, alongside experience of managing people. A tall order, or in reality is this the mix of skills required every day by the managers of our early childhood settings, whether they are playgroups, day-care centres, nursery schools, children centres or childminders providing a service in their own homes? Management today is complex and the introduction of new legislation (Children Act 2004; Childcare Bill 2005) means more demands on the managers of our settings.

This chapter considers some of the issues that face managers and discusses ways in which they can use the issues discussed in the different sections to support their role in providing a quality learning environment for the child.

Preparation for inspections

Until April 2005 inspections in England were planned in advance and the settings were notified when their Care Standards or Nursery Education Inspections would take place. The system of inspection was complex, with the National Standards for Day Care and Child-minding being used as the assessment criteria for the care inspection and the Curriculum Guidance for the Foundation Stage used for assessment by OFSTED to judge the quality of provision for children aged 3 to 4 years accessing the free entitlement for nursery education. There was, however, time to prepare staff, notify parents, update documentation and so on before the day of the inspection. The new OFSTED regulatory framework, introduced on 1 September 2005, has changed the frequency and nature of inspections. There will now be no warning about when the inspector will call – except for childminders who will be given a few days' notice, to ensure they are at home.

This change has evolved alongside other changes resulting from the Children Act 2004. In preparing for inspection, managers will now have to take responsibility for many organisational and administrative tasks, as part of the regulatory process, as well as ensuring the quality of provision for the child. These include ensuring all staff are adequately cleared as a 'suitable person' (Standard 1) and through its organisation (Standard 2) the setting has a commitment to continual improvement, including the qualifications of staff. Keeping good records and having appropriate documentation (Standard 14) are also assessed.

Inspectors will take account of how the setting, or childcarer is working with the *Birth to Three Matters* framework, as well as the *Curriculum Guidance for the Foundation Stage*.

These changes reflect the ethos of the Children Act 2004 and its Green Paper *Every Child Matters* (HMT, 2003) ensuring that children are safe and well cared for. Inspectors, upon entering a setting will ask the question 'What is it like for a child here?' and will write their report under the five outcomes that form the basis of the Act. These are:

- being healthy
- staying safe
- enjoying and achieving
- making a positive contribution
- economic well-being.

The OFSTED document, *Early Years: Firm Foundations* (OFSTED, 2005b), reports on the findings of all OFSTED inspections in the two-year period between April 2003 and March 2005. This document is useful for managers in their preparation for inspection, as it sets out the findings under four of the *Every Child Matters* Outcomes and demonstrates how providers, by meeting the relevant standards, are able to provide good outcomes for children.

These are summarised as:

1. *Being healthy.* The outcome for 'being healthy' involves children being physically, mentally and emotionally healthy, and leading healthy lifestyles.

   - The most relevant national standards and six areas of learning in the curriculum for the Foundation Stage relate to:

     - Health (Standard 7);
     - Food and Drink (Standard 8);
     - Physical development.

   - In settings where outcomes are good, children:

     - learn about the importance of healthy eating;
     - are provided with nutritious, balanced meals and snacks appropriate to their individual dietary needs;
     - are protected from infection and are well taken care of if they have an accident or become ill;
     - take part in regular physical play, both indoors and outside. (OFSTED, 2005b: 6)

2. *Staying safe.* The outcome for 'staying safe' is about children having security, stability and care that protects them from mistreatment and neglect, accidental injury, bullying, discrimination and anti-social behaviour.

   - The most relevant national standards relate to:

     - Physical environment (Standard 4);
     - Equipment (Standard 5);
     - Safety (Standard 6);
     - Child protection (Standard 13).

   - In settings where outcomes are good, children:

- are protected by adults who are suitable and vigilant;
- are secure and well supervised in a clean and maintained environment;
- use safe and suitable toys and equipment that stimulate and challenge them. (OFSTED, 2005b: 9)

3. *Enjoying and achieving.* The outcome for children 'enjoying and achieving' involves children enjoying play experiences that help them develop and achieve. The relevant national standard relates to care, learning and play (Standard 3), all areas of learning are relevant.

- In settings where outcomes are good, children:
  - are happy and settled;
  - are involved in a broad range of planned activities and spontaneous events, which support their development and overall learning;
  - are confident to make decisions, explore and investigate, and relate well to others;
  - respond well to adults who are interested in what they do, and play. (OFSTED, 2005b: 12)

4. *Making a positive contribution.* The outcome for children 'making a positive contribution' involves children making positive relationships, engaging in positive behaviour, being involved in what goes on around them and gaining in self-confidence.

- The relevant national standards and areas of learning relate to:
  - Equal opportunities (Standard 9);
  - Special Needs (Standard 10);
  - Behaviour (Standard 11);
  - Partnership with parents (Standard 12);
  - Personal, social and emotional development;
  - Knowledge and understanding of the world.

- In settings where outcomes are good, children:
  - behave well as they learn to consider others and what is expected of them;
  - benefit from activities and resources which help them to value diversity;
  - are valued and included;
  - have their individual needs met by adults who work in close partnership with parents and carers. (OFSTED, 2005b: 16)

The regulatory changes that took place on 3 October 2005 place additional responsibilities on the manager, through amendments to the National Standards. These include:

A written complaints procedure which must be shared with parents. Managers have a duty to investigate complaints, providing a record of all complaints stating –

- date of the complaint;
- the nature of the complaint;
- the standard it relates to;
- within 28 days to give an account of the action taken;
- the record must be kept for 10 years. (OFSTED, 2005a: 3–13)

Another regulatory change places the responsibility of the Registered Person (usually the manager) to ensure the suitability of the day-care staff. The Office for Standards in Education will check at inspection the robustness of the systems the manager has in place to test the suitability of the staff they employ. This could be through evidence to show:

- quality of systems in place for Criminal Records Bureau process
- interview process
- process for obtaining references
- induction process
- employment history and qualifications of staff.

More emphasis is also placed on settings taking responsibly for their own organisation, and is inspected under the outcome 'Economic well-being'. Inspectors will consider:

- Standard 1 – suitable person
- Standard 2 – organisation
- Standard 14 – documentation.

They will also comment on how well the setting is being led and managed.

There are now four inspection grades, which are the same across all settings that OFSTED inspects. These are:

- Outstanding
  This reflects:

  - exceptional settings
  - excellent outcomes for children
  - exemplary practice
  - no recommendations.

- Good
  This reflects:

  - successful settings
  - effectiveness in meeting the outcomes for children
  - practice that is worth reinforcing and developing
  - at least one recommendation.

- Satisfactory
  This reflects:

  - acceptable settings
  - the setting meets the outcomes for children
  - scope for improvement
  - at least one recommendation.

- Inadequate – category 1
  This reflects:

  - weak settings
  - unsatisfactory outcomes for children
  - cause for concern
  - notice of action to improve.

What does this mean? A setting receiving an action will be re-inspected within 6–12 months, but this could be sooner.

- Inadequate – category 2
  This reflects:

  - highly ineffective settings
  - unsatisfactory outcomes for children
  - urgent attention is needed
  - enforcement action
  - external help and support.

What does this mean? The Office for Standards in Education will write formally to the local authority to inform them and recommend the need for help and support, as there is no evidence that the provision can make the improvements needed by itself. Re-inspection will be within 3–6 months or as specified in any enforcement action, whichever is sooner.

Preparing for inspection need not be an onerous task – part of the manager's role is to ensure that all aspects to be inspected are part of daily practice. The following suggestions might be helpful:

- Complete the self-assessment form and update it regularly (see 'self-assessment' section of this chapter).
- Check that you and your staff are familiar with all relevant documentation (see 'writing a policy' section of this chapter).
- Make sure that you have put right any weaknesses that were identified in your last inspection (check your last report).
- Check that you have *all* the required records.
- Keep any information about how parents and carers view your service and any improvements that you have made as a result.
- Make sure that you have available any record you keep of complaints about the care you provide.
- Ensure you have notified OFSTED of any significant changes to your provision.

The following sections of this chapter address issues to support managers in their complex role of meeting required outcomes that ensure a quality experience for children and their families.

Self-assessment

Managers and their staff frequently question why they need to undertake self-assessment, as they find it difficult to make a judgement about their provision and the service they provide. This is not unusual – most people find self-assessment difficult, as it is not easy to be critical about your own work. Self-assessment needs to be thought of as an extension of good reflective early childhood practice.

The daily practice of early childhood practitioners involves understanding through observation and reflection, the development of the children and identifying the learning that takes place to enable them to develop the learning. Self-assessment is the way that managers and practitioners, as a team, engage in the quality improvement of their practice. They identify together, through observation and reflection, what the setting is good at and what it needs to do to improve the quality. An action plan can then be developed.

Self-assessment provides:

- all members of staff with an understanding of the organisational arrangements
- systems for ensuring the quality of the experience for the child, under the recognised outcomes
- a programme of review and evaluation
- an action plan with measurable and achievable targets
- a link to staff development and training.

The self-assessment required by OFSTED at the inspection is a concise form (which can be downloaded from the OFSTED website) and needs to be regularly updated. It is important to be able to justify why you made the judgements for self-grading and this will be easier as self-assessment is an integral aspect of a recognised Quality Assurance scheme (see later section of this chapter) as reflection will become regular practice.

Another framework that can support managers in making informed judgements for self-assessment is the DfES Sure Start Unit's *Key Elements of Effective Practice* (KEEP) (DfES, 2005e). This document supports the continuous improvement of:

- relationships with both children and adults
- understanding of the individual and diverse ways that children develop and learn
- knowledge and understanding in order to actively support and extend children's learning in and across all areas and aspects of learning
- practice in meeting all children's needs, learning styles and interests
- work with parents, carers and the wider community
- work with other professionals within and beyond the setting (DfES, 2005e: 3).

Key Elements of Effective Practice can be used to support self-assessment, appraisal, quality assurance, performance management and provides a 'management tool for building capacity, develop job descriptions and for self-review by individuals' (DfES, 2005e: 8). More information and support for using the KEEP framework can be obtained from local authority Early Years and Childcare Teams.

Writing a policy

One of the questions on the OFSTED self-assessment form asks managers 'Have you got the following documents ready to show the Inspector?' and lists a series of questions that relate to aspects of the policies that the setting needs to have in place as a requirement by the Day Care and Childminding (National Standards) (England) Regulations 2003 (DfES/OWP, 2003).

It is, however, the manager's responsibility to ensure that policies are not just written to meet the inspector's approval and tick the box on the self-assessment form. Managers need to have evidence of policy in practice. This is most effective when all staff and parents have been involved in developing and adopting the policy in the first instance.

Many early childhood settings have access to policy documents that have been produced by the national organisation to which they are affiliated – such as the Pre-school Learning Alliance, which has produced the publication *'Policies for Early Years Settings* in consultation with OFSTED' (PLA, 2005). This document advises that 'all staff and parents should be involved in adopting, implementing and reviewing policies, so that all the adults involved can influence the way the setting is run' (PLA, 2005, Introduction). The organisation goes on to suggest that the following process be undertaken.

- *Adopting policies*
  - Copies of the policy to be adopted should be made available to all parents and staff.
  - A meeting to discuss and adopt the policy should be held. This will enable everyone to discuss and agree the policy's aim and methods.

- *Implementing policies*
  - All new parents and staff should be introduced to the setting's policies.
  - It should be explained to all parents that the policies are the rules for running the setting and being a member involves agreeing to them.

- *Reviewing policies*
  - Each policy should be continually monitored by collecting evidence about the results of its implementation.
  - The evidence should be used to make any necessary changes to the policy and/or the way it is implemented.
  - All staff and parents should contribute to the evidence collected and share in decisions about any necessary changes (Pre-school Learning Alliance, 2005).

Quality assurance

The local authority recognises that settings might need support and guidance in undertaking a Quality Assurance scheme, so it has developed it's own 'Quality Framework' to introduce settings to reflective practice and the self-Assessment process needed to achieve National Accreditation. The Local Framework is used as a 'stepping-stone' to a National Scheme, such as the Effective Early Learning Programme Quality Assurance Scheme (EEL).

The example of this local authority is typical of others across the country, as was evidenced in a report from the National Children's Bureau, *Integration in Practice* (Jamieson et al., 2000), which reviewed the quality improvement practices being used by local authorities at that time. Since 2000, many more local and national quality assurance schemes have developed. The DfES ring-fenced funding to local authorities to ensure they supported settings in achieving a recognised quality standard from one of the nationally accredited schemes. Although this funding is no longer ring–fenced, many local authorities continue to recognise the importance of supporting settings both financially and through mentoring to continue the quality improvement process. They recognise the benefits as being:

- *For children*

  - Good quality provision benefits children by positively affecting their cognitive, social and emotional development.
  - All young children, therefore deserve the highest quality care that we can provide.

- *For parents*

  - In choosing and engaging with early childhood services, parents need a recognised way of knowing that these settings are taking part in an accredited continuous quality improvement scheme.
  - This knowledge provides reassurance and confidence in the setting.

- *For staff*

  - All staff become involved in the continuous improvement process.
  - This provides an effective team building mechanism.

- *For the setting*

  - It provides a 'living document' that can be used for reference, training and a consistent approach to policy and procedure.
  - It provides evidence to support OFSTED inspections by providing a regularly updated approach to collating evidence for quality improvement.
  - It provides a means by which to value diversity and be consistent with anti-discriminatory practices and the principles of equal opportunities.
  - It addresses management practices which influences staff turnover rates, job satisfaction and staff development.

Where settings are involved in systematic quality improvement processes, such as nationally accredited quality assurance schemes, local authorities are able to support and monitor the quality of provision within their area. This provides data by which they can plan future support and training.

Managers need this type of support and encouragement, as leading staff teams through the quality improvement process is hard work, but vital if we are to have the best possible environments and learning experiences for our children.

Legislation

Within the early childhood sector, managers are generally only concerned with the practical aspects of legislation that affects them on a daily basis. This is usually by ensuring that their setting meets the requirements of the National Standards for Day care and Childminding, alongside delivery of the *Curriculum Guidance for the Foundation Stage* (CGFS, 2000), to provide good quality care and education.

The National Standards are set in the regulations of the Day Care and Childminding (National Standards) (England) Regulations 2003 No. 1996 and other regulations under Part XA of the Children Act 1989. These standards represent a baseline of quality below which no provider may fall, so the role of the manager is to ensure that they underpin a continuous improvement of quality within their setting.

There are 14 National Standards. These are:

- Standard 1 – Suitable Person
- Standard 2 – Organisation
- Standard 3 – Care, Learning and Play
- Standard 4 – Physical Environment
- Standard 5 – Equipment
- Standard 6 – Safety
- Standard 7 – Health
- Standard 8 – Food and Drink
- Standard 9 – Equal Opportunities
- Standard 10 – Special Needs (including special educational needs and disabilities)
- Standard 11 – Behaviour
- Standard 12 – Working in Partnership with Parents and Carers
- Standard 13 – Child Protection
- Standard 14 – Documentation.

Each standard describes a quality outcome and has a set of supporting criteria giving information about how the outcome can be achieved. The Registered Person in each setting is required, by the Children Act 1989 to meet these standards and have regard to the supporting criteria. The law also requires that OFSTED has regard to these when they inspect the setting.

Although the 14 standards remain the same, the criteria that supports them differs between the five categories of Day Care and Childminding provision. These are:

- Full Day Care
- Sessional Day Care
- Crèches
- Out of School Care
- Childminding.

Alongside the requirements in the Children Act 1989 for settings to meet the National Standards, the act also places a requirement on local authorities to provide guidance and support, through pre-registration meetings for those wanting to become a childminder.

The requirement of settings to deliver high-quality educational provision for 3- and 4-year-old children who access the free entitlement to nursery education grant is also set out in the legislation. Under the School Standard and Framework Act 1998, local authorities were required to establish Early Years Development Partnerships, setting out their duty to provide funding for the nursery education for 4-year-olds, which would be inspected for quality by OFSTED. It was also a requirement that local authorities and settings providing nursery education have regard to the *Special Educational Needs Code of Practice for* (DfES, 2001).

The Education Act 2002 extended the remit of nursery education to include 'funded nursery education' for 3-year-olds. The funding, like that for 4-year-olds was to be administered by the local authority through a Code of Practice which set out terms and conditions of the grant to which settings had to agree. This Act was also important for establishing the Foundation Stage as part of the National Curriculum, making it a Key Stage in the same way as Key Stage 1 and Key Stage 2. It placed the *Curriculum Guidance for the Foundation Stage* (CGFS, 2000) as the core document to be used for all funded nursery education for children aged 3 years to those at the end of the Reception year in school, or setting. The Act also established that OFSTED would inspect the quality of learning experiences for the child across all six areas of the curriculum, which it states as being:

1. Personal, social and emotional development.
2. Communication, language and literacy.
3. Mathematical development.
4. Knowledge and understanding of the world.
5. Physical development.
6. Creative development.

The 2002 Education Act also renamed the Early Years Development Partnerships as the Early Years Development and Childcare Partnerships (EYDCP), adding to the local authority a duty in respect to childcare.

In 2003 consultation began on the Green Paper *Every Child Matters* that resulted from the findings of the Climbié report. The recommendations of this paper, which became law in the Children Act 2004, have resulted in the creation of Children's Services Departments across the country, with the reorganisation of services to provide an integrated approach to service delivery. This is evidenced in the development of the first Children's Centres and Extended Schools across the country, and changing the way of working for many managers and practitioners in the early childhood sector.

The Children Act 2004 also established the five outcomes mentioned earlier in this chapter, against which services are now planned, monitored, evaluated and inspected.

Further changes to the early childhood sector are proposed in the Childcare Bill 2005 (that were set out in detail in the *Ten Year Strategy for Childcare,* HMT et al., 2004). The planned changes will impact on all practitioners as they propose:

- to place a new duty on local authorities to secure sufficient childcare for children up to the September after the child turns 14 (16 for disabled children)

- the entitlement of free part-time nursery education to be extended from 33 weeks a year to 38 weeks a year from 2008 and from 12.5 hours a week to 15 hours a week by 2010 (beginning in 2007), with an eventual goal of 20 hours a week
- by 2010 all parents of school-aged children to have year-round access to childcare from 8 a.m. to 6 p.m., with the result that most childcare for school-aged children will be linked to an extended school, although not necessarily provided by it
- to create a new legal framework to remove the current distinction between care and education and the separate regulatory and inspection requirements that exist for each. This will bring together the *Birth to Three Matters* framework and the *Curriculum Guidance for the Foundation Stage* as well as the associated National Standards into a single quality framework, which currently has the working title of the Early Development and Learning Framework. Under this framework, OFSTED will inspect integrated care and education as a single entity and make one judgement.

These legislative changes will mean different ways of working for many managers, but local authority staff will be involved in support and training at local level.

External monitoring and appraisal

All managers are required to undertake, as part of their role, performance management and appraisals. Settings that are affiliated to national organisations may adopt their policy on both performance management and appraisal, and many of the aspects already discussed in this chapter, such as self-assessment, quality assurance schemes and KEEP can provide evidence to support both of these systems.

One local authority has developed the criteria of KEEP into a framework into which each practitioner, as well as local authority staff, can note evidence to support their performance and training within each section. This provides an ongoing record for the practitioner to take to the annual appraisal meeting, or to a six-monthly review, from which to develop future targets and training plans.

The evidence also supports different forms of external monitoring. This chapter has considered in depth the external monitoring undertaken by OFSTED as this is common to all settings, but external moderation can be in many different forms and for different members of the staff team. Managers will be directly involved in visits by local authority staff who might visit on a regular basis to reflect on the setting's position regarding the provision of childcare or to support delivery of the *Birth to Three Matters* framework and the *Curriculum Guidance for the Foundation Stage*. They might ask your permission to bring the Regional Advisor for the Foundation Stage or other visitors to celebrate your good practice.

If a setting delivers the Foundation Stage for children who complete the Foundation Stage Profile at the end of Reception class (or equivalent provision), then they will also be involved in external moderation of the assessment that they have made. This will usually be undertaken by members of the local authority staff as well as expert Foundation Stage Qualified teachers, who will undertake shared observations with the practitioners and discuss the judgements that are made. External moderation also takes place when the setting completes a Nationally Accredited Quality Assurance Scheme. Managers and practitioners who have rigorously implemented a continuous approach to quality improvement across all members and aspects of the setting will have all evidence in place for this assessment.

External assessment, linked to staff undertaking further qualifications will be a familiar part of the work of many settings. Managers will need to consider the implications of all these visitors; they will need time and space in which to either spend time with the person involved in the meeting or assessment, or with the manager to provide feedback. In many settings it is difficult to find space that is not being used, but time to talk to the visitor ensures clarity of thought and the ability to concentrate on the issues without distraction.

Working with other professionals

Following a local authority Best Value Review into provision for children with additional needs and disabilities the group that had formed to consider the needs of children from birth to six years, decided to continue working to develop an 'All about me' folder that one of the parents said was desperately needed. The group comprised health, education, and social care staff as well as parents and carers. They met regularly to design the folder under the guidance of the parents and carers and finally produced a document that would record all visits to and by the professionals involved with their child. It also held the child's Health record book and the Record of Achievement used by the nursery to record observed achievements in the Foundation Stage. It was piloted within a Sure Start Local Programme area and was so successful that it is now being funded by the EYDCP for all children with additional needs.

This example shows how different professionals, practitioners and parent/carers can work together for the benefit of the children in their care. It is also an example of what the Children Act 2004 would regard as integrated working that was based on consultation with the users of services about their needs.

Managers need to think about developing this way of working, as many early childhood settings will be located within or affiliated to Children's Centres and Extended Schools where there will be an integrated approach to service delivery. One of the first difficulties to be overcome will be to clarify the different 'language' that the different professions use, and managers can do this together, to help their staff to feel secure when meeting with the staff from different agencies. One of the first challenges presented to the workforce in the integration agenda will affect all settings that are registered to deliver full day care as they will be directly involved in providing a seamless experience for the child between the 'care' and 'education' elements of the child's day, as required by the Childcare Bill 2005. Despite the different training backgrounds that might exist, a common language, linked to the proposed Early Years Foundation Stage will provide managers with a new strategy, alongside the other aspects discussed in this chapter, on which to build a strong, well-qualified workforce that provides a high-quality provision for the child.

CHAPTER 30

DEVELOPING AND MANAGING THE PROFESSIONAL ROLE

Janet Moyles and Siân Adams

Janet Moyles PhD is Professor Emeritus at Anglia Ruskin University. She has worked as an early years teacher and head, and has written widely. She has directed several research projects including *Jills of All Trades?* (ATL, 1996), *Too Busy to Play?* (Leicester, 1997–2000), *SPEEL (Study of Pedagogical Effectiveness in Early Learning)* (DfES, 2002) and *Recreating the Reception Year* (ATL, 2004).

Siân Adams PhD has a background totally rooted in the early years. Siân was engaged in several research projects with Janet Moyles relating to effective, playful pedagogy in the early years, including *Recreating the Reception Year* (ATL, 2004). Her latest book, co-authored with Janet Moyles, is *Images of Violence* (Featherstone Publications, 2005).

Aims

To develop understanding of:

- ☐ and consider what it means to be 'professional' in early education
- ☐ and explore basic competences in terms of attitudes, knowledge, understanding and skills
- ☐ and examine strategies for developing competence and managing the practitioner's role.

Introduction

In this chapter, we will explore a range of issues to do with the professional role and its development. The first section explores professionalism and the second section relates to identified basic 'competences', that is, the attitudes, knowledge, understanding and skills needed by early years practitioners. The third section examines how to develop and extend the professional role and the fourth section investigates how to manage and develop oneself and others. These four sections are underpinned by our 'Story of Jane', which explores the content of the four sections in relation to one practitioner. Jane happens to be a nursery nurse but could be any kind of worker in the early years.

'I'm just a nursery nurse!' The story of Jane

Jane (aged 32 years) has been a nursery nurse in the same nursery for 15 years. She is competent, comfortable and established in her role, enthusiastic and respected by staff, children and parents alike. She sees her role as providing activities for children within established routines, with the teaching role occupied by the teacher. When asked about her attitude to children she says 'Oh, I love the children – it's great to see them happy in the nursery. And I really get on well with the parents.' She is content that she does a good job and knows intuitively what is expected of her. She admits that her curriculum knowledge is 'shaky' but is insistent that the children are 'settling well, which is what matters'. She reads *Nursery Education* in the staffroom and has attended courses about hygiene and health and safety. Jane is able to talk about her role at the level of practice. She leaves the analysis and evaluation of her role in providing for children's learning and development to senior staff.

On the setting's recommendation, Jane accepts an invitation to join a research project. From the beginning, it is clear that she has an open attitude and a willingness and eagerness to think about her role and engage with other professionals in the project team, although she insists that she is 'just a nursery nurse'! Monthly research meetings offer Jane

(Continued)

(Continued)

time to explore various aspects of her practice and she values the time and space to think deeply about children's learning and the context of her own development as a practitioner. In the research group she also has to cope with her own strengths and weaknesses in ways that have not been necessary in the nursery, making her realise how much she still has to learn – and how exciting that prospect is! Jane also recognises that her professional development is mainly in her own hands. As someone keen to do well, she uses the research forum to explore her own attitudes, knowledge, understanding and skills in order to develop both her competences and strategies for extending and managing her role more effectively.

What does it mean to be a professional in early education?

The English government's flagship documents *Every Child Matters* (DfES, 2005b) and the *Common Core of Skills and Knowledge for the Children's Workforce Framework* (DfES, 2005a) both demand high-quality practitioners who adopt professional roles and responsibilities. While it may be obvious that, if children are to succeed in their early years and later life, they need the highest-level interactions with adults (Edgington, 2004; Sylva et al., 2004), some practitioners struggle to get to grips with their role as 'professionals'. We are still asking the question 'What does it mean to be professional in the early years?' (Fumoto et al., 2004). To many, it would appear that, in the cameo above, Jane was acting 'professionally' before she joined the research project. She was carrying out her role effectively, understood it in terms of others around her, engaged in management-directed appraisal and generally knew how to provide interesting activities for children. Is this 'technical competence' sufficient in the context of being an early years professional in the twenty-first century?

It seems to us from undertaking our own research (Adams et al., 2003; Moyles and Adams, 2001; Moyles and Musgrove, 2003; Moyles and Suschitzky, 1997; Moyles et al., 2002) and that of others (for example, Atkinson and Claxton, 2000; Rodd, 1998) that the professional role has changed significantly over the past few years, especially in early years. All practitioners now need to think about themselves not just in relation to practice but in relation to the broader concept of being a professional (see, for example, Day, 2005; Ghaye and Ghaye, 1998). Helsby (1995) makes a useful distinction between 'being professional' and 'behaving professionally', the former related to pay, status and autonomy and the latter to dedication, commitment and highly skilled practice. Professional behaviour is, to us, a key determinant of effective practice. Declaring that 'I'm just a nursery nurse' undermines the crucial role that such practitioners undertake and, more importantly, can mean that the nursery nurse feels that fulfilling day-to-day practice is sufficient in itself. But as the final report of the EPPE Project emphasises: 'Effective pedagogy includes interaction traditionally associated with the term "teaching", the provision of instructive learning environments and "sustained shared thinking" to extend children's learning' (see Sylva et al., 2004). This type of practice certainly requires thinking practitioners.

As we can see in reviewing Jane's position, she found through engagement in the research project, that there is much more to being and behaving professionally. Behaving as a professional means having sufficient knowledge and understanding of children, their learning and development, to be able to challenge everyday practice and to adapt it where relevant through continual interrogation and analysis of what best meets children's needs. Moreover, it also means that practitioners must have the ability to scrutinise their own actions and reactions to establish their impact upon children and upon those in the wider context of the settings in which they operate. As Goodfellow (2004: 68) points out 'It is important to address hidden qualities and dimensions of our professional practice if we are to improve our way of being professional'. This is exactly what Jane began to do through engaging in the research project: she began to confront many aspects of her role and found that it was both more motivating and felt more 'professional' to have a clear personal understanding of her strengths and weaknesses and also to understand her own role more thoroughly. As a result, she was, in turn, more able to relate to the strengths and weaknesses of the children with whom she played and worked, and to understand in greater depth how to provide for sustained development and learning.

Jane was also supported in her own professional development through being part of a process that documented areas of key thinking in relation to one of her main activities, that of playing with children (Moyles and Adams, 2001). Initially, Jane and others felt that making provision for play was sufficient to ensure that children learned. When they viewed videos of play activities in their own settings, however, it quickly became evident that practitioners have a major role in ensuring that play activities are translated into learning outcomes. This enabled Jane and the group to look closely at their own roles, which, in turn, inevitably led them to critiquing their own practices and, more importantly, their thinking about day-to-day practices. This led to both a form of self- and peer-assessment which all those within the research found supportive and helpful in their professional thinking and development.

The kind of framework developed in StEPs (Moyles and Adams, 2001) was just one of a number of such frameworks which, over the past few years, have been available to practitioners and against which they can now undertake different forms of self-assessment (and peer-assessment) of their professional roles. In Jane's nursery prior to her involvement in the research, appraisals and self-assessments were reliant mainly on a system of established relationships. These are fine and important in creating a good ethos in any setting. Combined with other forms of high-quality assessment they are a powerful force for developing professionalism. This is where analysis of the professional role is so important: it establishes where each individual 'is' within the various frameworks and within the overall adult group within a setting. Knowing everyone's individual strengths and weaknesses helps all to work together effectively for the children.

What are the basic competences necessary for early years professionals?

While much emphasis was given in the early days of developing an early years curriculum to children's developmental needs, it was quickly recognised that effectiveness in those areas depends heavily upon how adults both interact with children and perceive themselves within those interactions, which, of course, includes aspects such as planning to meet individual needs and planning for one's own professional development. Various frameworks, including that developed by the present authors in the *Study of Pedagogical Effectiveness in Early Learning* project (SPEEL) (Moyles et al., 2002) and the Siraj-Blatchford et al. Research into Effective Pedagogy in the Early Years project (REPEY) (Siraj-Blatchford et al., 2002), have led to the presentation by the DfES of the new *Key Elements of Effective Practice* document (KEEP) (DfES 2005e).

Key Elements of Effective Practice uses six headings to outline the key elements, all focused on the early years professional:

1. Understanding of the individual and diverse ways that children develop and learn.
2. Relationships with both children and adults.
3. Knowledge and understanding in order to actively support and extend children's learning in and across all areas and aspects of learning.
4. Practice in meeting all children's needs, learning styles and interests.
5. Work with other professionals within and beyond the setting.
6. Work with parents, carers and the wider community (DfES, 2005e: 5).

We argue that, in many ways, these six headings do not go far enough in emphasising the need for practitioners to have a profound understanding of themselves, which we believe is crucial to being able to call oneself a professional. However, almost by default, these key elements show that being able to claim high levels of effectiveness requires a real depth of understanding both of children and practice, which inevitably means understanding one's own position in generating and sustaining such effectiveness. The KEEP document does emphasise:

> Effective practice … requires committed, enthusiastic and reflective practitioners with a breadth and depth of knowledge, skills and understanding. Effective practitioners use their own learning to improve their work with young children and their families in ways which are sensitive, positive and non-judgemental. Therefore, through initial and on-going training and development, practitioners need to develop, demonstrate and continuously improve … (DfES, 2005e: 5)

As Jane discovered, realising your own effectiveness depends on being able to analyse what it is you currently do, what this means in terms of outcomes for children and others within the context of the setting and how practice can be extended and developed. This is, of course, a cyclical and ongoing process and one which needs sustained and co-ordinated effort. While KEEP is intended as an 'evaluation tool for local authorities' (ibid.: 7), self-assessment (and, we would also argue, peer-assessment) is a vital process in which the professional must adopt honesty, self-respect and an understanding of their role in relation to that of others (see later in this chapter).

In SPEEL (Moyles, et al., 2002) the present authors worked with practitioners in trying to establish the components of effective pedagogy in the early years. As well as similar headings to those above in KEEP, the research generated 127 key statements covering:

- learning and teaching interactions
- the learning and teaching context
- planning, assessment and evaluation
- practitioners' beliefs and values in relation to children's entitlements and their own roles and practice
- practitioners' knowledge and understanding
- practitioners capacity to be reflective and thoughtful
- practitioners' personal qualities.

We found that, of all these, the practitioners' capacity to be reflective and thoughtful dominated other aspects in so far as all other aspects depended critically on this ability. (We also found that 'effective management and team-work … are crucial to individual practitioners being able to fulfil their roles effectively' (Moyles, et al., 2002), as we have seen in previous chapters of this book). In the SPEEL project (as in StEPs) it was a real surprise to practitioners to be challenged on quite straightforward elements of their practice, for example, why we provide a home-area in a setting or what children learn through playing with water. Both of these generated much discussion – and much learning – for practitioners, as they articulated, and sometimes defended, their views, beliefs and values.

In the Essex Effective Practice Evaluation Scheme (Early Years) (Moyles and Musgrove, 2003), the key statements from SPEEL were extended and converted into an evaluation scheme against which practitioners could rate themselves on a continuum from 'adequate' to 'exemplary'. Under a heading 'Developing professionally', for example, practitioners self-evaluate in relation to:

1. How they are able to reflect on their own professional development.
2. Their professional awareness.
3. Their professional development opportunities.

In relation to 1 above, as an example, the four progressive statements are:

Acceptable — Thinks in general terms about the quality of own pedagogy.

Good — Examines periodically the quality of own pedagogy and the extent of own knowledge and understanding. Acknowledges own strengths and weaknesses and thinks through necessary changes to practice. Relates such self-knowledge to training and professional development needs.

Very good — Reflects regularly upon own pedagogy, professional awareness and knowledge and understanding of early years practice. Considers changes at both practical and conceptual levels. Identifies specific training and professional development needs.

Exemplary — Challenges own pedagogy through critical and informed analysis of practice and thinking. Monitors own professional development needs and plans necessary involvement in training and development opportunities, including reading relevant research.

In total, there are 264 sets of effectiveness statements and ample evidence, through cameos and examples, is given to support practitioners in determining their levels of professional development. As a practical example in relation to statements given above, Jane would have initially been operating at an 'acceptable' level but, after involvement in professional development, would have advanced to 'very good' on the scale.

The next two sections look more specifically at how practitioners might approach the evaluation of their professional role and what it looks and feels like to be part of the development and management of the professional role, using Jane's experiences as the mainstay.

Developing and extending the professional role – understandings and strategies

As we have seen, developing a professional role involves practitioners seeing themselves as professionals rather than 'only helpers' or 'just early years' – no doubt many early years practitioners have heard those words escape from their lips!

The status related to working in the Foundation Stage, with all its challenges and complexities of understanding the developing child, has often been under-rated. Therefore, it can be helpful if practitioners take an active role in recognising, assessing and promoting a sense of empowerment and confidence within their professional role.

Returning to Jane, it is possible that, in her first few years as a nursery nurse, Jane thought in general terms about her role, rather than in specific terms about the quality of her own pedagogy and effectiveness. For example, she might:

- consider the success of children's involvement in the home-area based on their enjoyment
- assess how successful the activity might be in terms of how she, as a practitioner, feels about it
- think further about training opportunities in order to develop her expertise as a nursery nurse having recognised her own curriculum knowledge as somewhat shaky.

However, with experience and through the informed, focused support of others within and beyond the setting, she might begin to develop her professional role in more specific ways (Adams, 2000). She might, for example:

- look more closely at what children *learn* when they are playing, as well as consider their emotional welfare
- reflect upon ways in which she can successfully support children's learning through play so that she gradually becomes critically aware of what constitutes a 'good job'
- take time to explore how she might update her own knowledge of the curriculum and how children learn through playful experiences.

In adopting a constructively critical approach to her practice, Jane is more likely to see herself as a professional, with training needs and aspirations relating to the complex role of working with young children, rather than standing still in professional terms as 'just a nursery nurse'.

So, what factors contribute to Jane's maturing professionalism? How does she promote a sense of self-efficacy, with its implications for self-esteem, motivation, commitment and job satisfaction (Pajares, 2003)?

The very process of reflecting on how she impacts upon children's learning provides us with evidence of her maturing professional role and an increased pedagogical awareness of her own attitude, knowledge, understanding and skills. It is important to remember that young children do not develop or learn tidily or chronologically! Consequently, ensuring that pedagogical dilemmas – those moments when it is difficult to know quite how to respond to a child's comments or behaviours – demand informed responses. For example, how does Jane determine what children are learning when they enter the home-area? How does she decide if, when and how to support their play so that all children continue to be enriched and challenged? How does she respond if her own values are challenged by children's behaviours (Adams and Moyles, 2005)?

In the story about Jane, we saw that she displays an interest in her professional development in attending courses and reading literature provided in the staffroom, but she leaves more informed considerations of children's learning to senior staff. It is significant that, initially, Jane's professional development (reading literature, attending courses on health and safety), while informing vital aspects of her role, does not also extend her shaky knowledge of the curriculum or child development. So it is inevitable and appropriate that more complex considerations are left to those who are more appropriately informed or qualified.

But this does not need to limit Jane's professional understanding or development. Jane has made significant steps towards extending her professional role through:

- beginning to develop a critical and reflective approach to her practice
- extending her knowledge, understanding and skills in specific, focused areas.

She can further develop her role as a nursery nurse by taking an active role in being a manager of her own learning and supporting others in their development and learning.

Being a manager ... being managed

There are several indications that Jane is beginning to assume responsibility for aspects of her own learning.

1. Jane *accepts* the invitation to join the research project. We make an assumption that this is an informed decision and, with that ownership, Jane is likely to be highly motivated to engage in the project-related issues and challenges.
2. She displays an *eagerness to think* about her role. A supportive manager would have made this opportunity available to Jane, and we read she is responding with enthusiasm and commitment.

3. She manages her diary so that she can commit *regular time* in which to explore specific aspects of her practice.

4. She is prepared to confront her own 'not knowing' as well as acknowledge and build on her *strengths*.

5. She displays evidence of her willingness to be challenged with her *open attitude* and acceptance of the invitation to join the research group (Adams, 2000). It is important not to undermine the discomfort associated with being challenged: it is not always easy to accept a state of 'not knowing' and we sense Jane's unease in her comments that she's 'just a nursery nurse'.

6. She recognises that, although her manager has made this opportunity available, her *professional development is mainly in her own hands.* Jane is responsible for developing and maximising her 'own potential as an effective early years practitioner' (Moyles and Musgrove, 2002: 93).

7. Within the research project Jane also benefits from *engaging with other professionals in the project team. Working with* informed others allows Jane to benefit from different dynamic perspectives of those informed others working within her professional community. Sharing, talking about and articulating aspects of practice with colleagues also helps to surface previously intuitive pedagogy (Atkinson and Claxton, 2000).

It is likely that, with additional informed support, Jane's insecure curriculum knowledge will be developed so that she will be able to make more effective, confident responses to the children's activities. As research continues to explore the developing child, then the professional's pedagogical stance must in turn develop to reflect the current constructs of young children. Part of Jane's challenge is to accommodate the change in her perception of her professional role: from nurturing to also teaching. Without Jane's willingness to respond to challenge, she would deny children the benefit of contemporary understanding of how young children learn.

Effective and reflective practice is dependent on informed, focused support (Adams, 2000). Through discussing contemporary issues with informed, supportive colleagues, Jane has discovered a context in which she is respected and encouraged to justify and provide a rationale for her own practice (Moyles and Musgrove, 2002: 91). She also welcomes opportunities to ensure that practice is informed by current and informed understanding of how children learn (Kyriakides, 2002).

Jane's proactive role in her own professional development and as manager of her own learning will help to develop both her competences and her strategies for extending and managing her role more effectively. In allowing others to support her, she has, in turn, enabled them to develop their own professional thinking and behaviours.

Conclusion

As we have seen, in this and other chapters, the early years professional role is somewhat awesome in its demands and the breadth and depth of its content, even if some still believe it to be an easy option! Doing our best for the children and families is what makes the whole process of professional development vital, exciting and stimulating. Children need and deserve the best practitioners. Those people are the ones who understand themselves as professionals and have the confidence and competence continually to examine their own attitudes, knowledge, understanding and skills as determined in the KEEP document.

EXERCISE 30.1

1. Ask a peer to observe you with a group of children, preferably with a video, perhaps using one of the sections of the Common Core. Observe the video together and discuss what evidence there is of you meeting the standards.
2. Using the same section of the Common Core, write down examples of how you are able to show competence, strengths and understanding within the content of the chosen section.
3. Analyse 1 and 2 above in terms of what you could improve, perhaps using your peer colleague for support.
4. Consider how you feel about the analysis of your strengths and weaknesses (in 2 and 3 above). Does it make you feel empowered in your role? How can you use this information in appraisal?
5. Jane determined to extend her knowledge; make provision for use of time and engage with other professionals. See whether you can:

   (a) identify a specific area in which you can develop your knowledge
   (b) plan how you will commit regular time
   (c) determine how you will communicate more effectively with colleagues through training; research projects, higher/further education activities; LEA links; staff meetings.

Glossary

Effectiveness	Being the best you can in the early years practitioner role.
Pedagogy	The art and science of learning and teaching.
Peer-assessment	Having one's role analysed and evaluated by a peer.
Professional/professionalism	Behaving in a professional manner, that is, accepting responsibility for one's own actions and reactions.
Reflective	Thinking about one's role and practice with the intention of analysing, evaluating and making relevant changes.
Self-assessment	Analysing and evaluating one's own role.

Key skills

Capacity to reflect
Development of supportive relationships
Observation and analysis of practice
Self-assessment

Further reading

Atkinson, T. and Claxton, G. (2000) (eds) *The Intuitive Practitioner.* Buckingham: Open University Press.
This is a wonderful collection of papers which explore the professional world of the practitioner in relation to the dynamic relationship between reason and intuition in the context of practice. The various authors demonstrate that intuition, as well as knowledge, have a vital role in the development of professional judgement and expertise.

Brubacher, J., Case, C. and Reagan, T. (1994) *Becoming a Reflective Educator.* London: Sage Publications.
This book provides a superb balance of informed discussion and an abundance of practical examples of practitioners striving to adopt a reflective approach to practice. The authors liken the lengthy reflective process to the stage 'after a toy [rabbit] has lost its hair and becomes shabby, so becoming a truly reflective teacher involves time, experience and, inevitably, a bit of wear around the edges' (p. 25).

Day, C. (2004) *A Passion for Teaching.* London: RoutledgeFalmer.
While this is essentially a book about qualified teachers, everything it says applies to all early years practitioners. Christopher Day demonstrates that passionate teachers are aware of the challenge of the broader social contexts in which they work, have a sense of identity and believe they can make a difference to children. He asserts that teachers with passion are those who are committed, enthusiastic and intellectually and emotionally energetic in their work.

Early Years: An International Journal of Research and Development.
This journal provides a range of opportunities to explore and engage with other practitioners' reflections. For example, the Fumoto et al. (2004) article in the references.

Edgington, M. (2004) *The Foundation Stage Teacher in Action.* London: Paul Chapman Publishing.
The author is very well known in early years circles and this book is a must-have for those who work with young children. It describes the qualities needed of the early years professional and gives practical guidance on developing pedagogic skills.

REFERENCES

Abbott, A. and Langston, A. (eds) (2005) *Birth to Three Matters: Supporting the Framework of Effective Practice*. Maidenhead: Open University Press.

Abbott, L. and Moylett, H. (1997) *Working With Under Threes: Responding to Children's Needs*. Buckingham: Open University Press.

Adams, S. (2000) 'An investigation of the deconstruction and reconstruction processes within the context of reflective pedagogical practice and with the content of play', unpublished PhD thesis, University of Leicester School of Education.

Adams, S. and Moyles, J. (2005) *Images of Violence*. Husbands Bosworth: Featherstone Education.

Adams, S., Alexander, E., Drummond, M.-J. and Moyles, J. (2003) *Inside the Foundation Stage: Recreating the Reception Year*. Report on research commissioned by the Association of Teachers and Lecturers, London.

Ainsworth, M.D.S., Blehar, M.C., Wakes, E. and Stayton, D. (1978) *Patterns of Attachment: A Psychological Study of the Strange Situation*. Hillsdale, NJ: Erlbaum Associates.

Alexander, R. (2000) *Culture and Pedagogy, International Comparisons in Primary Education*. Oxford: Blackwell.

Alfrey, C. (ed.) (2003) *Understanding Children's Learning: A Text for Teaching Assistants*. London: David Fulton.

Anning, A. and Ring, K. (2004) *Making Sense of Children's Drawings*. Maidenhead: Open University Press.

Association for Science Education (2001) *Be Safe*. Hatfield: ASE.

Athey, C. (1991) *Extending Thought in Young Children: A Parent–Teacher Partnership*. London: Paul Chapman Publishing.

Atkinson, T. and Claxton, G. (2000) *The Intuitive Practitioner*. Buckingham: Open University Press.

Baker, C. (2000) *A Parents' and Teachers' Guide to Bilingualism*. Clevedon, Boston, Toronto and Sydney: Multilingual Matters Ltd.

Barsotti, C. (2004) 'Walking on threads of silk, an interview with Loris Malaguzzi', in P. Moss (ed.), *Children in Europe*. Edinburgh: Children in Scotland.

Bazalgette, J. (2002) 'Integration in behaviour', a presentation for the Consultant Leaders Development Programme of the National College for School Leadership, Grubb Institute, London.

Bentham, S. (2006) *A Teaching Assistants' Guide to Managing Behaviour in the Classroom*. London: Routledge.

Blunkett, D. (1999) 'Foreword', in *The National Curriculum*. London: DfEE/QCA.

Bowlby, J. (1951) *Maternal Care and Mental Health*. Geneva: World Health Organisation.

Bowlby, J. (1953) *Child Care and the Growth of Love*. London: Penguin.

Boyatzis, R. (1999) 'Self-directed change and learning as a necessary meta-competency for success and effectiveness in the twenty-first century', in R. Sims and J. Veres III (eds), *Keys to Employee Success in Coming Decades*. London: Quorum Books. pp. 15–31.

Bretherton, I. (1992) 'The origins of attachment: John Bowlby and Mary Ainsworth', *Developmental Psychology*, 28: 759–75.

Brindle, D. (2004) 'Clash of cultures', *Society Guardian*, 19 May. Also at http://society.guardian.co.uk. children/story/0,,1219562,00.html.

British Educational Research Association (BERA) Early Years Special Interest Group (2003) *Early Years Research: Pedagogy, Curriculum and Adult Roles, Training and Professionalism*. Nottingham: BERA.

Bronfenbrenner, U. (1979) *The Ecology of Human Development: Experiments by Nature and Design*. Cambridge, MA, and London: Harvard University Press.

Brooker, L. (2002) *Starting School – Young Children Learning Cultures*. Buckingham: Open University Press.

Brooker, L. and Broadbent, L. (2003) 'Personal, social and emotional development: the child makes meaning in a social world', in J. Riley (ed.), *Learning in the Early Years*. London: Sage.

Brown, B. (1998) *Unlearning Discrimination in the Early Years*. Stoke-on-Trent: Trentham Books.

Brown, B. (2001) *Combating Discrimination Persona Dolls in Action* (Video and Support Book). London: Persona Doll Training.

Brown, B. (2004) *Celebrating Diversity: inclusion in practice* (Video and Support Book). London: Persona Doll Training.

Brown, F. (ed.) (2003) *Playwork Theory and Practice*. Buckingham: Open University Press.

Bruce, T. (1991) *Time to Play in Early Childhood Education*. London: Hodder & Stoughton.

Bruce, T. (2001) *Learning through Play: Babies, Toddlers and the Foundation Years*. London: Hodder Arnold.

Bruce, T. (2004a) *Developing Learning in Early Childhood*. London: Paul Chapman Publishing.

Bruce, T. (2004b) *Cultivating Creativity: Babies, Toddlers and Young Children*. London: Hodder Arnold.

Bruce, T. (2005) *Early Childhood Education*. 3rd edition. London: Hodder Arnold.

Bruce, T. and Meggitt, C. (2002) *Child Care and Education*. 3rd edition. London: Hodder & Stoughton.

Bruner, J. (1960) *The Process of Education*. Cambridge, MA: Harvard University Press.

Bruner, J. (1996) *The Culture of Education*. Cambridge, MA: Harvard University Press.

Burningham, J. (1982) *Avocado Baby*. London: Jonathan Cape.

Buzan, T. and Buzan, B. (2003) *The Mind Map Book: Radiant Thinking – Major Evolution in Human Thought*. London: BBC Books.

Carr, M. (2001) *Learning Stories: Assessment in Early Childhood Settings*. London: Paul Chapman Publishing.

Carr, M. and May, H. (2000) 'Te Whariki: curriculum voices', in H. Penn (ed.), *Early Childhood Services, Theory, Policy and Practice*. Buckingham: Open University Press.

Carruthers, E. and Worthington, M. (2006) *Children's Mathematics: Making Marks, Making Meaning*. 2nd edition. London: Paul Chapman Publishing.

Centre for Studies on Inclusive Education (2005) 'Inclusion basics', http://inclusion.uwe.ac.uk/csie/csiehome.htm.

CGFS (2000) See QCA, DfEE, (2000)

'Children's Workforce Strategy: a strategy to build a world-class workforce for children and young people', www.dfes.gov.uk/consultations.

Chomsky, N. (1975) *Reflections on Language*. New York: Pantheon Books.

Clark, A. and Moss, P. (2001) *Listening to Young Children: The Mosaic Approach*. London: National Children's Bureau Enterprises Ltd.

Claxton, G. (1999) *Building Learning Power*. Bristol: Teaching and Learning Organisation.

Communicating Matters (2005) A DfES course at level 3 for those with two or more years of experience.

Dahlburg, G., Moss, P. and Pence, A. (1999) *Beyond Quality in Early Childhood Education and Care*. London: RoutledgeFalmer.

Damasio, A. (2004) *Looking for Spinoza*. London: Vintage/Random Press.

Das Gupta, P. (1994) 'Images of childhood and theories of child development', in Oates, J. (ed.), *The Foundations of Child Development*. Buckingham: Open University Press.

David, T. and Goouch, K. (2001) 'Early literacy teaching: "The Third Way"', *Education*, 3–13 June.

David, T., Goouch, K., Powell, S. and Abbott, L. (2003) *Birth to Three Matters: A Review of the Literature*. Research Report 444. London: DfES Publications.

David, T., Raban, B., Ure, C., Goouch, K., Jago, M., Barriere, I. and Lambirth, A. (2000) *Making Sense of Early Literacy*. Stoke-on-Trent: Trentham Books.

Davies, M. (2003) *Movement and Dance in Early Childhood*. 2nd edition. London: Paul Chapman Publishing.

Day, C. (2005) *A Passion for Teaching*. London: RoutledgeFalmer.

Department for Education and Employment (DfEE) (1989) *The National Curriculum*. London: DfEE.

Department for Education and Employment (DfEE) (1998) *The National Literacy Strategy Framework for Teaching*. London: DfEE.

Department for Education and Employment (DfEE) (1999) 'The National Curriculum: a handbook for teachers in England, Key Stages 1 and 2', www.nc.uk.net.

Department for Education and Employment and Qualifications and Curriculum Authority (DfEE and QCA) (1999) *The National Curriculum: Handbook for Primary Teachers in England*. London: DfEE/QCA.

Department for Education and Skills (DfES) (2001) *Special Educational Needs Code of Practice*. London: DfES.

Department for Education and Skills (DfES) (2002) *Birth to Three Matters: A Framework to Support Children in their Earliest Years*. London: DfES Publications.

Department for Education and Skills (DfES) (2003) *Excellence and Enjoyment: A Strategy for Primary Schools*. London: DfES/QCA.

Department for Education and Skills (DfES) (2004a) *Every Child Matters: Change for Children*. London: DfES. Also at www.everychildmatters.gov.uk.

Department for Education and Skills (DfES) (2004b) *Excellence & Enjoyment in Primary Years Containing Learning and Teaching – Professional Development Materials*. London: DfES.

Department for Education and Skills (DfES) (2004c) *Choice for Parents, the Best Start for Children: A Ten Year Struggle for Childcare*. London: HMSO.

Department for Education and Skills (DfES) (2004d) *Every Child Matters: Next Steps*. London: DfES. Also at www.everychildmatters.gov.uk.

Department for Education and Skills (DfES) (2004e) *A New Relationship with Schools: Improving Performance through School Self-Evaluation*. London: DfES.

Department for Education and Skills (DfES) (2004f) *The Effective Provision of Pre-School Education Project: Findings from Pre-School to end of Key Stage 1. Final Report*. London: DfES/Sure Start.

Department for Education and Skills (DfES) (2005a) Foundation Stage Parents: Partners in Learning folder, DfES 1210-2005G.

Department for Education and Skills (DfES) (2005b) *Every Child Matters*. London: DfES.

Department for Education and Skills (DfES) (2005c) *Children's Workforce Strategy, Consultation Paper*. London: DfES.

Department for Education and Skills (DfES) (2005d) *Childcare Bill Consultation Paper*. London: DfES. Also at www.dfes.gov.uk/consultations/.

Department for Education and Skills (DfES) (2005e) *KEEP – Key Elements of Effective Practice*. London: DfES/Sure Start.

Department for Education and Skills (DfES) (2005f) *Common Core of Skills and Knowledge for the Children's Workforce*. Nottingham: DfES Publications.

Department for Education and Skills and Department for Work and Pensions (DfES/DWP) (2003) *Full Day Care: National Standards for Under Eights Day Care and Childminding*. Nottingham: DfES Publications.

Department for Education and Skills (DfES), Sure Start and Qualifications and Curriculum Authority (QCA) (2003) *Continuing the Learning Journey*. London: DfES/Sure Start Publications.

Department of Health (DoH) (2003) *Keeping Children Safe – the Government's Response to the Victoria Climbié Inquiry Report and the Joint Chief Inspectors' Report Safeguarding Children* (Cm 5861). London: TSO.

Department of Health (DoH) and Home Office (2003) *The Victoria Climbié Inquiry: Report of an Inquiry by Lord Laming* (Cm 5730). London: TSO.

Desforges, C. (2003) *The Impact of Parental Involvement, Parental Support and Family Education on Pupil Achievement and Adjustment: A Review of the Literature.* DfES Research Report 433, www. dfes.gov.uk/research.

Dewey, J. (1899) *The School and Society.* Chicago, IL: University of Chicago Press.

Doherty-Sneddon, G. (2003) *Children's Unspoken Language.* London: Jessica Kingsley.

Donaldson, M. (1978) *Children's Minds.* London: Fontana Press.

Drummond, M.J. (2002) 'Listening to young children talking', www.earlychildhood.org.uk/download/ keynote.

Duffy, B. (1998) *Supporting Creativity and Imagination in the Early Years.* Maidenhead: Open University Press.

Duffy, B. (2005) *Supporting Creativity and Imagination in the Early Years.* 2nd edition. Maidenhead: Open University Press/McGraw-Hill.

Dunn, J. (1988) *The Beginnings of Social Understanding.* Oxford: Blackwell.

Dweck, C. (1988) *Self-Theories: Their Role in Motivation, Personality and Development.* London: Taylor and Francis.

Early Childhood Forum (2003) *Policy Statement: Definition of Inclusion.* Leaflet.

Early Years Trainers Anti-Racist Network (EYTARN) (2001) *A Policy for Excellence: Developing a Policy for Equality in Early Years Settings.* London: EYTARN.

Easen, P., Kendall, K. and Shaw, J. (1992) 'Parents and educators: dialogue and development through partnership', *Children & Society*, 6(4): 282–96.

Edgington, M. (1998) *The Nursery Teacher in Action.* 2nd edition. London: Paul Chapman Publishing.

Edgington, M. (2004) *The Foundation Stage Teacher in Action.* 3rd edition. London: Paul Chapman Publishing.

Education and Employment Committee (2000–01) *First Report, Early Years*, vols 1 and 2. London: HMSO.

Edwards, C., Gandini, L. and Foreman, G. (1998) *The Hundred Languages of Children.* New York: Ablex.

Elkington, J. (2005) Personal communication.

EPPE and REPEY: summary reports of these two research papers are available as downloadable PDF files from various sources, for example: www.ioe.ac.uk/cdl/eppe/pdfe/eppe_brief2503.pdf and www.surestart. gov.uk/_doc/0-B51527.pdf.

Equal Opportunities Commission (2005) 'Occupational Segregation: Working Paper Series, No. 35, Men in childcare', www.eoc.org.uk.

Evangelou, M., Brooks. G., Smith, S. and Jennings, D. (2005) *The Birth to School Study: A Longitudinal Evaluation of the Peers Early Education Partnership (PEEP) 1998–2005.* Nottingham: DfES Publications.

Fagen, R. (1975) 'Modelling how and why play works', in J. Bruner, A. Jolly and K. Sylva (eds), *Play – its Role in Development and Evolution.* London: Penguin.

ferl.becta, http://ferl.becta.org.uk/display.cfm?resID=7593&page=633&catID=657.

Finch, S. (1999) quoted by J. Moorhead in 'Out of the mouths of babes', *Guardian*, 2 June, p. 9.

Frabetti, R. (2005) 'Eyes and silences', *Early Childhood Practice: The Journal for Multi-Professional Practice*, 7(1): 63–70.

Frost, J.L., Wortham, S.C. and Reifel, S. (2005) *Play and Child Development.* 2nd edition. Upper Saddle River, NJ: Pearson Merrill Prentice Hall.

Fullan, M. (2001) *Leading in a Culture of Change.* San Francisco, CA: Jossey-Bass.

Fullan, M. (2003) *The Moral Imperative of School Leadership.* Thousand Oaks, CA: Corwin Press.

Fumoto, H., Hargreaves, D.J. and Maxwell, S. (2004) 'The concept of teaching: a reappraisal', *Early Years*, 24(2): 179–91.

Gardner, H. (1993) *Frames of Mind: The Theory of Multiple Intelligences.* 2nd edition. London: Fontana.

General Teaching Council and National College of School Leadership(GTC and NCSL) (2005) 'Networks the potential for teacher learning', TPLF05: P-NETW-0905, info@gtce.org.uk, www.gtce.org.uk.

Ghaye, A. and Gaye, K. (1998) *Teaching and Learning through Critical Reflective Practice*. London: David Fulton.

Goddard Blyth, S. (2004) *The Well Balanced Child: Movement and Early Learning*. Stroud: Hawthorn Press.

Goldsworthy, A., Watson, R. and Wood Robinson, V. (1998) 'Sometimes it's not fair', *Primary Science Review*, 53, May/June: 15–17.

Goleman, D. (1996) *Emotional Intelligence*. London: Bloomsbury.

Goleman, D. (1999) *Working with Emotional Intelligence*. London: Bloomsbury.

Goleman, D., Boyatzis, R., and McKee, A. (2002) *The New Leaders: Transforming the Art of Leadership into the Science of Results*. London: Time Warner.

Goodfellow, J. (2004) 'Documenting professional practice through the use of a professional portfolio', *Early Years: An International Journal of Research and Development*, 24(1): 63–74.

Grainger, T., Goouch, K. and Lambirth, A. (2005) *Creativity and Writing, Developing Voice and Verve in the Classroom*. London: Routledge.

Greenland, P. (2005) *Developmental Movement Play: Emerging Themes from a Six-Year Project Exploring Physical Development Practice in the Early Years*. Leeds: JABADAO Publications.

Gura, P.C. (ed.) (1992) *Exploring Learning: Young Children and Blockplay*. London: Paul Chapman Publishing.

Harrison, R. (1994) 'Barriers to learning in the organisation', in R. Boot, J. Lawrence and J. Morris (eds), *Managing the Unknown by Creating New Futures*. London: McGraw-Hill. pp. 185–205.

Heath, S.B. (1983) *Ways with Words: Language, Life and Work in Communities and Classrooms*. Cambridge: Cambridge University Press.

Helsby, G. (1995) 'Teachers' constructions of professionalism in England in the 1990s', *Journal of Education for Teaching*, 21(3): 317–32.

Hendy, L. and Toon, L. (2001) *Supporting Drama and Imaginative Play in the Early Years*. Buckingham: Open University Press.

Her Majesty's Stationery Office (HMSO) (2001) *Special Educational Needs and Disability Act*. London: The Stationery Office.

Higgins, S. and Packard, N. (2004) *Meeting the Standards in Primary ICT*. London: RoutledgeFalmer.

HM Treasury (2003) *Every Child Matters* (Cm 5860). London: TSO.

HM Treasury, Department for Education and Skills, Department for Work and Pensions and Department of Trade and Industry (2004) *Choice for Parents, the Best Start for Children: A Ten Year Strategy for Childcare*. London: HMT, DfES, DWP and DTI.

Holland, P. (2003) *We Don't Play With Guns Here*. Maidenhead: Open University Press.

Hughes, B. (1996) *Play Environments: A Question of Quality*. London: PLAYLINK.

Hughes, B. (2001) *Evolutionary Playwork and Reflective Analytic Practice*. London: Routledge.

Hughes, B. (2002) *A Playworker's Taxonomy of Play Types*. 2nd edition. London: PlayLink.

Huizinga, J. (1938) *Homo Ludens: A study of the play. Element in Culture*. Boston: Beacon.

Hutchin, V. (1999) *Right from the Start, Effective Planning and Assessment*. London: Hodder & Stoughton Educational

Hutchin, V. (2003) *Observing and Assessing for the Foundation Stage Profile*. London: Hodder & Stoughton Educational.

Hyder, T. and Kenway, P. (1995) *An Equal Future: A Guide to Anti-Sexist Practice in the Early Years*. London: National Early Years Network.

Innovation Unit (2004) Picture This workshop pack (DfES/0904/2004). Nottingham: DfES Publications.

Isaacs, S. (1935) *The Psychological Aspects of Child Development*. London: Evans Brooks Ltd, published in association with University of London Institute of Education.

JABADAO (2005) *Developmental Movement Play*. Leeds: National Centre for Movement, Learning and Health.

Jack, G. and Jordan, B. (1999) 'Social capital and child welfare', *Children & Society*, 13: 242–56.

Jaffke, F. (1996) *Work and Play in Early Childhood*. London: Floris Books.

Jamieson, A., Cordeaux, C. and Wilkinson, L. (2000) *Integration in Practice*. London: National Children's Bureau.

Jennings, J. (2001) 'A broad vision and a narrow focus', *Early Childhood Practice: The Journal for MultiProfessional Partnerships*, 4(1): 50–60.

Kalliala, M. (2005) *Play Culture in a Changing World*. Maidenhead: Open University Press.

Kelly, M. and Ayto, R. (2004) *One More Sheep*. London: Hodder Children's Books.

Key Elements of Effective Practice (KEEP) (order ref. DfES-1201-2004G), www.standards.dfes.gov.uk/primary/publications/foundationstage/keep/pns_fs120105keep.pdf.

Knowles, M. (1970) *The Modern Practice of Adult Education: From Pedagogy to Andragogy*. Cambridge: Cambridge Book Company.

Koshy, V. (2005) *Action Research for Improving Practice: A Practical Guide*. London: Sage Publications.

Kyriakides, L. (2002) 'A research based model for the development of policy on baseline assessment', *British Educational Research Journal*, 28(6): 805–26.

Laevers, F. (1994) 'The innovative project: experiential education 1976–1995', Research Centre for Early Childhood and Primary Education, Katholieke Universiteit, Leuven, Belgium.

Lane, J. (2005) 'Why settings must ensure they are safe havens for children', vol. 7, Issue 6 October, *Early Years Educator*, special free download. www.intered.UKCOM/index.php?site=eye

Langstead, O. (1994) 'Looking at quality from the child's perspective', in P. Moss, and A. Pence (eds), *Valuing Quality in Early Childhood Services: New Approaches to Defining Quality*. London: Paul Chapman Publishing.

Learning and Teaching (LT) Scotland, (2005) *Birth to Three: Supporting our Youngest Children*. ISBN 1-84399-061. Edinburgh: HMSO.

Leeson, C. (2004) 'In praise of reflective practice' in J. Willan, R. Parker-Rees and J. Savage (eds), *Early Childhood Studies*. Exeter: Learning Matters.

Lester, S. and Russell, W. (2002) *Play for Real*. Manchester City Council, unpublished.

Lewis, J.S. (undated, private publication) *Retails Trading: The Philosophy and Practice of John Spedan Lewis – an Anthology*. High Wycombe: Merritt and Hatcher, for John Lewis and Company Limited.

Light, P., Sheldon, S. and Woodhead, M. (1991) *Learning to Think*. London: Routledge.

Lloyd, T. (2000) *Reading for the Future: Boys' and Fathers' Views of Reading*. London: Save the Children.

MacGilchrist, B., Myers, K. and Reed, J (2004) *The Intelligent School*. 2nd edition. London: Sage Publications.

Mackay, G. (2002) 'The disappearance of disability? Thoughts on a changing culture', *British Journal of Special Education*, 29(4): 159–63.

MacPherson, W. (1999) *The Stephen Lawrence Inquiry*. London: The Stationery Office.

Makin, L. and Whitehead, M. (2004) *How to Develop Children's Early Literacy: A Guide for Professional Carers and Educators*. London: Paul Chapman Publishing.

Malaguzzi, L. (1996) *The Hundred Languages of Children*. Reggio Children s.r.l – Via Bligny 1/A – 42100 Reggio Emilia, Italy. www.reggiochildren.it

Mallett, M. (2005) *The Primary English Encyclopaedia: The Heart of the Curriculum*. 2nd edition. London: David Fulton.

Marsden, L. and Woodridge, J., with Drummond, M.J. and Hill, L. (2005) *Looking Closely at Learning and Teaching: A Journey of Development*. Huddersfield: Early Excellence. Also at www.earlyexcellence.com.

Mason, M. and Davies, A. (eds) (1993) *Inclusion, the Way Forward: A Guide to Integration for Young Disabled Children*. London: VOLCUF.

Masson, J. (2000) 'Researching children's perspectives: legal issues', in T.J. Lewis and G. Lindsay (eds), *Researching Children's Perspectives*. Buckingham: Open University Press.

Matthews, J. (2003) *Drawing and Painting: Children and Visual Representation*. 2nd edition. London: Paul Chapman Publishing.

Mayall, B. (2003) *Sociologies of Childhood and Educational Thinking: Professional Lecture*. London: Institute of Education.

McAuliffe, A. (2005) 'Ready for school?', *Nursery World*, 29 September, pp. 22–3.

McKellar, P. (1957) *Imagination and Thinking*. London: Cohen and West.

McNaughton, G. (1996) 'The gender factor', in B. Creaser and E. Dau (eds), *The Anti-Bias Approach in the Early Years*. Sydney. Harper Educational.

Mezirow, J. (1981) 'A critical theory of adult learning and education', *Adult Education*, 32(1): 124–38.

Mills, C. and Mills, D. (1998) *Britain's Early Years Disaster*. London: Channel Four Television.

Moyles, J. (1989) *Just Playing? The Role and Status of Play in Early Childhood Education*. Buckingham: Open University Press.

Moyles, J. and Adams, S. (2001) *StEPs: Statements of Entitlement to Play*. Buckingham: Open University Press.

Moyles, J. and Musgrove, A. (2003) 'EEPES (EY) Essex, Chelmsford APU/Essex County Council.

Moyles, J. and Suschitzky, W. (1997) *The Buck Stops Here! Nursery Nurses and Teachers Working Together*. Leicester: University of Leicester/Esmée Fairbairn Trust.

Moyles, J., Adams, S. and Musgrove, A. (2002) *SPEEL: Study of Pedagogical Effectiveness in Early Learning*. Report No. 363. London: DfES.

National Assessment Authority (NAA) (2005) *Continuing the Learning Journey*. London: QCA.

National Children's Bureau (NCB) (2002) 'Including children in social research', *Highlight*, no. 193.

National Children's Bureau (NCB) (2003) 'Guidelines for research', www.ncb.org.uk.

National College for School Leadership (NCSL) (2003) *Tutor Readings for Leading from the Middle*. Nottingham: NCSL.

National Playing Fields Association (NPFA), Children's Play Council and Play Link (2000) *Best Play: What Play Provision Should do for Children*. London: NPFA.

National Remodelling Team (NRT) (2003) *Touching Tomorrow: Remodelling Resources*. V4.1. London: NRT.

Norwich, B. (1996) 'Special needs education or education for all: connective specialisation and ideological impurity', *British Journal of Special Education*, 23(3): 100–4.

Nottingham Play Forum (1994) *Playscheme Training Pack*. Nottingham: Nottingham Play Forum.

Nutbrown, C. (1994) *Threads of Thinking*. London: Paul Chapman Publishing.

Ockleford, A. (1996) *All Join In! A Framework for Making Music with Children and Young People Who Are Visually Impaired and Having Learning Difficulties*. London: RNIB.

Office for Standards in Education (OFSTED) (2000) 'Evaluating educational inclusion: guidance for inspectors and schools' (HMI 235), www.ofsted.gov.uk/publications.

Office for Standards in Education (OFSTED) (2005a) *Day Care and Childminding: Guidance to the National Standards, Revisions to Certain Criteria, October 2002*. London: OFSTED.

Office for Standards in Education (OFSTED) (2005b) *Early Years: Firm Foundations*. London: OFSTED.

Office for Standards in Education (OFSTED) (2005c) *The Framework for Inspecting Schools in England from September 2005*. London: OFSTED.

Oogly Boogly, www.ooglyboogly.org.uk.

Opie, I. and Opie, P. (1988) *The Singing Game*. Oxford and New York: Oxford University Press.

Organisation for Economic Co-operation and Development (OECD) (2000) *Starting Strong*. Paris: OECD.

Orr, R. (2003) *My Right to Play: A Child with Complex Needs*. Maidenhead: Open University Press.

Ouvry, M. (2004) *Sounds like Playing: Music and the Early Years Curriculum*. London: Early Education. Also at www.early-education,org.uk.

Pahl, K. and Rowsell, J. (2005) *Literacy and Education: Understanding the New Literacy Studies in the Classroom*. London: Paul Chapman Publishing.

Paley, V. (1984) *Boys and Girls: Superheroes in the Doll Corner*. Chicago, IL: University of Chicago Press.

Paley, V.G. (1988) *Bad Guys Don't Have Birthdays*. Chicago, IL: University Press of Chicago.

Paley, V.G. (2004) *A Child's Work*. Chicago, IL: University Press of Chicago.

Paley, V.G. (1990) *The Boy Who Would be a Helicopter*. Cambridge, MA: Harvard University Press.

Pascal, C. and Bertram, A.D. (1997) *Effective Early Learning: Case Studies in Improvement*. London: Hodder & Stoughton.

Pascal, C. and Bertram, T. (1999) 'Assessing what matters in the early years', in J. Fisher (ed.), *The Foundations of Learning*. Buckingham: Open University Press.

Pajares, F. (2003) 'Self efficacy beliefs, motivation and achievement in writing: a review of the literature', *Reading and Writing Quarterly*, 19(2): 139–58.

Pen Green Research, Development and Training Base, (2000) *Involving Parents in their Children's Learning*. Corby: Pen Green Centre.

Penn, H. (1997) *Comparing Nurseries: Staff and Children in Italy, Spain and the UK*. London: Paul Chapman Publishing.

Piaget, J. (1951) *Play, Dreams and Imitation in Childhood*. London: Heinemann.

Piaget, J. and Inhelder, B. (1969) *The Psychology of the Child*. New York: Basic Books.

Play Safety Forum (2002) *Managing Risk in Play Provision: A Position Statement*. London: Children's Play Council.

Pollard, A. (2004) 'Towards a sociology of learning in primary schools', in S. Ball (ed.), *The RoutledgeFalmer Reader in Sociology of Education*. London: RoutledgeFalmer.

Pound, L. (1999) *Supporting Mathematical Development in the Early Years*. Buckingham: Open University Press.

Pre-School Learning Alliance (PLA) (2005) *Policies for Early Years Settings*. London: Pre-School Learning Alliance.

Pring, R. (2004) *Philosophy of Education, Aims, Theory, Common Sense and Research*. London: Continuum.

Project Zero (2001) *Making Learning Visible*. Cambridge, MA: Reggio Children and Harvard Graduate School of Education.

Pugh, G., DeAth, E. and Smith, C. (1994) *Confident Parents, Confident Children*. London: National Children's Bureau.

Pugh, G., Hickson, D.J. and Hinings, C.R. (eds) (1983) *Writers on Organisations*. 3rd edition. London: Penguin Books.

Qualifications and Curriculum Authority (QCA) (1999) *The National Numeracy Strategy: Teaching Written Calculations*. London: QCA/DfES.

Qualifications and Curriculum Authority (QCA) (2000) *Curriculum Guidance for the Foundation Stage* (QCA/00/587). London: QCA/DfES.

Qualifications and Curriculum Authority (QCA) (2002) *Creativity, Find It, Promote It*. London: DfES/QCA.

Qualifications and Curriculum Authority (QCA) (2003) *Foundation Stage Profile Handbook* (QCA/03/1006). Sudbury: QCA.

Qualifications and Curriculum Authority (QCA) (2005) 'Pathways to learning for new arrivals', www.qca.org.uk.

Rich, D., Casanova, D., Dixon, A., Drummond, M.J., Durrant, A. and Myer, C. (2005) *First Hand Experience: What Matters to Children*. Clopton, Suffolk: Rich Learning Opportunities.

Rinaldi, C. (1998) 'The thought that sustains educational action', www.sightlines-initiative (originally in *Rechild*, April 1998).

Roberts, R. (1995) *Self-Esteem and Successful Early Learning*. London: Hodder & Stoughton.

Roberts, R. (2002) *Developing Self-Esteem in Young Children*. London: Paul Chapman Publishing/Sage.

Roberts-Holmes, G. (2005) *Doing Your Early Years Research Project: A Step by Step Guide*. London: Sage Publications.

Robinson, M. (2003) *From Birth to One: The Year of Opportunity*. Buckingham: Open University Press.

Rodd, J. (1998) *Leadership in Early Childhood: The Pathway to Professionalism*. Buckingham: Open University Press.

Rodd, J. (2001) 'Can young children learn to learn?', *Early Years Educator*, 3(6): 16–18.

Rogers, B. (2003) *Behaviour Management: A Whole-School Approach*. London: Paul Chapman Publishing.

Rogers, C. (1983) *Freedom to Learn for the 80s*. London: Charles E. Merrill.

Russell, W. (2004) *Play and Playwork Principles 1 Workbook*. Cheltenham: University of Gloucestershire.

Sanders, D., White, G., Burge, B., Eames, A., McEune, R. and Grayson, H. (2005) *A Study of the Transition from the Foundation Stage to Key Stage 1*. Slough: NFER/Sure Start.

Schaffer, H.R. and Emerson, P.F. (1964) 'The development of social attachment in infancy', *Monographs of the Society for Research in Child Development*, 29(serial number 94).

Schon, D. (1983) *The Reflective Practitioner*. New York: Basic Books.

Sensory Integration Network (2003) *Sensory Integration Information Booklet: A Resource for Parents and Therapists*. Dublin: SI Network.

Sherry, J.L. (2004) 'Media effects theory and the nature/nurture debate: a historical overview and directions for future research', *Media Psychology*, 66: 83–109.

Siraj-Blatchford, I. (1994) *The Early Years: Laying the Foundations for Racial Equality*. Stoke-on-Trent: Trentham Books.

Siraj-Blatchford, I., Sylva, K., Mattock, S., Gilden, R. and Bell, D. (2002) *Researching Effective Pedagogy in the Early Years* (REPEY). DfES Research Report 356. London: HMSO.

Siraj-Blatchford, I., Sylva, K., Taggart, B., Melhuish, E., Sammons, P. and Elliott, K. (2003). *Effective Provision of Pre-school Education (EPPE) Project 1997–2003: Technical Paper 10, Intensive Case Studies of Practice Across the Foundation Stage*, Institute of Education, University of London.

SkillsActive (2004) *Playwork People*. London: SkillsActive. Available online at www.playwork.org.uk.

Southway Early Childhood Centre (1996) 'The key experiences', unpublished document.

Sparioso, M. (1989) *Dionysus Reborn*. Ithaca, NY: Cornell University Press.

Sturrock, G. and Else, P. (2005) *Therapeutic Playwork Readers One and Two*. Sheffield: Ludemos Associates.

Sure Start (2002) *Birth to Three Matters Framework*. London: HMSO.

Sutton-Smith, B. (1997) *The Ambiguity of Play*. London: Harvard University Press.

Sylva, K., Melhuish, E., Sammons, P., Siraj-Blatchford, I. and. Taggart, B. (2004) *The Effective Provision of Pre-School Education (EPPE) Project. Technical Paper 12. Final Report (A Longitudinal Study Funded by the DfES 1997–2004)*. London: DfES/Institute of Education, University of London.

Sylva, K., Melhuish, E., Sammons, P., Siraj-Blatchford, I. and Taggart, B. (2005) 'The Effective Provision of Pre-School Education (EPPE) Project', presented at the Fifth Warwick International Early Years Conference, March.

Taggart, B., Sammons, P., Sylva, K., Melhuish, E., Siraj-Blatchford, I. and Elliot, K. (2003) *The Effective Provision of Pre-school Education Project*. London: DfES.

'Ten year strategy: choice for parents, the best start for children' (ISBN-1-84532-056-5), www.hmtreasury.gov.uk/media/8F5/35/pbr04childcare_480.pdf.

Theatre-Rites, www.theatre-rites.co.uk.

Tizard, B. and Hughes, M. (1984) *Young Children Learning*. London: Fontana.

Tizard, B. and Hughes, M. (2002) *Young Children Learning*. 2nd edition. Oxford: Blackwell.

Tizard, B., Phelps, J. and Plewis, I. (1976) 'Play in pre-school centres: effects on play of the child's social class and of the educational orientation of the centre', *Journal of Child Psychology and Psychiatry*, 18: 21–38.

Trevarthen, C. (1998) 'A child's need to learn a culture', in M. Woodhead, D. Faulkner and K. Littleton (eds), *Cultural Worlds of Early Childhood*. London: Routledge.

Trevarthen, C. (2003) 'Infancy, mind', in R. Gregory (ed.), *Oxford Companion to the Mind*. Oxford: Oxford University Press.

Vecchi, V. (2004) 'The multiple fonts of knowledge', in P. Moss (ed.), *Children in Europe*. Edinburgh: Children in Scotland.

Vygotsky, L.S. (1978) *Mind in Society*. Cambridge, MA: Harvard University Press.

Wade, B. and Moore, M. (2000) *Baby Power: Maximise your Baby's Potential through Books*. Handforth, Cheshire: Egmont World.

Wells, G. (1987) *The Meaning Makers: Children Learning Language and Using Language to Learn*. London: Hodder & Stoughton.

Whalley, M. (1997) *Working with Parents*. London: Hodder & Stoughton.

Whitebread, D. (ed.) (2003) *Teaching and Learning in the Early Years*. 2nd edition. London: Routledge.

Whitehead, M. (2002) *Developing Language and Literacy with Young Children*. London: Paul Chapman Publishing.

Wilkinson, R.G. (2005) *The Impact of Inequality: How to Make Sick Societies Healthier*. London: Routledge.

Wilson, R.A. (1998) *Special Educational Needs in the Early Years*. London: Routledge.

Woolf, F. and Belloli, J. (2005) *Reflect and Review: The Arts and Creativity in the Early Years*. London: Arts Council England. Also at www.artsmark.org.uk.

Zohar, D. and Marshall, I. (2001) *Spiritual Intelligence: The Ultimate Intelligence*. London: Bloomsbury.

INDEX

Added to a page number 'f' denotes a figure and 't' denotes a table.